영어 독해의 전략과 실제

영어 독해의 전략과 실제

김용도 지음

한국문화사

영어 독해의 전략과 실제

초판인쇄 2014년 2월 20일
초판발행 2014년 2월 25일

지은이 김 용 도
펴낸이 김 진 수
펴낸곳 **한국문화사**
등   록 1991년 11월 9일 제2-1276호
주   소 서울특별시 성동구 광나루로 130 서울숲IT캐슬 1310호
전   화 (02)464-7708 / 3409-4488
전   송 (02)499-0846
이메일 hkm7708@hanmail.net
홈페이지 www.hankookmunhwasa.co.kr

책값은 뒤표지에 있습니다.

잘못된 책은 바꾸어 드립니다.
이 책의 내용은 저작권법에 따라 보호받고 있습니다.

ISBN   978-89-6817-168-0   93740

머리말

너무나 빠르게 진화하는 스마트 폰과 같은 전자기기가 우리의 일상생활을 좌지우지 한다. 전자기기가 우리 일상생활의 많은 일처리에서 상상을 초월할 정도로 시·공간적 처리노력을 절약하게 해주는 동시에 이 전자기기를 통해 들어오는 많은 정보를 단시간에 처리하도록 요구한다.

이 책은 영어를 통한 정보를 단시간에 효율적이면서도 효과적으로 처리하게 해주는 독해전략을 내재화 하도록 의도한 책이다. 이 책은 영어 글에 대해 단순히 한국어로 옮겨 놓는 번역 차원의 독해 학습지도서가 아니다. 이 책은 가령 한통의 통지서를 받는 순간으로부터 읽은 후 사후처리까지를 의미하는 총 5단계(15절차)의 효율효과적 처리를 습관화 하도록 한다.

이 독해전략 기저에는 작자의 쓰기인지과정과 독자의 읽기인지과정이 함께 반영되어 있다. 작자의 쓰기인지과정은 출력 현상이고 독자의 읽기인지과정은 입력 현상이라는 차이가 있지만 대상인 텍스트(즉 글)는 동일하고, 따라서 텍스트는 작자 생산의 산물인 동시에 독자 이해의 대상이기 때문이다. 작자의 쓰기인지과정이 반영된 독해 접근방법이 이 책이 의미하는 독해전략이다.

독해의 전략이라는 이름의 I부는 단계별로 학습하는 곳이고, 독해의 실제라는 이름의 II부는 통합적으로 학습하는 곳이다. 단계별 독해(I부)는 5단계(15절차)를 의미하는 5장(15절차)로 구성되는데, 각 단계별(절차별)로 독해전략을 학습내재화 하는데 초점이 있다. 이 학습내재화는 해당 단계에서 독해처리의 전략을 학습하여 내재화하는 것이다. 통합적 독해(II부)는 I부의 5단계(15절차) 독해전략 학습내재화를 종합적으로 적용하여 독해전략을 심화하는데 초점이 있다.

단계별 독해(I부)에서 절(section)은 기초 이론적 설명 부분과 독해 자료 부분으로 구성되고, 독해 자료 부분은 영어본문, 어휘해설, 본문해설, 국역 등으로 구성된다. 따라서 학습자는 첫 기초 이론적 설명을 이해한 후 이 이론적 설명을 적용하여 영어 본문을 독해처리하면 된다. 독해처리 하는 동안에 필요하면 어휘해설, 본문해설, 국역을 참고할 수 있다.

  통합적 독해(Ⅱ부)는 다양한 영어 글로 구성된다. 먼저 글의 영역을 의미하는 여섯 장(chapter)으로 구성되고, 장은 글 종류를 의미하는 절로 구성되고 절은 실제 다양한 글 유형으로 구성된다. 따라서 학습자는 다양한 영어 글(영역⇌종류⇌유형⇌개별텍스트)을 대상으로 5단계(15절차)를 적용한 학습을 통하여 글 처리능력을 향상시키면 된다.

  이 책의 목적에 의한 구성을 따라 학습을 진행하는 학습자는 이 시대에 꼭 필요한 영어 독해전략을 익혀 유용하게 이용할 수 있기를 기대된다.

  끝으로 이 책의 출판을 맡아 준 한국문화사 김진수 사장님과 임직원에게 감사하게 생각한다.

2014년 2월 10일
저자 김 용 도

차례

■ 머리말 / V

제I부 독해의 전략 ········ 1

제1장 윤곽 확인 ········ 3
제1절 양식구성 확인 ········ 5
제2절 작자 의도 예측 ········ 21
제3절 본문 크기 확인 ········ 44

제2장 절 독해 ········ 65
제1절 구성성분 어휘의미 리콜 ········ 65
제2절 어휘의미들의 구성처리 ········ 80
제3절 주제어휘와 초점어휘 확인 ········ 94

제3장 단락 독해 ········ 105
제1절 절마디 관계 이해 ········ 105
제2절 단락의 내용흐름 파악 ········ 117
제3절 단락의 주제 확인 ········ 124

제4장 본문 독해 ········ 134
제1절 단위 마디의 관계식별 ········ 134
제2절 본문의 내용흐름 파악 ········ 146
제3절 본문의 주제 확인 ········ 162

제5장 독해사후 처리 ········ 174
제1절 글의 의도 확인 ········ 174
제2절 본문구성의 패턴 요약 ········ 188
제3절 마무리 수행 ········ 208

제II부 독해의 실제 ····· 219

제1장 통신 영역 ····· 224
- 제1절 대화 ····· 224
- 제2절 편지 ····· 232
- 제3절 email ····· 239
- 제4절 통지 ····· 247
- 제5절 메모 ····· 259
- 제6절 기타 ····· 266

제2장 시사 영역 ····· 271
- 제1절 일간 ····· 271
- 제2절 주간 ····· 272
- 제3절 월간 ····· 275
- 제4절 시간 ····· 281
- 제5절 부정기 ····· 283
- 제6절 기타 ····· 292

제3장 홍보 영역 ····· 295
- 제1절 광고 ····· 295
- 제2절 전단 ····· 303
- 제3절 표어 ····· 305
- 제4절 초청 ····· 308
- 제5절 행사 ····· 314
- 제6절 호소 ····· 318
- 제7절 기타 ····· 322

제4장 확인 영역 ····· 324
- 제1절 이력 ····· 324
- 제2절 계약 ····· 330
- 제3절 신고 ····· 343
- 제4절 증서 ····· 345
- 제5절 조서 ····· 353

제5장 주장 영역 ····· 360
- 제1절 논문 ····· 360
- 제2절 사설 ····· 373
- 제3절 평론 ····· 377

제4절　토론 ································· 383
　　제5절　연설 ································· 393
　　제6절　선언 ································· 400
제6장　효과 영역 ································· 403
　　제1절　우화 ································· 403
　　제2절　설화 ································· 408
　　제3절　속담 ································· 412
　　제4절　희곡 ································· 414
　　제5절　교과 ································· 425
　　제6절　준칙 ································· 431
　　제7절　수상 ································· 444
　　제8절　흥미 ································· 455
　　제9절　기타 ································· 462

- 참고문헌 ································· 465
- 찾아보기 ································· 466

제 I 부
독해의 전략

제1장
윤곽 확인

영어 글을 독해한다는 것은 작자가 자신의 쓰기목적 아래 써 놓은 다음 (1)과 같은 영어텍스트를 대상으로 독자가 자신의 독해목적 아래 필요한 내용을 이해하는 것을 의미한다.

Galaxies are the major building blocks of the universe. A galaxy is a giant family of many millions of stars, and it is held together by its own gravitational field. Most of the material universe is organized into galaxies of stars, together with gas and dust.

There are three main types of galaxy: spiral, elliptical, and irregular. The Milky Way is a spiral galaxy: a flattish disc of stars with two spiral arms emerging from its central nucleus. About one-quarter of all galaxies have this shape. Spiral galaxies are well supplied with the interstellar gas in which new stars from : as the rotating spiral pattern sweeps around the galaxy it compresses gas and dust, triggering the formation of bright young stars in its arms. The elliptical galaxies have a symmetrical elliptical or spheroidal shape with no obvious structure. Most of their member stars are very old and since ellipticals are devoid of interstellar gas, no new stars are forming in them.

The biggest and brightest galaxies in the universe are ellipticals with masses of about times that of the sun: these giants may frequently be sources of strong radio emission, in which case they are called radio galaxies. About two-thirds of all galaxies are elliptical. Irregular galaxies comprise about one-tenth of all galaxies and they come in many subclasses.

Measurement in space is quite different from measurement on earth. Some terrestrial distances can be expressed as intervals of time : the time to fly one continent to another or the time it takes to drive to work, for example. By comparison with these familiar yardsticks, the distances to the galaxies are incomprehensibly large, but they too are made more manageable by using a time calibration, in this case the distance that light travels in one year. On such a scale the nearest giant spiral galaxy, the Andromeda galaxy, is two million light years away. The most distant luminous objects seen by telescopes are probably ten thousand million light years away. Their light was already halfway here before the Earth even formed. The light from the nearby Virgo galaxy set out when reptiles still dominated the animal world.

> 어휘해설 •building block: 구성(하는) 블록(구역); •is held together: 함께 붙들려 있다; •gravitational field: 중력장; •The Milky Way: 특정의 은하수 이름; •disc: 평원, 평판; •spiral: 나선형; •elliptical: 타원형(의); •irregular: 부정형; •flattish disc: •편편한 판; •rotating spiral: 회전하는 나선형; •sweep: 휩쓸다; •compress: 압축하다; •trigger: 유발하다, 일으키다; •symmetrical: 대칭적인; •devoid: 텅 빈; •mass: 질량; •radio emission: 전자파 방출; •spheroidal: 구형의; •old (star): 늙은(별); •radio galaxies: 전파 은하계; •measurement: 계량법(화), 계산법; •terrestrial: 지구의, 지상의; •yardstick: 야드 자; •time calibration: 시간측도; •luminous: 빛을 발하는; •Virgo galaxy: 처녀 은하계; •reptile: 파충류.

5단계(15절차)의 연속적 현상이 한 차례의 독해과정이다. 앞 (1)과 같은 글을 대상으로 한 장(chapter)에서 한 단계(step)만을, 한 절(section)에서는 한 절차(process)만을 다룬다.

독자가 영어 독해자료를 접하는 첫 단계에서 어떻게 해야 하는가? 독해자료의 구성윤곽을 확인하는 것이다. 구성윤곽의 확인은 1)독해자료의 양식구성을 확인하고, 2)작자의 의도를 예측하고, 3)본문의 크기를 확인하는 세 절차를 거치는 것이다.

제1절 양식구성 확인

첫 절차인 양식구성 확인은 어떻게 하는가? 독자 앞에 독해자료가 있음은 쓴 작자, 가상의 독자, 써야 할 이유(즉 의도 혹은 목적)[1], 쓴 때와 장소, 그리고 쓴 결과물이 독자 앞에 전달된 방법이 있었기 때문이다.[2] 첫 절차에서는 이 의사소통 6요소 관점에서 독자는 독해자료에 대하여 누가 누구에게 썼으며, 언제 어디서 썼으며, 무엇(가령: 제목)을 써서 어떤 방법(예: e-mail)으로 전달했는가[3]를 확인하는 것이다.

양식구성의 여섯 요소는 글의 종류에 따라서 변인(생략, 부가, 이동)이 작용하여 다양하게 구성된다. 가령, 개별서신에서는 수신자가 특정인이 되어 중요하게 간주되어 반드시 나타나지만, 신문의 사설에서는 독자가 불특정 다수가 되어 중요하게는 간주되지 않으며 보통 나타나지 않는다. 여섯 요소의 출현위치도 취급의 중요도에 따라 다르다. 조직단체의 보편적 공식 서한문의 경우 조직단체의 이름이 맨 위 중앙에 나타나고 수신자가 그 아래 왼쪽에 나타난다.[4] 따라서 다양한 글의 양식을 경험해 두는 것이 필요하다.

(1) **Institute of Secretaries**

Wilson House, West Street, London SW12AR

Telephone 0181 987 2432

Fax 0181 987 2556

LD/ST

12 May 19__

---

1) 여기서는 이유를 포함하여 의도와 목적을 본질적으로 동일한 개념으로 간주하며, 글의 탄생과정 관점에서 차별화할 수도 있는데, 이유는 발생동기 차원, 의도는 발생된 심적 차원, 목적은 언어적 표현 차원으로 간주한다.
2) 이 접근방법은 존재론적 관점이다(김용도 2011:161).
3) 이 독해재료(글) 양식구성의 요소는 문 구성의 기능요소(예: 주어, 술어동사, 목적어, 보어 등)에 비교되며, 존재론적 의사소통과정의 6요소라고 부른다(김용도 2011:161).
4) 김용도(2011:160)는 양식구성에 대하여 규칙화를 시도했다.

Mrs Lesley Nunn
15 Windsor Road
Manchester
M2 9GJ

Dear Lesley

19__ SECRETARIES CONFERENCE, 8/9 OCTOBER 19__

As a valued member of the Institute of Secretaries, I have pleasure in inviting you to

.

.

.

Louise Dunscome

LOUISE DUNSCOME (Mrs)
Conference Secretary

Encs

> 어휘해설 •Institute of Secretaries: 조직체 이름; •valued member: 주요 구성원.
>
> 양식구성해설   1)상단 중앙의 작자(상호, 주소, 전화번호, 팩스), 2)상단 왼쪽의 작자(이니셜), 3)작성 때(일/월/년), 4)수신자(성명, 주소), 5)본문(축약), 6)작자(서명, 이름, 직위), 7)본문의 일부인 첨부물로 구성됨. 쓴 장소는 나타나지 않고(즉 생략되고), 방법은 지면(서한문)임.
>
> 부분국역   (본문 한 문장)주요 직원으로서 직원강습회의에 저희가 귀하를 초청하게 되어서 기쁩니다.

(2) **Friend or Foe?**

1 ⁵⁾A fox slipped in climbing a fence. To save himself from falling he clutched at a brier-bush. The thorns made his paws bleed, and in his pain he cried out: "Oh dear! I turned to you for help and you have made me worse off than I was before." "Yes, my friend!" said the brier. "You made a bad mistake when you tried to lay hold of me. I lay hold of everyone myself."

2 The incident illustrates the folly of those who run for aid to people whose nature it is to hurt rather than to help.

어휘해설 •slip: 미끄러지다; •clutch: 움켜잡다; •brier-bush: 가시나무 덤불; •thorn: 가시; •paw: 동물의 발; •Oh dear: 이런, 세상에; •worse off에서 off는 completely, utterly의 뜻으로 동사나 형용사의 의미를 강화 시킨다; •lay (catch, get, seize, take) hold of: ~을 잡다(쥐다); •folly: 어리석음.

양식구성해설 제목이 있는 본문만으로 구성.

전문국역 **1** 여우 한 마리가 울타리를 기어오르다 미끄러졌다. 떨어지지 않으려고 여우는 가시나무 덤불을 움켜잡았다. 가시에 찔려 발에서 피가 나자 여우는 고통스럽게 외쳤다. "이런 세상에! 나는 너에게 도움을 청했는데 나를 이전보다 더욱 궁지에 몰아넣다니." "그래, 이 친구야! 나를 붙잡으려 했던 것은 너의 대단한 실수였어. 왜냐하면 나 자신이 모든 것을 붙잡고 늘어지니까." 라고 가시나무가 말했다. **2** 이 이야기는 그 본질상 도움을 주기는커녕 피해를 주는 사람들에게 도움을 청하는 사람들의 어리석음을 실례로 보여주는 것이다. (이솝의 우화)

---

(3) **EDITORIAL**
N.K.'s missile gamble

1 Almost a year has passed since North Korea's new leader Kim Jong-un took power following his father's death on Dec. 17, 2011. The Swiss-educated young man was widely expected to take his impoverished nation in a new direction and show a leadership different from his father's iron fisted rule.

---

5) 영어 글 속에 있는 **1** 과 같은 번호는 저자가 필요한 곳인 경우 편의상 임의로 부여한 것임.

2 Since his enthronement, the 20-something leader has repeatedly pledged to focus on building the economy and raising the standard of living, saying that it is an objective laid out for him by his father.

3 As recently as August, Kim told a visiting Chinese delegation that one key goal of the Workers' Party was to develop the economy and improve livelihoods so that the North Korean people could lead happy and civilized lives.

...생략...

4 He should realize that his missile threat won't change the policies of Washington or Seoul. The North's missiles can neither change the destiny of his nation nor improve the lives of his people.

5 Therefore, Kim should stop his missile gamble. More importantly, he should give up the ambition of becoming a nuclear power. What he needs to do is to look to Myanmar and see how a pariah state can break from isolation and get assistance from other countries.

어휘해설 •gamble: 도박; •impoverished: 가난에 빠진; •iron fisted rule: 철권통치; •enthronement: 즉위; •20-something leader: 20대의 지도자; •pledge: 약속하다; •objective: 목표; •delegation: 대표단; •missile gamble: 미사일도박; •nuclear power: 핵 강국; •pariah state: 낙오국가.

양식구성해설 글의 종류(editorial/사설)가 표시되어 있고, 제목이 있는 본문만으로 구성됨.

전문국역 **1** 북한의 새 지도자 김정은이 2011년 12월 17일 그의 아버지 사망 후 권력을 잡은 지 근 1년이 지났다. 스위스에서 교육을 받은 젊은 지도자는 가난에 빠진 국가를 새로운 방향으로 이끌고 아버지의 철권통치와는 다른 지도력을 보여줄 것으로 널리 기대됐다. **2** 그의 즉위 이후 20대의 이 지도자는 경제를 개발하고 생활수준을 높이는 데 초점을 맞출 것을 약속하면서 이것이 그의 아버지가 자신에게 제시한 목표라고 말했다. **3** 8월까지만 해도 김정은은 방북했던 중국 대표들에게 노동당의 핵심 목표는 북한 주민들이 행복하고 안락한 생활을 할 수 있도록 경제를 개발하고 생활수준을 향상시키는 것이라고 말했다. ---생략--- **4** 그의 미사일 위협이 미국 또는 한국의 정책을 바꾸지 못할 것이라는 점을 인식해야 한다. 북한 미사일은 북한의 운명도, 국민들의 삶도 개선시킬 수 없다. **5** 따라서 김정은은 미사일 도박을 중단해야 한다. 더욱 중요한 것은 그는 핵 강국이 되려는 야심을 포기해야 한다. 그가 해야 할 일은 미얀마에 눈을 돌려 낙오 국가가 어떻게 고립에서 벗어나 다른 국가로부터 지원을 얻을 수 있는지를 지켜보는 일이다.

(4)

JB SIMPSON & CO LTD
18 Deansgate, Sheffield S11 2BR
Telephone 0114 234234
Fax: 0114 234235

Order no 237   Date 7 July 19—

Nylon Fabrics Ltd
18 Brazenose Street
MANCHESTER
M60 8AS

Please supply:

Quantity	Item(s)	Catalogue Number	Price
25	Bed Sheets (106 cm) blue	75	£5.50 each
25	Bed Sheets (120 cm) primrose	82	£5.00 each
50	Pillow Cases blue	117	£2.90 each
50	Pillow Cases primrose	121	£2.90 each

(signed)

for J B Simpson & Co Ltd

어휘해설 •quantity: 량; •bed sheet: 침대시트; •£5.50 each: 개당 50 파운드; •pillow case: 베개 커버; •primrose: 연 노란색.

양식구성해설 1)발신자 소속 조직체(이름, 주소, 전화 및 팩스 번호), 2)발신자의 주문서 번호, 3)작성일, 4)수신자 소속 조직체(이름, 주소), 5)내용(주문내용), 6)수신자의 확인 사인 란으로 구성.

국역 생략.

(5) Dear Ms Hansen

1 Thank you for your letter of 18 August and for the samples of cotton underwear you very kindly sent to me.

2 I appreciate the good quality of these garments, but unfortunately your prices appear to be on the high side even for garments of this quality. To accept the prices you quote would leave me with only a small profit on my sales since this is an area in which the principal demand is for articles in the medium price range.

3 I like the quality of your goods and would welcome the opportunity to do business with you. May I suggest that perhaps you could make some allowance on your quoted prices which would help to introduce your goods to my customers. If you cannot do so, then I must regretfully decline your offer as it stands.

4 I hope to hear from you soon.

5 Yours sincerely

어휘해설 •cotton underwear: 목화 내의; •garment: 옷, 의복; •quote: (가격)부르다; •profit: 이익, 수익; •principal demand: 기본수요; •medium price range: 중급 가격 범위; •do business: 영업하다; •make allowance: 참작하다; •decline: 거절하다; •as it stands: 그대로의.

양식구성해설 수신자 이름과 본문만으로 구성됨.

부분국역 **2** 이 의복의 품질이 좋다는 것을 잘 알겠습니다만, 이 정도 품질의 옷에 대하여 가격이 높은 것 같습니다. 저희 입장에서 주요 고객이 중급 가격 수준의 영역이기 때문에, 귀하가 부르는 가격을 받아들인다면, 저희가 팔 경우 이윤이 별로 남지 않습니다.

---

(6) As you know, we have become far more successful than anyone expected when we opened for business a year ago. During the lunch and the dinner rush we always have a long line of customers waiting to get a seat. As it happens, the gift shop next door has gone out of business and we decided to lease that space and expand the dining area. The increased capacity should eventually lead to higher pay for everyone. However, we will have to stay closed for the first two weeks of October. I'm telling you as far in advance as possible in case you need to arrange for some part-time work during the renovations.

> **어휘해설** •As it happens: 마침; •gift shop: 선물가게; •go out of business: 폐업하다; •lease: 임대하다, 빌리다; •dining area: 식사 장소; •lead to: -한 결과를 초래하다; •closed: 문을 닫은; •in advance: 미리; •arrange for: (여기서는) 신청하다; •renovation: 쇄신, 혁신, 수리.
>
> **양식구성해설** 본문만으로 구성됨.
>
> **전문국역** 여러분들도 알다시피, 우리는 우리가 1년 전에 사업을 시작했을 때 사람들이 예상했던 것보다 훨씬 성공적으로 해 오고 있습니다. 점심과 저녁 붐비는 시간에는 자리에 앉으려고 기다리는 긴 줄의 손님이 항상 있습니다. 마침 옆에 선물 가게가 폐업을 해서 그 공간을 임대하여 식사 장소를 늘리기로 결정하였습니다. 수용능력이 늘어나게 되면 결국 이는 여러분들의 임금 인상으로 이어질 것입니다. 하지만 10월 첫 2주 동안에는 문을 닫아야 할 것으로 생각됩니다. 수리 작업이 있는 기간 동안에 파트타임 일이 필요하신 분들을 위해 최대한 미리 말씀드리고자 하는 것입니다.

(7) ## Television still most powerful among news media outlets: study

By Bae Ji-sook

1 Korea's three largest-circulation daily newspapers account for more than half of all newspapers' power to influence public opinion, a government panel concluded Thursday.

2 Television proved to be the most powerful media outlet, while conventional print media is losing ground to online media.

3 This is the first time a survey on the concentration of media outlets' power to influence the formation of public opinion has been conducted with the aim of getting "an objective view of the media market."

4 According to the three-year study by a panel under the Ministry of Culture, Sports and Tourism, television marked 47.2 percent in weighted concentration ratio – a measure of influence based on market share and strength of impact - followed by online news outlets at 26 percent and newspapers at 17.3 percent, showing that people paid the most attention to the small screen.

5 TV news and investigative programs were shown to be influential among people of all generations while newspapers attract older people and youngsters were drawn to online outlets.

6 Among the 70 daily newspapers in the country, the three largest dailies – Chosun, JoongAng and Donga - held 57.6 percent of the concentration ratio. Chosun marked 23.7 percent, JoongAng 17.9 percent and Donga took 16 percent. Only seven other papers recorded 2 percent concentration ratio.

7 When it comes to online news outlet, Chosun.com, the website for the Chosun Ilbo newspaper, topped the chart with 7.6 percent followed by the websites for JoogAng Ilbo, 6.8 percent, and Yonhap News, 5.9 percent.

8 State-run broadcaster KBS accounted for 29 percent of concentrate ratio, followed by broadcasting networks MBC at 10.7 percent, and SBS at 7.5 percent. Chosun Ilbo newspaper and its affiliates including the general programming cable channel TV Chosun marked 7 percent concentration ratio followed by JoongAng and its affiliates, 5.4 percent, Donga and its affiliates 5.3 percent, Maeil Economic Daily and its affiliates, 4.6 percent, Yonhap News Agency and its affiliates, 2.4 percent, and YTN and its affiliates, 2.3 percent.

9 The research was conducted on 70 daily newspapers, 10 TV stations with 11 channels, 13 radio stations with 19 channels, and 117 online news websites between 2011 and 2012. The outlets' shares on readership, viewing, listening and duration time as well as a survey of 7,000 people and others were reflected in the final results.

10 "We believe the research could contribute to a 'plurality' in the media market by looking at the strongest and the weakest. The second report is due to come in 2016, and will include social media services such as Twitter or Facebook and use of smartphones as media platforms," said Chungnam National University professor Cho Sung-kyum, who headed the panel. (*baejisook@heraldcorp.com*)

어휘해설 •outlet: 출구; •circulation: 발행; •account for: 설명하다, 떠맡고 있다; •public opinion: 여론; •panel: 조사단; •weighted concentration ratio: 무게 중심(집중) 비율; •measure: 수치 정도; •market share: 시장점유율; •strength of impact: 영향력; •the chart: 순위표; •State-run broadcaster: 국영방송사; •affiliate: 계열사; •is due to root: ~ 예정이다; •shares: 점유율; •media platform: 미디어 소프트웨어.

양식구성해설   작자와 본문(제목 있음)만으로 구성됨.

전문국역   텔레비전이 뉴스 미디어 중에서 아직 가장 강력함 **1** 한국의 발행부수 3대 일간신문이 여론에 미치는 영향으로 신문 전체 영향의 절반 이상을 떠맡고 있다고 정부 조사위원회가 결론 내렸다. **2** 텔레비전이 가장 강력한 미디어인 반면에, 전통적인 인쇄 미디어는 온라인 미디어에게 자리를 잃어가고 있다. **3** "미디어시장에 대한 객관적 견해"를 물을 목적으로 여론형성에 영향을 미치는 미디어 영향의 정도에 관한 조사를 실시한 것은 이번이 처음이다. **4** 문화스포츠관광부 산하 조사위원회의 3년에 걸친 연구에 따르면, 가중 집중 비율-시장점유율과 영향력에 기초한 영향정도-에서 TV가 47.2%, 이어 온라인뉴스 26%, 신문 17.3%로 나타나, 사람들은 자그마한 스크린에 가장 많은 집중을 보였다. **5** TV뉴스와 조사프로그램은 영향력이 모든 세대의 사람들에게 미치는 것으로 나타났으며, 반면에 신문은 보다 나이 많은 사람들에게 매력이 있었고, 젊은이들은 온라인 매체에 끌렸다. **6** 우리나라 일간신문 70개 중에서 3대 일간지-조선, 중앙과 동아-가 57.6%의 집중비율을 가졌다. 조선은 23.7%, 중앙은 17.9%, 동아는 15%를 나타냈다. 다른 7개의 신문만이 2%의 집중비율을 기록했다. **7** 온라인뉴스는 조선일보의 웹사이트인 Chosun.com이 최상위 순위로 7.7%, 다음이 중앙일보 웹사이트 6.8%, 연합뉴스 5.9%순이었다. **8** 국영방송 KBS가 29%의 집중비율을, 다음이 MBC방송네트워크가 10.7%, 그리고 SBS가 5.9%를 나타냈다. 조선일보와 일반프로그램 케이블 채널 TV조선을 포함하는 그 계열사가 7%의 집중비율을 나타냈고, 다음이 중앙일보와 그 계열사가 5.4%, 동아와 그 계열사가 5.3%, 매일경제와 그 계열사가 4.6%, 연합뉴스사와 그 계열사가 2.4%, YTN과 그 계열사가 2.3%를 나타냈다. **9** 이 연구는 70개 일간신문, 11개 채널을 가진 10개 TV방송국, 19개 채널을 가진 13개 라디오 방송국, 그리고 117개의 온라인 웹사이트를 대상으로 2011년도와 2012년도 사이에 이루어졌다. 이 전달매체들의 읽기, 시청, 청취 및 지속 시간의 시간 점유율과 7,000명에 대한 설문조사와 기타의 내용이 최종 결과에 반영되었다. **10** "우리는 이 연구는 최강 매체와 최약 매체를 보게 됨으로서 미디어시장에서 '수다성(plurality: 수 차이의 의미)'에 기여할 것으로 믿는다. 두 번째 보고서는 2016년에 있을 예정이며, 트위트나 페이스 북과 그리고 미디어 소프트웨어로서의 스마트폰과 같은 사회적 미디어들을 포함하게 될 것이다"라고 충남대학교 교수 조성겸 조사위원회 위원장이 말했다.

(8)   **Book reviews 50 years of Korean-Swiss ties**[6]

1 The book "50 Years: Switzerland-Korea," published by the Swiss Embassy in Korea in May 2012, celebrates half a century of shared history between the two nations.

2 The publication reviews the innovations, initiative and passion they developed as

---

6) 책 표지의 사진은 생략함.

partners in areas of trade, science, academia, politics and culture, and profiles individuals who contributed to burgeoning ties over the many decades.

3 An electronic version is available for free at www.swissembassynews.kr/ index.asp. The first 30 people to email the embassy at seo.vertretung@eda.admin.ch will receive a free hard copy, too.

4 What counts most in bilateral relations between countries are the people who contributed to the many fields of cooperation - especially those engaged in business, politics, science and culture.

5 Switzerland is a very old direct democracy, and has maintained peace and neutrality for hundreds of years. Although Korea made miraculous achievements in economic development and the establishment of a vibrant democracy, the Korean Peninsula is still exposed to military tensions.

6 This year Switzerland marks another milestone: the 60th anniversary of the Neutral Nations Supervisory Commission. For 60 years Switzerland has contributed to this body with its presence in the DMZ to observe the maintenance of the 1953 armistice agreement.

7 The commemoration of 50 years of diplomatic ties is a good chance to take stock of the past and reflect on how to further strengthen the Swiss-Korean partnership in the future.   (ephilip2011@heraldcorp.com)

어휘해설 •shared history: 함께한 역사; •innovations, initiative and passion: 기술혁신, 창의정신, 그리고 열정; •profile: 프로파일, 소개하다, 인물평을 쓰다; •burgeon: 싹이 나게 하다; •count: 중요하다; •neutrality: 중립성; •vibrant: 진동하는; •milestone: 이정표; •Neutral Nations Supervisory Commission: 중립국감시위원회; •this body: 이 위원회; •its presence: 주둔; •observe the maintenance: 유지하다; •armistice agreement: 군사정전 협정; •commemoration: 기념, 기념식, 축하; •take stock of ~: ~을 평가하다.

양식구성해설 제목이 있는 본문과 작자 두 요소로 구성됨.

전문국역 책이 한-스 유대관계 50년을 되돌아보다. **1** 2012년 5월 주한 스위스대사관에서 발행한 "50년: 스위스-대한민국"은 두 나라 사이 함께한 반세기 역사를 기린다. **2** 출판물은 무역, 과학, 정치 및 문화의 영역에서 두 나라가 발전시킨 기술혁신, 창의정신, 그리고 열정을 개관하고, 그리고 수십 년에 걸쳐 돈독해져온 유대에 기여한 인물들을 소개한다. **3** 전자버전이 www.swissembassynews.kr/index.asp에서 무료로 이용가능하다. 대사관 메일주소

> seo.vertretung@eda.admin.ch로 보내오는 첫 30명은 또한 하드커버인 책을 받게 될 것이다. ④ 두 나라 사이 양측 관계에서 가장 중요한 것은 여러 협력 분야에서 기여한 사람들, 특히 기업, 정치, 과학 및 문화에서 기여한 사람들이다. ⑤ 스위스는 아주 오래된 직접민주주의 국가이고, 수백 년 동안 평화와 중립국의 입장을 유지해 왔다. 한국이 경제 분야에서 기적의 업적을 이루었고 요동치는 민주주의를 확립해 왔지만, 한반도는 아직도 군사적 긴장에 노출되어 있다. ⑥ 금년은 스위스가 또 하나의 이정표-중립국감시위원회 60주년-을 나타낸다. 스위스는 1953년에 맞은 군사정전협정 유지를 지키기 위해 DMZ 주둔에 60년 동안 기여해 왔다. ⑦ 50년의 외교적 유대의 기념식은 과거를 평가해보고, 그리고 앞으로 스-한 파트너십을 어떻게 더 강화할 것인가에 대해 숙고해 볼 좋은 기회이다.

(9) Barack Obama is the 44th President of the United States. He is the first African-American President. Obama previously served as a United States Senator from Illinois, from January 2005 until he resigned after the election to the presidency in November, 2008.

　　Barack Obama was born to a Kenyan father and an American mother in Honolulu, Hawaii on August 4, 1961. His parents met while they were studying at the University of Hawaii. They separated when he was 2 years old. His father returned alone to Kenya, where he worked as a government economist. He wrote to his son regularly, but visited his son only once. His mother later married an Indonesian, and young Obama moved to Jakarta in 1967 with his mother and stepfather. Obama stayed in Indonesia for 4 years, before returning to Honolulu to live with his grandparents.

　　Obama studied Political Science and specialized in International Relations at Columbia University in New York City. In 1988, He entered Harvard Law School, where he became the first African—American editor of the Harvard Law Review. He graduated from Harvard Law School in 1991. Obama met Michelle Robinson in 1989, and they married in 1992. The couple has two daughters. Obama held several positions professionally between 1993 and 2004. He worked as a lawyer for a law firm and worked as a part—time lecturer at the University of Chicago Law School. Obama also served as a board member at a charitable organization. In 2004, he was elected to the U.S. Senate as a Democrat, and in 2008, he sought the Democratic nomination for the U. S. Presidency.

On November 4, 2008, Barack Obama won the 44th Presidency of the United States, becoming the first African—American to win the victory. "This is your victory. Change has come to America.", he said after winning the election. "The road ahead will be long. Our climb will be steep. We may not get there in one year or even in one term. But America, I have never been more hopeful than I am tonight that we will get there. I promise you, we will get there!"

> 어휘해설 •African-American: 아프리카계 미국인; •serve: 봉사하다, 근무하다; •board member: 이사회 위원; •charitable organization: 자선단체.
>
> 양식구성해설 본문만으로 구성됨.
>
> 부분국역 (끝 단락) 2008년 4월, 버락 오바마는 미국 44대 대통령에 당선되어, 대통령이 된 최초 아프리카계 미국인이 되었다. "이것은 여러분의 승리입니다. 미국에 변화가 일어났습니다."라고 당선된 후 말했다. "앞 갈 길은 멀 것입니다. 우리의 오르는 길은 가파릅니다. 우리는 일 년 만에 혹은 임기 중에 그기에 이르지 못할 수도 있습니다. 그러나 미국, 나는 오늘밤 우리는 그기에 이르게 될 것이라는 희망 그 이상은 결코 가지지 않습니다. 저는 여러분에게 약속합니다. 우리가 그기에 이를 것이라는 것을!"

(10) Existential Life Lessons from David Bowie and Mahatma Ghandi "Ch— ch— ch — changes"

David Bowie

Why is it that many bands are one—hit wonders or have a brief, shining period of success and then fade into oblivion only to be heard from again on compilations and TV shows, such as "Rock of the 80s?"

Because they don't change; they allow themselves to become stale and outdated.

David Bowie — Ziggy Stardust — rock star, actor, and icon is arguably one of the most malleable pop culture figures of all time. He has migrated from one generation to the next with unabashed transformation, living, in effect, his own lyrics to "Changes": singing "time may change me, but I can't trace time."

Librarianship, like Bowie, is arguably one of the most malleable professions in recent years. Looking at Bowie as an example, we know that we must continue to embrace change in order to stay relevant to this and future generations. And, also like Bowie, while we embrace change, we must continue to be what people love about libraries - we certainly don't want to turn off our loyal fan base.

As a result, we still introduce people to the love of reading, but we also introduce people to computers, email and the Internet. We have story hours for children and parents, and we also have classes on how to surf the Internet designed specifically for parents and children (as well as for many other age groups). We provide reading lists for all ages, as well as lists of Web sites.

While libraries and librarians could have turned their backs on the digital revolution, we instead embraced this major change and, if anything, helped to propel it forward. Libraries are, after all, playing an increasingly important role by providing free access to information resources and technology to everyone. Is there anything else out there that can make that claim?

Libraries will continue to be the great equalizer in our society by providing this free access to information, and also by showing people how to access the information they need - whether it's on the Web or buried somewhere in an ancient book. Teaching others how to find, use and evaluate information is a unique skill that librarians bring to a society suffering from information overload.

You must be the change you wish to see in the world. — Ghandi

So far, we have been leaders in the digital revolution. Yet I keep hearing the question, "Won't the Internet make libraries obsolete?" As we all can attest, new technology is making libraries even more vitally important, especially in rural and under-served communities throughout Montana where people often do not have access to the Internet at home.

Libraries have always been places of opportunity, self—help and lifelong learning where we can find what we need for our health, school, jobs and family. And with today's library technology, libraries are reaching beyond their walls to connect to the larger, global community. Polson reaches Paris and Big Sky accesses Beijing. Today's library technology means that information from around the world is just a few clicks away and affords us opportunities like never before.

There is no doubt that libraries are changing, and will continue to change as new ways of managing information become available. The libraries that we know and love today will likely be very different places with very different offerings in just a few years. Changing and moving forward is continuous, hard work. Librarians must continue to embrace change, while simultaneously leading the way for change in information management — being the change we wish to see in the world.

source: Ontana State Library

어휘해설 •Why is it that~에서 it는 가주어이고 that절은 진주어절이다; •band: (음악의) 밴드; •one-hit wonder; 한번 히트로 빤짝함; •brief, shining period of success: 한 순간 성공시기; •oblivion: (세상 등에서) 잊혀진 상태; •compilation: 편집(편찬) (된 것); •stale: 진부한, 퀴퀴한; •outdated: 시대에 뒤떨어진; •malleable: 적응성 있는; •figures: 인물들; •migrate: 이주하다, 이동하다; •unabashed: 부끄러워하지 않는, 겁먹지 않는; •lyrics: 가사; •librarianship: 사서직; •turn off loyal fan base: 충직한 팬 토대를 싫증내다, 그만두다; •surf: ~을 서핑하다; •propel: 가속하다; •equalizer: 동등하게 하는 것; •information overload: 정보과부하; •obsolete: 폐기물; •attest: 증명(증언)하다; •self-help: 자조, 자립(자치); •Polson: 폴스카(폴란드의 폴란드어); •Big Sky: 피츠버그, 도시; •embrace: 수용하다.

양식구성해설 제목이 있는 본문과 출처로 구성됨.

부분국역 (첫 4행)밴드들이 한 번의 히트로 경이의 사건이 되거나 한 번의 빼어난 성공시기를 가진 뒤 잊혀지고 시들어져서 예를 들어 '80년대 락 음악'처럼 단지 편집 판과 TV쇼에서 다시 한 번 듣게 될 뿐이다.//그들은 변하지 않기 때문에, 그들은 스스로 퀴퀴하게 되고 시대에 뒤떨어지게 된다.

(11) **The Key To Creativity, According To Steve Jobs**

By Jeff Dunn on October 21, 2011@edudemic

I've been viewing the Steve Jobs narration of the 'Think Different' ad as well as his 2005 Stanford Commencement address over the past few days. It's served to inspire me, take on new tasks, and generally try things a bit differently. I've felt more creative than I have in recent memory.

If you're not in the mood for a little Steve Jobs multimedia, why not try some good old fashioned text? Earlier today, Brit Morin (great Tumblr to follow) posted this wonderful quote from Jobs on how he thinks creative minds operate.

One of the biggest themes to what Jobs said in many public addresses has been to 'connect the dots' and to critically think about everything you do. According to him, that's a rare trait that many of us do not enjoy. I hope you use this quote to become inspired and to start, well, thinking differently. You never know what you'll find.

"Creativity is just connecting things. When you ask creative people how they did something, they feel a little guilty because they didn't really do it, they just saw something.

It seemed obvious to them after a while. That's because they were able to connect experiences they've had and synthesize new things. And the reason they were able to do that was that they've had more experiences or they have thought more about their experiences than other people.

Unfortunately, that's too rare a commodity. A lot of people in our industry haven't had very diverse experiences.

So they don't have enough dots to connect, and they end up with very linear solutions without a broad perspective on the problem. The broader one's understanding of the human experience, the better design we will have."

- Steve Jobs, Wired, February, 1995

어휘해설 •commencement: (미 대학의)졸업식; •inspire: 영감을 주다; •quote: 인용(문); •post: 게시하다, 공시하다; •dot: 도트, 점, 조각; •trait: 특징, 특성, 특질, 솜씨; •synthesize: 종합(통합, 합성)하다; •commodity: 상품, 산물, 유용한(편리한) 것.

양식구성해설 제목, 저자, 작성일, 출처, 인물사진, 본문으로 구성됨.

부분국역 (첫 문장)나는 '생각을 달리하라'라는 광고에서 스티브 잡의 말을 들었고, 수일 전에 2005년 스탠포드 졸업식 연설을 들었다.

(12)

> 어휘해설 •Caffyns Brighton: 영업소 이름; •miss out: 놓치다; •limited numbers: 한정된 차 대수.
>
> 양식구성해설 광고전단지 내에 본문에 속하는 광고내용과 광고주가 혼합되어 구성됨.
>
> 부분국역 (중간 광고문구)새 차와 중고차 (할인 판매) 행사가 12월 20부터 시작합니다.

(13) 1) Walls have ears.

2) To see is to believe.

3) Time and tide wait for no man.

4) Talk of the devil and you'll hear the flutter of his wings.

5) As one sows so shall he reap.

6) Mend the barn after the horse is stolen.

> 어휘해설   •tide: 조수, 조류; •flutter: 날개 짓; •sow: 씨를 뿌리다; •reap: 수확하다; •barn: 외양간.
>
> 양식구성해설   속담 리스트.
>
> 부분국역   (1번 속담)낮 말은 새가 듣고, 밤 말은 쥐가 듣는다.

제2절 작자 의도 예측

양식구성 확인 다음에 독자는 어떻게 해야 하는가? 작자 의도를 예측하는 것이다. 글은 대체로 목적에 따라 적합한 양식으로 관습화 되어 있으며, 글의 이름 또한 글의 목적을 대개 드러낸다. 따라서 독자는 일단 글의 양식과 이름으로부터 작자 의도를 예측하는 것이 필요하다. 작자 의도 예측 시점은 양식구성 확인 단계와 동시에, 혹은 양식구성 확인 직후이다. 양식에 기초한 작자 의도 (목적, 혹은 기능)의 개념체계는 다음과 같다.[7]

목적(대 분류)	목적(중 분류)	목적(개별 텍스트)
1) 사실전달	안내(문), 신문과 방송의 뉴스, 보고, 공지(문), 공고(문), 선언(문), 식사(문), 판결(문), 안내(방송), 포스터, 초청(장) 등	
2) 해설	설명(문), 안내(서), 해명(서), 강의, 강연, 교과서 등	
3) 주장	연설, 논설, 신문사설, 토론, 칼럼 등	
4) 준칙	법조문, 규칙, 회칙, 정관 등	
5) 협의	회의, 토의, 의논 등	
6) 호소	호소문, 탄원서, 건의문, 청원서, 진정서 등	
7) 수상	일기, 기행, 독후감, 평론, 감상문 등	
8) 사건규명	청문회, 심문, 소사 등	
9) 선전	광고문, 홍보물, 시연회, 강연회 등	
10) 환심	칭찬, 고백 등	

---

[7] 개별텍스트는 해당 글의 목적을 가리킨다(가령: 비행기탑승 안내).

11) 흥미　　유머, 수수께끼, 희곡, 시나리오, 연극, 영화, 퀴즈, 코미디 등
12) 교훈　　속담, 전설, 일화, 우화 등
13) 기타　　대화, 서한문, 만화 등

(1) Dear Sir or Madam

1 On 1 September we returned to you by parcel post one cassette tape recorder, Model EK76, Serial Number 048617, one of a consignment of 12 delivered on 5 August and charged on your invoice number 5624 dated 2 August. The customer who bought this recorder complained about its performance. It was for this reason that we returned it to you after satisfying ourselves that the complaint was justified.

2 We have received no acknowledgement of the returned recorder or of the letter we sent to you on 1 September. It may be that you are trying to obtain a replacement for us. If this is the case and a replacement is not immediately available, please send us a credit note for the invoiced cost of the returned recorder, namely £175.

3 We hope to hear from you soon.

Yours faithfully

어휘해설　•parcel post: 소포우편물; •consignment: 위탁(탁송)물; •charge: 요금을 지불하다, 요금을 청구하다; •performance: 작동; •acknowledgement: 수취증명; •replacement: 교환 품; •credit note: 대변 전표.

의도예측　허두(Dear)에 나타나는 수신자 이름과 본문만 나타나고 있다. 지면 공적 서한문임. 조직체의 업무적 내용 전달이 목적인 것으로 예측됨.

부분국역　**1** 9월1일자에 저희가 귀하에게 모델 EK76, 연번 048617인 카세트테이프 레코드 1개를 소포우편물로 돌려보내 드렸습니다....

---

(2) Dear

1 We are sorry to learn from your letter of 16 September of the need to return one of the recorders supplied to you and charged on our invoice number 5624.

We received your letter of 1 September but regret that we have no trace of the returned recorder. It would help if you could describe the kind of container in which it was packed and state exactly how it was addressed and the method of delivery used. As soon as we receive this information we will make a thorough investigation.

2 Meanwhile I am sure you will understand that we cannot either provide a free replacement or grant the credit you request. If you could wait for about 10 days, we could replace the tape recorder but would have to charge it to your account if our further inquiries should prove unsuccessful.

Yours sincerely

어휘해설 •charge: 요금을 청구하다; •trace: 흔적, 자국, 기록; •pack: (포장)꾸리다; •container: 용기; •free replacement: 무료 교환 품; •the credit: 외상, 증명; •grant: 수여하다, 주다; •thorough investigation: 철저한 조사; •inquiries: 조사내용.

의도예측   허두(Dear-)로 시작하고, 끝맺는 인사말로 된 본문만 있음. 앞 (1)에 대한 답장이다. 지면서한문. 작자의 의사전달이 목적인 것으로 예측.

부분국역   **1** 귀하에게 공급되고 요금이 청구된 레코드 중 하나를 돌려보낼 필요가 있다는 송장 번호 5624에 대한 귀하의 편지를 받게 되어 미안합니다....

---

(3)
STANTON CHASE
I N T E R N A T I O N A L
Executive Search Consultants

Do You Require Executives?
Stanton Chase Korea is ready to assist you!

Industrial
Chemical
Healthcare
Technology
Manufacturing

Financial Service

Consumer Products

Natural Resource & Energy

WWW.stantonchase.com

Telephone: +82 2 551 0203   Email: seoul@stantonchase.com

스탠튼 체이스 코리아

> 어휘해설   •Executives: 관리직원; •industrial: 산업; •healthcare: 보건.
>
> 의도예측   상단에 작자 관련 요소(상호), 중간에 본문, 하단에 작자 관련 요소(웹주소, 전화번호, 멜 주소, 상호)로 구성되어 있는데, 상단 상호에서 컨설턴트 회사로 이해되고. 컨설턴트 중역 제공이 목적인 광고로 예측됨.
>
> 부분국역   <중간 2문장>귀하께서는 관리직원이 필요하십니까? 스탠튼 체이스 코리아가 귀하를 도와드릴 준비가 되어 있습니다.

(4)   **SOUR GRAPES**

1 A hungry fox tried to reach some clusters of grapes which he saw hanging from a vine trained on a tree, but they were too high. So he went off and comforted himself by saying: "They weren't ripe anyhow."

2 In the same way some man, when they fail through their own incapacity, blame circumstances.

> 어휘해설   •trained on: ~로 뻗어 오른; •cluster: 송이, 다발; •go off: 떠나다.
>
> 의도예측   제목이 있는 본문만으로 구성되어 있음. 의도가 예측되지 않음.
>
> 전문국역   신포도 **1** 배고픈 여우가 나무 위에 뻗어 있는 포도 넝쿨에서 포도송이를 발견하고는 따먹으려고 애썼지만 포도송이가 너무 높게 매달려 있었다. 그래서 여우는 떠나면서 스스로 위로하기를, "저 포도송이들은 어차피 익지도 않았을 거야." **2** 이와 마찬가지로 사람들은 자신들의 능력부족으로 무슨 일에 실패했을 때 그 원인을 주위의 탓으로 돌려버린다.

(5) **RELIGIOUS SERVICES**

To apply for a free ad, send your ad text to: khnews@heraldcorp.com

CHRISTIANITY

Seoul International Baptist Church (02-793-6267)

English-language church service offered. Sunday activities include morning worship and Bible study for all ages. Located near Itaewon and a 5-minute walk from Yongsan U.S. military base. Contact Pastor Dan Armistead for more information

Young Nak Presbyterian Church (02-2286-0228)

International worship in English located in downtown Seoul. Sunday at 10 a.m. and 3 p.m. in the Mission Chapel room 505. Contact to Pastor Bill Majors for more information. Visit www.mywe.com

BUDDHISM

Ahnkook Zen Center

Brief practice and discussion of Buddhism in English. Saturdays at 2:30 p.m. except national holidays. Special instruction available from Zen Master Soo Bool. Located near Exit 2 on Anguk Subway Station on Subway Line No.2. Visit www.ahnkookzen.org

ISLAM

The Seoul Central Masjid (02-794-7307)

Juma Prayers in Korean, Arabic and English at 1 p.m. every Friday. Salam prayers are offered five times on weekdays. Exit 3, Itaewon Station, turn left to Seoul Bogwang Elementary School. Visit www.koreaislam.org

HINDUISM

ISKON Seoul Temple (010-2448-6441)

Darshan daily at 7 p.m. Aarti & Kirtan, Sundays at 5-8 p.m. Bhagavd Gita classes in English, Hindi, 'Korean followed by Prasadam Feast in Haebangchon. Situated near

Itaewon. Visit www.krishnakorea.com

JUDAISM

Chabad Jewish Community Center

Rabbi Osher Litzman (010-7730-3770) Services every Sunday, 4-5:30 p.m. fee is required 20.00 per class. Located in Itaewon. Get out at exit #1. Walk straight for 180m, turn right to go uphill toward "Samsung museum of art" For more information http://jewishkorea.com/

어휘해설 •religious services: 종교예배; •International Baptist Church: 국제침례교회; •Presbyterian Church: 장로교회; •morning worship: 오전예배; •bible study: 성경공부; •pastor: 목사; •zen: (불교) 선; •practice: 예배; •special instruction: 특별 설교; •masjid: 회교 성원; •Prasadam: 프라사담(신 또는 성자에게 바치는 음식).

의도예측 제목인 '종교예배'와 여러 종교의 광고 안내문으로 구성되어 있기 때문에 예배 참여 안내문으로 예측됨.

국역 생략.

---

(6) Park warns N.K. against additional nuke tests[8]

By Lee Joo-hee

1 President-elect Park Geun-hye strongly warned against North Korea's additional provocation such as a nuclear test, calling Pyongyang's nuclear ambition a "path toward collapse."

2 "None of the third, fourth or fifth nuclear tests by North Korea will elevate its negotiating power," Park said during the presidential transition committee's debate arranged by the sub-panel on foreign affair's, unification and defense. The meeting was held a day after the North conducted the third, more powerful nuclear test.

3 "The North may, in the future, demand a disarmament negotiation instead of a

---

8) Korea Herald(2013.2.14) 4면 일부의 내용을 여기 양식 속에 옮겨온 것임

denuclearization negotiation by claiming itself to be a nuclear state, but that will be a misjudgment," Park said.

4 Underscoring that more nuclear tests will lead the North to a path of collapse through deeper isolation from the international community. Park affirmed her determination to fortify the South's "comprehensive defense capability that fits the changing strategic environment."

5 Park also expressed commitment to her "trustpolitik" platform.

6 "I believe there are many who believe the trust-building process should be revised (upon the nuclear crisis). But the process is fundamentally based on strong deterrence and it is not an appeasement policy."

7 Park stated that while the policy will remain the same, it may be forced to change if the North resorts to further provocation.

8 "The important philosophy of the trustpolitik is to create a trust that a provocation will be met with corresponding price, and that a willingness to become a responsible member of the international society will be followed by definite opportunities and support."

9 Trustpolitik pushed by Park defines a step-by-step approach to North Korea in parallel with the denuclearization, and that remains constant through political transitions and unexpected domestic or international events, beginning with humanitarian aid to low-level economic cooperation to longer-term projects involving large-scale infrastructure investment.

10 Park also urged the participants to seek measures to build trust with neighboring countries by taking the example from the Helsinki process of Europe - to run trust-building and economic cooperation in parallel by extending bilateral relations with major nations to trilateral and multilateral cooperation.

어휘해설 •President-elect: 대통령 당선자; •provocation: 도발, 도전; •nuclear test: 핵실험;• presidential transition committee: 대통령직 인수위원회; •sub-panel: 하위분과; • disarmament negotiation: 군축협상; •denuclearization: 비핵화; •underscore(=underline): 강조하다; •determination to: ~에 대한 결심; •fortify: 요새화하다, 강하게 하다; •commitment: 공약; •"trustpolitik" platform: 신뢰정책 강령; •trust-building process: 신뢰프로세스; •

deterrence: 저지, 단념; •appeasement policy: 유화 정책; •resort to: 의지하다, 호소하다; •corresponding price: 상응하는 대가; •pushed by: 추진되는; •in parallel with~: ~와 병행해서; •humanitarian aid: 인도적인 도움; •low-level economic cooperation: 낮은 단계 경제협력; •urge: 촉구하다; •measures: 대책; •trilateral and multilateral cooperation: 3자 및 다자 협력.

의도예측 제목이 있는 본문으로 구성되어 있는데, 제목으로 볼 때, 주장을 목적으로 하는 텍스트로 예측됨.

전문국역 ① 박근혜 대통령당선자는 핵실험과 같은 북한의 추가 도발에 대해 강력하게 경고하고, 핵 야욕을 몰락으로 가는 길이라고 했다. ② '북한의 3차, 4차, 혹은 5차 핵실험 어느 것도 협상력을 높이지 못할 것이다.'라고 대통령 인수위 외무, 통일 및 국방 하위분과 토론회에서 말했다. 이 토론회는 북한이 3차, 더 강력한 핵실험을 감행한 다음날 개최되었다. ③ "북한은, 향후에, 스스로를 핵 국가라고 주장하면서 비핵화 협상 대신에 군축협상을 요구할지도 모르지만, 그것은 오판이다."라고 박은 말했다. ④ 더 많은 핵실험은 국제사회로부터 더 고립되게 함으로서 북한을 붕괴의 길로 가게 할 것이다. 박은 남한의 "변하는 전략적 환경에 맞는 종합 방위 능력"을 강화하려는 자신의 결심을 확인했다. ⑤ 박은 또한 자신의 "신뢰정책" 강령에 대한 공약을 나타냈다. ⑥ "신뢰 증진프로세스가 수정되어야 한다(핵 위기에 대해)고 믿는 사람들이 있다고 믿고 있다. 그러나 그 프로세스는 근본적으로 강력한 저지에 기초하고 있고 그리고 프로세스는 유화정책이 아니다." ⑦ 박은 그 정책은 그대로 이면서 만약에 북한이 앞으로 더 도발에 의존한다면 이 정책은 힘을 발휘하게 될 것이라고 말했다. ⑧ "신뢰정책의 중요한 철학은 야욕은 상응하는 대가를 지불하게 되고, 국제사회의 책임 있는 일원이 되려는 의지에는 일정의 기회와 지원이 따른다는 신뢰를 창조하는 것이다." ⑨ 박이 추진하는 신뢰정책은 비핵화와 병행하여 북한에 대한 스텝-바이-스텝 접근방법이라고 정의하며, 그 정책은 정치적 분야 및 예기치 않은 내적인 사건 혹은 국제적인 사건에도 지속적으로 적용되는데, 인도적 도움에서 시작하여 낮은 단계의 경제협력을 거쳐 대규모의 인프라구조 투자를 포함하는 장기적 프로젝트에 이르기까지 적용된다. ⑩ 박은 또한 유럽의 헬싱키 프로세스를 예로 들면서 참여자들로 하여금 이웃 국가들과 함께 신뢰를 구축할 대책을 찾기를 촉구했다 - 강대국들과의 양자 관계를 3자 및 다자 협력으로 확대함으로서 신뢰구축과 경제협력을 병행할 것을 촉구했다.

(7)   Profiles of minister-nominees

Seo Nam-soo
Education

Seo, 60, is set to become the first educational bureaucrat to take helm of the ministry, whose previous chiefs have all been outside experts and politicians.

He has more than 30 years of experiences in the Education Ministry and affiliated offices.

Seo, a native of Seoul, first joined the ministry in 1979 after passing the administrative service exam in 1978.

He served for nearly 20 years until 1999 before taking the vice-superintendent seat at the Gyeonggi Province Office of Education.

He also worked as vice superintendent for the Seoul Metropolitan Office of Education from 2005-2007, before serving as vice minister at the Education Ministry from 2007 for about a year under the late former President Roh Moohyun's administration.

(5968story@heraldcorp.com)

Hwang Kyo-an
Justice

Hwang, 56, is former head of Busan High Prosecutors' Office and well known for his firm commitment to public safety.

A native of Seoul, Hwang, 56, passed the state-run bar exam in 1981 and built his career in prosecution's service on improving public security for many years.

The nominee is also known as a man of principle and has been praised of his rational work style and leadership. Hwang is the author of a guidebook to National Security Law and a devout Christian who attended a seminary to fulfill his knowledge both on law and religion.

He served many posts but retired as chief of Busan High Prosecutors' Office as after failing to become a prosecutor general, the highest post in, prosecution, during the Lee Myung-bak administration. Hwang currently works for Bae, Kim & Lee.

(christory@heraldcorp.com)

Kim Byung-kwan
Defense

Kim. 65, is former deputy commander of the South Korea-U.S. Combined Forces Command and an expert on the Korea-U.S. military alliance.

Kim established a firm relationship with Burwell Bell, then the commander of U.S. Forces Korea, and continued smooth military cooperation between the two countries despite the difference. in diplomatic stance toward North Korea and difficulties in the process of signing the Korea-U.S. Free Trade Agreement.

A native of Gimhae, South Gyeongsang Province, Kim entered Seoul National University

to major in chemical engineering, but dropped out of the school to attend Korea Military Academy the following year. Kim entered the academy at the top of his class and also graduated summa cum laude. (*christory@heraldcorp.com*)

Yoo Jeong-bok
Security, public administration

Yoo, 55, former minister of food, agriculture, forestry and fisheries, is one of the closest aides to President-elect Park Geun-hye.

The veteran bureaucrat and third-term lawmaker served as top secretary to Park from 2008 to 2010 when she reduced her political activities following her defeat to President Lee Myung-bak in the residential nomination race of the Grand National Party.

He is currently the deputy chief of the preparatory committee for her inauguration.

The nominee started his public career at the Ministry of Home Affairs (now the Ministry of Pubic Administration and Security) in 1979 and served as governor for Gimpo County. He became a lawmaker in 2004 and led the Ministry of Food, Agriculture, Forestry and Fisheries for a year in 2010. (*wone0102@heraldcorp.com*)

Yu Jin-ryong
Culture, sports and tourism

Yu, a former vice culture minister and the current dean of Hallyu Graduate School at the Catholic University of Korea, has been named as the new culture minister.

Yu received his bachelor's degree in commerce and trade from Seoul National University, and a Ph.D in public administration from Hanyang University.

Yu became a public official in 1978 and served a number of positions in the nation's cultural sector, including the secretary-general of Korea National University of Arts, and deputy secretary general for planning and management of the culture ministry.

He was appointed as vice culture minister in 2006, during the Roh Moo-hyun administration. However, he served the position for only six months.

(dyc@heraldcorp.com)

어휘해설 •nominee: 임명된 자; •set to: 정하다, 배치하다; •educational bureaucrat: 교육관료; •take helm of: ~을 잡다; •whose previous chiefs: 교육부의 이전 장관들; •affiliated: 관련된; •administrative service exam: 행정고시; •superintendent: 지휘자, 장; •vice minister: 차관;// •High Prosecutors' Office: 고등검찰청; •prosecution's service: 검찰업무; •public safety: 공안; •firm commitment: 강직한 수행; •state-run bar exam: 국가 사법 시험; •public security: 공공보안; •man of principle: 원칙주의자; •rational work style and leadership: 합리적 업무 스타일과 리더십; •National Security Law: 국가보안법; •devout Christian: 독실한 기독교인; •seminary: 신학대; •post: 자리; •prosecutor general: 검찰총장; •Bae, Kim & Lee: 배김이 법무법인;//•deputy commander of the South Korea-U.S. Combined Forces Command: 한미연합사 부사령관; •expert on Korea-U.S. military alliance: 한미군사동맹 전략가; •diplomatic stance: 외교적 입장; •Korea-U.S. Free Trade Agreement: 한미무역협정; •chemical engineering: 화공과; •dropped out of: 자퇴했다; •Military Academy: 육사; •summa cum laude: 최우등생으로;//•Security, public administration: 안전행정부; •food, agriculture, forestry and fisheries: 농림수산식품; •closest aides: 최측근; •veteran bureaucrat and third-term lawmaker: 베테랑 관료 및 3선 국회의원; •top secretary: 비서실장; •residential nomination race: 대통령지명경선; •Grand National Party: 한나라당; •deputy chief of the preparatory committee for her inauguration: 취임준비위 부위원장; •Ministry of Home Affairs: 내무부; •Pubic Administration and Security: 행정안전;// •vice culture minister: 문화부차관; •dean of Hallyu Graduate School: 한류대학원 원장; •secretary-general: 비서관; •planning and management of the culture ministry: 문화부 기획관리.

의도예측 제목 '장관 피임명자 프로파일' 아래 대상자 이름 및 구체 내용으로 구성되어 있는 양식으로 인물을 소개하는 목적으로 예측됨.

부분국역 <교육부>서(60세)는 이전 장관들 모두 외부 전문가 및 정치인들이였던 교육부를 맡는 첫 교육관료 출신이다. 그는 교육부와 관련 단체에서 30년 이상의 경험을 가지고 있다. 서울이 고향인 그는 1978년 행정고시에 패스한 이후 1979년 처음 교육부에 발을 들여 놓았다. 그는 경기도 교육청 부교육감을 맡은 이후 1999년까지 거의 20년 동안 근무해왔다. 그는 또한 2005-2007서울교육청에서 부교육감으로 근무했고, 그 이전 2007년부터 고 전 노무현 정부 아래에서 약 1년 동안 교육부에서 부교육감으로 근무했었다.

(8) **Albert Einstein**

Albert Einstein is regarded as the most influential physicist and intellectual of all time.

Einstein developed the special and general theories of relativity.

Albert Einstein were born on March 14, 1879 in Wurttelnberg, Germany. Einstein's parents were middle—class Jews. His father ran an electrochemical factory. Although Einstein had early speech difficulties, he was a top student in elementary school. In 1888, he entered the Luitpold—Gymnasium. There Einstein clashed with authorities and hated the school's strict rules and teaching methods. He later wrote that his creativity was lost because of strict learning methods. His father sent him to Aarau in northern Switzerland to finish secondary school. In 1896, he enrolled in mathematics and physics teaching diploma program at the Polytechnic in Zurich. Einstein also wrote his first "scientific paper" at that time.

After graduating, Einstein tried to get a teaching post, only to get a job at a patent office in Berne. On April 30, 1905, he finished his thesis, and was awarded a Ph. D degree by the University of Zurich. By 1908, he was recognized as a leading scientist, and appointed lecturer at the University of Berne. The next year, he quit the patent office and the lectureship, and took the position of a part—time physics lecturer at the University of Zurich. In 1911, based on his new theory of general relativity, he had calculated that light from another star would be bent by the sun's gravity. In 1914, he went back to Germany after he was appointed director of the Kaiser Wilhelm Institute for Physics. He won the Nobel Prize for Physics in 1921. In 1933, Einstein was forced to immigrate to the United States because of the Nazis. He took up a position at the Institute for Advanced Study at Princeton. He later became an American citizen in 1940.

On April 18, 1955, Albert Einstein died of internal bleeding in Princeton at the age of 76. Throughout his career, Einstein published hundreds of books and articles about physics. Hc is considered the father of modern physics.

> 어휘해설 •theories of relativity: 상대성 이론; •middle—class: 중류; •electrochemical: 전기화학의; •clash: 충돌하다; •enroll: 등록하다; Polytechnic: 응용전문학교; •teaching post: 교수직; •patent: 특허의, 확실한; •leading scientist: 주임과학자; •quit: 그만두다; •bleeding: 출혈.
> 의도예측 본문의 제목이 Albert Einstein으로 되어 있어 전기로 예측됨.
> 부분국역 (첫 2문장)Albert Einstein은 인류역사에서 가장 영향력 있는 물리학자이자 지식인으로 간주되고 있다. Einstein은 상대성에 관한 특별한 이론들과 일반 이론을 발전시켰다.

(9)

Please come celebrate with us on our happiest day of our life.
We would be honored if you would come and be witnesses of our wedding.

| KANEKO TOSHIHARU
KANEKO YOKO | ' Daughter | KANEKO AYA |
| KIM SECWON
SHIN CHUNOG | ' Son | KIM JONGHYUN |

DATE : 2013. 10. 13.(9.9) SUN PM12:00
LOCATION : 587, Tanbang-dong, Seo-gu, Daejeon, Korea

> 어휘해설 •celebrate: 식블 거행하다; •honor: 존경하다, 경의를 표하다.
> 의도예측 작자부분이 중심 내용으로 되어 있는 본문 및 양식으로 보아 초대장으로 예측됨.
> 전문국역 생략.

(10)   **Preparing for a Successful Negotiation**

1. Parties & Issues

Who (representing what institution) will be in the meeting?
With what degree of responsibility and power to decide?
What are the issues to be dealt with?

2. Alternatives

If no agreement is achieved what alternatives do we have?
What alternatives would they have?
Can we improve our alternatives prior negotiation?

3. Interests

What motivates both parties to negotiate?
What are our interests? What are their interests?
Do we have interests in common?
Do we have opposite interests?

4. Options

What options are we ready to generate?

5. Legitimacy

What objective criteria help us support our options?
What is our sense of fairness?

6. Communication

What questions are needed to be asked?
How should those questions be posed?
What are the messages to send?

7. **Relationship**

   What is it like between the parts?

   How would we like to keep it?

   What can we do (or avoid) to progress in the relationship?

8. **Commitment**

   What are the topics needed to be addressed before committing to a final agreement?

어휘해설 •alternative: 대안; •opposite interests: 손해; •legitimacy: 적법성; •sense of fairness: 공익성, 공평성; •pose: 드러내다; •commitment: 공약, 서약.

의도예측 제목이 있는 본문만의 구성에서 제목의 뜻 '성공적인 협상 준비하기'이 행위목록 예측.

부분국역 (첫 2문장)누가 미팅에 올 것인가? 결정의 책임과 파워는 어느 정도인가?

(11) THIS IS YOUR **LIFE.**
DO WHAT YOU LOVE,
AND DO IT OFTEN.
IF YOU DON'T LIKE SOMETHING, CHANGE IT.
IF YOU DON'T LIKE YOUR JOB, QUIT.
IF YOU DON'T HAVE ENOUGH TIME, STOP WATCHING TV.
IF YOU ARE LOOKING FOR THE LOVE OF YOUR LIFE, STOP;
THEY WILL BE WAITING FOR YOU WHEN YOU
START DOING THINGS YOU LOVE.
STOP OVER ANALYZING, ALL EMOTIONS ARE BEAUTIFUL.
LIFE IS SIMPLE. WHEN YOU EAT, APPRECIATE EVERY LAST BITE.
OPEN YOUR MIND, ARMS, AND HEART TO NEW THINGS
AND PEOPLE, WE ARE UNITED IN OUR DIFFERENCES.
ASK THE NEXT PERSON YOU SEE WHAT THEIR PASSION IS,
AND SHARE YOUR INSPIRING DREAM WITH THEM.
TRAVEL OFTEN; GETTING LOST WILL HELP YOU FIND YOURSELF.
SOME OPPORTUNITIES ONLY COME ONCE, SEIZE THEM.
LIFE IS ABOUT THE PEOPLE YOU MEET, AND
THE THINGS YOU CREATE WITH THEM
SO GO OUT AND START CREATING.
LIFE IS SHORT. LIVE YOUR DREAM AND SHARE YOUR PASSION.

"THE HOLSTEE MANIFESTO" ©2009   WRITTEN BY DAVE, MIKE & FABIAN   DESIGN BY RACHAEL   WWW.HOLSTEE.COM/MANIFESTO

어휘해설	•quit: 그만두다; •appreciate: 정당하게 평가하다, 이해하다; •share: 공유하다.
의도예측	제목이 없는 구성과 글자체로 보아 디자인이 광고 내지 선언으로 예측됨.
부분국역	(첫 3행)이것이 당신의 인생이다. 당신이 좋아하는 것을 하라. 그것을 자주 하라.

(12) DRIVER'S HANDBOOK
Division of Motor Vehicles
North Carolina Department of Transportation

N O R T H C A R O L I N A

Motor vehicle laws are subject to change by the North Carolina General Assembly. Revised May 2009 The North Carolina Driver's Handbook and the Manual de Manejo de Carolina del Norte are available online at www.ncdot.gov/dmv/driver_services/rivershandbook/.

Dear Fellow Motorist:

As you earn your North Carolina driver license, you will be joining 6.5 million drivers across the state. Your preparation and practice will enable you to travel to places of uncommon beauty and diversity across this state. Remember, please, that you also are responsible for driving by the rules of the road and for keeping vigil over other drivers and dangers around you. By obeying the traffic laws and looking out for your fellow traveler, you can help prevent the 214,000 crashes and 1,400 fatalities we have on our highways each year. This handbook was written to help prepare you for the driver license examination. It offers valuable safe driving techniques which will help keep you out of harm's way. If you need additional assistance, contact your nearest driver license office or go online to www.ncdot.gov/dmv.

Safe driving,
Bev Perdue
Governor
Eugene A. Conti, Jr.
Secretary of Transportation
State of North Carolina
Department of Transportation
Division of Motor Vehicles

> 어휘해설　•handbook: 안내문; •be subject to~: ~지배를 받다; •preparation and practice: 연수와 실제; •rules of the road: 도로(교통)법규; •vigil: 철야, 불면; •looking out for: 배려하다; •fatality: 재해, 재난, 사망자; •driver licence examination: 운전면허시험.
>
> 의도예측　서한문의 양식, 첫 큰 글자체 '운전자 안내서'로부터 안내로 예측됨.
>
> 부분국역　(첫 문장)북 캐롤라이나 교통부, 자동차과, 운전자 안내서. 자동차 법은 북 캐롤라이나 의회에 의한 개정 내용을 따른다. 개정된 2009년 5월 북 캐롤라이나 운전자 안내서 및 매뉴얼 de Manejo del Norte가 온라인 www.ncdot.gov/dmv/driver_services/drivershandbook/에서 볼 수 있다.

(13)

P:310.285.5822
F:310.285.8423
137 N.Larchmont Blvd. #708
Los Angeles, CA 90004
animaladvatcatesalliance.org

June 11, 2009

Andrea Kohler, Esq.
County of Kern
District Attorney's Office
1215 Truxtun Avenue
Bakesfield, California 93301

Re: People v. Bemis, et al.

Dear Ms. Kohler

We, the directors of Animal Advocates Alliance, would like to commend you on your recent successful prosecution of Cynthia Bemis and Cynthia Trapani on charges of felony animal cruelty. The undersigned personally took part in the evacuation of Ms. Bemis' dogs from her property in Mojave, and were shocked and saddened at the horrific conditions in which these innocent animals had kept for so many years.

As you know, Ms. Bemis and Ms. Trpani have a long history of animal cruelty and neglect, and have been cited numerous times in Kern, San Bernardino, and Los Angels counties for animal-related offenses. As you are also no doubt aware, animal hoarders have a high rate of recidivism, as has been proven by Ms. Bemis and Ms. Trapani over the years. Despite constant efforts by animal control officers in three counties to prevent these women from abusing countless dogs and cats, Ms. Bemis and Ms. Trapani continued to "collect" hundreds of animals, often moving them from county to county to avoid legal ramifications.

Accordingly, we respectfully request that your department seek the maximum penalty allowed under the California Penal Code of six to nine years imprisonment. Unless Ms. Bemis and Ms. Trapani are physically removed from society, they will undoubtedly continue their pattern of animal abuse and neglect. While it is undeniable that incarceration is costly, and county budgets are tight, it is important to consider that Ms. Bemis' and Ms. Trapani's animal hoarding activities have already cost the taxpayers many thousands of dollars. In addition to the numerous hours county workers have spent attempting to protect these animals, for which they have received due compensation, thirty-five of the most severely abused "Bemis Dogs" were cared for in county shelters for as many as *three years* while this case slowly wound its way through the court system.

In addition, although the animal rescue community has worked tirelessly to find rescues or homes for the nearly two-hundred dogs and cats that remained on the Bemis property at the time of the conviction, approximately fifty are still waiting. If placements are not found in the immediate future for these fifty, they will soon become the responsibility of various county animal shelters as well. Clearly, if Ms. Bemis and Ms. Trapani are not incarcerated for their crimes, they will continue to hoard and abuse animals, and the taxpayers will continue to foot the bill. Rescue and other humane groups such as ours, which have little funding as it is, will continue to be adversely affected, as the funds used to facilitate the rescue of these animals could be applied towards other humane efforts. Most importantly, however, countless dogs and cats will continue to suffer at the hands of these two women.

Thank you so very much for seeking justice for these animals. It is our sincere hope that your department will continue to aggressively pursue all cases of animal cruelty, and will strive to impose the maximum allowable penalties in order to communicate the message that animal abuse and neglect will not be tolerated in Kern County.

Best regards

Lee Goldberg
Lee Goldberg
Director, Animal Advocates Alliance

Michele Westhoff
Michele Westhoff
Director, Animal Advocates Alliance

cc: Edward R. Jagels, Esq., Kern County District Attorney

Animal Advocates Alliance is a California 501(c)(3) non-profit corporation dedicated to promoting the humane treatment of animals through legal advocacy, humane education initiatives, and support of animal rescue and adoption.

어휘해설 •Animal Advocates Alliance: 동물옹호자연대; •advocacy: 지지, 옹호; •alliance: 결연, 협정, 협력(회), 인척, 유사성, 동족; •Esq.: esquire(귀하, 님)의 약자; •director: 중역, 이사; •command: 칭찬하다; •prosecution: 기소, 고발; •on charges of~: ~의 책임을 물어; felony: 흉악범죄, 중죄; •evacuation: 배변, 배설물; •sadden: 슬퍼하다; •horrific: 끔찍한; •animal related offences: 동물 관련 범죄; •animal hoarder: 동물학대; •recidivism: 상습범죄성; abuse: 비난하다; •ramification: 영향, 효과; •maximum penalty: 최대처벌; •imprisonment: 투옥, 구속; •incarceration: 투옥, 감금; •taxpayer: 납세(의무)자; •tirelessly: 끈기 있게; •conviction: 유죄판결; •humane: 인간적인, 인도적인; •pursue: 뒤쫓다; •non-profit corporation: 비영리단체.

의도예측 서한문의 양식, 동물그림, 상호가 동물애호 관련 내용으로 예측됨.

> 부분국역   (본문 첫 문장)Animal Advocates Alliance의 중역들인 저희는 중죄의 동물 살상 책임으로 Cynthia Bemis 및 Cynthia Trapani에 대한 당신의 최근 성공적인 고발에 대해 당신에게 칭찬하고자 합니다.

(14)   **Petition**

We urge the United States government to reject the global warming agreement that was written in Kyoto, Japan in December, 1997, and any other similar proposals. The proposed limits on greenhouse gases would harm the environment, hinder the advance of science and technology, and damage the health and welfare of mankind.

There is no convincing scientific evidence that human release of carbon dioxide, methane, or other greenhouse gases is causing or will, in the foreseeable future, cause catastrophic heating of the Earth's atmosphere and disruption of the Earth's climate Moreover, there is substantial scientific evidence that increases in atmospheric carbon dioxide produce many beneficial effects upon the natural plant and animal environments of the Earth.

_____ ◆ Please send more petition cards for mc to distribute.
    Please sign here

My academic degree is B.S. M.S. Ph.D. in the field of_____

            I have specialized scientific experience in:

_____
Name

_____
Street

_____
City, State, and Zip

> 어휘해설 •petition: 청원(탄원, 진정)(서); •urge: 촉구하다; •global warming agreement: 지구 온난화 합의서; •convince: 납득시키다, 설득시키다; •carbon dioxide: 이산화탄소; •foreseeable: 예견할 수 있는; •catastrophic: 파국의, 대재해의; •disruption: 파멸, 붕괴; •Zip: 우편번호.
>
> 의도예측 탄원서 양식 작성법으로 예측됨.
>
> 부분국역 (첫 문장)우리는 미국 정부에게 1977년 일본, 도쿄에서 서명된 지구 온난화 합의서를 거부할 것을 촉구합니다.

(15) **The Diary of Anne Frank Summary**

How It All Goes Down

On her thirteenth birthday, Anne Frank's parents give her a diary. She's excited because she wants someone, or something, in which to confide all of her secret thoughts. Even though she has a rich social life, she feels misunderstood by everyone she knows. Anne starts writing about daily events, her thoughts, school grades, boys, all that. But, within a month, her entire life changes.

As Jews in German-occupied Holland, the Frank family fears for their lives. When Anne's sister, Margot, is called to appear before the authorities, which would almost surely mean she was being sent to a concentration camp, Anne and her family go into hiding. They move into a little section of Anne's father's office building that is walled off and hidden behind a swinging bookcase. The little diagram of the office building and "Secret Annex" along with the Thursday, July 9, 1942 entry gives us the layout.

For two years, the Frank family lives in this Secret Annex. Mr. and Mrs. van Daan and their son Peter (who is a few years older than Anne) are also in hiding with the Franks. Later, Mr. Dussel' an elderly dentist moves in, and Anne has to share her bedroom with him. Anne's adolescence is spent hidden from the outside world. She's cooped up in tiny rooms, tiptoeing around during the day and becoming shell-shocked from the sounds of bombs and gunfire at night.

Luckily, the Franks have tons of reading material and a radio. Anne grows in her knowledge of politics and literature, and she puts tons of energy into studying and writing. At the same time, she grows further and further away from the other members of the Annex.

We see a real change in Anne when she begins hanging out in the attic with Peter van Daan. Around this time she starts having dreams about a boy she was in love with, another Peter, Peter Schiff. She sometimes even gets the two Peters confused in her head.

She comes to see Peter (of the Annex) as much more than she first thought. She finds him sensitive and caring, and they talk about everything, including sex. Eventually their relationship changes. Anne and Peter's passion turns into a friendship and a source of comfort for them both.

Another big change for Anne happens when the war seems to be ending. She hears that personal accounts such as her diary will be in demand after the war ends. We see a return to her earlier optimism as she begins editing her diary with vigor and excitement.

Unfortunately, this does not last. Even as Anne becomes more and more sensitive to the suffering going on in the world, her own suffering becomes unbearable. She feels completely alone. She thinks everyone hates her. She feels constantly criticized. And there is no escape. At one point, she thinks it might have been belter it she and her family had all died instead of hiding in the Annex. As Anne becomes harder on those around her, she also becomes harder on herself, berating herself for being mean to the other members of the Annex.

There her diary ends. Two short months after Anne's fifteenth birthday, and two days after he last diary entry, the secret Annex is raided. We don't know Anne's thoughts or feelings at that point any time after, but we know things got worse.

As you probably already know, Anne and the other members of the Annex were sent to various concentration camps. Anne's father, Otto Frank, was the sole survivor.

어휘해설   •How it all goes down: 이 모든 것이 어떻게 받아들여지나; •confide: 신뢰하다, 털어놓다; •German-occupied Holland: 독일에 의해 점령된 네덜란드; •concentration camp: 집단 캠프; •wall off: 벽으로 차단하다; •swinging bookcase: 흔들거리는 책장; •adolescence: 청년기, 청년다움; •coop: 가두다; •shell-shocked: 깜짝 놀란, 전쟁신경증에 걸린; •hang out: 매여 있다; •attic: 다락방; •caring: 남을 배려할 줄 아는; •berate: 호되게 꾸짖다; •for being mean

  to the other members of the Annex: Annnex의 다른 구성원들에게 비열하게 되는 것 때문에;
•raid: 습격하다.

의도예측 제목이 있는 본문에서 제목으로 보아 Anne Frank의 일기에 관한 내용으로 예측.

부분국역 (본문 첫 부분)Anne Frank의 열세 번째 생일날, 그녀의 부모님은 그녀에게 일기장을 사준다. 그녀는 자신의 모든 비밀을 털어놓고 싶은 누군가, 혹은 무엇인가를 원했기 때문에 흥분된다. 비록 그녀는 풍부한 사회생활을 하지만, 자기를 알고 있는 모든 사람들에 의하여 잘못 이해되고 있다고 느낀다. Anne는 일일 사건들, 생각들, 학교성적, 남학생들, 그 모든 것을 쓰기 시작한다. 그러나 한 달 만에 그녀의 전체 생활이 변한다.//독일 사람들로 메워진 Holland에서 유태인으로서 Frank 가족은 자기들 생활을 두려워한다.

제3절 본문 크기 확인

  독자가 독해재료의 양식구성을 확인하고 작자의 의도를 예측한 다음에는 어떻게 해야 하는가? 독자는 지나쳐 버릴 수도 있고(가령, 관련이 없는 이유로), 읽게 될 수도 있다. 읽게 될 경우 시간 관점에서 지금 읽느냐 나중에 읽느냐를 결정하게 될 것이다. 지금이든 나중이든 읽고자 하는 경우, 이 읽는 단계에서는 어떻게 해야 하는가? 정직한 문장들로 되어 있는 본문의 크기를 확인하는 것이다. 본문 크기의 확인은 본문의 물리적 크기와 계층적 층을 확인하는 것이다. 가령, 본문이 문인지, 문들로 된 단락인지, 들여쓰기에 의한 혹은 행간을 띄운 단락들로 된 절(section)인지, 여러 절들로 된 장(chapter)인지를 확인하는 것이다. 이 확인은 읽을 본문의 분량, 내용분야, 난이도, 소요시간을 짐작하게 해준다.

(1) One ill word asks another.

어휘해설 생략.
크기해설 한 문장 길이.
전문해석 가는 말이 고와야, 오는 말도 곱다.

(2) You must learn creep before you go.

> 어휘해설　•creep: 기다.
> 크기해설　한 문장 길이.
> 전문해석　걷기 전에 기는 것부터 배우라.

(3) Six million dollars is a small amount in the gasoline market. The United States will consume over 20 million barrels of oil a day. Replacing some of oil with ethanol seems, so far, to be most feasible solution to reducing the country's dependence on petroleum. Today, most cars on the road can use a mix of 10 percent ethanol and 90 percent gasoline. But the car industry is rapidly changing to a higher mix of ethanol.

> 어휘해설　•gasoline: 가솔린, 휘발유; •ethanol: 에탄올; •so far: 이제(여기, 지금, 이점 까지)는
> •feasible: 실행할 수 있는, 가능한; •petroleum: 석유.
> 크기해설　본문 한 단락 크기.
> 전문국역　6백만 달러가 가솔린 시장에서는 적은 량이다. 미국은 하루에 2천만 배럴 이상을 소비할 것이다. 석유 일부를 에탄올로 대치하는 것은, 이제, 국가가 석유에 의존하는 것을 줄이는 그럴듯한 해결책인 것 같다. 도로를 달리는 대부분의 차량은 10%의 에탄올과 90% 가솔린을 혼합한 것을 사용한다. 그러나 자동차 회사는 에탄올을 보다 많이 혼합하는 수준으로 빨리 전환하고 있다.

(4) Dear Lesley

19- SECRETARIES CONFERENCE, 8/9 OCTOBER 19-

As a valued member of the Institute of Secretaries, I have pleasure in inviting you to attend our special conference to be held at the Clifton Hotel, London on Tuesday/Wednesday 8/9 October 19-.

This intensive, practical conference for professional secretaries aims to:

- increase your managerial and office productivity
- improve your communication skills
- bring you up-to-date with the latest technology and techniques
- enable networking with other secretaries

The seminar is power-packed with a distinguished panel of professional speakers who will give expert advice on many useful topics. A programme is enclosed giving full details of this seminar which I know you will not want to miss.

If you would like to join us, please complete the enclosed registration form and return it to me before 30 June with your fee of £50 per person.

I look forward to seeing you again at this exciting conference.

Yours sincerely

어휘해설 •secretaries conference: 사무직원 회의; •valued member: 정규 직원; •Institute of Secretaries: 사무원; •intensive: 집중적인; •practical: 실무의; •managerial: 관리의; •office productivity: 직무생산성; •up-to-date with the latest~: 최근의 ~로 업데이트 시키다; •-packed: 꽉 찬, 넘치는; •registration form: 등록양식.

크기해설   허사, 제목, 끝 인사말을 각각 단락으로 간주하여 8단락(행간으로 표시) 크기.

부분국역   ...전문 사무직원들을 위한 집중 실무 회의의 목적은 다음과 같습니다: 관리 및 사무 생산성 향상... 세미나는 여러 유익한 주제에 관해 전문적인 조언을 줄 전문 강사들을 초청하는 구별되는 소위원회로 파워 넘친다. 프로그램이 첨부되는데, 세미나에 대한 상세내용을 제공해준다... 참여하고 싶으면, 동봉된 등록양식을 작성하여 저에게 보내주기 바랍니다....

---

(5)

1 When their children begin talking about dieting, most parents smile indulgently and do not worry. In figure-conscious America, it is quite natural for young people to desire a slim figure. However, for some teenagers, dieting is no laughing matter. For them, dieting is not a momentary whim to be pursued and forgotten; instead, it is the symptom of a serious emotional disorder called anorexia nervosa, a disease that can have terrible, even fatal consequences.

2 The disease usually strikes adolescent and preadolescent girls-who have no reason to diet. They are not overweight, nor have they been told to diet by their doctors, they are not preparing to take part in specialized sports activities requiring a slender figure. These girls stop eating because, despite all evidence to the contrary, they believe they are fat. Determined to lose the imaginary excess poundage, they refuse to eat more than a few morsels of food. Usually, the weight loss is raped, sometimes more than fifty pounds in a few months.

3 Some teenagers who are obsessed with the need to diet seek treatment because they or, more typically, their parents realize that the diet is leading to starvation. Others do not seek treatment but simply begin eating normally again on their own. However, because the disease comes in waves, or bouts, a few victims manage to keep it a secret and so avoid both exposure and treatment.

4 Unfortunately, members of this group are in the most serious danger. Although they may be able to keep their secret into adult-hood, the disease, if untreated, almost always goes out of control, with tragic results. In fact, some victims-like gymnast Christy Henrich and pop singer Karen Carpenter-died from the physical effects of prolonged starvation, Mortality rates are high; One in ten anorexia patients will die within ten years of the disease's onset.

5 To date, the actual cause of the starvation disease has not been determined. According to one theory, teenagers may be starving themselves in order to rebel against parental authority. Traditionally, the refusal to eat has been a young child's weapon against parental discipline. The parent may plead and even demand that the child eat, but by refusing, the child demonstrates his or her power over the situation. Unconsciously, teenagers who diet to the point of starvation may be attempting to teach their parents the same lesson : Control is not in the hands of the parents.

6 According to another theory, anorexia may indicate a young girl's deep-rooted fear of growing up, from this perspective, starving the body can be viewed as a way of maintaining its childish contours and rejecting adult femininity. Yet another hypotheses views the disease as a form of self-punishment. The victims may have extraordinarily high standards of perfection and punish themselves for failing to meet their goals.

어휘해설 •indulgently: 관대하게; •figure-conscious: 몸매를 의식하는; •slim: 호리호리한; •whim: 변덕; •anorexia nervosa: 거식증; •strike: ~에게 닥치다; •adolescent: 젊은이; •preadolescent: 사춘기 이전; •slender: 날씬한; •imaginary excess poundage: 상상을 한 과체중의 파운드; •morsel: 한입, 가벼운 식사; •weight loss: 체중감량; •rape: 강탈하다; •obsess: 들리다, 붙다, 괴롭히다; •comes in waves, or bouts: 파상적으로 혹은 발작적으로 오다; •gymnast: 체육교사; •mortality rate: 사망률; •has not been determined: 밝혀지지 않았다; •rebel against: 반항하다; •parental discipline: 부모 훈육; •plead: 항변하다; •disease's onset: 질병의 공격; •to date: 오늘날까지; •starvation disease: 굶는 병; •to the point of~: ~라고 말할 정도까지; •childish contour: 어린이다운 곡선; •adult femininity: 성인여성임; •self-punishment: 자기채벌; •extraordinarily: 특별히, 이례적으로; •high standards of perfection: 지나친 완벽의 기준.

크기해설 본문은 여섯 단락의 크기(약 1쪽 분량).

전문번역 ① 자기 아이들이 다이어트에 대해 이야기하기 시작할 때, 대부분의 부모님들은 관대하게 미소를 지으며 걱정을 하지 않는다. 몸매를 의식하는 미국에서는 젊은이들이 호리호리한 몸매를 갈망하는 것은 아주 당연하다. 그러나 일부 10대들에서는 다이어트가 웃을 일이 아니다. 그들에게 있어 다이어트는 추구하다가 잊어버릴 임시적 변덕이 아니다. 오히려 다이어트는 거식증-무섭고도 심지어 치명적인 결과를 가져올 수 있는 질병-이라고 부르는 심각한 감정혼란이다. ② 거식증은 보통 젊고 사춘기의 여성-다이어트를 할 이유가 없는-에게 온다. 그들은 과체중이 아니고, 그리고 그들은 의사로부터 다이어트 하라는 조언도 듣지 않았고, 그들은 날씬한 몸매를 가져다주는 특별 스포츠 활동에 참여할 준비를 하고 있지 않다. 이런 소녀들이 먹지 않는 이유는 그 반대의 모든 증거에도 불구하고, 자기들은 살이 찌다고 믿기 때문이다. 상상의 과체중 파운드 무게를 줄이기로 결심한 그들은 몇 모금의 식사 이상은 먹기를 거부한다. 보통은 체중 감량이 억지로 이루어지는데, 때때로는 2-3개월 만에 50파운드 이상 감량된다. ③ 다이어트의 필요에 괴로워하는 일부 10대들은 치료 쪽을 찾는데, 이유는 그들이 혹은 더 전형적으로는 그들의 부모가 다이어트가 굶어죽게 되는 경우로 이어진다고 인식하기 때문이다. 다른 10대들은 치료 쪽을 택하지 않고 단순히 자신의 방식대로 다시 먹기 시작한다. 그러나 질병이 파상적으로 오기 때문에 소수의 희생자들은 질병을 비밀로 하면서 노출과 치료를 피한다. ④ 불행하게도 이 그룹의 여성들이 가장 심각한 위험에 처한다. 비록 그들이 그들의 비밀을 성인임 척하여 억제해두면, 그 질병은 만약 치료를 안 받을 경우, 거의 항상 통제 불가하게 되어 비극적인 결과를 초래한다. 사실, 어떤 희생자들은 – 체육교사 Christy Henrich와 팝가수 Karen Carpenter와 같이 – 오래 끌은 굶주림의 신체적 결과로 죽는다. 사망률은 높다. 거식증 환자 10명 중 1명이 그 병의 발병 10년 안에 죽을 것이다. ⑤ 오늘날까지 굶주림 병의 실제 원인은 밝혀지지 않았다. 한 이론에 따르면, 10대들은 부모의 권위에 반항하기 위해서 스스로 굶을 수도 있다. 전통적으로 먹기를 거부하는 것은 부모의 훈육에 반하는 어린 아이의 무기였다. 부모는 항변하고 아이가 먹으라고 요구하기까지 하지만 아이는 거절함으로서 그 상황에 대하여 자신의 힘을 과시한다. 무의식적으로, 굶어 죽을 정도까지 다이어트 하는 10대들은 자기 부모에게 똑 같은 식으로 가르치려고 할 수도 있다: 통제는 부모님의 수중에 있지 않습니다. ⑥ 다른 한 이론에 따르면, 거식증은 성장에 대해 깊이 뿌리박혀 있는 젊은 여성의 공포를 나타낼 수도 있고, 자기 관점에서 신체를 굶기는 것은 어린이의 윤곽(모습)을 유지하면서 성인여성을 거부하는 방식으로 볼 수도 있다. 그러나 또 하나의 가설은 그 질병을 자기체벌의 형태로 본다. 그 희생자들은 특이하게 지나친 완벽의 기준을 견지하여 자신의 목적을 충족시키지 못한 것에 대하여 자기를 체벌하는 것일 수도 있다.

(6) **A LESSON LEARNT TOO LATE**

A bird in a cage at a window used to sing at night-time. A bat which heard her came up and asked why she never sang by day, but only at night. She explained that there was a good reason: it was while she was singing once in the daytime that she was captured, and this had taught her a lesson. "It's no good taking precautions now." said the bat. "You should have been careful before you were caught."

어휘해설   •bat: 박쥐; •precaution: 사전조심.
크기해설   제목(소 잃고 외양간 고치기)이 있는 본문 한 단락의 크기.
전문국역   창문 옆에 매달려 있는 새장 안에서 새 한 마리가 밤에만 노래를 부르곤 했다. 그 노래를 들은 박쥐가 다가와서 어째서 낮에는 전혀 노래를 부르지 않다가 하필 밤에만 노래를 부르냐고 물었다. 새는 당연히 그럴만한 사연이 있다고 말했다. 자기는 한때 낮 동안에 노래를 부르다가 잡혔으며 그래서 이것이 그에게 교훈이 되었다는 설명이었다. "이제야 조심해 보았댔자 무슨 소용이 있겠나. 자네는 잡히기 전에 조심했어야 했는데 말일세."하고 박쥐가 말했다.

(7) **"The Handyman's Special"**

By Timothy Josiah Morris Peltz, who attended a medium-sized private school in Lawrenceille, New Jersey.

1 I made my first trip to Costa Rica when I was fifteen. I spent a summer living with a Costa Rican family in the capital city of San Jose and studying at a language school. I was eager to absorb as much of the culture as I possibly could, and so for dinner on my first night in the country I stuffed myself with the most popular traditional dish, *gallo pinto*, or rice and beans.

2 The next morning I woke up early and walked a few blocks to the Costa Rican Language and Dance Academy. I was placed in a class, and for the rest of the morning I studied Spanish verbs and phrases. We broke for lunch at noon, and as the school emptied out I stayed behind in class to finish up a grammar exercise. I hadn't eaten breakfast and was hungry for some more *gallo pinto*, but just as I was walking out the door to go to lunch I felt nature call.

3 I remembered seeing the women's bathroom as I came in, but I didn't see one for the men. I wandered the halls. I saw no men's bathroom. I became desperate. Still no men's bathroom. I looked left, then right, swallowed my pride and slipped into the ladies' room.

4 It was only meant for one person, but wasn't at all small. It had several beautiful antique fixtures, such as a claw-foot porcelain bathtub (with a pile of rusty hangers in it) and an old toilet with a gold-plated handle.

5 I sat down and did what I had forgotten one generally does after eating lots of beans. I finished up (remembering to throw the toilet paper in the wastebasket, as is done in Costa Rica to keep the pipes from clogging) and pulled the gold-plated handle. Nothing happened. Huh, that's funny. Tried again. Nothing.

6 For years my father worked as a maintenance man at a summer camp, and had a great deal of experience with plumbing. I, however, had been sheltered from the world of waste removal and had been too concerned with the high pursuit of academia to learn my father's art. It took being stuck in the ladies' bathroom of a strange school in a foreign country with a full, broken toilet to make me realize the error of my ways.

7 There was no one around; I could have just slipped back out and no one would have known I was the culprit. But I knew I would dishonor my father if I walked away (it wouldn't reflect too well on me as a person either), so I decided I would try my best to deal with the situation.

8 For the first time in my life, I opened up the cover at the back of the toilet. I studied the mechanism for a minute and realized that there needed to be something that would connect the handle to the plug that drains the water. I looked around the room, grabbed a hanger from the bathtub, twisted it into a straight piece of wire, attached one end to the stopper and one to the handle, and flushed. I heard the swishing sound of success as the contents of the toilet disappeared into never-never land.

9 That day I learned what my father already knew, that life calls for an understanding not only of lofty topics, but of more practical matters as well. Most importantly, I learned not to run away from sticky situations, but to deal with them with grace, persistence, and a sense of humor. This was the first in a series of realizations about the importance of public service at the most clown-and-dirty levels, the beginning of a personal transformation that would lead to my returning to Costa Rica the next summer to revive a recycling program in the Monteverde Cloud Forest.

10 But that was a ways in the future. For the moment, I needed to eat and get back to class. With newfound confidence and sense of purpose, I ran to the restaurant across the street and gobbled down a big plate of beans.

어휘해설   •stuff: 배불리 먹다; •broke for lunch: 점심식사를 했다; •stayed behind in class: 수업 후 남았다; •wander: 돌아다니다, 배회하다; •nature call: 생리적 요구가 부르다; •swallowed one's pride: 자존심을 억제하다; •n't at all: 전혀 ~하지 않은; •antique fixture: 골동 비품; •claw-foot porcelain bathtub: 발이 있는 도자기 욕탕; •rusty hanger: 녹이 쓴 고리; •gold-plated handle: 금붙이가 있는 손잡이; •keep the pipes from clog: 파이프가 막히지 않게 하다; •maintenance man: 관리인; •plumb: 배관수리공하다; •waste removal: 쓰레기 제거; •culprit: 범죄자, 피의자; •drain: 배수하다, 방수하다; •grab: 꽉 잡다; •flush: 왈칵 흐르다; •lofty: 고상한; •sticky: 끈적끈적한, 곤란한; •clown-and-dirty: 천하고 더러운; •ways: 방향; •recycling program: 재생 프로그램; •gobbled: 게걸스레 먹다.

크기해설   저자를 표현하는 부분과 제목이 있는 본문 1쪽 남짓의 크기.

선문국역   The Handyman's Special(잡역부의 특별함). 저자 Timothy Josiah Morris Peltz는 New Jersey주 Lawrenceille에서 중간 크기의 학교에 다녔음. **1** 나는 15살 때 코스타리카로 첫 여행을 했다. 나는 San Jose라는 수도에서 코스타리카 시민의 집에서 생활하고 언어연수원에 공부하면서 여름을 보냈다. 나는 내가 할 수 있는 한 그 문화의 많은 것을 열심히 흡수하려고 했으며, 그래서 정찬은 그 나라 첫 날 밤 가장 전통적인 식사인 *gallo pinto*, 즉 밥과

콩을 배불리 먹었다. ② 그 다음날 아침 나는 일찍 일어났으며 몇 블록을 걸어 코스타리카 언어 및 무용 학원으로 갔다. 나는 한 반에 배정되었으며 남은 오전 시간대에는 스페인어의 동사와 구를 공부했다. 우리는 정오에 점심식사를 했으며, 수업을 마친 다음에 나는 문법 연습문제를 끝내기 위하여 뒤에 남았었다. 나는 아침을 먹지 않았었기 때문에 배가고파 *gallo pinto*를 좀 더 먹었다. 그러나 정찬을 먹으러 교실 문을 걸어 나갈 때 나는 생리적 요구가 부르는 것을 느꼈다(즉 화장실에 가고 싶었다). ③ 나는 들어설 때 여자화장실이었음이 기억이 났다. 그러나 남자용 화장실이 보이지 않았다. 나는 홀을 돌아다녔다. 나는 남자 화장실을 보지 못했다. 나는 절망적이었다. 계속 남자화장실이 나타나지 않았다. 나는 왼쪽으로 보고 오른쪽으로 보았고, 자존심을 억제하고 숙녀화장실로 미끄러져 들어갔다. ④ 화장실은 1인용이라고 표시되어 있었지만 전혀 작지 않았다. 화장실에는 발이 있는 도자기 욕탕(욕탕 내 녹이 슨 여러 손잡이와 함께)과 금붙이가 달린 손잡이가 있는 변기 등 여러 아름다운 골동 비품들이 있었다. ⑤ 나는 앉아서 그리고 콩을 많이 먹은 후에 사람들에게 일반적으로 일어나는 현상을 내가 잊고 있었던 것을 했다. 나는 일을 끝냈고(파이프가 막히지 않도록 코스타리카에서 하는 대로 화장지를 쓰레기통에 던지는 것을 기억하면서) 그리고 금붙이가 달린 손잡이를 당겼다. 아무 일도 일어나지 않았다. 후, 이것은 이상한데, 다시 시도했다. 아무 일도 일어나지 않았다. ⑥ 여러 해 동안 나의 아버지는 여름 캠프 장에서 관리인으로 일을 했고, 그래서 배관수리에 많은 경험을 가지고 있었다. 그러나 나는 쓰레기청소 세계로부터 숨었었고, 그리고 또한 고급의 학문추구에 관심이 많아 아버지의 기술을 배우지 못했다. 외국의 낯선 학교에서 완전히 고장 난 여자화장실에 맞부딪혀 나로 하여금 내 (사고)방식의 잘못을 깨닫게 했다. ⑦ 주위에 아무도 없었다. 나는 바로 슬쩍 빠져나갈 수 있었고, 아무도 내가 범인이라는 것을 몰랐을 것이다. 그러나 내가 걸어 나가버린다면(그것이 역시 한 인간으로서의 나에 대해 나를 잘 반영해 주지 않는다) 나는 아버지를 존경하지 않게 되는 것임을 알았고, 그래서 나는 그 상황을 다루기 위해 최선을 다하기로 결정했다. ⑧ 내 인생에 처음으로, 나는 화장실 뒤에 있는 덮개를 열었다. 나는 잠시 장치를 살폈고 그리고 물을 배수하게 하는 플러그에 핸들을 연결시키는 무엇인가가 있어야 된다는 것을 깨달았다. 나는 주위를 두리번거리다가 변기통에 달린 손잡이를 꽉 잡고 그것을 전선이 있는 쪽으로 틀었고, 한쪽 끝을 안전장치에 다른 한쪽은 손잡이에 붙였는데 왈칵 흘렀다. 나는 화장실 내용물이 끝없는 지면으로 사라질 때 획 소리 나는 성취의 소리를 들었다. ⑨ 그날 나는 나의 아버지가 이미 알고 계셨던 것을 배웠고, 인생이란 고상한 주제들에 대한 이해뿐만 아니라 또한 보다 실제적인 문제들에 대한 이해도 요구한다는 것을 배웠다. 가장 중요한 것으로 나는 끈적끈적한 상황으로부터 도망칠 것이 아니라 그 상황을 호의, 인내, 유머감각을 가지고 다루는 것을 배웠다. 이번이 가정 천하고 더러운 수준의 공공서비스의 중요성에 관한 일련의 현실에서 처음이고, 그리고 Monteverde Cloud Forest에 재생프로그램을 받아들여 그 다음 여름 코스타리카로 다시 돌아오게 하는 개인 변화의 계기가 되었다. ⑩ 그러나 그것은 미래의 방향이었다. 현재로는 나는 식사를 하고 교실로 돌아갈 필요가 있었다. 새로 발견된 자신감과 목적의식을 갖고 나는 식당을 향해 길을 달려가서 큰 접시의 콩을 게걸스레 먹었다.

(8)   **Ban Ki-moon**

Ban Ki-moon is the 8th Secretary-General of the United Nations.

Ban Ki-moon was born on June 13, 1944 in Eumseong, Chungchungbuk-do. In his school days, he studied English so hard that his friends said he was crazy about English. His eagerness for studying English impressed an American engineer's wife, so she helped him practice it. Basically he was quiet, but very talkative in practicing English. His hard work paid off in the end. When he was in the third year at high school, Ban won the VISTA(Visit International Student to America) competition. Students from 43 different countries including Ban visited America. They were invited to the White House to meet U.S. President John F. Kennedy. The experience led a country-bred boy to pursue a public career as a diplomat.

Ban majored in international relations at Seoul National University. After graduating from the university, he joined the Korean Ministry of Foreign Affairs and Trade the same year. He earned a master's degree from the Kennedy School of Government at Harvard University. For over 25 years, Ban served in a variety of diplomatic posts inside and outside of Korea. He was also actively involved in issues relating to inter-Korean relations. In 2001, he worked for the United Nations. After that, he returned to Korea and served as Minister of Foreign Affairs and Trade. In 2005, he played a leading role as Foreign Minister to promote peace and stability of the Korean Peninsula.

In 2007, Ban became the second Asian to hold the post of Secretary-General of the U.N. Many people say that Ban is a consensus builder who would be able to work harmoniously with everyone. He received countless prizes, medals and honors from all over the world. Now, he is working hard to make the world a better, more peaceful place.

> 어휘해설 •Secretary-General: 사무총장; •crazy: 미친, 열중한, 괴상한; •impress: 감명을 주다, 인상을 주다; •pay off: 보답하다; •diplomatic post: 외무(교)의 자리; •consensus: 일치, 조화, 합의.
>
> 크기해설 제목이 있고 세 단락으로 된 본문 크기.
>
> 부분국역 (첫 부분)반기문은 여덟 번째 UN 사무총장이다.// 반기문은 충청북도 음성에서 1944년 6월 13일 태어났다. 고등학교 다닐 때, 그는 영어를 매우 열심히 공부를 해서 그의 친구들은 그가 영어에 미쳤다고 했다.

(9) Police Say Game Sites Hotbed of Cyber Crime

More than half of online crimes are related to game sites and the perpetrators are getting younger, the police said yesterday.

The latest trends in cyber crimes are that they are getting more generalized and organized, Chang Yoon-shik, chief of Cyber Crime Investigation Team 1 at the National Police Agency (NPA), told The Korea Times yesterday.

The NPA yesterday announced the number of online crimes this year had reached more than 40,000 by the end of July, an 18 percent increase from that of same period last year.

Previously cyber crimes were something that were committed only by computer specialists, but now teenagers are taking part in such crimes, and even those with no computer skills or backgrounds such as organized criminals are now taking part in cyber crime, Chang said. Organized crime rings simply hire or conspire with computer experts because it makes money.

According to Chang, online game sites are the most frequent targets of cyber crimes. Out of some 40,000 cyber crimes committed this year, more than 22,000 were online game related, according to the NPA.

This is because these online games are not treated just as online games, and their money not treated as imaginary money, Chang said. A lot of cyber crimes involve cyber money, but people are buying and selling this cyber money with real cash.

Chang was cautious about saying whether online game sites are responsible for such crimes taking place offline.

The world inside the Internet is another real time and space for these people. They can't buy real money or items with their cyber money, but they still buy and sell this money because they are rich and powerful as long as they are online, he said.

But a number of cyber crimes involving cyber gaming money show that cyber money is tradable for hard money. On July 3, the NPA arrested two hackers, including a 22-year-old college student identified as Choi, on charges of manipulating the server of an Internet game service provider to obtain 60 quadrillion won in cyber money and exchange it for 1.5 billion won in real money.

어휘해설 •hotbed: 온상; •perpetrator: 가해자, 범인, 하수인; •commit: 저지르다, 의무 지우다; •computer specialist: 컴퓨터 전문가; •conspire: 음모를 꾸미다; •imaginary money: 가공의 돈; •offline: 오프라인으로; •tradable: 교환 가능한; •hard money: 실제의 돈; •manipulate: 처리하다, 조작하다, 조종하다; •quadrillion: 천조의.

크기해설 제목이 있는 1쪽 분량 정도의 본문 크기.

부분국역 (첫 부분)경찰은 게임 사이트가 사이버범죄의 온상이라고 말한다. 온라인 범죄의 절반 이상이 게임 사이트와 관련되어 있고, 범인들은 더욱 젊어지고 있다고 경찰이 어제 말했다.// 사이버범죄의 최근 경향은 범죄가 더욱 보편화되고 있고 조직화되고 있다고 경찰청 사이버범죄 수사1팀장인 장윤식이 어제 코리아타임즈에서 말했다.//

(10)

For Women

- A neutral colored suit in navy or another dark color with a skirt
- Skirt length should be a little below the knee and never shorter than above the knee
- Blouses should be cotton or silk (white or light pastel color)
- Pantyhose should be flawless (no runs) and conservative in color. (You may want to bring an extra pair with you)
- Basic pumps with 1"-2" heel (No strappy sandals or platforms!)
- Simple Accessories. No visible body piercing (nose rings, eyebrow rings, etc.)
- Make-up should be minimal and in conservative tones
- minimal cologne or perfume
- Light briefcase or portfolio case

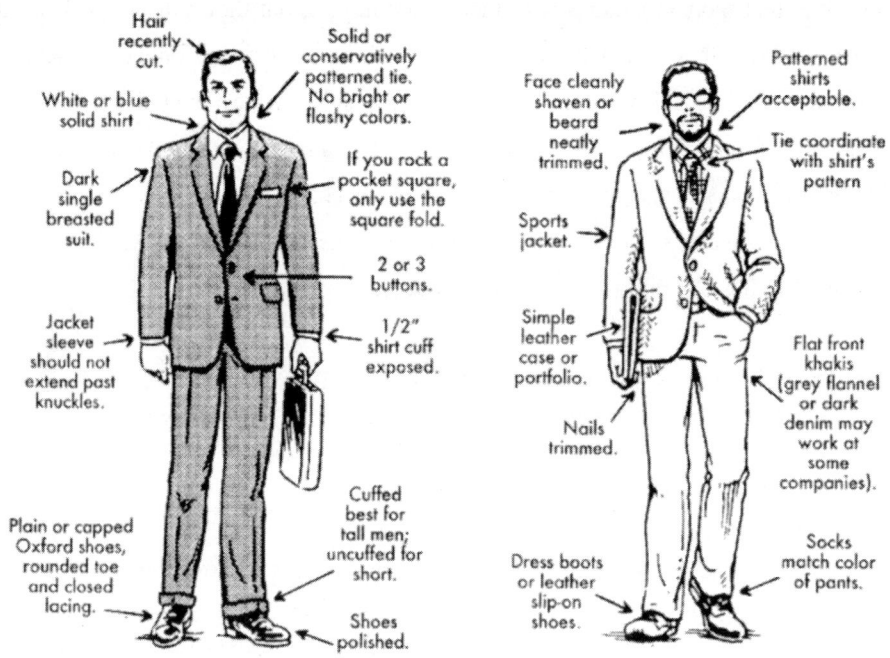

어휘해설　•pantyhose: 팬티스타킹; •flawless: 흠이 없는, 완전한; •pump: 펌퍼, 양수기, 퍼올리다; •strappy: 곤포용의 큰 테이프; •platform: 뚜꺼운 밑창; •peircing: 날카로운, 통찰력 있는; •cologne: 오드 콜로뉴; •perfume: 향기, 방향, 향료, 향수; •portfolio: 서류 가방; •single breasted: 단추를 한 줄로 한; •attire: 옷, 의상; •knuckle: 관절, 마디, 모서리; •flashy: 화려한; •rock: 멋지게 입다; •manliness: 남자다움, 씩씩함; •cuff: 소맷부리, 접어 젖힌 아랫단; •trim: 깎아 다듬다; portfolio: 손가방, 서류 가방; •slip-on: 슬립온 식의, 간편한; •pattern: 무늬, 도안; •khakis: 카키색 바지(제복, 군복); •flannel: 플란넬, 면포; •socks: 양말; •pants: 바지; •polish: 딱다, 빤짝이게 하다, ~을 문질러 없애다; •denim: 데님, 능직의 두꺼운 면포; •pastel: 부드럽고 옅은.

크기해설　제목이 있는 1쪽 분량 정도의 본문 크기.

부분국역　취직 인터뷰를 위한 복장방법, 공식 비즈니스 인터뷰 복장, 케쥬얼 잡 인터뷰 복장, 스커트 차림에 회색 혹은 짙은 해군복.

(11) DAVID A. PATERSON ANDREA W EVANS
GOVERNOR CHAIRWOMAN & CEO

STATE OF NEW YORK
EXECUTIVE DEPARTMENT
DIVISION OF PAROLE
97 CENTRAL AVENUE
ALBANY, NY 12206

December 31, 2009

Ms. Mona Graves
88 G 0305
Albion Correctional Facility
3595 State School Road
Albion, NY 14411-9399

Dear Ms. Graves:

A grant of executive clemency involves the Governor's intervention in the normal course of the criminal justice process. Such action constitutes extraordinary relief and is taken in only the most compelling of circumstances.

Prior to any determination being made in a particular case, there is a comprehensive compilation of information and assessment of all known relevant factors.

After a careful review of this case, it has been determined that there is insufficient basis to warrant the exercise of the Governor's clemency powers. While I cannot disclose the nature of the deliberations, I can assure you that all aspects of this case were considered.

While most inmates can reapply one year from their denial notification, please review the Governor's Guidelines for Review of Executive Clemency Applications, which is available in your facility's inmate law library, to determine if you continue to meet the eligibility criteria.

Sincerely

Francis J. Herman
Francis J. Herman
Director
Executive Clemency Bureau

FJH/kow

> 어휘해설   •Executive Department: 행정처; •parole: 입국허가; •grant: 수여, 허가, 인가, 양도; •executive: 행정부, 집행부, 행정관; •intervention: 중재, 조정, 간섭; •clemency: 인정 있는 행위; •intervention: 간섭, 개입; •extraordinary relief: 특별 구원; •compelling: 강제적인, 설득력이 있는; •compilation: 축적, 집적; •assessment: 평가; •warrant: 보증; •inmate: 수감자; •notification: 통지(문), 통고(문), 공고(문); •eligibility: 적격(성), 적임(성), 자격.
>
> 크기해설   짧은 4 단락의 본문.
>
> 전문국역   행정처 관대조치(가석방)의 허가는 정상적인 범인 재판과정에서 주지사의 중재를 포함합니다. 그러한 조치는 특별 구제이며 가장 설득력이 있는 상황에서만 받아들여집니다.//특별한 경우 내려지는 결정에 앞서서, 알려져 있는 모든 관련 요소들에 관한 종합적 자료에 대한 정보와 평가가 있습니다.//이번 사건에 대하여 조심스럽게 검토를 한 후, 내려진 결정은 주지사의 관대조치를 보증할만한 근거가 충분하지 못하다는 것입니다. 본인이 그 고려사항들에 대한 성격을 밝힐 수는 없지만, 본인은 이번 사건에 대한 모든 측면들이 고려되었음을 귀하에게 확인해 드립니다.//대부분의 수감자들은 거부 통지를 받은 1년 후에는 재신청할 수 있는 데, 가석방 검토를 위해서는 주지사의 가이드라인을 검토하시기 바라는데, 이 가이드라인 검토는 수감자 법률도서관에서 가능합니다. 귀하가 자격기준을 계속해서 충족시키는지를 결정하기 바랍니다.//

(12) 1. Husband : Honey, why are you wearing your wedding ring on the wrong finger?
   Wife: Because I married the wrong man!

  2. A guy went to a party without his wife. He heard another guy say to his wife, "Pass the sugar, Honey." and "Pass the honey, Sugar." He thought this sort of

speech is a good idea. The next morning when he and his wife are eating breakfast, he said to his wife, "Pass the bacon, Pig."

3. Police Officer : When I saw you driving down the road, I guessed 55 at least.

   Man: You're wrong, officer, it's only my hat that makes me look that old.

4. Patient: Doctor, I have a serious memory problem. I can't remember anything!

   Doctor: So, since when did you have this problem?

   Patient: What problem?

5. Daughter: Dad, can you write in the dark?

   Dad: I think so. What is it you want me to write?

   Daughter: Your name on this report card.

6. Customer: Waiter, this lobster's only got one claw.

   Waiter: I expect he's been in a fight, sir.

   Customer: Well, then, please bring me the winner!

7. A man telephoned an airline office in New York and asked, "How long does it take to fly to Boston?"

   The clerk said, "Just a minute."

   "Thank you," the man said and hung up.

8. From his death bed, the husband called his wife and said, "One month after I die I want you to marry Mr. Drone." "Drone! But he is your enemy!" "Yes, I know that! I've suffered all these years so let him suffer now."

9. A man inserted an 'ad' in the classified ads ; "Wife wanted." The next day he received a hundred letters. They all said the same thing : "You can have mine."

10. Newly-wed: Do you want dinner?

    Spouse: Sure, what are my choices?

    Newly-wed: Yes and no.

어휘해설   •guy: 녀석, 남자, 놈; •report card: 성적표; •lobster: 대하, 바다가제; •claw: 갈고리 발톱; •airline office: 항공사; •death bed: 임종; •classified ad: 분류광고; •Newly-wed: 신혼자.

크기해설   1쪽 분량의 본문.

> 부분국역　(첫 부분)남편-허니, 왜 당신은 결혼반지를 엉뚱한 손가락에 끼고 있어요?
> 아내-왜냐하면 나는 잘못된 남자와 결혼했기 때문입니다!
> 　　(wrong의 의미를 이용한 말장난)

(13) 1. Why is the letter "t" like an island?

　→ Because it is in the middle of "water"

2. Which is it the swifter, heat or cold?

　heat : because you can catch cold

3. What is it that is deaf, dumb, and blind and always tells the truth?

　It is mirror

4. There is a creature on the earth that moves first with four feet and then with two and finally with three, through more weakly then with two. What is it?

　It is man

5. Which is the longest word in the English language?

　Smiles: because there is one mile between the first and last letter

6. What is it?

　We are twins.

　Each of us has a round body and a long leg.

　We have to work together.

　When we cover your eyes, you can see better.

　We sit on your nose when we work.

　* glasses (안경)

7. What is it?

　I am a beautiful girl.

　I am wearing a dress that is fashionable.

　I am standing in the show window.

　I am popular with ladies rather than gentlemen.

　Don't think of marrying me because I am not a living person.

　* mannequin

8. What is it?

　Without me, human could not be as smart as they are.

I have been teaching humans everything.

I have letters and pictures in me.

Students carry me to school.

I am made of paper.

* book

어휘해설	•swift: 빠른.
크기해설	본문 1쪽 분량.
부분국역	문자 't'가 왜 섬과 같은가? 그것은 'water' 가운데 있기 때문이다.

(14) **CHAPTER I GENERAL PROVISIONS**

Article 1

(1) The Republic of Korea shall be a democratic republic.

(2) The sovereignty of the Republic of Korea shall reside in the people, and all state authority Shall emanate from the people.

Article 2

(1) Nationality in the Republic of Korea shall be prescribed by *Act*.

(2) It shall be the duty of the State to protect citizens residing abroad as prescribed by *Act*.

Article 3

The territory of the Republic of Korea shall consist of the Korean peninsula and its adjacent island.

어휘해설	•sovereignty: 주권, 통치권; •emanate. 퍼지다, 나오다.
크기해설	본문 1/2쪽 분량.
부분국역	(첫 부분)대한민국 공화국은 민주공화국이다. 대한민국의 주권은 국민에게 있고, 국가 모든 권력은 국민으로부터 나온다.

(15)   **Obama Pivots To Reclaim Reputation as
Negotiator-In-Chief**

President Barack Obama has a new message for congressional Republicans today: let's talk.

"I will look for willing partners wherever I can go to get important work done," the president said Thursday morning, announcing he intends to work with Congress to pass an annual budget, comprehensive immigration reform, and a farm bill.

Fresh off his victory over House Republicans in twin fiscal crises, the president is preparing an about-face after weeks of swearing off any negotiations with the GOP to fund the government and raise the debt limit. Not only that, but he is also setting the stage to criticize the opposition if they decline to put everything on the table.

It's the completion of a months-long White House strategy on the debt limit that whittled away at the president's preferred public image as moderate dealmaker. After getting rolled in 2011, Obama swore to his staff that he wouldn't again get held hostage over the debt limit. Earlier this year, Obama laid down that no-negotiation promise in a statement on the New Year's fiscal cliff deal, and he stood by it. There were no serious talks. No secret back-channel negotiations. No Joe Biden. Aides on both sides of Pennsylvania Ave. described meetings with congressional leaders last week as more to please the media than a reflection of any attempt to make progress.

Aides admit they were wary of the impact of Obama's hardline position during the shutdown, especially as Republicans passed piecemeal bills to reopen slices of the federal government last week. Business leaders called on the president to throw Republicans a lifeline. Senate Democrats instinctively rushed to cut rogue deals. They fretted the rebuke from the "David Gergen caucus" of beltway pundits. But more than anything, it posed a danger to the Obama brand. He ran for office in 2008 insisting that he was open to negotiating with Iran without preconditions. He had pledged to change the way business is done in Washington and bridge the partisan divides.

As the afterglow of an end to the shutdown quickly faded, Obama turned his focus to the next crisis in a morning address at the White House, taking a swing at the tea party and extending an olive branch to moderate Republicans.

"You don't like a particular policy or a particular president, then argue for your position," Obama said in a shot at the GOP. "Go out there and win an election."

"Sometimes we'll be just too far apart to forge an agreement," Obama added. "But that should not hold back our efforts in areas where we do agree. We shouldn't fail to act on areas that we do agree or could agree just because we don't think it's good politics, just because the extremes in our party don't like the word 'compromise.'"

It was an echo of his message from the night before. "I am willing to work with anybody, I am eager to work with anybody--Democrat or Republican, House or Senate members~on any idea that will grow our economy, create new jobs, strengthen the middle class, and get our fiscal house in order for the long term," Obama said Wednesday evening before the House voted to reopen the government. On Thursday he laid out his remaining priorities, though nobody at the White House is holding their breath that Republicans will change course.

According to White House officials, the president will adopt the same strategy for dealing with the upcoming crises as he has in the past. He still won't negotiate over the debt limit, but he is open to reaching a budget deal if Republicans are willing to put everything on the table. "The President has insisted that in these budget negotiations that he's been calling for all year, everything has to be on the table, and that will be his position going forward," White House Press Secretary Jay Carney said Wednesday.

By Zeke J. Miller

어휘해설 •pivot: 방향을 바꾸다, 회전하다; •reputation: 평판, 세평, 명성, 신망; •negotiator-In-Chief: 협상대표자; •willing partner: 뜻 있는 파트너; •fiscal crises: 회계 위기; •about-face: 180도 전환, 정반대로 바꾸기; •swear off: 맹세하다, 선언하다; •debt limit: 채무 한계; •whittle: (예산)깎다, 줄이다; •back-channel: 정상적이 아닌, 정규적이 아닌; •wary of: 신중한; •piecemeal bills: 개별 법안; •fret: 안달하다.

크기해설 제목이 있는 본문 약 1.5쪽 분량.

부분국역 (첫 부분)Barack Obama 대통령이 오늘 의회 공화당의원들에게 보낼 새 메시지를 준비하다: 대화합시다.//"저는 혼자 할 수 있는 중요한 일을 할 수 있는 곳은 어디든지 뜻 있는 파트너를 찾겠습니다."라고 대통령은 목요일 아침 말하고, 연간예산, 종합 이민 개혁, 그리고 농업법안을 통과시키기 위해 의회와 함께 할 의향임을 선언했다.

제2장

절 독해

독자가 독해재료의 윤곽을 확인한 다음에는, 즉 양식구성을 확인하고 작자의도를 예측하고 본문크기를 확인한 다음에는 어떻게 해야 하는가? 본문 첫 부문의 첫 절(clause)[1]에 접근하는 것이다. 즉 절을 독해하는 것이다. 이것을 절 독해 단계라고 부른다. 절 독해 단계는 선적인 순서를 따라 1)어휘들의 의미를 리콜하여(즉 기억 혹은 사전확인 등으로부터 알아내어) 2)이 어휘의미들을 연결시켜서 절을 구성하고 3)절 단위의 주제어휘와 초점어휘를 확인하는 세 절차를 거친다.

제1절 구성성분 어휘의미 리콜

절 독해 단계의 첫 절차는 읽는 어휘의 의미를 리콜하는 것이다. 어휘의 의미리콜은 의미를 두뇌로부터 기억해 내든지 사전을 찾아 확인하든지 등의 방법으로 알아내는 것을 의미한다. 이 어휘의미 리콜에는 어휘의 위치, 형태, 기능을 이해하는 것이 도움이 되는데, 이 위치, 형태, 기능 등을 이용하는 것은 어휘를 잊혀 지지 않도록

---

[1] 단문 차원이든 중/복문 속의 절 차원이든 한 번의 주술 단위를 가리킨다.

동기화 하는데 의도가 있다. 위치의 이해는 문장에서의 문법 구조적 위치(가령: 주어 다음의 위치로 동사 위치)의 이해를 가리킨다. 형태의 이해는 1)기초적 단위(형태소, 단순어)의 뜻 이해, 2)구성의 이해(<u>접두사+어근(단어)+접미사 혹은 단어+단어</u>)[2], 3) 음, 철자, 기타 등 이해를 가리킨다. 기능의 이해는 통사적 기능(가령: 주어, 술어동사, 목적어, 보어, 수식어, 기타 등)의 역할 이해를 가리킨다.

(1) The reason general relativity broke down at the Big Bang was that it was not compatible with quantum theory.

> 어휘리콜[3]   •relativity: 상대성이론←1)general(일반)의 수식을 받고, 2)broke down at(깨뜨렸다/안 어울렸다)의 주어이고, 3)뒤에 Big Bang(우주대폭발)을 목적어로 취하고, 4)relativity가 속한 절이 앞 The reason(그 이유)을 수식하고, relativity뒤에 quantum theory(양자이론) 의미가 따른다; •quantum: 양자←quant(ity) (분)량.
> 전문국역   일반 상대성이론이 빅뱅(우주대폭발)에 적용되지 않는 이유는 빅뱅이 양자이론과 양립하지 않기 때문이다.

(2) Belt pouches were less popular in fashion-conscious Milan, where only 4% of men used them, and belt pouches were non-existent in Tokyo.

> 어휘리콜   •Belt pouches: 휴대전화 케이스←Belt: 벨트+pouch: 주머니; •fashion-conscious: 패션에 민감한←fashion: 패션+conscious: 깨어있는, 의식적인, 민감한; •non-existent: 존재하지 않는←non: 부정+exist: 존재하다+-ent: 형용사화 접미사.
> 전문국역   벨트 파우치는 패션에 민감한 이탈리아 밀라노에서는 인기가 덜 했었는데, 그곳에서는 단 4퍼센트의 남성들만 사용을 했으며, 벨트 파우치가 일본에서는 존재하지도 않았다.

(3) The breakthrough technologies of the 787 Dreamliner have given birth to a new and remarkable 747.

> 어휘리콜   •breakthrough: 돌파, 성공, 타결, 혁신←break: 부수다+through: 뚫기.

---

2) 직면하는 어휘에 대한 구성을 보고자 할 경우 구성분석을 보다 잘 제시하는 사전을 이용하는 것도 한 방법이다.
3) 1-3절에서 사용한 용어 '어휘해설' 대신 '어휘리콜(어휘 뜻 불러내기)'을 사용한다.

전문국역　787 Dreamliner의 혁신기술은 새롭고도 주목할 만한 747을 낳았다.

(4) One bacterium that survives keeps replication because it is not susceptible to the drug treatment.

어휘리콜　•bacterium: 박테리아←'박테리-'라는 발음으로부터; •replication: 복사, 복제←접두사 re-(다시-); •susceptible: 걸리기 쉬운←접두사 sus-(sub-): 아래.
전문국역　살아있는 박테리아는 약물 치료에 영향을 받지 않기 때문에 계속 복제가 된다.

(5) The function of the historian is neither to love the past nor to emancipate himself from the past, but to master and understand it as the key to the understanding of the present.

어휘리콜　•emancipate: 사람을 지배 속박으로부터 해방시키다←접두사 e-: 이탈, 밖으로; man (사람).
전문국역　역사가의 역할은 과거를 사랑하는 것이 아니고, 또 과거로부터 자신을 해방시키는 것도 아니라, 과거의 이해를 향한 열쇠로서 과거를 마스트하고 이해하는 것이다.

(6) The two stood bemused in the middle of the parking lot at Disneyland, trying to remember where they had parked their car.

어휘리콜　•bemused: 생각에 잠긴, 멍한←be: 있음+muse: 명상하다, 묵상하다+-d: 형용사화 접미사.
전문국역　두 사람은 디즈니랜드 주차장 중앙에서 멍하니 서서 자기들 차를 주차했던 곳을 기억해 내려 하고 있었다.

(7) Herbal medicine is perhaps the fastest growing category of complementary and alternative medicine. A few herbs have become more popular and/or proved more effective than their synthetic counterpart, while others have raised concerns about potential adverse herb-drug interactions.

> **어휘리콜** •Herbal medicine: 한약←herb: 풀, 풀잎, 약초+-al: 형용사화+medicine: 약; •alternative: 대안의, 대체의←alter: 변경하다+native: 토산의, 천연의; •synthetic counterpart ←synthetic: 종합적인, 합성의+counterpart: 상응하는 것; •adverse: 반대하는, 적의의← ad-: 변화+verse: 시, 운문; •herb-drug interactions: 약초들의 상호작용←herb-drug: 약초 +interactions: 상호작용.
>
> **전문국역** 한약은 아마 가장 빨리 성장하는 대체 의학인지도 모른다. 몇 가지 약초들은 합성약(즉 양약)보다 더 인기가 있고 더 효과적이었지만, 반면에 다른 약초들은 그들의 상호작용에 의하여 해를 줄 수 있다는 우려를 야기했다.

(8) We could make bigger-sized cars, but with high oil prices, they just wouldn't be cost effective.

> **어휘리콜** •bigger-sized: 사이즈가 더 큰←bigger: 더 큰+sized: 크기.
>
> **전문국역** 우리는 사이즈가 더 큰 차를 만들 수도 있다. 그러나 오일 값이 비싸기 때문에 그것은 비용 면에서 비효율적이다.

(9) A clear majority of executives intend to invest more time and money in emerging markets over the next three years than in developed markets.

> **어휘리콜** •emerging: 신흥의←emerge: 나타나다+-ing: 형용사화 접미사.
>
> **전문국역** 확실히 대다수의 이사진들은 더 많은 시간과 돈을 향후 3년간 선진(국)시장보다 신흥 시장에 투자하고자 한다.

(10) Each day, Pillsbury products and other General Mills brands appear in millions of shopping carts around the world.

> **어휘리콜** •shopping carts: 쇼핑 카트←shopping: 쇼핑+carts: 카트.
>
> **전문국역** 매일, Pillsbury 제품과 다른 General Mills 브랜드는 전 세계 수백만의 쇼핑카트에서 보인다.

(11) The defense attorney attempted to rebut the prosecutor's claim that the defendant's fingerprints, hair, clothing, signature, wallet, wrist-watch, credit cards and car had

been found at the scene of crime.

> 어휘리콜 • defense attorney: 피고 측 변호사←defense: 방어+attorney: 변호사; •rebut: 반박하다; •prosecutor: 검사←prosecute: 수행하다+-or: 행위자.
>
> 전문국역 피고 측 변호사는 피고의 지문, 머리카락, 옷, 서명, 지갑, 손목시계, 신용카드, 그리고 자동차가 범죄현장에서 발견되었다는 검사의 주장에 대한 반증을 들어 반박을 하려고 시도했다.

(12) History, as always, acts as a useful damper on overconfidence. Whole shelves of studies have been written on the mutual familiarity of German and British elite in the decades before World War 1, which did nothing to prevent the two nations going at each other like frenzied dogs. The point is simple. China may amaze us today, but nothing about its future is certain.

> 어휘리콜 • damper: 기세를 꺾는 자←damp: 실망, 낙담+-er: 사람; •overconfidence: 과신, 자만심←over: 위, 초과+confidence: 자신; •shelves of studies: 수많은 연구; •frenzied dogs: 미친 개들.
>
> 전문국역 언제나 마찬가지로, 역사는 자만심에 대해선 유용한 방해꾼으로 역할을 한다. 수많은 연구가 1차 대전 수십 년 전에 영국과 독일 엘리트들의 상호 친밀한 관계에 관해 쓰였다. 그 상호간의 친밀한 관계도 두 나라가 서로 미친개처럼 공격하는 것을 막는데 아무 역할을 못했다. 핵심은 간단하다. 중국은 오늘날 우리들을 놀라게 할지도 모르지만, 미래에 관한 것은 아무것도 확실한 것이 없다.

(13) The number of ethanol plants has grown to 119 from 56 in 2001 and 86 more are under construction.

> 어휘리콜 • under construction: 건설 중인←under: 아래+construction: 건설.
>
> 전문국역 에탄올 공장의 숫자는 2001년의 56개에서 현재 119개로 늘어났으며 86개 이상이 건설 중이다.

(14) While many job seekers may rely on prayer for success, career experts warn against discussing faith when meeting with hiring managers.

> **어휘리콜** • career expert: 직업 전문가←career: 경력, 직업+expert: 전문가.
> **전문국역** 많은 구직자들이 성공을 위해 기도에 의지를 하기는 하지만, 직업 전문가들은 구인 담당자들과 만날 때 믿음에 대해 말하는 것에 대해 경고한다.

(15) School officials in Nebraska recognize that it is virtually impossible to keep children off the Internet these days. Instead, they are using safeguard to help protect students from online dangers.

> **어휘리콜** • off: 분리의 개념; • safeguard: 보호 장치←safe: 안전+guard: 보호자.
> **전문국역** 미국 네브래스카 주 학교 직원들은 요사이 아이들을 인터넷에서 떼어 놓기가 실제적으로 불가능하다는 것을 인식하고 있다. 그 대신 학생들을 온라인 위험에서 보호하기 위한 안전장치를 이용하고 있다.

(16) The chemical composition of ink is one indicator of authenticity in a map or drawing, but it's not the only one. It is certainly not dependable enough to be the sole factor in indicating whether a work is genuine or forgery.

> **어휘리콜** • composition: 구성←compose: 구성하다+-tion: 명사화접미사; • authenticity: 확실성, 신빙성←author: 저자, 작자; • genuine: 진짜의←gene: 유전자; • forgery: 위조, 위조의←forge: 용광로, 제조하다+-ery: 접미사.
> **전문국역** 잉크의 화학적 성분은 지도나 그림의 진품을 가릴 수 있는 표시기이다. 그러나 그것이 유일한 것만은 아니다. 그것(잉크의 화학적 성분)은 하나의 작품이 진품이냐 위조품이냐를 가리는 데에 유일한 요소로 충분히 의존할만하지 못하다.

(17) As their brains mature neurologically, infants become more capable of distinguishing the shapes and textures of the objects around them.

> **어휘리콜** • neurologically: 신경학적으로←neuro: 신경+log: 학, 론; • texture: 짜임새, 구성, 조직←text: 직물+-ure: 접미사.
> **전문국역** 그들(유아들)의 뇌가 신경학적으로 성숙하기 때문에, 유아들은 자기들 주변 사물의 형태와 구조를 더욱 구별할 수 있다.

(18) Home of the world's largest chocolate-manufacturing plant, Hershey, Pennsylvania, was originally known as Derry Church, but its name was changed in 1906 to honor one of its most famous residents.

> 어휘리콜 • resident: 거주자←reside: 거주하다+-ent: 사람.
>
> 전문국역 세계에서 최대 초콜릿 제조공장인 Pennsylvania주 Hershey는 원래 Derry Church로 알려져 있었지만, 이 이름이 가장 유명한 거주자의 한 사람을 기리기 위하여 1906년에 바뀌게 되었다.

(19) There is probably no story more dramatic that of baseball's great hitter and right fielder, Hank Aaron.

> 어휘리콜 • fielder: 야수, 외야수←field: 들, 논+-er: 사람.
>
> 전문국역 야구의 강타자이자 우익수인 Hank Aaron에 관한 드라마틱한 이야기 보다 더 드라마틱한 이야기는 아마 없을 것이다.

(20) An initial screening of the nominees will be made by the Kelly Foundation during December and January. A personal interview with each other nominee will be held during this period at a location convenient to both the nominee and the Foundation.

> 어휘리콜 • nominee: 지명자←nomin: 이름+-ee: 불리는 사람.
>
> 전문국역 지명자들에 대한 첫 검토는 12월과 1월 중에 Kelly Foundation에서 있을 것이다. 각 후보자에 대한 개인면접은 이 기간에 후보자와 재단 양쪽에 모두 편한 장소에서 진행될 것이다.

(21) Early in February, approximately forty-five finalists will be selected from the total pool of nominees.

> 어휘리콜 • approximately: 가까이←appro: 접근; • pool: 협동자금, 요원←pool: 물웅덩이, 저수지.
>
> 전문국역 2월 초에 대략 45명의 최종 후보자들이 전체 후보자들 중에서 선정될 것이다.

어휘리콜을 통해 어휘를 익히는 접근방법은 문장 단위의 독해과정 보다는 그 상위 글 단위의 독해과정을 통하는 것이 더 유익할 수도 있다. 후자는 내용지식을 바탕으로 하기 때문이다.

(22)

1 Early studies of anatomy were hampered by the authorities' disapproval of dissections, and by the lack of refrigeration. By the 1500's in Europe the collected knowledge about the human body had been codified and was the exclusive domain of the Doctors of Physick, a group of scholars who went to great lengths to prevent medical information from spreading. To this end, the Doctors stored their knowledge in obscure languages such as Greek, Latin, and Arabic. The Doctors, by not allowing the works of anatomy to be translated into common tongues, remained invincible to intellectual assaults by laymen. Not only did Doctors of Physick refuse to supplement the bodily lore they learned at the university with practical observations, but they also charged ludicrous amounts to treat their patients.

2 The doctors generally prescribed two different treatments for disease, blood letting for those with physical disorders, and point branding for those in need of psychiatric care. The treatments involved using leeches and needles respectively, and often caused patients to end up worse off than they were prior to treatment. Given these conditions, the common people opted to patronize the village apothecary, who was typically a local grocer selling ineffectual herbal remedies.

3 Protected by an imposing guild system, the citadel of medicine was finally cracked by Paracelsus, a rogue physician of the sixteenth century. Paracelsus was a self-taught medicine man who instructed his own students at the University of Basal in a local dialect instead of Latin, and actually burned copies of books on the traditional principles of medicine. Teaching only from his own experience as a doctor who had treated hundreds of patients, he enraged his fellow professors by freely disseminating the safeguarded wisdom of his profession among the common men. This not only violated the Hippocratic oath, in which the Doctor of Physick swore to guard his professional knowledge, but it also eventually proved detrimental to Paracelsus' career.

4 In 1528, Paracelsus was thrown out from the University, but the damage to medical tradition had already been done. The works of Paracelsus were published after his death, and among other things they completely altered the European notion of disease, overturning the then-popular opinion that disease was caused by unbalanced "humors" within a patient's body. But this was just the beginning of the far-reaching impact Paracelsus had on Western medicine.

어휘리콜 •anatomy: 해부학←ana-: 분리, 조각+-tomy: 절제, 절개; •hamper: 방해하다←ham: 엉터리; •dissection: 해부(체)←dissect: 해부하다, 분석하다+-tion: 명사화접미사; •authority: 당국, 관청←author: 저자+-ity: 명사화접미사; •refrigeration: 냉장고←re-: 반복+frigid: 추운+-ation: 명사화접미사; •codify: 편찬하다, 성문화하다, 요약하다←code: 법전, 부호, 기호+ify: 동사화접미사; •exclusive: 배타적인, 유일한, 전문적인←ex-: 밖+clusive: 포함하는; •go to great lengths: 철저하게 하다; •obscure: 희미한, 어려운, 감지할 수 없는←ob-: 반대, 저항; •invincible: 정복할 수 없는, 무적의←in-: 부정+vincible: 정복할 수 있는, 이길 수 있는; •assault: 습격, 공격; •laymen: 보통사람←lay: 놓다, 지형, 바닥+men: 사람; •lore: 지식, 학문; •ludicrous: 익살맞은, 우스운; •lettings: 임대(물)←let: 놓다; •blood letting: 방열, 유혈; •physical disorders: 신체상의 상처; •point branding: 중요사항 표출; •psychiatric care: 정신과 치료; •leeches: 의사용의 거머리, 흡혈귀; •needle: 바늘; •patronize: 보호하다, 고객이 되다, 은인인 척하다←patron: 부친+-ize: 동사화접미사; •apothecary: 약제사, 약방, 약국←apothe: 약제+cary: 나르다; •ineffectual herbal remedies: 효과가 없는 약초 치료제←effect: 효과+herb: 풀잎+remedy: 치료; •imposing: 위압하는, 당당한, 인상적인←impose: 강요하다+-ing: 형용사화접미사; •citadel: 성체, 요새←cit: 시민, 일반인; •crack: 찰싹 소리 내다, 금가게 하다; •rogue: 악한, 불량배; •enrage: 화나게 하다←en: 동사화접두사+rage: 분노; •disseminate: 널리 퍼뜨리다, 보급하다←dis: 비, 분리, 제거+eminate: 저명한, 뛰어난; •detrimental: 유해한, 손해되는←detriment: 손해, 손상, 손해원인 혹은 유해물+-al: 형용사화접미사; •overturn: 뒤집어엎다←over: 위+turn: 돌리다.

전문국역 **1** 해부학 초기 연구는 당국의 해부 불인정 및 냉동시설의 결핍으로 방해를 받았다. 1500년대까지 유럽에서는 인체에 관해 축적된 지식이 요약되었고, 외과 의사들의, 즉 의학정보를 널리 퍼지지 않게 철저히 한 의사들 그룹의, 배타적인 영역이 되었다. 이런 목적으로 의사들은 그들의 지식을 그리스어, 라틴어, 그리고 아랍어와 같은 감지할 수 없는 언어로 보관했다. 의사들은, 해부학 연구내용이 보통의 언어로 번역되는 것을 허용하지 않음으로써, 보통 사람에 의한 지적 공격에 무적의 상태로 남아있었다. 외과 의사들은 실험연구로 대학에서 배운 인체지식을 보충 하는 것을 거부했을 뿐 아니라, 그들은 환자를 치료하기 위해 익살스러운 부분을 추가했다. **2** 의사들은 일반적으로 질병에 대해서 두 가지 다른 치료법을 사용했는데, 신체적 상처 환자들에 대해서는 출혈이 되게 하고, 그리고 정신과 치료를 필요로 하는 환자에게는 중요사항이 떠오르게 했다. 치료방법들은 거머리와 바늘 사용을 포함했고, 그리하여 종종 환자들로 하여금 치료받기 이전보다 더 악화시켰다. 이런 조건에서 보통사람들은 전형적으로 효과가 없는 약초 치료제를 팔고 있는 마을 잡화상인 마을 약국의 고객이 되었다. ③ 위압적인 길드 체제의 보호를 받는 의약이라는 요새는 결국 16세기 악한 외과의 사인 Paracelsus에 의하여 금이 가게 되었다. Paracelsus는 독학한 의사로, Basal대학에서 라틴어 대신에 지역 언어로 자기 학생들에게 가르쳤으며, 전통적인 의학원리에 관한 책들을 태워버렸다. 수백 명 환자를 치료한 의사로서 자기 자신의 경험에 의해서만 가르친 그는 보호해 온 전문적 지혜를 보통 사람들에게 마음대로 퍼뜨려 자기 동료 교수들을 분노케 했다. 이것은 전문지식을 보호하기로 맹세한 히포크라스 선서를 어겼을 뿐만 아니라, 이 사건은 결국 Paracelsus의 경력에 확실히 손해가 되었다. ④ 1528년에 Paracelsus는 대학으로부터 추방되었으나, 의학적 전통에 대한 (손)해는 이미 그 이전 입었다. Paracelsus의 연구들은 그가 죽은 후 발간되었고, 다른 것들 중에서 그 연구들은 유럽의 질병 개념을 변화시켰으며, 질병이 환자 체내 어울리지 않는 유머에 의하여 발병된다는 당시 대중적 견해를 뒤집어엎었다. 그러나 이 정도는 단지 Paracelsus가 서방 의학에 미친 광범위한 영향의 시작이었다.

(23)

1 The Human Genome Project began in 1990, and its first phase was completed in June of 2000 — two years ahead of schedule. The project was carried out by researchers funded by the U.S. Department of Energy, the National Institutes of Health, and Celera Genomics, a privately owned company. Researchers in Japan, the United Kingdom, Italy, France, and Russia also participated, with their efforts coordinated by U.S. scientists. The purpose of the project was to identify and order every human gene and to understand each gene's chemical structure. Ultimately, the project hopes to provide a better understanding of each gene's function in health and disease. Many expect the results to provide a basis for genetic forms of medicine.

2 DNA is made up of nucleotides, of which there are four types. Genes are discrete stretches of nucleotides that carry the information cells use to construct proteins. Researchers were surprised to discover that the human genome consists of only 30,000 to 40,000 genes; the original estimate was 100,000. Human genes actually only take up about 5 to 10 percent of human DNA; the rest may carry information about when to construct proteins, but the function is largely unknown.

3 The Human Genome Project constructed two types of gene mapping: a physical map and a map showing genetic linkages. The physical map located genes in relation to known DNA sequences that served as landmarks. A detailed physical map was needed before sequencing could begin—sequencing, or ordering the nucleotides that make up DNA, was the most technically challenging part of the project. The Project also created a genetic linkage map that provides the relative location of genes on the basis of how frequently they are inherited together. Genes that are closer together are more likely to be inherited together.

4 Medical researchers' hopes for practical applications of the research seemed to be borne out even before the mapping was finished. Some companies began to offer inexpensive and easy to administer genetic tests that can show predisposition to a variety of illnesses, including breast cancer, cystic fibrosis, and liver disease. Another potential objective of genome research could be to analyze the effects of changes in genetic programming (switching elements of DNA) on an organism, or replacing a mutated gene with a healthy one. These changes are what scientists envision for the future of genetically based medicine. However, these positive results also point to some of the problems with the project.

5 The human genome draft project cost three hundred million dollars, but with the ever-increasing rate of medical advances, it might be possible to reduce this cost. Reducing the cost significantly might make it feasible to identify any person's genome for the sake of research or treatment. Many patient advocates are concerned that individuals' genetic predispositions could be used to justify refusing to give them health insurance—or even a job. Or, specific genome data could potentially highlight the differences among different groups of people and different races. Such information might be used to fuel racial prejudices. Some feel that the ethics of genome research needs to be examined more carefully in the future. These ethical questions are the next phase of work for the Human Genome Project.

6 Another primary goal of future research is the complete computerization of biology. Putting information about how genes affect or cause diseases along with scientific literature in a giant database cross-referenced with other databases will allow scientists to accurately predict and control genetic diseases in humans. There would also be many important benefits for biological researchers. For example, if a researcher investigating a particular disease has narrowed down his search to a particular gene, he could visit the human genome database and explore what other scientists have written about this gene. This information could potentially include its structure, its functions, potentially harmful mutations, interactions with other genes, other diseases associated with this gene, or even its evolutionary relationships to other human genes or to genes in lab animals.

어휘리콜 •Human Genome Project: 인간 게놈 프로젝트; •carry out: 수행하다←carry: 나르다＋out: 밖으로; •Gene: 유전자; •coordinate: 동등한, 대등하게 하다←co-: 공동＋ordinate: 세로좌표; •nucleotide: 뉴클리오티드-핵산(DNA, RNA)의 기본단위; •discrete: 별개의, 분리된; •cells use: 세포가 이용하다; •protein: 단백질; •take up: 차지하다; •about when to construct: 언제 구성할지에 관한; •gene mapping: 유전자 지도; •genetic linkage: 유전적 결합; •locate: 알아내다; •landmark: 경계표; •sequencing: 배열; •sequencing, or ordering: 배열하거나 순서화 하는 것은; •more likely to: 확률이 높은; •bear out: 낳다, 가져오다; •administer: 관리하다, 통제하다; •genetic test: 유전자 검사; •predisposition: 경향, 성질; •breast cancer: 유방암; •cystic fibrosis: 낭포성 섬유증; •liver disease: 간질환; •organism: 유기체; •mutated gene: 돌연변이 유전자; •envision: 상상하다; •draft: 초안, 밑그림; •fuel: 연료, 연료를 공급하다, 부추기다; •point to: -을 지적하다.

전문국역 **1** 인간 게놈 프로젝트가 1990년에 시작되었으며, 그 첫 국면이 2,000년 6월-연구일정 2년 앞서-완성되었다. 그 프로젝트는 미 국립보건원인 에너지국과 사기업인 Celera Genomics의 지원에 의하여 수행되었다. 일본, 영국, 이태리, 프랑스, 그리고 러시아의 연구원들이 미국 과학자들과 공동의 노력으로 참여했다. 프로젝트의 목적은 모든 인간 유전자를 확인하고 순서화 하는 것이고, 그리고 각 유전인자의 화학적 구조를 이해하는 것이었다. 궁극적으로 그 프로젝트는 건강과 질병에서 각 유전자의 기능에 대해 더 나은 지식제공을 기대하는 것이다. 많은 사람들은 그 결과가 의약의 유전인자적 형태를 위한 기초를 제공해 줄 것으로 기대한다. **2** DNA는 네 가지 유형이 있는 뉴클리오티드로 구성되어 있다. 유전인자들은 구별되는 뉴클리오티드의 연결 모습인데, 이 연결 모습은 정보세포들이 단백질을 구성할 수 있도록 정보를 실어 나른다. 연구자들은 인간 게놈이 30,000 내지 40,000개의 유전자로 구성되어 있다는 것을 발견하고 놀랐다. 원래의 평가는 100,000개 이었다. 인간 유전자는 실제로 인간 DNA의 5 내지 10% 만을 취한다. 그 나머지는 단백질을 구성할 때 정보를 주위로 실어 나른다. 그러나 그 기능은 알려져 있지 않다. **3** 인간 게놈 프로젝트는 2 가지 유형의 유전자 지도를 구축했는데, 인체 지도와 유전자 연결 지도이다. 인체 지도는 이정표로 기여하는 이미 알려진 DNA 연속체들과 관련된 유전자들을 나타낸다. 상세 인체 지도가 연결 작업이 시작될 수 있기 전에, 즉 DNA를 형성하는 뉴클리오티드를 연결하기, 즉 순서화하는 것이 시작되기 전에 필요했다. 프로젝트는 또한 유전자들이 얼마나 빈번하게 함께 상속되는가에 기초하여 유전자들의 상대적 위치를 제공해주는 유전자 연결 지도를 만들어 냈다. 밀접한 유전자들은 함께 상속되어질 가능성이 더 높을 것이다. ④ 연구내용의 실제 적용에 대한 의사들의 기대가 지도 완성 이전에 나올 것 같았다. 일부 회사들은 유방암, 낭포성 섬유증 및 간질환을 포함하는 다양한 질병에 대해 성향을 보여줄 수 있는 유전자 검사를 통제할 값싸고 쉬운 방법을 제공하기 시작했다. 게놈 연구의 또 한 가지 잠재적 목적은 유기체에 미치는 유전자 프로그램밍 변화(DNA의 요소를 바꿈으로서)의 영향, 혹은 돌연변이 유전자를 건강한 유전자로 대치하는 변화의 영향을 분석하는 것일 수 있다. 이러한 변화는 과학자들이 유전적으로 기초한 의약의 미래를 위하여 상상하는 것이다. 그러나 이러한 긍정적인 결과는 또한 그 프로젝트의 문제점을 시사한다. ⑤ 인간 게놈 밑그림 프로젝트는 3억 달러 경비이지만, 의학 발전의 지속적 증가로 이 경비를 낮추는 것이 가능할 것이다. 경비를 낮추는 것은 중요하게도 연구나 치료 목적을 위해서 인간의 게놈을 확인하는 것이 가능하게 할 것이다. 많은 환자 옹호자들은 개개인들의 유전적 성향이 자기들에게 의료보험을 주는 것 혹은 직업까지 주는 것을 거절하는 데에 정당화하는데 사용될 수 있을 것이라는 데에 관심이 있다. 혹은 특정 게놈 데이터는 잠재적으로는 인간 그룹들 사이 혹은 종족 사이의 차이를 두드러지게 할 수 있다. 그러한 정보는 인종적 편견을 부추기는 데에 사용될 지도 모른다. 어떤 사람들이 느끼는 바는 게놈 연구의 윤리가 향후 더 조심스럽게 검토되어 질 필요가 있다는 것이다. 이러한 윤리적 문제들은 인간 게놈 연구의 다음 연구 단계 몫이다. ⑥ 향후 연구의 또 하나의 목적은 생물의 완전한 전산화이다. 유전인자들이 과학문헌과 함께 질병에 어떻게 영향을 미치고 유발시키는가에 관한 정보를 다른 데이터베이스들과 상호 연결되어진 거대한 데이터베이스에 입력한다는 것은 과학자들로 하여금 인간의 유전적 질병을 정확하게 예측하고 통제하게 할 것이다. 또한 생물학 연구자들에게 여러 중요한 이점들이 있다. 예를 들면, 한 특정 질병을 연구하는 연구자가 자기의 연구를 특정 한 유전인자로 좁힐 수 있다면, 그는 인간 게놈 베이스에 방문해서 다른 과학자들이 이 유전인자에 대해서 어떻게 썼는가를 탐구할 수 있을 것이다. 이 정보에는 잠재적으로 유전자의 구조, 유전인자의 기능, 잠재적으로 해로운 돌연변이, 다른 유전인자와의 상호교류, 이 유전인자와 관련 있는 다른 질병, 혹은 심지어 다른 인간의 종 혹은 실험실 동물의 유전인자와의 진화 관련성을 포함된다.

(24) **THE IRONY OF FATE**

A thirsty stag came to a spring, and after drinking noticed his own reflection in the water. He felt proud of his great and curiously fashioned antlers, but was very dissatisfied with his slender weak-looking legs. While he was still lost in thought a lion appeared and ran to him. He fled and easily outdistanced it—for the deer's strength is in his legs the lion's in his courageous heat. As long as the ground was open, the stag kept safely in front; but when they reached wooded country his antlers got entangled in the branches of **a** tree, so that he could not run farther and was caught by the lion. As he was about to be killed, "Alas!" he thought, "my legs, which I feared would fail me, were my preservation, and the antlers that filled me with such confidence are destroying me." It often happens, when we are in danger, that the friends whose loyalty we doubted prove our saviours, while those in whom we put implicit trust betray us.

> 어휘리콜 •stag: 수사슴; •antler: 수사슴의 뿔; •slender: 호리호리한, 가냘픈; •weak-looking: 빈약해 보이는; •be lost in thought: 생각에 잠기다; •flee: 달아나다; •outdistance: ~월등히 앞서다←out: 밖으로+distance: 거리; •get entangle-:-에 뒤엉키다; •preservation: 보존, 보호; •loyalty: 신의; •saviour: 구세주; •betray: 배신하다.
>
> 전문국역 운명의 장난/갈증이 난 수사슴이 샘터로 다가와서 목을 축이고 난 뒤에 물속에 되비친 제 모습을 응시하였다. 사슴은 자기의 거대하고 진기하게 생긴 뿔에 대해선 자부심을 느꼈지만 가느다랗고 빈약해 보이는 다리에는 몹시 불만이었다. 사슴이 한참 생각에 잠겨 있을 때 사자가 나타나 그에게 덤벼들었다. 사슴은 있는 힘을 다해 도망쳤으며 쉽사리 사자를 훨씬 앞서게 되었다. 왜냐하면 사슴이 유리한 것은 그의 다리 때문이며 사자의 장점은 배짱 두둑한 그의 심장덕분이기 때문이다. 땅이 툭 트여 있을 동안엔 수사슴은 안전하게 앞서갈 수 있었다. 그러나 나무가 빽빽이 들어찬 지역에 이르자 수사슴의 뿔이 나뭇가지에 뒤엉켜 버림으로 인해 사슴은 더 이상 도망가지 못하고 마침내는 사자에게 붙들리고 말았다. 막 잡아먹히려는 순간에 사슴은 생각했다. "아 슬프다! 나의 기대를 저버릴까봐 걱정했던 다리가 나를 보호해 주었다면 자신감으로 뿌듯하게 채워 주었던 이 뿔이 나의 목숨을 빼앗아가도록 만들다니."// 위험에 처했을 때 우리가 의심스러워했던 친구들의 신의야말로 우리의 구원임이 드러나는 반면 맹목적으로 신뢰했던 친구들이 우리를 배신하는 것은 흔히 있는 일이다.//

(25) **DECLARATION OF INTENT**

We gather today in solemn dedication as atheist free minds to establish a society for the enjoyment and advancement of atheism in Austin, Texas. We accept and celebrate the material nature of reality which allowed the evolutionary development of life that made possible our personal lives on humanity's home planet. We accept and celebrate fully our intellectual emotional, and physical humanity for the brief time that our minds are alive.

With this Declaration of Intent, we express our desire and hope for a more sane, rational, and progressive future for humanity. We dedicate ourselves to achieving and enjoying to the fullest possible extent the potential for personal liberty that exists within every human. We dedicate ourselves to effectively expressing our vision on civic and social affairs within the greater Austin area for the purpose of moving society toward a material realist approach to human affairs.

Therefore, we dedicate ourselves to the development of a social and activist organization that will meet the needs of Austin atheists and provide a society to nurture our hopes. In accordance with our intent, we, the atheist free minds of Austin, Texas dedicate ourselves to our hopes for and vision of a more realist future by establishing the:

ATHEIST COMMUNITY OF AUSTIN

어휘리콜　•declaration: 공표, 고지, 선포; •solemn: 신성한; •dedication: 헌납(식), 봉납(식); •atheism: 무신론; •sane: 분별력 있는; •nurture: 키우다, 육성하다.

전문국역　취지 선언/우리는 오늘 Texas, Austin에서 무신론의 즐거움과 발전을 위한 사회를 건설하고자 무신론자 자유인들로서 신성한 봉헌식에 모였다. 우리는 인간의 지구 혹성 위에서 우리 개인의 생활을 가능케 한 혁신적인 생활의 발전을 허용하는 현실의 물질적 본질을 받아들이고 축하한다. 우리는 우리의 마인드가 살아있는 짧은 시간동안 우리의 지적, 정서적, 그리고 신체적 인간다움을 충분히 받아들이고 축하한다.//이 취지 선언으로, 우리는 인간다움을 향한 더 분별력이 있고, 더 합리적이고, 그리고 더 진보적인 미래를 위해 우리의 욕망과 희망을 표현한다. 우리는 모든 인간 안에 내재하는 개인적 자유를 향해 잠재력을 가능한 한 최대로 성취하고 즐기는 데에 우리 스스로를 바친다. 우리는 인간의 문제에 대하여 물질적 실제 접근 방향으로 시회를 움직일 목적을 위해 위대한 Austin 영역 내 시민/사회적 문제에 관해 우리의 비전을 효과적으로 표현하는 데에 우리 스스로를 바친다.//그러므로, 우리는 Austin 무신론자의 욕구를 충족시키고, 그리고 우리의 희망을 키울 사회적 및 실천적 조직의 발전에 우리 스스로를 바친다. 우리의 취지에 따라, 우리, Texas Austin 무신론자 자유인은 ATHEIST COMMUNIST OF AUSTIN을 세움으로서 보다 현실적 미래의 우리의 희망과 비전에 우리 스스로를 바친다.

제2절 어휘의미들의 구성처리

절(Clause: C)에서 읽어나가는 어휘들에 대하여 의미들이 리콜 되면 독자는 어떻게 해야 하는가? 다음 예문에서 보는 것처럼 리콜 되는 의미들을 합하여 한 차례의 주술단위가 완성되도록 구성하는 것이다.

예문: Thousands of people hope to meet the president.
수천 명의 사람들이(S) ←바란다(tV) ←대통령 만나기를(dO).

절단위가 완성되도록 합하게 되는 의미단위들, 즉 구성성분에는 어떤 것들이 있으며, 어떤 순서로 합해 지는가? 절을 구성하는 구성성분 13개와 순서변인요소 3개가 있는데, 다음 배열패턴에서 보는 바와 같다.

배열패턴: C→{(s/cN) (s/cMxy) (W) (P) (S) (i/t/ptV) (dO/sC/sA) (iO/oC/oA)
↳{(Ad) (De) (Mo)}[4]
(cxM) (.?/!)}

C: 절; s/cN: 문/절 접속어; s/cMxy: 문/절 수식어(xy는 수식범위)[5]; W: 의문사; P: 조동사; S: 주어; i/t/ptV: 자/타/수동타동 동사; dO: 직접목적어; sC: 주격보어; sA: 주격부사어; iO: 간접목적어; oC: 목적보어; oA: 목적격부사어; cxM: 구성성분 수식어(피수식어로부터 떨어져 있는 경우의 수식어 임); ./?/!: 세 종지부호. Ad: 부가; De: 삭제; Mo: 이동

앞 배열패턴은 구성성분들이 정직하게는 밑줄 윗부분의 순서로 배열되지만 밑줄 아래에 있는 변인요소에 의하여 비 정직하게 배열될 수도 있음을 함축하고 있다. 이 말은 구성성분들은 전형적으로 자신의 일반적인 위치(즉 원래의 위치)에 한번만 나타나지만 부가(Addition: Ad, 예: 동격)되거나, 삭제(Deletion: De)되거나, 혹은 이동

---
[4] 대문자들만 발음화하면 '엔/엠/더블유/피/에스/브이//오/시/에이//오/시/에이//엠//아/데/모'가 된다.
[5] s/cMxy에서 xy는 M이 수식하는 문/절의 범위(가령: 절1번부터 3번까지이면 xy는 13이 됨)를 의미한다.

(Movement: Mo)되기도 한다는 뜻이다. 자신의 원래의 위치에 나타나지 않은 요소도 나타난 그 위치(부가 위치, 삭제 위치, 이동된 위치)에서 의미를 리콜하여 이전의 독해내용에 합한다.

독해처리에서 기본적으로는 이 배열패턴에서의 단위들 단위(예: W)로 독해하여 합해나가다가 독자의 독해처리 숙련도가 높아짐에 따라 독해처리 단위를 크게 확장해 갈 수 있다. 1)처음에는 13분법(앞 패턴의 구성요소들)으로, 다음은 3분법[예: {(s/cN) (s/cMxy) (W) (P)} {(S) (i/t/tpV)} {(dO/sC/sA) (iO/oC/oA) (cxM)}]으로 나누어서 할 수도 있고, 2분법[예: {(s/cN) (s/cMxy) (W) (P) (S) (i/t/ptV)} {(dO/sC/sA) (iO/oC/oA) (cxM)}]으로 나누어서 할 수도 있고, 3)몇 분법적이든 단위가 아닌 곳에 나누어서 할 수도 있고, 4)혹은 더 나아가서 나누지 않은 전체 단위로 독해처리 할 수도 있다.

(1) ---. But the opposite was seen in East asia.

> **구성처리**   문간접속어(sentence coNnective: sN)가 나타난다면 문단위에서 일반적으로 문 전반부 위치에 나타난다. (1)에서 문장의 첫 단어 밑줄 친 부분에 대해 '그러나' 의미를 리콜하고, 선행문에 대하여 뒤 문을 접속('대조관계')시킨다.
> **전문국역**   그러나 그 반대가 동아시아에서 보였다.

(2) There should be a law which forbids couples to have more than two children.

> **구성처리**   절간접속어(clause coNnective: cN)가 나타난다면 절단위에서 일반적으로 절 전반부에 나타난다. (2)에서 절의 첫 단어 밑줄 친 부분에 대해 '~한 법' 혹은 '그리고 그 법' 의미를 리콜하고, 앞 절에 대하여 뒤 절을 접속('명사한정')시킨다.[6]
> **전문국역**   부부로 하여금 아이를 둘 이상 가지는 것을 금하는 법이 있어야만 한다.

(3) Given strong wage growth in recent years, sales of food, drink and tobacco inRussia will jump by nearly 18% 2013.

---

6) 향후는 앞 (1)의 문간접속어는 절간접속에 포함시킨다.

> 구성처리   문이나 절의 수식어(sentence/clause Modifier: scM)가 나타난다면 일반적으로 문/절 전반부에 나타난다. (3)에서 밑줄 친 부분에 대해 '최근 몇 년간의 큰 임금인상을 고려해 볼 때' 의미를 리콜하고, 뒤에 나오는 문/절 전체에 수식관계로 연결시킨다.
>
> 전문국역   최근 여러 해에 걸쳐 높은 임금 상승이 있었기 때문에 러시아에서 식품, 음료수, 담배 값이 2013년도에는 거의 18% 오를 것이다.

(4) <u>When</u> did the problem start?

> 구성처리   의문사(Wh-: W)가 나타난다면 일반적으로 문/절 전반부에 나타난다. (4)에서 밑줄 친 부분에 대해 '언제' 의미를 리콜하고, 내용의문문으로 진행한다는 것을 예측한다.
>
> 전문국역   언제 그 문제가 시작(발생)되었는가?

(5) What else <u>do</u> you have?

> 구성처리   조작사(oPerator: P)가 나타난다면 일반적으로 문/절 전반부에 나타난다. (5)에서 밑줄 친 부분에 대해 '현재' 의미를 리콜하고, 직전의 독해내용 '그 밖에 무엇'에 합한다.
>
> 전문국역   그 밖에 당신은 무엇을 가지고 있습니까?

(6) In Shanghai, <u>men and women</u> routinely change into pajamas after work and walk around in public.

> 어휘리콜   •routinely: 일상적으로, 기계적으로, 판에 박힌 듯이.
>
> 구성처리   주어(Subject: S)가 나타난다면 일반적으로 문/절 전반부에 나타난다. (6)에서 밑줄 친부분에 대해 '남자와 여자들이' 의미를 리콜하고, 이전의 독해내용 '상하이에서는'에 합한다.
>
> 전문국역   상하이에서는 남자와 여자들이 직장에서 퇴근한 후 파자마로 갈아입고 공공연히 돌아다닌다.

(7) Each year the sanctuary <u>is visited</u> by thousands of school children.

> 어휘리콜   •sanctuary: 성전.
>
> 구성처리   동사(자동사/intransitive Verb: iV, 타동사/trans Verb: tV, 수동타동사/passive

transitive Verb: ptV)가 나타난다면 일반적으로 주어 다음에 나타난다. (7)에서 밑줄 친 부분에 대해 '방문 받았다' 의미를 리콜하고, 이전의 독해내용에 합한다.

전문국역   매년 그 신전은 수천 명의 학교 어린이들의 방문을 받는다.

(8) The six municipalities of the Red Lake-Bayonne region will celebrate <u>the 2nd Annual Art Festival</u> from July 20th to September 2nd.

어휘리콜   •municipality: 지자체.

구성처리   직접목적어(direct Object: dO)가 나타난다면 일반적으로 동사 다음에 나타난다. (8)에서 밑줄 친 부분에 대해 '두 번째 연례 예술축제' 의미를 리콜하고, 이전의 독해내용에 합한다.

전문국역   Red Lake-Bayonne 지역 여섯 지자체들은 7월 20일부터 9월 2일까지 두 번째 연례 예술축제를 거행할 것이다.

(9) We are excited about the upcoming conference on solar energy at the Hopeland Hotel in Mayfair this Saturday, January 7. Hopefully you have already registered. The listed cost is <u>$30 per person</u>, but SEE employees get a 50% discount.

구성처리   주격보어(subject Complement: sC)가 나타난다면 일반적으로 동사 다음에 나타난다. (9)에서 밑줄 친 부분에 대해 '1인당 30$' 의미를 리콜하고, 이전의 독해내용에 합한다.

전문국역   우리는 이번 1월 7일 토요일 Mayfair에 있는 Hopeland 호텔에서 있을 태양에너지에 관한 회의에 대해 흥분된다. 기대했던 대로 당신은 이미 등록했다. 등록비는 1인당 30$이지만 SEE 근로자는 50% 할인된다.

(10) Dr Blackett is <u>in Tokyo</u>.

구성처리   주격부사어(subject Adverbial: sA)가 나타난다면 일반적으로 동사 다음에 나타난다. (10)에서 밑줄 친 부분에 대해 '도쿄에' 의미를 리콜하고, 이전의 독해내용에 합한다.

전문국역   Blackett 박사는 Tokyo에 있다.

(11) They are demanding that a new clause be added to the contract which will give <u>them</u> a share of the profits.

> 구성처리 　간접목적어(indirect Object: iO)가 나타난다면 일반적으로 동사 바로 뒤 혹은 직접목적어 뒤에 나타난다. (11)에서 밑줄 친 부분에 대해 '그들에게' 의미를 리콜하고, 이전의 독해내용에 합한다.
> 전문국역 　그들은 그들에게 이익의 몫을 줄 새로운 조항이 계약서에 부가되어야 한다고 주장하고 있다.

(12) Willie's jokes made her uneasy.

> 구성처리 　목적보어(object Complement: oC)가 나타나면 일반적으로 직접목적어 다음에 나타난다. (12)에서 밑줄 친 부분에 대해 '불편한' 의미를 리콜하고, 이전의 독해내용에 합한다.
> 전문국역 　Willie의 조우커는 그녀를 불편하게 했다.

(13) He put the vase in the cabinet without a word.

> 구성처리 　목적격부사어(object Adverbial: oA)가 나타난다면 일반적으로 목적어 다음에 나타난다. (13)에서 밑줄 친 부분에 대해 '캐비닛 안에' 의미를 리콜하고, 이전의 독해내용에 합한다.
> 전문국역 　그는 꽃병을 말도 없이 캐비닛 안에 놓았다.

(14) To make the most of your life, you must keep the vision of eternity continually in your mind and the value of it in your heart.

> 구성처리 　구성성분 x 수식어(constituent x Modifier: cxM)가 나타난다면 일반적으로 구성성분 x에 인접하여 나타나지만(예: 문 These new manufacturing methods brought about an increase in production에서 구성성분 an increase를 수식하는 in production. 이런 경우는 전체 an increase in production을 직접목적어 한 단위로 독해 처리함), 분리되어 나타나는 경우 여러 위치에서 나타날 수 있다. 분리되어 나타나는 경우 분리수식어의 의미를 리콜하여 이전의 독해내용에 합한다. (14)에서 술어동사의 분리수식어인 밑줄 친 부분에 대해 '지속적으로 당신의 마음에' 의미를 리콜하고, 이전의 독해내용에 합한다.
> 전문국역 　여러분의 인생을 최대로 활용하기 위하여, 여러분은 영원에 대한 비전을 여러분의 마음속에 지속적으로 간직하고 그것에 대한 가치도 여러분의 마음속에 간직해야 한다.

(15) Football, his only interest in life, has brought him many friends.

> 구성처리   (15)에서 명사 Football 다음에 나타나는 명사적 표현 his only interest in life를 부가(동격관계)로 식별하고, 동시에 '자기 인생의 유일한 관심사' 의미를 리콜하여 이전의 독해내용에 합한다.
> 전문국역   축구, 즉 인생에서 그의 유일한 관심사가 그에게 많은 친구가 생기게 해주었다.

(16) User can easily buy iPhones that are sold overseas and brought into China for resale, though not 3G models.

> 구성처리   (16)에서 though절 독해에 진입하여 '주어+be(they/iPhones are)'가 생략되었음을 식별함과 동시에 그 의미 '아이폰들이 있다'를 리콜하여 이전의 독해내용에 합한다.
> 전문국역   3세대 모델은 아니지만, 리세일로 해외에서 팔리며 중국에 리세일로 들어온 아이폰을 사용자는 쉽게 살 수 있다.

(17) If you would like to eat lunch in the banquet room, an additional $10 will be/charged. Attached is a schedule for the conference.

> 구성처리   (17)에서 조작사(oP)가 본동사 뒤로, 동시에 주어(S)가 조작사 뒤로 이동했음을 이해하고, 밑줄 친 부분에 대해 '회의 스케줄이 있음' 의미를 리콜하고, 이전의 독해내용에 합한다.
> 전문국역   연회실에서 점심식사를 하고 싶으면 추가 10$를 내야 합니다. 회의의 일정이 첨부되어 있습니다.

지금까지 절 구성의 개별 요소 확인처리에 초점을 두었는데, 다음부터는 절 처리 과정에서 선적인 순서를 따라 모든 구성요소를 함께 처리한다.

(18) China will take steps toward improving intellectual property protection
     중국은(S)/조치를 취할 것이다(tV+dO)/지적재산권 보호를 높이는 방향으로(cMtV)/
     by reexamining an Internet music distribution protocol.
     인터넷 음악 배포 프로토콜을 재점검함으로서(cM'cMtV')[7]

---

[7] tV는 타동사, cMtV는 타동사수식어, cM'cMtV'는 타동사수식어의 수식어를 각각 표시함.

(19) Goldman Sachs estimates that Toyota's operating profit will slump 40 percent
　　　골드만삭스는(S)/평가한다(tV)/~를(dOt)8)///(cN)/도요타의 운영수익이(S)/ 올 회계연도에 40% 둔화되어
this fiscal year $13 billion, which is well below the carmaker's forecast of
　130억 달러에 이를 것이다(iV)//　　　이것은(cN&S)9)/자동차제조사 예상치 160억보다 훨씬 낮다(iV)
$16 billion.

(20) Surveys show that "life satisfaction" has been improving in recent years in line
　　조사는(S)/보여준다(tV)/~을(dOt)//삶의 만족도가(S)/1990년대의 급락이후에 경제회복과 더불어 개선되었다(iV)
of with economic recovery, after plunging in the 1990s.
* plunge: 뛰어들다, 빠지다.

(21) Japan will need to take more action to protect its economy from the effect of
　　　일본은(S)/자국 경제를 보호하기 위해 더 많은 조치를 취할 필요가 있을 것이다(iV)/세계적인 재정위기
의 영향으로부터.)
the global financial crisis(cMiV).

(22) Policy makers have long studied whether substantial amounts of money to poorer
　　　정책입안자들은(S)/오랫동안 연구해왔다(tV)/~를(dOt)//~인지 아닌지(cN)/더 가난한 국가들에게 실질적인
nations is helpful to bringing about their social infrastructure. Most economists
지원액이(S)/사회적 인프라를 갖추는 데에 도움이 되는지를(iV)./대부분의 경제학자들이(S)/느끼다(tV)/
feel that, at best, aid has produced only incompetence.
　　~를(dOt)//~를(cN)/기껏해야(cMV)/원조가 불완전함을 낳는다(tV)./)

　　구성성분 표기도 함께 다루었던 앞 (18)-(22)에 이어서 다음 (23)부터는 구성성분 표기는 하지 않고 독해처리를 다룬다.

(23) Please be there at least thirty minutes prior to the first demonstration if you are
　　　　적어도 30분 전에 오십시오/　　　　　　　　첫 실연 이전/　　　　만약 당신이

---

8) (dOt)는 진목적어와 가목적어의 관계에 비유되는 것으로 뒤에 나올 직접목적어(dO) 절을 의미하는 흔적(trace:t)을 의미한다.
9) cN&S 는 절접속어(cN)와 주어(S)를 겸한다는 것을 의미.

setting up a demonstration booth. If you are giving a speech, please be at the hotel
실연부스를 설치한다면./　　　　　　당신이 연설을 하신다면/　　　　한 시간 전에 호텔에
an hour before the morning refreshments are served in order to participate in
　오십시오/　　　　　아침 다과가 제공되기/　　　　　연설자의 최종연습에
the speaker's rehearsal.
참여하기 위해서/

(24) At this stage in the worldwide fight against depression, it is useful to stop and
　현 단계에서는/　불황을 퇴치하기 위해 전 세계적인 싸움을 하고 있는/ 잠시 생각해 보는 것도 도움이
consider just how conservative the policies implemented by the world's central
　된다/　　　얼마나 보수적이었는가를/
banks, treasuries and government budget offices have been. Almost everything that
세계의 중앙은행들, 재무부, 그리고 정부 예산처에서 도입된 정책이/　　그들이 지금까지 한 일/
they have done — spending increases, tax cuts, bank recapitalization, purchases of
즉 소비증가, 세금 감면, 은행자본 재구성, 부실자산 매입, 공개적인 시장 활동, 그리고 다른 통화 공급
risky assets, open market operations, other money supply expansions — has
확대와 같은 /하나의 정책과정을 답습한 것이다/
followed a policy path that is nearly 200 years old, dating back to the earliest
거의 200년이나 된,/ 즉 산업혁명 초기단계까지 거슬러 올라가는/
days of the Industrial Revolution.

> 어휘리콜　•depression: 의기소침, (경기)불황; •conservative: 보수적인; •implement: 이행하다,
> 효력을 주다; •treasury: 보고, 금고, 재무부; •asset: 자산(항목), 이점.

(25) The big bang is the most popular theory about the creation of the universe./
빅뱅은 우주의 생성에 관한 가장 널리 알려져 있는 이론이다.
According to this theory,/ the whole universe was created in a spilt second in
이 이론에 따르면,/　　　우주 전체는 한 순간(찰라)에 한 번의 거대한 폭발로 생겨났다.
one huge explosion./ All matter was squeezed together into a tiny, super-hot, dense
모든 물질이 압착되어져서 작으면서도 고열의 밀집된 공 모양이 되었는데,

ball/ that was smaller than an atom. The ball gradually expanded as it cooled,
이 공 모양은 원자보다도 더 작았다.　　　　이 공 모양은 차가워지자 점점 팽창해져서

it exploded, releasing energy and matter in all directions./ We cannot see the big
결국 에너지와 물질을 모든 방향으로 방출시켜 버렸다.　　　　우리는 빅뱅을 볼 수는 없는데,

bang/ because it would have happened billions of years ago./ But we can see/
그 이유는 수십억 년 전에 일어났을 것이기 때문이다.　　그러나 우리는 볼 수 있다 우주가 점점 더

that the universe is growing steadily bigger./ All the galaxies are speeding away
커지고 있는 것을./　　　　　　　　　　모든 은하는 서로서로 멀어지고 있다.

from each other/ as the universe expands.
우주가 팽창함에 따라

> 어휘리콜　•big bang: 우주 대 폭발; •spilt second: 순간, 찰라; •squeeze: 압착시키다; •release: 방출시키다; •galaxy: 은하.

(26) Avalanches are among the world's most dangerous natural disasters./ Fortunately,
　　　눈사태는 세계에서 가장 위험한 자연재해 속에 들어간다.

they usually occur in remote mountain areas,/ where they threaten neither human
다행스럽게도, 눈사태는 보통 먼 산악지역에서 일어나는데,　　이 산악지역에서는 인간의 생명과

life nor property./ Occasionally, however, an avalanche can strike without
재산을 위협하지 않는다.　그러나 경우에 따라서는 눈사태가 예고 없이 발생하고,

warning,/ taking hikers and skiers by surprise./ This is precisely what happened
놀랍게도 하이커와 스키어들을 집어 삼킨다.　　　　상태는 정확하게 1세기 이상 전에 일어났던 것으로

more than a century ago/ when a small of mountain climbers tried to scale the
그때 소규모 등산가 그룹이 거대한 높은 산 정상인 Mont Blanc에 올라가려고 시도했을 때이다.

huge alpine peak Mont Blanc./ Suddenly they were overtaken by an avalanche/
　　　　　　　　　　　　　　그들은 눈사태를 맞았는데

that left only a few survivors./ Three members of the party were buried in the
단지 몇 사람만 생존하게 되었다. 그 일원 중 3명은 눈 속에 묻혔다.

snow./ When, after almost half a century,/ the bodies were found,/ they were
　　　　그의 반세기 이후에　　　　　시체들이 발견되었는데,

perfectly preserved./ They were so well preserved, in fact,/ that a surviving
완벽하게 보존되어 있었다.   사실 시체들은 아주 잘 보존되어 있어서,

member of the original party, by then an old man, was able to recognize them.
당시 노인이 된 생존자들은 그 시체들을 알아 볼 수 있었다.

어휘리콜   •Avalanch: 사태, 쇄도; •overtake: ~를 뒤따라 잡다; •alpine peak: 높은 산 정상.

(27) Why is it that some people need Novocain just to get their teeth cleaned, while
왜 그런가? 어떤 사람들에게는 자기 치아를 깨끗이 하는 데에 국부마취약이 필요하고,

others allow the dentist to drill without benefit of painkillers? The answer is that
반면에 다른 사람들은 치과의사로 하여금 통증제거제의 도움 없이 구멍을 내도록 하는데.   대답은 이렇다-

people differ in their tolerance for pain, and this may be one reason why doctors
사람들은 통증을 참는데 차이가 있음,   이것이 이유일지 모른다- 의사들이 통증을

don't seem to know how to effectively treat pain. In 1993, an Annals of Internal
효과적으로 다루는 방법을 아는 것 같지 않은 이유.   1993년, 국제의학조사의 연보가 게재한 바,

Medicine survey found that 86 percent of the cancer physicians questioned
설문에 답한 암 치료 의사의 86%는 믿고 있다는 것이다.

believed their patients had received inadequate pain medication. As Richard B. Patt, an
환자들이 부적절한 통증치료를 받았음.   마취학자인 Richard B. Patt가

anesthesiologist, noted in an interview, "We do a lousy job with pain." The truth
인터뷰에서 말했다.   "우리는 비열한 통증치료 작업을 합니다"라고.

is that there's no x-ray or blood test to identify pain. Instead, doctors have to
사실은 통증을 확인할 엑스레이가 없거나 혈액검사가 없다.   대신에, 의사들은

rely on a zero to ten rating scale, with ten being the worst possible pain
0(영)에서 10까지의 통증 정도 차에 의존해야 한다. 10이 상상할 수 없을 정도의 가장 심한 통증 수준

imaginable. Yet here again, unbearable pain for one person may be quite bearable
이라고 할 경우. 그런데 다시 한 번 말하면, 이 사람에게 참을 수 없을 정도의 통증은 다른 사람에게도

for another. Thus, many doctors don't always pay enough attention when a patient
심한 통증이 될 수 있다. 그래서 많은 의사들은 항상은 충분한 주의를 하는 것은 아니다

insists that he or she is in pain.
환자가 고통스럽다고 말할 때.

어휘리콜 •Why is it that(왜 그런가?)~; •it와 that절은 가주어와 진주어; •Novocain: 국부마취약; •painkiller: 통증제거제; •anesthesiologist: 마취학자; •lousy: 이투성이의, 불결한.

(28) Because of years of restrictions on hunting, the wild deer population in the United States is higher than ever. These regulations, which include bans on hunting in many places and strict limits on the number of deer killed, have allowed the animals to thrive. Their rate of reproduction, too, has contributed to the large population. One doe usually gives birth to twins every year. Further more, reduced numbers of natural predators' such as wolves, along with a series of mild winters, have resulted in a lower mortality rate. Deer have also managed to adapt successfully to human destruction of their habitats. Even when forests are cut down, deer manage to find enough food and shelter in the remaining vegetation. They also venture into the new suburbs that replace their woodland home, causing deer-vehicle accidents to increase significantly. Deer also damage crops and gardens and wipe out plant species. Because hunters help reduce deer overpopulation and its effects, suburban residents who used to disapprove of hunting now appreciate the positive benefits of keeping deer populations under control.

> 어휘리콜 •restriction: 제약; •wild deer population: 야생사슴 수; •regulation: 규제; •thrive: 번창하다; •predator: 육식동물; •mortality rate: 사망률; •habitat: 서식지; •shelter woodland: 숲 보금자리; •deer-vehicle accident: 사슴이 차량에 치이는 사고; •overpopulation: 과잉 개체수.

(29) Whether military or civilian, most professional training programs stress the importance of self-confidence. Believe in your-self and you will succeed. But, in some cases, the opposite is true. There are people whose success stems not from self-confidence but from feelings of failure. Feeling inadequate, these people push themselves harder and harder, forcing themselves to achieve. In this way, failure becomes, paradoxically, a source of success. At least this was the view of the famed writer and critic Edmund Wilson. As examples, Wilson cited the philosopher Karl Marx and the poet Edna St. Vincent Millay, two people have driven to succeed by feelings of inadequacy and failure.

군사적이든 민간적이든, 대부분의 훈련 프로그램은 자신감의 중요성을 강화시켜준다. 여러분의 자신을 믿으세요, 그러면 여러분은 성공할 것입니다. 그러나 어떤 경우에는 그 반대일 수 있다. 자기들의 성공이 자신감에 기원하지 않고 실패감에 기원하는 사람들이 있다. 이런 사람들은, 부적당하다고 믿고, 스스로를 열심히 노력하게 하고, 스스로를 성공으로 밀어붙인다. 이런 면에서, 실패가, 역설적으로, 성공의 원천이 된다. 적어도 이것은 이름 있는 작자이자 비평가 Edmund Wilson의 견해이다. 예로, Wilson은 철학자 Karl Marx와 시인 Edna St. Vincent Millay를 인용했는데, 이 두 사람은 부적당함과 실패의 감정으로 성공했다.

> 어휘리콜 •civilian: 민간적인; •self-confidence: 자신감; •stem: 기원하다; •paradoxically: 역설적으로; •famed: 유명한, 이름 있는; •inadequacy: 부적당함.

(30) Many educators believe that the internet will prove to be a powerful tool for learning. However, others are not so convinced. Some teachers are worried about the

많은 교육자들은 믿고 있다-인터넷이 학습의 강력한 도구로 입증이 될 것. 그러나, 또 다른 사람들은 그렇게는 확신하지 않고 있다. 어떤 교사들은

growing number of websites with names like "House of Cheat." In exchange for
"House of Cheat"와 같은 이름이 있는 웹사이트의 증가를 우려하고 있다.   이용료 대신으로
a fee, these websites offer students term papers on everything from the cost of
         그 웹사이트들은   학생들에게   모든 것에 관한 텀페이퍼를   아이 갖는 비용으로부터
having a baby to the death of Chief Crazy Horse. Although most of these sites
Chief Crazy Horse의 죽음에 이르기까지의 제공하고 있다.   비록 이 대부분의 사이트들은
include disclaimers insisting that the papers are not intended to be plagiarized and
그 페이퍼들이 한 학생의 이름   아래 표절되어 보내지도록 의도되지 않았다고 주장하는
submitted under a student name, it's not clear that such disclaimers will totally
경고문을 포함하지만   표절에 해당하는 것을 완전히 무시한다는 것은 분명치 않다.
discourage what amounts to intellectual theft. In the long run, teachers worried
                                            결국, 인터넷으로부터 다운받은 과제물들에
about term papers being down-loaded from the Internet can only hope that their
대해 걱정하는 교사들은 단지 그들의 학생들이 착하기 때문에 자기들의 이름을 다른 사람의 작품에
students are simply too honest to put their names on someone else's work and
넣지 않을 것으로 기대할 뿐이고,   그리고
that websites like the House of Cheat will disappear for lack of interest.
"House of Cheat"와 같은 웹사이트가 관심부족으로 사라질 것으로 기대할 뿐이다.

어휘리콜   •In exchange for: ~대신으로; •disclaimer: 경고문; •plagiarize: 표절하다.

다음 (31)에서는 구성성분 표기와 국역이 없는 영어만을 대상으로 독해 처리한다.

(31)   **Successful Presentations −**
        Tips to Help You Make an Impact on an Audience

Tip No. 1 : Consider what you want to say
   When given the opportunity to pitch a new idea or product, we tend to naturally assume that a 'presentation' will be the best method. But is it? Sometimes, perhaps a demonstration, free trial, brainstorming session, outlet visit, or even a succinct,

benefits-led letter [with, of course, a follow-up phone call] may be more appropriate.

Tip No. 2 : Prepare, Prepare, Prepare

Preparation is vital for success. Do you know how many will be in the audience? Do you have enough seats, hard copies, samples, etc. for everyone? What is their current level of knowledge? How will you get their attention? How will you manage questions, as you go along or at the end? Where will you stand? Can you arrange a rehearsal at the venue?

Tip No. 3 : Involve the audience

A successful presentation is to present with an audience not at an audience. In your preparation, look at areas where you could get audience participation, maybe plan to ask them a question or get them involved in a product demonstration. An audience's attention span is very short. So always look for ways to grab and maintain their attention.

Tip No. 4 : Less is more

Aim to communicate a maximum of four key points successfully, rather than several poorly. Your preparation and delivery will benefit from having fewer key points, and your audience will more easily grasp your critical themes and ideas. If you have to communicate more than four points, perhaps consider doing two separate presentations or find another way of getting these other points across (perhaps via a leave piece, handout or e-mail).

Tip No. 5 : Use notes sparingly

After thorough rehearsal, the need for highly detailed notes should be removed. However there may be a need sometimes to have the 'security blanket' of a few key notes, perhaps highlighted on small prompt cards. The key thing here to remember is that notes should be used to support the presentation and not replace it or get in the way of you delivering with impact.

Tip No. 6 : YOU are the presentation
The best presentation tool you have is not your slides or props but YOU - the way you engage the audience, how you make and maintain eye contact with them, your enthusiasm, the volume and pitch of your voice, your use of silence, the depth of your listening skills. Never forget! You are the presentation.

> **어휘리콜**   •impact: 충동, 영향, 효과; •pitch: 말하다, 던지다; •demonstration: 실물 제시; •free trial: 무료 시연; •brainstorming: 각자가 자유롭게 착상을 내놓는 회의 법, 창조적 집단 회의법; •outlet: 출구, 배출구, 판로, 대리점; •succinct: 간결한, 딱 맞는; •vital: 긴요한, 중요한; •venue: 현장, 행위지; •grab: 붙잡다, 꽉 쥐다; •sparingly: 절약하여; •security blanket: 안전을 보장하는 것; •prop: 지주, 의지가 되는 것.
>
> **부분국역**   (첫 부분)성공적인 발표-청중에게 효과를 주는데 도움이 될 조건//새로운 아이디어나 제품을 말할 기회가 주어진다면, 우리는 당연히 '발표'가 최선의 방법이라고 생각하는 경향이 있다. 그런데 그런가? 때로는 아마도, 실물 제시, 무료 시연, 창조적 집단회의, 진열장 방문, 혹은 간단하고도 장점을 적은 서신[물론, 응답 전화]가 더 적당할 수도 있다.

제3절   주제어휘와 초점어휘 확인

절 단위를 구성한 다음, 즉 어휘의미들을 합한 다음에는 어떻게 해야 하는가? 영어의 경우 절에서 일반적으로 메시지 부분이 있고 이 메시지 부분은 이야기꺼리를 의미하는 주제부분과 이 이야기꺼리에 관한 초점부분으로 구성되기도 한다. 주제부분에서 가장 핵심적인 어휘를 주제어휘, 초점부분에서 가장 핵심적인 어휘를 초점어휘라고 한다. 독자는 절의 구성처리와 동시에 혹은 직후에는 이 주제어휘와 초점어휘를 보다 적은 수의 어휘 덩어리로 확인하는 것이 필요하다. 절 구성에 사용된 모든 어휘들은 절 내에서 역할과 정보도(정보 새로움의 정도)가 다르다. 영어의 경우 좌에서 우로 갈수록 정보도가 높아진다.

절에서 주제어휘와 초점어휘가 나타나는 위치는 문법적 구조, 언어적 문맥, 상황적 맥락, 그리고 작자의 구조 스타일로 인하여 원칙적으로는 다양하다고 할 수 있지만 영어의 경우 주제어휘는 가능한 앞쪽에, 초점어휘는 가능한 뒤쪽에 놓이는 경향이 강하다.

(1) The heavy rain prevented us from playing baseball.

키워드	주제어휘는 heavy rain, 초점어휘는 playing baseball이다.
전문국역	많은 비가 우리로 하여금 야구를 못하게 했다.

(2) Thanks to the '68 generation, Western youth by 1989 had all manner of personal freedom just as capitalism pervaded our societies.

키워드	주제어휘는 Western youth, 초점어휘는 personal freedom이다.
전문국역	'68년대 세대 덕분으로 1989년경에 서방의 젊은이들은 자본주의가 우리 사회 곳곳에 스며들었을 때 모든 종류의 개인적인 자유를 가지게 되었다.

(3) Nice apartments in this part of town are hard to come by.

어휘리콜	•come by: 손에 넣다.
키워드	주제어휘는 Nice apartments, 초점어휘는 hard to come by이다.
전문국역	이 도시의 이 구역에서는 좋은 아파트를 얻기가 어렵다.

(4) Despite the problems, they loved the house, warts and all.

어휘리콜	•warts and all: 남김없이 모두.
키워드	주제어휘는 they, 초점어휘는 the house이다.
전문국역	그 문제들에도 불구하고, 그들은 그 집을 남김없이 모두 좋아한다.

(5) Rechargeable batteries are more expensive than ordinary ones.

키워드	주제어휘는 Rechargeable batteries, 초점어휘는 more expensive이다.
전문국역	재충전 가능한 배터리는 보통 배터리보다 더 비싸다.

(6) Fortunately, I had memorized her telephone number and was able to ring her from the station.

> 키워드　　주제어휘는 I, 초점어휘는 able to ring이다.
> 전문국역　다행스럽게도 난 그녀의 전화번호가 기억나서 기차역에서 그녀에게 전화할 수 있었지.

절들이 연결된 문장에서는 문장 단위에서 핵절을 확인하고, 이 핵절에서 주제어휘와 초점어휘를 확인한다.10)

(7) The rumor says he will be promoted sooner or later.

> 어휘리콜　•*The rumor says*는 전달절로 기능하고, 나머지는 메시지 절.
> 키워드　　주제어휘는 he, 초점어휘는 promoted이다.
> 전문국역　그는 조만간 승진할 것이란 소문이 있다.

(8) I found it stupid to drive under the influence.

> 어휘리콜　•*I found*는 인지절, 나머지는 메시지 절.
> 키워드　　주제어휘는 it(drive under the influence), 초점어휘는 stupid이다.
> 전문국역　음주 운전하는 것은 어리석은 짓이라는 것을 알았다.

(9) It's more money, because it comes with all the bells and whistles.

> 어휘리콜　•because절 내에서 문의 주제어휘(it)와 초점어휘(the bells and whistles)도 가능하다. bells and whistles: 있으면 좋은 것, 덤.
> 키워드　　주제어휘는 It, 초점어휘는 more money이다.
> 전문국역　그것은 더 많은 돈이다. 왜냐하면 그것은 덤이기 때문이다.

---

10) 이론적으로는 절 내에서 주제어휘와 초점어휘를 식별하고, 절간의 관계를 식별하고, 다음에 (정보)핵절을 식별한 후 이 정보핵절의 주제어휘와 초점어휘를 문의 주제어휘와 초점어휘로 확인해야 하는데, 독해테크닉 상 정보핵절을 식별하고 이 정보핵절에서 주제어휘와 초점어휘를 확인하면 된다.

(10) Her doctor has told her to take things easy until she gets her strength back.

어휘리콜	•Her doctor: 그녀의 주치의; •gets her strength back: 그녀의 힘을 회복하다.
키워드	주제어휘는 둘째의 her, 초점어휘는 take things easy이다.
전문국역	그녀의 주치의는 그녀에게 그녀의 힘을 회복할 때까지 모든 것을 편하게 하라고 했다.

(11) Can you please give me a ball park figure of the salary you expect?

어휘리콜	•ball park figure: 근사치.
키워드	주제어휘는 me, 초점어휘는 ball park figure of use salary이다.
전문국역	당신은 당신이 생각하는 월급의 근사치를 저에게 주실 수 있겠습니까?

(12) The shop assistant lost the cords to the new vacuum cleaners so they couldn't be sold - all of them had to be written off as a loss.

어휘리콜	•write ~ off: (장부에서) 감가상각 처리하다.
키워드	주제어휘는 they(진공청소기), 초점주제는 n't be sold이다.
전문국역	그 가게 점원이 새 진공청소기의 줄을 잃어버렸기 때문에 그 진공청소기들은 팔수가 없었다-모두 손실 처리해야만 했다.

(13) You should buy that stock now, because in the long run that company will be very successful.

어휘리콜	•in the long run: 결국.
키워드	주제어휘는 You, 초점어휘는 buy이다.
전문국역	당신은 그 주식을 지금 사야하는데, 그 이유는 결국 그 회사가 매우 성공할 것이기 때문이다.

(14) It's good to strike while the iron is hot so you don't miss out on the good price.

어휘리콜	•strike while the iron is hot: 기회가 있을 때 행동을 취하다.

키워드	주제어휘는 you, 초점어휘는 good price이다.
전문국역	좋은 가격에서 놓치지 않도록 기회가 있을 때 행동을 취하는 것이 좋다.

(15) Although he was known to be extremely reserved in his public behavior, scholars have discovered that his diaries were written. with uncommon frankness.

어휘리콜	•reserved in his public behavior: 공적인 행동에서는 내성적인; •uncommon frankness: 보기드믄 솔직함.
키워드	주제어휘는 his diaries, 초점어휘는 uncommon frankness이다.
전문국역	비록 그는 대중적인 행동에서 매우 내성적인 것으로 알려져 있지만, 학자들은 그의 일기가 보기 드문 솔직함으로 써졌다는 것을 발견했다.

(16) I wonder if you would be so kind as to send me further details and an application form.

어휘리콜	•I wonder if: ~ 인지 궁금하다.
키워드	주제어휘는 me, 초점어휘는 details and an application form이다.
전문국역	저는 당신이 더 많은 상세내용과 지원서양식을 저에게 친절히 보내 주실 수 있는지 궁금합니다.

(17) We need to start studying. Our test is just around the corner.

어휘리콜	•just around the corner: 곧, 가까운 미래에.
키워드	주제어휘는 Our test, 초점어휘는 just around the corner이다.
전문국역	우리는 공부를 시작할 필요가 있다. 우리의 시험이 얼마 남지 않았다.

(18) The waiter told us not to worry about the check; it was on the house.

어휘리콜	•on the house: 회사부담의, 무료의.
키워드	주제어휘는 it(check), 초점어휘는 on the house이다.
전문국역	그 웨이터는 우리에게 그 수표에 대해 걱정하지 말라고 했다. 그것은 회사부담이었다.

(19) 1)Take Bill Gates for **example**,/ 2)The public has been **exited**/ 3)about what he has achieved/ 4)and been **thankful** for him,/ 5)but people hope/ 6)that he creates **something more**/ 7)that will provide a higher degree of convenience to our lives and work./ 8)He made the computer operating system "**DOS**," and went on to build a revolutionary one, "**Windows**"/9)yet people still require **something** of him/ 10)and he is constantly pressured to **develop** something different because of public demand, in addition to his **spirit of challenge**./

> 어휘리콜 •revolutionary: 혁신적인; •constantly: 지속적으로.
> 키워드[11]
> 전문국역 사례로 Bill Gates를 보자. 대중은 그가 성취한 것에 대해 흥분했고 그에게 감사했지만, 사람들은 그가 우리의 생활과 일 작업에서 더 편리한 것을 제공해주는 것을 더 많이 창조해 주기를 희망한다. 그는 컴퓨터 운영체제 DOS를 개발했고, 계속해서 혁명적인 것, 윈도우를 만들어냈다. 그러나 사람들은 아직도 그에게서 무언가를 요구한다. 그는 끊임없이 그의 도전정신 외에도 대중의 요구 때문에 다른 무엇을 개발하기 위해 압박을 받는다.

(20) Arguments about the need for national or cultural identity are often seen as being **opposed to those about the need for mutual intelligibility**. But this is **misleading**. It isperfectly possible to develop a situation in which intelligibility and identity happily**co-exist**. This situation is the **familiar one** of bilingualism - but a bilingualism where one of the languages within a speaker is the **global language**, providing access to the world community, and the other is a well-resourced **regional language**, providing access to a local community. The two functions can be seen as **complementary**, responding to different needs. And it is because the functions are so **different** that a world of linguistic diversity can in principle continue to exist in a world united by a common language.

> 어휘리콜 •mutual intelligibility: 상호 의사소통성
> 전문국역 민족적 또는 문화적 정체성이 필요하다는 주장이 상호의사소통성이 필요하다는 주장

---

11) 여기서부터는 편의상 영어텍스트 상에서 표시 한다(밑줄은 주제어휘, 밑줄과 볼드체는 **초점어휘**).

과 상반되는 것으로 생각하는 경우가 종종 있다. 그러나 이것은 잘못된 것이다. 의사소통성과 정체성이 조화롭게 공존하는 상황은 완전히 가능하다. 이것이 이중 언어를 사용하는 경우에는 일반적인 상황이다. 이중 언어의 경우에는, 한 사람이 사용하는 두 언어 중 하나가 세계어여서 세계 공동체에 쉽게 접근할 수 있게 하고, 나머지 한 언어는 풍부한 자료를 지닌 지역어여서 지역 공동체에 쉽게 접근할 수 있게 한다. 이 두 가지 기능은 서로 다른 필요에 부응하면서 상호보완적인 역할을 한다고 볼 수 있다. 그리고 그것은 두 기능이 서로 상당히 달라서, 공용어로 통합된 세계에서 언어적 다양성을 지닌 세계가 원칙적으로 계속 존재할 수 있기 때문이다.

(21)

1 There is an old saying in America that the only <u>two things</u> people can count on are **death and taxes**. But for the 65 percent of Americans who live in urban areas of 50,000 people or more, there is <u>one more</u> suer thing to add to that list; **traffic**. More than <u>two-thirds</u> of the population inhabit just **2.6 percent** of our nation's land, and the <u>number</u> is steadily <u>rising</u>. Many <u>people</u> live and work in **sprawling suburbs**, so the total <u>number of miles</u> Americans drive every year has nearly **doubled** in the last two decades. The <u>highway system</u>, however, has **not expanded** accordingly. In fact, <u>Americans</u> waste more than **4.6 billion hours** every year stuck in bumper-to bumper traffic jams. A University of Maryland study showed that on weekdays, <u>parents</u> spend **more time in their cars** than they spend with their children.

2 The problem is the worst, of course, in America's **major cities**. In <u>Washington, D. C.</u> the average motorist now loses **eighty-two hours** per year to traffic jams. In <u>Los Angeles</u>, it's **seventy-six** hours. In a recent survey, <u>residents of Atlanta</u> named traffic congestion as their city's **number one problem**.

3 But <u>lost time</u> is **not the only consequence** of the growing traffic problem in the United States. <u>The lock</u> contributes to **air pollution** and wastes **gasoline**. <u>Traffic jams </u>also lead to increased **stress** and even to "**road rage**" when busy, time-pressed Americans find themselves pinned in their cars for extended periods of time. <u>Individuals and businesses</u> **lose money** when employees become stalled in a sea of cars and can't get to work on time. As a matter of fact, the effects of traffic have become so serious that several different <u>solutions</u> are now **being implemented**.

어휘리콜
- stuck (들러붙은)과거분사; •count on: 의지하다, 기대하다; •stall: 오도 가도 못하다;
- sprawl: 버둥거리다, 기다; •lock: 교통정체; •traffic jam: 교통 혼잡; •road rage: 도로짜증;
- pin: 갇히다; •sea of cars: 승용차 물결.

전문국역 **1** 인간이 기대할 수 있는 유일한 두 가지는 죽음과 세금이라는 속담이 미국에 있다. 그러나 5만 명 이상의 도시지역 거주 미국인 65%에게는 추가해야 할 확실한 것이 하나 더 있는데, 교통이다. 인구 2/3 이상이 국토의 2.6%에서 거주하고 있으며, 그 수가 꾸준히 증가하고 있다. 많은 사람들은 버둥거리는 시 근교에 살면서 일하고 있으며, 그래서 미국인들이 매년 운전하는 마일의 수가 지난 20년 만에 거의 두 배가 되었다. 그러나 고속도로 망은 그에 맞게 확장되지 않았다. 사실, 미국인들은 범퍼와 범퍼가 붙은 교통지옥에 끼어서 매년 46억 시간을 허비한다. Maryland대학의 한 연구는 주중에 부모님들이 애들과 함께 시간을 보내는 것보다 자기들 차 안에서 더 많은 시간을 보낸다는 것을 보여주었다. **2** 물론 이 문제는 미국의 주요 도시들에서 가장 나쁜 경우이다. 워싱턴 D.C에서 보통의 운전자는 요즘 1년에 교통 혼잡에서 82시간을 낭비한다. 로스앤젤레스에서는 그것이 76시간이다. 최근의 조사에서는, 애틀랜타 주민들은 교통 혼잡을 그들 도시의 넘버 원 문제라고 부른다. **3** 그러나 잃어버리는 시간이 미국에서 증가하는 교통문제의 유일한 결과는 아니다. 교통정체는 공기오염을 가중시키고 연료를 낭비한다. 교통 혼잡은 바쁘고도 시간에 기는 미국인들이 스스로 그들 차 안에 갇히게 되어 연장되는 시간 또한 스트레스와 도로짜증을 증가시킨다. 근로자들이 승용차 물결 속에서 오도 가도 못하여 시간에 맞게 직장에 이르지 못할 때, 개인들과 기업들은 돈을 낭비하게 된다. 실제로, 교통의 영향은 너무 심각하여 여러 다른 해결방안이 지금 강구되고 있다.

(22)

Is Local News Really News?

1 News is frequently defined as the telling of **factual stories**, meant to inform the public about significant events. Thus, when you turn on your local television newscast every evening, you probably expect to hear about **recent events** in your community. You might even consider yourself an informed citizen because you're in the habit of **watching your local news program**. However, while watching your local news, it's unlikely that you will see or hear many reports about **significant events concerning politics, culture, business, and government**. Instead, You're probably learning about **violent crimes, major accidents, deadly disasters, and celebrity breakups**.

2 In half-hour local news broadcast, only about fifteen minutes are left once the time for **commercials, weather, sports, traffic**, and bantering by news anchors is

subtracted. This is **not much time** to relate all of the news of the day. Therefore, each individual news story is necessarily quite **short**. In fact, studies have shown that 70 percent of all news stories are no more than **a minute** long. Forty-three percent are less than **thirty seconds** long. Only about 16 percent of stories are longer **than two minutes**; in the television news industry, any story more than a minute and a half long is billed as an "**in- depth**" **report**.

3 Typically the television news anchors who introduce or read these stories are **not experts** in any of the fields-such as education, the environment, business, government, and health-that are covered. Most are hired not for their understanding of the news but for their **ability to read a story** well while conveying the specific emotion (anger, fear, sympathy, admiration, disgust, etc.) appropriate to that story. The reporters who gather the stories are **not experts** either. They are hired primarily for their **ability to communicate** well on camera, as well as for their **writing skill and general common sense** Plus, Reporters are under tremendous **pressure** to produce a story. They are usually **assigned a particular story** about midmorning; then they have but a few hours to **gather the facts** and **write the story** so that it can be edited with video and ready for a 5:00 or 6:00 p.m. broadcast. As a result, reporters have **little time for research**, and their sources tend to be **thin**: only 25 percent of TV news stories have more **than one source**. Not surprisingly, news directors **avoid assigning** hundreds of important stories that would require some real research.

4 The truth is that television news broadcasts **feature stories** that readily lend themselves to videotape footage and pictures. This is why there's so **little coverage of events** that ate important but difficult to illustrate, such as political speeches, school board meetings, or city council sessions. One survey revealed that only about 7 percent of news stories cover **economic issues**. Another study of 6,000 news stories showed that only 9 percent of them concerned **poverty or welfare**. Instead, TV news focuses on events that are relatively **trivial but also very visual**, and it tends to sensationalize those events by making them look even **more dramatic** than they actually were.

5 In addition to avoiding nonvisual news stories, TV newscasts seldom include **negative stories** about their advertisers or about police officers and fire-fighters. According to one survey, more than half of news directors interviewed said that they had been **pressured** by advertisers to either kill critical stories or promote favorable ones. The largest number of consumer complaints concern **new car dealerships**, but because car dealers use a lot of commercial airtime, they are rarely subjected to a **news station's scrutiny**. Neither will viewers see many **critical stories** about grocery and clothing stores, shopping malls, bands, insurance and health care providers, soda manufacturers, or fast-food restaurants, all of which buy a significant amount of commercial airtime. Police and fire-fighters are also rarely cast in a **negative light** on local TV news stations because reporters need the cooperation of law enforcement and public safety officials to get the crime stories that are their lifeblood. That's why viewers see **few, if any, stories** about issues like radar traps, brutality, and/or police or fire-fighter mistakes.

어휘리콜 •deadly disaster: 치명적인 재앙; •are left: 배정되었다; •celebrity breakup: 유명인의 별거; •banter: 놀리다, 도전하다; •subtract: 빼다, 감하다, 제외하다; •bill: 계산에 넣다; •"in-depth" report: 심층리포트; •write the story: 이야기를 구성하다; •footage: 방송필름; •car dealers but a lot of commercial airtime와 they는 동격 관계; •radar trap: 속도위반 탐지 장치; •brutality: 잔인, 야만적 행위.

전문국역 **1** 지방 뉴스가 진짜 뉴스인가? 뉴스란 의미가 있는 사건에 관해 대중에게 알리기에 의미 있는 실제의 이야기를 말하는 것으로 자주 정의된다. 그러므로 여러분은 매일 저녁 지역 방송을 켤 때, 아마도 여러분의 지역사회에서 최근의 사건에 관해 듣기를 기대할 것이다. 여러분은 여러분의 지역뉴스 시청에 습관화되어 있기 때문에 여러분 자기 자신을 알려져 있는 한 시민으로 생각할지도 모른다. 그러나 지역뉴스를 시청하는 동시에 정치, 문화, 기업, 그리고 정부 관련 중요한 사건에 관한 여러 리포트를 보거나 들을 것 같지가 않다. 여러분들은 아마도 격렬한 범죄, 큰 사건, 치명적인 재난, 그리고 유명인의 별거에 관해서는 듣게 될 것 같다. **2** 반시간 지방뉴스방송에서는, 뉴스앵커에 의해서 사업, 일기, 스포츠, 교통, 재량의 시간이 제외된다면, 단지 15분만 할당되어 진다. 이 시간은 그날의 뉴스 전부를 관련시키기는 충분한 시간이 못된다. 그러므로 개개의 뉴스 스토리는 매우 짧다. 사실, 연구내용이 보여준 바에 의하면 모든 뉴스의 70%는 (1건에) 체 1분도 못되었다. 43%는 30초도 체 못 되었다. 단지 16%의 뉴스 내용만이 2분을 넘었다. TV뉴스 산업에서는 1분반 이상 되는 뉴스내용은 심층리포트로 넣는다. **3** 전형적으로 이러한 스토리를 도입하거나 읽는 TV뉴스 앵커는 모든 분야 - 커버되는 교육, 환경, 기업, 정부, 보건-의 전문가는 아니다. 대부분은 뉴스에 대한 그들의 이해 때문에 채용된 것이 아니라 뉴스내용에 적절한 특별한 감정(분노, 공포, 동정, 감탄, 혐오 등)을 전달하면서 내용을 잘 읽는 능력 때문에 채용되었다. 뉴스 내용을 모으는 리포터들 역시 전문가가 아니다. 리포터들은 그들의 쓰기 능력과 일반상식 때문이 아니라 우선 카메라에 잘 소통하는 능력 때문에 채용되었다. 더 붙여서, 리포터들은 내용을 생산해내는 엄청난 압박을 받고 있다. 그들은 보통 오전 중간쯤에 특정 내용에 사인을 한다. 그 다음에 단지 2-3시간 동안에 사실들을 모으고 스토리를 구성하고 오후 5시 혹은 6시 방송용으로 비디오로 편집 및 준비가 된다. 그 결과, 리포터들은 연구할 시간이 없고, 그 자료들은 빈약한 경향이 있다: 단지 TV 뉴스 스토리 25%만이 둘 이상의 자료를 가질 뿐이다. 놀라울 것 없이, 뉴스 보도본부장은 어떤 실제적 연구를 요구하는 수백 개의 중요 스토리에 사인하는 것을 피한다. ４ 사실은 TV뉴스는 장면과 그림을 비디오에 담기에 쉬운 경향이 있는 특종 스토리만 방송한다는 것이다. 이것은 중요하지만 어려운 사건, 예를 들면 정치연설, 학교이사회, 시의회회기 등 사건의 커버가 없다는 이유 때문이다. 한 연구조사가 보여주는 바로는 뉴스 스토리의 단지 약 7%만이 경제 이슈를 커버한다. 6,000뉴스 스토리에 대한 또 한 조사가 보여주는 바는 그 6,000뉴스 스토리의 단지 9%만이 가난과 안녕에 관련되고 있다는 것이다. 대신에, TV 뉴스는 비교적 사소하지만 시각적인 사건에 초점이 맞추어져 있으며, 사건의 실제에 보다는 사건을 보다 더 드라마틱하게 보이도록 함으로써 사건을 센세이션화 하는 경향이 있다. ５ 비 시각적인 뉴스 스토리를 회피하는 것 외에, TV 뉴스방송은 그들의 광고주나 경찰관과 소방관들에 관해서는 부정적인 스토리를 좀처럼 포함하지 않는다는 것이다. 한 조사에 따르면, 인터뷰에 응한 뉴스 본부장 절반 이상은 말하기를 자기들은 광고주들로부터 압박을 받아 비평적 스토리를 호의적인 스토리로, 더 호의적이게 한다는 것이다. 소비자 불평의 최대의 수는 신 차 영업에 관심을 갖지만, 차 딜러들은 많은 상업방송 시간을 이용하기 때문에 그들은 보도국의 검열을 거의 받지 않는다. 시청자들은 식료품가게와 의류가게, 쇼핑몰, 넥타이가게, 보험 및 헬스케어제공자, 소다제조업자, 혹은 패스트푸드 식당에 관한 비판적 스토리를 시청하지 않는데, 이들 모두가 많은 량의 상업방송 시간을 차지해 버린다. 경찰과 소방관들에게 또한 지역 TV뉴스방송국에 대하여 부정적 시각으로 방송되지 않는데, 이유는 리포터들은 법집행관들과 시민안전공무원들의 협조를 얻어 생혈인 범죄 스토리를 얻어야 하기 때문이다. 그것이 시청자가 속도위반 탐지 장치, 야만적 행위, 그리고/혹은 경찰 혹은 소방관 실수와 같은 이슈에 관한 스토리를 시청하지 않는 이유이다.

제3장

단락 독해

　본문 첫 부문의 첫 절(clause)을 독해하는 것은 절을 대상으로 선적인 순서를 따라 1)어휘의미들을 리콜하여 2)연결시켜서 절을 구성하고 3)주제어휘와 초점어휘를 확인하는 것임을 2장에서 보았다. 이런 절들이 보태어지면 그 나름의 특성을 지니는 단락이 형성되기 때문에 단락 독해에 들어서면 이런 특성을 바탕으로 하여 단락 독해 처리 차원으로 접어들어 가야 한다. 그러면 단락은 어떻게 독해해야 하는가? 읽어나가는 절들을 단락구성의 부분으로 간주하여 조립해가는 것이다. 즉 1)절마디의 관계를 이해하고, 2)단락내용의 흐름(즉 핵절들의 흐름)을 이해하고, 3)단락 끝에 이르러 단락의 주제문을 확인하는 것이다.

제1절　절마디 관계 이해

　선행절, 즉 독자가 직전에 읽은 한 차례의 주술단위에 후행절, 즉 지금 읽는 한 차례의 주술단위가 보태어질 때 절마디에 관계가 형성되고, 절마디에 관계가 형성되면 내용흐름이 형성되고, 내용흐름이 형성되면 단락의 주제가 확립된다. 따라서 단락 독해의 첫 작업은 이 절마디에 대해 관계(가령: 주장←예증)를 이해하는 것이다. 만약

이 절마디의 관계가 이해되지 않으면 내용흐름이 파악되지 않으며, 단락 끝에 도달했을 때 단락주제가 파악되지 않는다. 단락의 주제가 확인되지 않은 경우는 단락을 독해한 것이 아니라는 주장이 가능하다. 절마디의 관계 이해는 후행절 독해시작 이전에 파악되는 것이 좋으며, 또 실제 파악되기도 하지만, 경우에 따라서는 후행절 독해처리 중에 이해가 이루어지는 경우도 있고, 절들이 더 이해되어진 이후에 파악이 되는 경우도 있고, 더 나아가서 보태어져 나가는 문맥에 의하여 이전에 확인된 관계가 다른 관계로 변경되어 인지되는 경우도 발생한다. 절 사이의 관계방식에는 부가, 대조, 선택, 명사성분, 명사한정, 재설명, 추론, 열거, 전이, 시공, 인과, 주장예증, 일반구체, 목적수단, 조건결과, 문제해결, 요약전후 등이 있는데(김용도2011: 4-5장), 이 관계리스트를 활용할 수 있다. 상대가 합성문(중문, 복문)인 경우 합성문 속의 핵절을 대상으로 한다.

(1) The festival, sponsored by the Regional Arts Council in cooperation with local museums, galleries and restaurants, promotes artists living and working in the area. Music, dance and traditional crafts will also be featured.

> 어휘리콜 •craft: 재간, 재주; feature: ~을 특별한 볼거리로 하다.
> 마디관계 선행문의 의미에 대해 후행문의 의미가 부가관계(의미관계: 또한).
> 전문국역 축제는 Regional Arts Council이 지역 박물관, 화랑 그리고 식당과 함께 후원하는데, 그 지역에 살면서 작품 활동하는 예술가들을 홍보하게 됩니다. 음악, 춤과 전통적 재주가 또한 특별 볼거리가 될 것입니다.

(2) It sounds plausible, but I don't think it is possible in practice.

> 어휘리콜 •plausible: 그럴듯한; •in practice: 실제로.
> 마디관계 선행절(but 앞부분)의 의미에 대해 후행절(but 뒤 전부)의 의미가 대조관계(의미관계: 그러나).
> 전문국역 그것은 그럴 듯하게 들린다. 그러나 나는 그것이 실제로는 그럴 듯하다고 생각하지 않는다.

(3) You can boil yourself an egg or you can make some sandwiches.

어휘리콜	•boil: 끓이다.
마디관계	선행절(or 앞부분)의 의미에 대해 후행절(or 이후 전부)의 의미가 선택 관계(의미관계: 혹은).
전문국역	너는 자신이 달걀을 삶을 수도 있고 아니면 너는 샌드위치를 좀 만들 수도 있다.

(4) Whoever visited the concert is able to download the music for free.

어휘리콜	•download: 내려 받다.
마디관계	선행절의 의미(Whoever~concert)는 후행절의 의미에 대해 주어 명사성분의 관계(의미관계: ~은).
전문국역	그 음악회에 참석하는 사람은 누구나 그 음악을 무료로 내려 받을 수 있다.

(5) The common assumption is that imprisonment deters them from returning to a life of crime.

어휘리콜	•imprisonment: 투옥, 감금; •deter A from -ing: A가 -ing하는 것을 막다.
마디관계	앞 절에 대하여 that-절은 명사성분(보어절)의 관계.
전문국역	일반적인 가정에 따르면, 교도소에 가둔다는 것이 그들로 하여금 범죄의 삶으로 돌아가는 것을 막는다는 것이다.

(6) Being faint is not uncommon in elderly people who stand up suddenly.

어휘리콜	•faint: 어질어질한, 현기증이 나는.
마디관계	선행절(~people)의 의미에 대해 후행절(who 이하)의 의미가 명사한정의 관계(의미관계: ~한).
전문국역	현기증은 갑자기 일어서는 노인들에게 흔히 생긴다.

(7) We can't see her any more. In other words, she passed away.

어휘리콜	•pass away: 사라지다, 죽다.
마디관계	In other words 앞문에 대하여 뒤 문은 재설명관계

> 전문국역 　우리는 그녀를 더 이상 볼 수 없다. 다른 말로 말하면 그녀는 죽었다.

(8) Her boss' voice was very high in the meeting. That implies that he was angry.

> 어휘리콜 　•imply: 함축하다.
> 마디관계 　앞 문장에 대하여 뒤 문장은 추론관계.
> 전문국역 　그녀의 서장님이 어제 회의에서 목소리가 매우 높았다. 그것은 사장님이 화가 났음을 함축한다.

(9) I tell you first the economy ... and I tell you secondly that unemployment figures ...

> 어휘리콜 　•unemployment: 실업.
> 마디관계 　and 앞 절에 대하여 뒤 부분이 열거의 관계.
> 전문국역 　저는 여러분에게 먼저 경제가 ...을 이야기 하고, 그리고 실업자가 ...을 이야기 합니다.

(10) It's time someone cleaned up this city; we have one of the highest crime rates in the country.

> 어휘리콜 　•It's time은 직설법시제; •cleaned: 가정법시제.
> 마디관계 　세미콜론(;) 앞 절에 대해 뒤 절은 열거관계.
> 전문국역 　이제 누군가가 이 도시를 청소해야 할 때이다. 우리에게는 국내에서 가장 높은 범죄율을 가진 도시 중의 하나가 있다.

(11) I will explain Muller's situation. By the way, this visit of Muller's is strictly secret.

> 어휘리콜 　•Muller's: Muller 댁.
> 마디관계 　앞 문장에 대해 뒤 문장은 전이관계.
> 전문국역 　내가 Muller의 상황을 설명해주겠다. 그런데 이 Muller 댁 방문은 비밀이다.

(12) In the mid 1990, it was estimated that 9 million Americans were planning a summer

vacation alone. Since then, the number of solo travelers has increased.

> 어휘리콜 • estimate: 평가하다.
> 마디관계 선행문 속의 핵절인 that절의 의미에 대해 후행문의 의미가 전후 시간관계(의미관계: 그 후).
> 전문국역 1990년 중반, 900만 미국인이 혼자 여름휴가를 계획하고 있었던 것으로 평가되었다. 그 이후 혼자 여행자의 수가 증가했다.

(13) When the bomb exploded, everyone tried to get as far away as possible.

> 어휘리콜 • explode: 터지다.
> 마디관계 앞 절에 대하여 뒤 절은 시간관계(동시시간).
> 전문국역 폭탄이 터졌을 때 모든 사람들은 가능한 한 멀리 도망치려고 시도했다.

(14) Most of charismatic individuals are very persuasive. They can influence others easily.

> 어휘리콜 • charismatic: 카리스마적인, 지도력이 있는.
> 마디관계 선행문의 의미에 대해 후행문의 의미가 인과관계(의미관계: ~이므로~/~인 이 유는~).
> 전문국역 대부분의 카리스마적인 개개인들은 대단히 설득력이 있다. 그들은 다른 사람들에게 쉽게 영향을 미친다.

(15) There must be some discipline in the home. For example, I do not allow my daughter Zoe to play with my computer.

> 어휘리콜 • discipline: 규율.
> 마디관계 앞 문장에 대하여 뒤 문장은 주장예증관계.
> 전문국역 가정에는 어떤 규율이 있다. 예를 들면, 나는 내 딸 Zoe가 내 컴퓨터를 갖고 노는 것을 허락하지 않는다.

(16) She likes the country. Particularly she likes the east coast.

> 마디관계 앞 문장에 대해 뒤 문장은 일반구체관계.
> 전문국역 그녀는 그 나라를 좋아한다. 특히 그녀는 동해안을 좋아한다.

(17) The school closes earlier so that children can get home before dark.

> 마디관계 so 앞 절에 대하여 뒤 절은 목적수단관계.
> 전문국역 어린이들이 어둡기 전에 집에 도착할 수 있도록 학교는 보다 일찍 마친다.

(18) I will have read this book four times if I read it once again.

> 마디관계 선행절의 의미에 대해 후행절의 의미가 조건관계(의미관계: 만약 ~면).
> 전문국역 만약 내가 이 책을 다시 읽는다면, 나는 네 번 읽게 될 것이다.

(19) 'Is there anyone here?' I asked. There was no answer.

> 마디관계 앞 문장과 뒤 문장은 문제해결관계.
> 전문국역 '여기에 누구 있습니까?'라고 내가 물었다. 대답이 없었다.

(20) He broke his promise, and he did not say the reason. In short, we cannot trust him.

> 어휘리콜 •break one's promise: 약속을 어기다.
> 마디관계 In short 앞 문장과 뒤 문장은 요약관계.
> 전문국역 그는 자기 약속을 깨뜨렸고, 그 이유도 말하지 않았다. 요컨대, 우리는 그를 믿지 못한다.

(21) 1)For the Greeks, beauty was a virtue: a kind of excellence. 2)If it occurred to the Greeks to distinguish between a person's "inside" and "outside," they still expected that inner beauty would be matched by beauty of the other kind. 3)The well-born young Athenians who gathered around Socrates found it quite paradoxical that their hero was so intelligent, so honorable, so seductive-and so ugly.

> 어휘리콜 • match: 필적하다; • well-born: 좋은 가문 태생의; • paradoxical: 역설적인; •6)에서 it는 가목적어, that절이 진목적어; • seductive: 유혹하는.
>
> 마디관계 1)은 첫 단문, 문2)는 (즉 핵절인 that절은) 문1)에 대해 일반구체관계, 문3)은 (즉 핵절인 that절은) 문2)에 대해 대조의 관계.
>
> 전문국역 그리스인들에게 아름다움은 하나의 미덕이었다. 일종의 우월성이다. 그리스인들은 사람들의 "내면"과 "외면"을 구별하게 되는 경우에, 내면의 아름다움은 외면의 아름다움과 일치할 것이라 믿었다. 소크라테스 주위에 몰려들었던 좋은 가문의 아테네 젊은이들은 그들의 영웅이 너무나 지적이고 용감하고 명예롭고 또 매혹적이지만, 못생겼다는 것을 모순적이라고 생각했다.

(22) 1)We should behave towards our country 2)as women behave towards the men they love. 3)A loving wife will do anything for her husband except to stop criticizing and trying to improve him. 4)That is the right attitude for a citizen. 5)We should cast the same affectionate but sharp glance at our country. 6)We should love it, but also insist upon telling it all its faults. 7)The dangerous man is not the critic, but the noisy empty leader who encourages us to indulge in orgies of self-congratulation.

> 어휘리콜 • criticize: 비평하다, 욕하다; • sharp glance: 예리한(날카로운) 시선; • indulge in: 빠져들게 하다.
>
> 마디관계 1)은 첫 절, 2)는 1)에 대해 사례관계, 3)은 1)에 대해 예증관계, 4)는 (3)에 대해 부가관계, 5)는 4)에 대해 결과관계, 6)은 5)에 대해 열거관계, 7)은 6)에 대해 인과관계.
>
> 전문국역 우리는 여성들이 자기가 사랑하는 남편들을 위해 하는 것처럼 우리는 국가에 대해 그렇게 해야 한다. 여성들은 자기 남편에게 비판을 그치지 않고 자기 남편들을 개선시키려고 노력을 중단하지 않는 것을 제외하고는 무엇이든지 남편을 위해 하려고 한다. 그것은 한 시민으로서 올바른 태도다. 우리는 그와 같은 애정 어린 그러나 날카로운 시선으로 국가를 보아야 한다. 국가를 사랑하지만 국가의 잘못을 늘 지적해 주어야 한다. 위험스러운 사람은 비판가가 아니고 우리에게 자축의 파티에 탐닉하도록 권하는 시끄럽고 텅 빈 지도자이다.

(23) 1)Neanderthals lived in Europe and parts of Asia and thε Middle East between around 200,000 to 30,000 years ago. 2)For years, we didn't know much about them. 3)That changed 4)when the first virtually complete set of Neanderthal remains was discovered in 1856 in a limestone quarry in the Neander Valley near

Dusseldorf, Germany. 5)That's 6)where the name "Neanderthal" comes from. 7)And if you're wondering, 8)that is the German word for "valley."

> 어휘리콜 •remains: 유적; •limestone quarry: 석회암 채석장.
> 마디관계 1)은 선행절이 없는 첫 문장, 1)에 대해 2)는 부가관계, 2)에 대해 3)은 대조관계, 3)에 대해 4)는 시간관계, 5)는 4)의 일부에 대해 정의관계, 5)에 대해 6)은 명사성분관계, 7)은 6)에 대해 조건관계, 8)은 7에 대해 문제해결관계.
> 전문국역 네안데르탈인들은 약 20만 년 전과 3만 년 전 사이에 유럽, 아시아와 중동의 여러 지역에서 살았다. 오래 동안 우리는 네안데르탈인에 관해서 많이는 몰랐다. 실질적인 완벽한 최초의 네안데르탈 유적이 독일 뒤셀도르프 가까이 Neander Valley에서 1856년 발견되었을 때 상황이 변했다. 그곳이 "네안데르탈"이란 이름이 나온 곳이다. 그리고 만약 여러분이 궁금하다면, 그것은 "계곡"에 해당하는 독일어 단어(Neanderthal 뒤에 붙어 있는 thal "계곡")이다.

(24) 1)Neanderthals had stronger skeletons and larger bones than modern humans. 2)On average, their hands and arms were much stronger than those of modern humans. 3)They also had quite powerful legs. 4)As for their height, male Neanderthals stood 165 centimeters tall on average 5)while the females averaged about, um, about ten centimeters less in height than the males. 6)Neanderthals' heads were also shaped differently from those of modern humans.

> 어휘리콜 •skeleton: 골격; •on average: 평균하여.
> 마디관계 1)에 대해 2)는 부가관계, 2)에 대해 3)은 부과관계, 3)에 대해 4)는 부과관계, 4)에 대해 5)는 대조관계, 5)에 대해 6)은 부과관계.
> 전문국역 네안데르탈인은 현대 인간보다도 더 강한 골격과 더 큰 뼈를 지니고 있었다. 평균하여, 그들의 손과 팔은 현대 인간의 그것들보다 더 튼튼했다. 그들은 또한 아주 강한 다리를 가지고 있었다. 키의 경우, 남성 네안데르탈인은 평균하여 165센티미터이고 여성은 남성보다 평균 10센티미터 작았다. 네안데르탈의 머리는 또한 현대인들의 머리와 매우 다른 모양이었다.

(25) 1)Anthropologists are unsure of 2)whether or not Neanderthals could talk 3)and, if they could, 4)if they had language. 5)Their brains were big enough to suggest intelligence, 6)so the possibility exists 7)that they produced both speech and language. 8)Also, in some Neanderthal remains, a hyoid bone has been found.

9)That's the bone in our throats that's attached to the larynx 10)and that we use mainly to make speech.

> 어휘리콜 •hyoid: 설골의; •larynx: 인두.
>
> 마디관계 1)에 대해 2)는 명사성분관계, 3)은 4)에 대해 조건관계, 4)는 1)에 대해 명사성분관계, 5)는 1)에 대해 대조관계, 6)은 5)에 대한 결과관계, 7)은 6)에 대한 명사한정관계, 8)은 6)에 대해 부가관계, 9)는 8)에 대한 일반구체관계, 10)은 8)에 대한 부가관계이다.
>
> 전문국역 인류학자들은 네안데르탈인들이 말을 할 줄 알았는지 여부를 확신하지 못하며, 그들이 말을 할 수 있었더라도, 그들이 언어를 가지고 있었는지를 확신하지 못하고 있다. 그들의 뇌는 지능을 시사하기에 충분히 큰 뇌이었기에, 그들이 말과 언어를 생산했을 개연성은 있다. 또한 네안데르탈인의 어떤 유적지에서는, 설골의 뼈가 발견되었다. 그것은 목구멍 안에서 인두에 연결되어 있는 뼈이며, 주로 말을 생산하는데 사용되는 뼈이다.

(26) 1)Thank you for inviting me to speak to you today. 2)I'd like to take this opportunity to tell you about our Silver Service activities 3)and why we believe 4)it is important for everyone to be involved in helping the elderly in our community. 5)Did you know 6)that one in every six people over the age of 60 in this community needs some kind of help in his or her home? 7)Those of us 8)who have experience in this kind of work know 9)that our small "investments" in time and effort are nothing compared to the kind of satisfaction and fulfillment 10)we get in turn.

> 어휘리콜 •satisfaction and fulfillment: 만족과 성취.
>
> 마디관계 1)은 선행문이 없는 첫 문, 1)에 대해 2)는 일반구체관계, 5)는 2)에 대해 이유관계(주제도입), 6)은 5)에 대해 명사성분관계, 7)은 5)에 대해 문제해결의 관계.
>
> 전문국역 여러분들에게 말씀드릴 수 있도록 초대해 주셔서 감사합니다. 나는 이 기회에 여러분들에게 "실버 서비스" 활동에 관해 말씀드리고, 왜 우리 각자가 우리 사회에 있는 노인들을 돕는 일에 같이 참여하는 일이 중요하다고 믿는가에 대해 말씀 드리고 싶습니다. 이 사회에 60세 이상 되는 사람 여섯 명 가운데 한 사람이 자기 집에서 어떤 도움이 필요하다는 것을 알고 계셨는지요? 우리들 중에 이와 같은 종류의 일을 경험해본 사람은 적절한 시간의 작은 "투자"와 노력은 우리가 그 대가로 얻는 만족과 성취와 비교되는 것은 아무것도 없다는 것을 알고 있습니다.

(27) 1)Fortunately, psychologists believe 2)that books can serve as therapeutic tools ㅡ or at least as effective adjuncts to professional therapy ㅡ to help children come to terms with their parents' divorce. 3)According to educator-counselor Joanne Bernstein, stories 4)that confront life's problems with candor and credibility may provide insights, promote self-examination, and lead to changes in attitude and behavior. 5)One way 6)stories accomplish this is through identification. 7)Reading about the grief and anxiety of others, 8)she explains, can arouse sudden awareness as problems 9)that have not been consciously or completely recognized are allowed to surface. 10)Introduced to characters 11)who share their difficulties, children may feel less alienated and thus freer to discuss and resolve their own plight.

> **어휘리콜** •therapeutic(치료의); •candor(공정, 정직); •alienate(멀리하다); •plight(궁지, 곤경).
> **마디관계** 절마디 절 2)는 절 1)에 대해 명사성분, 절 3)은 선행문에 대해 일반구체, 절 4)는 선행절 절 3)에 대해 명사한정, 문 5)-6)는 선행문에 대해 주장예증, 절 6)은 절 5)에 대해 명사한정, 문 7)은 선행문에 대해 일반구체, 절 8)은 명사한정(삽입절), 절 9)는 절 7)에 대해 명사한정, 문 10)은 선행문에 대해 11)에 대해 조건관계, 절 11)은 절 10)에 대해 명사한정.
> **전문국역** 다행스럽게도, 책은 어린이들이 그들의 부모가 이혼하는 데 이를 감수하게끔 도와주기 위해 전문적인 치료도구이거나 또는 적어도 전문적 치료에 효과가 있는 부가물이라고 심리학자들은 믿는다. 교육자이자 카운슬러 Joanne Bernstein에 따르면, 공정과 신뢰성 관련 생활문제에 맞서는 이야기는 통찰력을 제공하고, 자기 성찰을 향상시키고, 태도와 행동의 변화를 초래한다. 이야기가 이것을 성취하는 한 가지 방법은 정체성 확인을 통해서다. 타인의 슬픔과 분노에 관한 글을 읽으면서, 의식적으로 혹은 완전하게는 인식되지 않았던 문제들이 표면으로 올라오게 함으로서, 그녀는 갑작스런 앎을 불러일으킬 수 있다. 어려움에 봉착해 있는 인물들에게 소개되어 지면, 아이들은 격리됨을 덜 느낄지도 모르고, 그래서 자기 자신의 곤경을 보다 더 자유로이 논의하고 해결할 수 있을지도 모른다.

(28) 1)First of all, nowadays, since many academic sciences are connected to each other ‐ and such was not so much the case in the past ‐ the ability to accept and learn something in other fields is necessary to achieving progress in academic fields. 2)I understand that the ability to accept and learn something in other fields is not the only factor that affects the development of science, but it is one of the more significant ones. 3)As science develops and becomes more specialized, many researchers need to work together to advance technologies, and to work together

more efficiently, they need to acquire knowledge in other fields and apply it to their own fields. 4)As a result, mixed sciences such as biochemistry, biomechanics, and neuroscience have emerged. 5)For all these reasons, I think the ability to cooperate is essential today.

> 어휘리콜　•specialized: 전문화 되는; •technology: 과학기술; •biochemistry: 생화학; • biomechanics: 생명공학; •neuroscience: 신경과학.
>
> 마디관계　문1)에 대하여 문2)는 부과관계, 문3)은 인과관계, 문4)는 인과관계, 문5)는 결과관계.
>
> 전문국역　첫째로, 오늘날, 많은 학문 분야는 서로 관련되어 있기 때문에- 그리고 과거에는 그러하지 않았는데- 다른 학문 분야에서 이해하고 배우는 능력은 학문 분야에서 진전을 성취하는 데에 필요하다. 다른 분야에서 이해하고 배우는 능력은 학문의 발전에 영향을 미치는 유일한 요소는 아니지만 보다 더 중요한 요소들 중의 하나라고 나는 이해한다. 학문이 발전하고 더욱 전문화됨에 따라서, 많은 연구자들은 함께 연구하여 기술을 전진시키고, 그리고 연구를 더욱 효율적으로 할 필요가 있으며, 다른 분야에서 지식을 습득하여 그것을 자신의 분야에 적용시킬 필요가 있다. 그 결과, 생화학, 생명공학, 신경과학과 같은 융합분야가 나타났다. 이런 이유들로 해서, 나는 협력하는 능력이 오늘날 필수적이라고 생각한다.

(29) 1)A recent report on the country's immigration policy should draw attention from the public as well as government policymakers as a catalyst for their far-sighted views on how to secure long-term sustainable growth and social vitality. 2)The report, submitted by the Migration Research and Training Center to the Justice Ministry, proposed increasing the number of foreign nationals here, which stood at 1.44 million last year, to 3 million by 2030. 3)If not, the paper predicted, the nation would begin to suffer from a severe workforce shortage, which would further decelerate its economic growth. 4)There have been a series of warnings of a possible demographic disaster.

> 어휘리콜　•신문사설의 일부임; •government policymakers: 정책입안자들; •catalyst: 촉매, 기폭제; •far-sighted: 선견지명이 있는; •sustainable: 지속가능한; •vitality: 활력; •demographic disaster: 인구재앙.
>
> 마디관계　문1)에 대해 문2)는 부가관계, 문 2)에 대해 문3)은 조건결과관계, 문 3)에 대해 문 4)는 요약관계.
>
> 전문국역　우리나라 이민정책에 관한 최근 보고서는 장기적 지속 가능한 성장과 사회적 활력을

확보하는 방안에 관한 선견지명이 있는 견해의 기폭제로서 정부 정책 관리들은 물론 국민들로부터 관심을 끌고 있다. 이민정책연구원이 법무부에 제출한 이 보고서는 지난해 144만 명이었던 국내 외국인 수를 2030년까지 3백만 명으로 늘릴 것을 제안했다. 그렇지 않으면 우리나라는 경제성장을 더욱 둔화시킬 심각한 인력부족을 겪기 시작할 것으로 이 보고서는 전망했다. 인구 재앙 가능성에 대해 잇따른 경고가 나오고 있다.

(30) 1)The expected shrinkage of the workforce has been cited as a main factor in many predictions that the nation's potential growth rate will continue to decline from the current level of 3.4 percent in the coming decades. 2)What is the most alarming to Koreans is last year's forecast by the Organization for Economic Cooperation and Development 5)that the birth rate for the country will fall to 1 percent by 2031, the lowest among the 34 OECD member states except for Luxemburg.

어휘리콜　•shrinkage: 부족; •workforce: 인력; •potential growth: 잠재성장; 신문사설의 일부임.
마디관계　문 1)에 대하여 문 2)는 부가관계.
전문국역　예상되는 인력부족 현상이 우리나라의 잠재적 성장률이 현 3.4% 수준에서 앞으로 수십 년 동안 계속 감소할 것이라는 여러 예측들 중에서 한 주요 요인으로 지적되어 왔다. 한국인들에게 자장 충격적인 것은 우리나라 출산율이 룩셈부르크를 제외한 34개 OECD 회원국 중 최저수준인 1%까지 하락할 것이라는 지난해 경제협력개발기구(OECD)의 전망이다.

(31) 1)In June last year, Korea became the world's seventh country with a population of more than 50 million to have its per capita income exceed $20,000. 2)A growing number of expatriates here have contributed to the nation achieving these landmark figures. 3)Without their continued role, it would be difficult for the country to maintain this status in future.

어휘리콜　신문사설의 일부임; •per capita: 1인당; •expatriate: 국적을 이탈하다, 이주인; • landmark figure: 기념비적인 수치.
마디관계　문1)에 대해 문2)는 결과원인, 문2)에 대해 3)은 조건결과의 관계.
전문국역　지난해 6월 한국은 1인당 국민소득 2만 불로서 인구 5,000만 명 이상을 가진 세계 7위 경제대국이 됐다. 갈수록 늘어나는 한국 거주 이주민 수는 우리나라가 이처럼 기념적인 수치를 달성하는데 기여해왔다. 이들의 지속적인 역할 없이는 우리나라가 미래에 이러한 지위를 유지하기는 어려울 것이다.

제2절 단락의 내용흐름 파악

 단락본문의 독해에서 문마디 관계의 이해와 동시 혹은 직후 내용흐름을 이해해 가야 한다. 이 내용흐름 이해작업은 정보핵절(가령: 복문인 경우 메시지절)의 주제어휘와 초점어휘의 연속을 확인하는 것이다. 이 작업의 한 테크닉은 각 정보핵절에서 먼저 초점어휘를 확인하고 다음에 이 초점어휘의 주체를 유도하는 것이다. 그 전형적인 결과는 정보핵절의 주제어휘들은 한 주제어휘로 일반화 된 것이고 초점어휘들은 병렬 된 것이다.

(1) 1)Job-related <u>stress</u> can lead to symptoms of **poor physical health** such as weight gain, fatigue and illness. 2)Both <u>diet and exercise</u> can contribute to the **alleviation** of these negative effects of stress. 3)The <u>first step</u> is **to eliminate junk food** from the diet. Instead of soda or a candy bar, **try a piece of fresh fruit**. 4)The <u>next step</u> is to make a **habit of exercising** every day. 5)And <u>you</u> should aim for **twenty to thirty minutes** of exercise a day. 6)The <u>key</u> is **to find a form of exercise** that you enjoy. 7)That way, <u>you</u> are more likely to **do it every day** and will receive **the maximum benefit**. 8)Both <u>diet and exercise</u> keep you feeling **energized, and protect** you from sickness. 9)Then <u>you</u> will be **better equipped** to deal with the sources of stress at your job.

    주제어휘　　　　　　　　초점어휘
    1) <u>stress</u>　　　　　　　　- **poor physical health**
    2) <u>diet and exercise</u>　　　- **alleviation**
    3) <u>first step</u>　　　　　　- **to eliminate junk food/Try fresh fruit**
    4) <u>next step</u>　　　　　　- **habit of exercising**
    5) <u>you</u>(=exercising)　　　- **twenty to thirty minutes**
    6) <u>key</u>(=exercising)　　　- **to find a form of exercise**
    7) <u>you</u>(diet and exercise) - **do it every day/the maximum benefit**
    8) <u>diet and exercise</u>　　　- **energized, and protect**
    9) <u>you</u>(=diet and exercise) - **better equipped** (=**better**)

어휘리콜　•poor physical health: 안 좋은 육체적 건강; •alleviation: 경감.

내용흐름　문1을 제외하고 대부분의 문이 diet and exercise에 관한 내용이기 때문에 문1은 그 머리말이고, 이 단락의 일반화 주제는 diet and exercise이다. 초점어휘의 흐름은 '스트레스 경감 절차는 정크푸드를 줄이고 신선한 과일 섭취하고, 운동 습관화하고, 운동은 20-30분하고, 적당한 운동 발견으로 최대 효과, 에너지 충전과 질병 방어'이다.

전문국역　일과 관련된 스트레스는 체중 증가, 피로 그리고 질병과 같은 좋지 않은 신체적 건강의 증상으로 이어질 수 있습니다. 식이요법과 운동 두 가지는 이와 같은 스트레스에 의한 부정적 영향을 경감시켜 주는데 기여 할 수 있습니다. 첫 번째 단계는 당신의 음식에서 정크푸드를 제거하는 것입니다. 소다수나 캔디바 대신에 신선한 과일 한 조각을 드세요. 다음 단계는 매일 운동을 하는 습관을 들이고, 하루에 20분에서 30분 정도를 목표로 하세요. 중요한 점은 당신이 좋아하는 운동을 찾으세요. 그렇게 하면 당신은 매일 그 운동을 할 가능성이 더욱 높고 또 최대의 혜택을 얻게 됩니다. 식이요법과 운동 이 두 가지는 당신이 건강한 체중을 유지하고, 계속 활력을 느끼게 해주며 또 질병으로부터 당신을 보호해 줄 수 있습니다. 그러면 당신은 일에서 스트레스를 더 잘 처리할 수 있습니다.

(2) 1)More and more **people** are turning away from their doctors and, indeed, going **to individuals** who have **no medical training** and who sell **unproven treatments**. 2)**They** go to quacks to get everything **from treatments for colds to cures for cancer**. 3)And **they** are putting themselves in **dangerous situations**. 4)Many people don't realize how **unsafe** it is **to use unproven treatments**. 5)First of all, the treatments usually **don't work**. 6)They may be harmless, but if someone uses these products instead of proven treatments, he or she may be **harmed**. 7)**Why**? 8)Because during the time the person is using the product, his or her illness may be **getting worse**. 9)**This** can even cause **the person to die**.

　　　　　주제어휘　　　　　　　　초점어휘

1) people　　　　　　　　　- **to no medical training individuals/unproven Treatments**

2) They(=people)　　　　　 - **from treatments for colds to cures for cancer**.

3) they(=people)　　　　　 - **dangerous situations**.

4) to use unproven treatments　- **unsafe**.

5) the treatments　　　　　- **don't work**.

6) he or she　　　　　　　- **harmed**.

7) Why?	- 불필요
8) illness	- **getting worse**.
9) This	- **the person to die**. 혹은
the person	- **to die**

> 어휘리콜 •quack: 돌팔이 의사.
>
> 내용흐름 모든 문장의 주제어휘는 사람(people)이다. 초점어휘의 흐름은 '(사람들이) 돌팔이의사에게 가서, 치료를 받고, 위험상황에 처하고, 안전하지 못하고, 효과 없고, 악화되어, 죽는다'이다.
>
> 전문국역 점점 더 많은 사람들이 의사들로부터 멀어져 가고 있다. 대신에 의학교육을 받지 않고 입증되지 않은 치료를 팔고 있는 사람들에게 가고 있다. 그들은 돌팔이 의사들에게 가서 감기에서 암에 이르기까지 모든 것을 얻는다. 그들은 자신들을 위험스러운 상태에 빠뜨리고 있다. 많은 사람들은 입증되지 않은 치료를 이용한다는 것이 얼마나 위험스러운가를 인식을 못하고 있다. 무엇보다(첫째로) 그와 같은 치료는 일반적으로 효과가 없다. 해가 없을지도 모른다. 그러나 만약 어떤 사람이 입증된 치료 대신에 그런 상품을 이용하면 피해를 입을 수도 있다. 왜냐하면 그것은 그 사람이 그런 상품을 이용하고 있는 동안에 그의 병은 더 악화가 되고 있을지도 모르기 때문이다. 이것은 심지어 그 사람을 죽게 만들 수도 있다.

(3) 1)Even now, <u>ancient India</u> is still **visible and accessible** to us in a very direct sense. 2)At the beginning of the twentieth century, some <u>Indian communities</u> still lived as all our primeval ancestors must once have lived, by **hunting and gathering**. 3)The <u>bullock- cart and the potter's wheel</u> of many villages today are much the **same as those used 4,000 years** ago. 4)A <u>caste-system</u> whose main lines were set by about 1,000 B.C. still **regulates the lives of millions**, and even of some <u>Indian Christians and Moslems Gods and goddesses</u> whose cults can be traced to the Stone Age are still **worshipped at village shrines**.

> 어휘리콜 •primeval: 원시의; •bullock-cart: 마차; •potter's wheel: 도공의 물레바퀴; •caste-system: 카스트제도; •main lines: 주요 혈통; •regulate: 지배하다; •cult: 예배, 숭배; •village shrine: 마을사당.
>
> 내용흐름[1]) 고대인도(주제어휘)는 시각적이고 접근가능하고, 사냥과 채집하는 커뮤니티 있고, 고대와 동일한 마차와 물레바퀴가 있고, 카스트제도, 마을사당 신앙숭배 등이 있다.
>
> 전문국역 오늘날에도, 고대의 인도가 매우 직접적인 의미에서 시각적이고도 접근가능하다. 우

---

1) 여기서부터는 도표를 생략함.

리 인류의 원시 조상들이 살았을 것으로 추정되는 대로, 사냥과 채집으로, 20세기 초에 몇몇 인도 지역사회들이 계속 존재했다. 오늘날 여러 마을에 있는 수소가 끄는 마차와 도공의 물레 바퀴는 4,000년 전에 사용된 것들과 꼭 같다. 주요 혈통이 약 1,000년 전에 형성된 카스트 제도가 아직도 수백만 명의 생활을 지배하고, 심지어 인디언 기독교인들과 모슬렘의 생활을 통제하고 있다. 석기시대로 추적될 수 있는 숭배 대상의 신과 여신들이 마을 사당에서 아직도 숭배되고 있다.

(4) 1)**One of the most famous houses** in the United States is **Monticello**. 2)It was the **home of Thomas Jefferson**, the third President of the United States. 3)Located on a hill near Charlottesville, Virginia, it has a **beautiful view** of the surrounding country side. 4)The house is famous, first of all, because it **belonged to a president**. 5)It is also a fine example of **early 19th century American architecture**. 6)Jefferson **designed it himself** in a style he had admired in Italy. 7)Many American buildings of that time, in fact, **imitated European styles**. 8)But while most were just imitations, his Monticello is **lovely in itself**. 9)Furthermore, the design combines a **graceful style** with a **typical American concern** for comfort and function.

어휘리콜 •architecture: 건축; •imitate: 모방하다.

내용흐름 몬티셀로(주제)는 에스퍼선의 집, 아름다운 경치, 대통령 소유, 19세기 초 미국 건축, 대통령에 의해 직접디자인 됨, 비 모방, 질적으로 멋짐, 우아한 스타일과 전형적 미국인의 관심의 결합(이상 초점들)이다.

전문국역 미국에서 가장 유명한 집들 중의 하나가 Monticello이다. 그것은 미국의 3대 대통령, Thomas Jefferson의 집이였다. Virginia주 Charlottesville 가까이 있는 언덕에 위치한 이 집은 주위 시골 쪽으로 아름다운 전경을 갖고 있다. 첫째로, 이 집은 유명한데, 이유는 대통령에 속하기 때문이다. 이 집은 또한 19세기 초 미국 구조물의 좋은 예이기 때문이다. Jefferson이 이태리에서 감탄했던 스타일로 이 집을 직접 설계했다. 당시에 많은 미국 빌딩들은, 사실, 유럽 스타일을 모방했었다. 그러나 대부분이 모방건물이지만, 그의 Monticello는 본질적으로 아름답다. 더 나아가서, 그 디자인이 편안함과 기능을 위해서 우아한 스타일을 전형적인 미국 관심사를 결합시키고 있다.

(5) Man is always left with a **crisis in decision**. The main test before him involves his **will to change** rather than his ability to change. That he is capable of change is **certain**. For there is no more **mutable or adaptable** animal in the world. We have

seen him **migrate** from one extreme clime to another. We have seen him step **out of backward societies and join advanced groups** within the space of a single generation. This is not to imply that the changes were necessarily always for the better; only that change was and is **possible**. But change requires **stimulus**; and mankind today needs to look no further for stimulus than its **own desire to stay alive**. The critical power of change, says Spengler, is directly linked to the **survival drive**. Once the instinct for survival is stimulated, the basic condition for change can **be met**.

> 어휘리콜 •crisis: 위기, 갈림길; •mutable: 변하기 쉬운; •migrate: 이주하다, 이동하다; •clime: 나라, 지방, 풍토; •survival drive: 생존의 충동.
>
> 내용흐름[2] 주제는 인간(의 변화)이고, 밑줄과 진한 글자체가 동시에 표시된 부분들의 연속이 내용흐름이다.[3]
>
> 전문국역 인간은 언제나 결정의 갈림길에 처한다. 자기 앞에 놓인 주요 시험은 변화의 능력 보다는 변화의 의지이다. 자기가 변할 수 있음은 확실하다. 세계에서 마음이 잘 변하는 혹은 적응을 잘 하는 동물은 더 이상 없기 때문이다. 우리는 인간이 한 극단적인 지역으로부터 다른 지역으로 이주하는 것을 보아왔다. 우리는 인간이 한 세대 안에서도 기존 사회로부터 빠져나와 선진 그룹으로 들어가는 것을 보았다. 이 말은 변화가 반드시 항상 더 좋다는 뜻은 아니며, 단지 변화가 있으며 변화가 가능하다는 것을 함축한다. 그러나 변화는 자극을 요구한다. 그리고 오늘날 인간은 생존해 있을 욕망 외 더 이상은 자극을 찾을 필요가 없다. Spengler 는 중요한 변화의 힘은 생존의 충동에 직결되어 있다고 한다. 생존을 위한 본능이 자극적이면, 변화의 기본 조건은 충족될 수 있다.

(6) Should we be concerned that the Copenhagen Climate Change Conference is not going to produce a **concrete plan** to reduce greenhouse-gas emissions? Lots of people clearly are. Indeed, while activists prepare to unfurl protect banners, politicians are scrambling for a **face-saving way** to declare. The summit may be a **blessing in disguise**, because when it comes to dealing with climate change, the last thing we need right now is yet another empty agreement and yet more moral posturing.

---

2) (5)번부터 (9)번까지는 학습자가 국문으로 내용을 연결해 볼 수 있다.
3) 여기서부터는 '한 화제(주제)에 대하여 관련 내용(초점들)을 머리에 바로 입력'하는 습관화가 필요함.

> **어휘리콜** •greenhouse-gas emission: 온실가스방출; •unfurl: 펴다, 올리다; •banner: 기; •scramble: 빼앗다, 얻으려고 다투다; •face-saving: 체면/면목을 세우는; •blessing in disguise: 외견상 불행해 보이는 행복.
>
> **내용흐름** 주제어휘는 Copenhagen Climate Change Conference(코펜하겐 기후 변화회의), 초점 어휘는 concrete plan, face-saving way, blessing in disguise이다.
>
> **전문국역** 우리가 이 코펜하겐 기후변화 회의에서 온실가스 방출을 줄이기 위한 구체적 계획을 내 놓으려고 하지 않는 일에 관여해야 합니까? 많은 사람들이 관여하고 있습니다. 진실로, 한편으로 활동가들이 항의 깃발을 들어 올릴 준비를 하고 있는 중에, 정치가들은 면목을 세우는 방법을 찾아내서 정상회의가 성공임을 선언하려고 애쓰고 있습니다. 정상회의가 가면을 쓴 축복일 수도 있는데, 이유는 정상회의가 기후변화를 다루면서, 우리가 지금 바로 할 필요가 있는 마지막 일은 또 하나의 내용 없는 합의이면서 더 도덕적인 자세이기 때문입니다.

(7) <u>Earth</u> may be unique in the universe for its **abundance of water,** amounting to 70 percent of its surface. But <u>the image</u> recalls the **old sailor's lament**. Water, water everywhere, but **not a drop to drink**. For the vast majority of <u>it</u> is **salty and unfit** for consumption. It is really remarkable that on the blue planet, on a planet as abundant with water as the one on which we find ourselves, **only three percent** of the water resources on the planet are <u>fresh water</u>.

> **어휘리콜** •amount to: ~에 달하다; •lament: 탄식, 넋두리; •consumption: 소비.
>
> **내용흐름** 각 문에서의 초점어휘는 진한 글자체이고, 이들의 연결이 내용흐름이고 주제는 지구 (의 물)이다.
>
> **전문국역** 지구는 우주에서 유일하게 물이 풍부한 존재인지도 모른다. 표면의 70%가 물이다. 그러나 이 모습은 옛날 선원의 넋두리를 연상시킨다. "물, 물, 모든 곳이 물이지만, 마실 물은 한 방울도 없다." 이 물의 대부분은 짠물이고 마시기에 적합하지 않다. "우리가 살고 있는 물로 가득한 지구상에서 오직 3%만이 마실 수 있는 물이라는 것은 정말로 주목할 만한 일이다.

(8) The <u>Balkanization</u> of nations is a **worldwide phenomenon** that the US has not escaped. <u>Regions and localities</u> are less and **less willing to incur costs** that will primarily help people in other parts of the same country. <u>Consider</u> the development of the coalfields of **Wyoming and Montana**. There is no question that most of the benefits will accrue to those living in urban areas in the rest of the country while

most of the <u>costs</u> will be imposed on those living in **that region**. As a result, the <u>local population</u> **objects**. More coal mining might be good for the US but <u>it</u> will be **bad for local constituents**. Therefore, <u>they</u> will impose as many **delays and uncertainties** as possible.

> 어휘리콜   •Balkanization: 소국분할(주의/정책); •incur: ~에 부딪히다, 당하다, 빚지다; •coalfield: 탄갱; •Wyoming: 미국 서부의 주 이름; •Montana: 미국 서부의 주 이름; •accrue: 저절로 생기다; •impose: 부과하다, 지우다; •coal mining: 채탄, 탄광업.
>
> 내용흐름   각 문장의 초점어휘의 연속, 즉 내용흐름은 진한글자체의 연속적 개념과 같고 주제는 Balkanization(소국분할)이다.
>
> 전문국역   소국분할주의는 미국이 피하지 않았던 전 세계적 현상이다. 지역들 및 지방들은 동일 국가 내 다른 지역들의 사람들을 돕게 될 비용을 덜 들이려고 한다. 와이오밍 주와 몬타나 주의 발전을 생각해보라. 대부분의 비용이 그 지역 거주 사람들에게 부과되는 한편, 대부분의 이익이 동일 국가 내 도시 지역 거주 사람들에게 돌아간다는 것은 의문의 여지가 없다. 그 결과, 지방 주민들은 반대한다. 채광이 미국 국가에는 좋은 것이지만 지방에는 나쁘다. 그러므로 지방들은 가능한 많은 지연과 불확실성을 강요한다.

(9) Contemporary events differ from history in that <u>we</u> do **not know the results** they will produce. Looking back, <u>we</u> can assess the **significance of past occurrences** and trace the **consequences** they have brought in their train. But while history runs its course, <u>it</u> is **not history** to us. It leads us into an unknown land but <u>rarely can we</u> get a **glimpse of what lies ahead**. It would be different if it were given to <u>us</u> **to live a second time** through the same events with all the knowledge of what we have seen before. How different would things appear to us, how important and often alarming would <u>changes</u> seem that **we now scarcely notice**! It is probably fortunate that <u>man</u> can **never have this experience and knows of no laws which history must obey**.

> 어휘리콜   •train: 연속, 연관.
>
> 내용흐름   주제는 we(우리 인간(의 인지))이고, 내용흐름은 진한 글자체의 연속적 개념이다.
>
> 전문국역   현재의 사건은 역사와 다른데, 현재의 사건들이 초래할 결과를 우리가 모른다는 점에 서다. 과거를 돌아보면, 우리는 과거에 일어난 것의 의미에 접근할 수 있고 연속선상에서 초래한 결과를 추적할 수 있다. 그러나 역사는 그 노정을 따라가지만, 그것이 우리 인간에게

> 는 역사가 아니다. 역사는 우리를 미지의 땅으로 인도하지만 우리는 결코 우리 앞에 놓여있는 것을 힐끗 볼 수 없다. 우리가 과거에 보았던 것에 대한 지식 모두를 가지고서 동일한 사건을 통해 잠시라고 살 수 있도록 역사가 우리에게 주어진다면 상황은 다를 수 있을 것이다. 사물이 우리 앞에 얼마나 다르게 나타나며, 지금 현재 우리가 주목하지 못하는 변화현상들이 얼마나 중요하게 그리고 얼마나 놀랍도록 나타나는가! 인간이 이러한 경험을 결코 할 수 없다는 것이 그리고 역사를 지배하는 법칙에 대해서 우리가 모른다는 것이 아마 다행일 것이다.

제3절 단락의 주제 확인

단락 독해에서 내용의 흐름을 이해한 다음에는 어떻게 해야 하는가? 문장(sentence)이 이야기꺼리(주제, 보통은 한 문장)와 이야기꺼리에 관한 내용(초점)으로 구성되는 것과 같이 단락도 이야기꺼리(주제)와 이야기꺼리에 관한 내용(초점, 보통 문장그룹)으로 구성된다. 따라서 독해가 단락의 끝에 이르는 순간 단락의 주제를 확인해야 한다. 주제를 확인하는 한 방법은 내용흐름(앞 2절의 내용) 확인으로부터 초점어휘들을 일반화시키고 이 일반화 초점어휘의 주체를 유도하면 된다. 결과는 <u>일반화된 주제어휘와 일반화된 초점어휘로 구성된 문장</u>이다. 이 일반화된 주제문장은 다른 문장들을 포괄하는 상위 개념의 문장이 된다(주제유도규칙).

(1) 1)When we're sick, <u>we</u> might be able **to avoid going to doctor's office** simply using something in our office. 2)More and more studies are finding that <u>certain foods and spices</u> can provide **effective relief** from common health problems. 3)In fact, <u>many physicians</u>, concerned about the overuse of antibiotics and the trend toward treatment overkill for even minor medical problems, are **recommending these simple cures**. 4)And <u>patients</u> are more than **willing to give them try**, given today's high medical costs.

어휘리콜 • spice: 양념; • antibiotics: 항생제; • overkill: 과다, 과잉.

주제확인 각 문장을 독해하면서 핵절의 주제어휘와 초점어휘를 확인하면 밑줄만으로 표시된 부분이 주제어휘들이고, 밑줄에 볼드체가 동시에 표시된 부분이 초점어휘들이다. 주제어휘들을 일반화 하면 '모든 사람'을 의미하는 we가 된다.(이상 2절의 내용) 그리고 초점어휘들을 일반화하면 **to avoid going to doctor's office**가 된다. 일반화 주제와 일반화 초점이 동시에 있는 첫 문장이 주제문이 된다. 이 첫 문장은 나머지 문들을 포괄하는 상위 개념의 문이다.

전문국역 우리들이 아플 때 우리들 사무실에 있는 다른 것을 쉽게 사용함으로써 병원에 가는 일을 피할 수 있을지 모른다. 점점 더 많은 연구에서 어떤 식품이나 양념도 일반적인 건강의 문제점을 어느 정도 감해줄 수 있다고 밝히고 있다. 사실 항생제 과용과 소소한 의학적 문제에 대해서도 지나친 치료의 추세에 대해 우려하고 있는 의사들은 이런 쉬운 치료를 추천하고 있다. 환자들은 오늘날 비싼 의료비를 감안해서 더욱 가까이 이런 것을 시험해 보고 싶어 한다.

주제유도규칙에 의하여 전체를 포괄하는 문장을 찾아 가는 독해를 진행하여 단락의 주제부분을 텍스트 위에 바로 표시해 볼 수 있다.

(2) 1)Welcome to Trinidad International Airport, where we will **refuel the aircraft** and **clean the cabin** before continuing on to Bermuda. 2)All passengers must **leave the plane** curing this time. 3)We would like to allow those of you who are connecting to **different flights to get of the aircraft first**, followed by passengers whose final destination is Trinidad, then, everyone else will be welcome to depart the aircraft. 4)Be sure to keep your **boarding pass with you at all time**. 5)Reboarding will begin at **2:05**. 6)You may **leave your carry-on luggage** under your seats or in the overhead compartment. 7)We are scheduled to **take off again at 2:25**, so please **listen for announcements** from the gate while you are in the airport.

어휘리콜 • refuel: 연료 재주입하다; • cabin: 선실; • reboard: 재 탑승하다.

주제확인 선적인 순서를 따라 각 문장을 독해하여 나머지 문장을 포섭하는 절을 유도하면 첫 문장이 주제문이 된다.

전문국역 트리니다드 국제공항에 오신 것을 환영하며 항공기 기체에 다시 주유를 하고 객실을 청소한 이후에 버뮤다로 계속 비행하도록 하겠습니다. 모든 승객 분들께서는 이 시간 동안 반드시 기체에서 내려주시기 바랍니다. 다른 비행기로 갈아타기 위해 비행기에서 내리고자

하는 손님들께서 먼저 내려주시고, 트리니다드가 최종 목적지이신 분들이 그 다음에 내려주시기 바랍니다. 그리고 나머지 분들께서 항공기에서 내려주시면 됩니다. 항상 탑승권을 소지하고 있어 주십시오. 재 탑승은 2시 5분에 시작됩니다. 기내 수화물은 좌석 아래 혹은 머리 위 짐칸에 두고 가셔도 좋습니다. 2시 25분에 출발할 예정이오니 공항에 계실 때 안내 방송을 잘 들어주시기 바랍니다.

(3) One example is Henry Ford. He did not invent the assembly line itself. Instead, he used his creativity to apply it to make cars on it. That made his company incredibly profitable. Another example is that there are many artists and other individuals who lack "good learning". Instead, they have huge amounts of creativity. These people range from Pablo Picasso to Steven Spielberg, but they all have two things in common: they were highly creative and highly successful. <u>As these cases illustrate, those with creativity can outperform those only with knowledge.</u>

어휘리콜 •invent the assembly line itself: 조립라인 자체를 발명하다; •range from A to B: A에서 B에 이르다; •outperform~: ~을 보다 잘하다.

주제확인 문장을 따라 독해하여 다른 문들의 내용을 포섭하는 문을 유도하면 끝 문장이 된다.

전문국역 한 사례가 Henry Ford이다. 그는 조립라인 자체를 발명하지 않았다. 대신, 그는 창조성을 발휘하여 조립라인 상에서 차동차를 만들기 위하여 그것을 적용했다. 그것이 그의 회사로 하여금 믿을 수 없을 정도로 이익이 나게 했다. 또 한 사례는 많은 학식은 부족한 많은 예술가들 등이 있다는 사실이다. 대신에 그들은 많은 창조성을 갖고 있다. 이들 사람들은 Pablo Picasso에서 Steven Spielberg에 이른다. 그러나 이들은 모두 두 가지를 공유하고 있다. 그들은 매우 창조적이고 매우 성공적이다. 이런 것들이 예증해준 것처럼, 창조성을 지닌 사람들은 지식만을 가진 사람들을 수행력에서 앞선다.

(4) <u>The modern shopping mall is a result of the evolution of concepts and ideas developed throughout almost a century.</u> First, simple suburban shopping strips were built in the 1920s, 1930s, and 1940s. They offered convenience to drivers who could easily park their cars while doing quite successful. The shopping strips eventually evolved into the shopping center.

어휘리콜 •shopping strip: 쇼핑가(strip: 가늘고 긴 것).

주제확인 문장을 따라 독해하여 다른 문장의 내용을 포섭하는 문장을 유도하면 첫 문장이 된다.

전문국역 현대 쇼핑몰은 약 1세기 동안에 개발된 개념과 이상이 진화된 결과이다. 첫째로 간단한 시외 쇼핑가는 1920년대와 1930년대, 그리고 1940년대에 지어진 것이다. 그들은 운전자들에게 한 자리에서 쇼핑을 하는 동안에 주차를 쉽게 할 수 있는 편의를 제공한다. 그 쇼핑가는 대단히 성공작이었다. 그 쇼핑가는 최종적으로 쇼핑센터로 진화되었다.

(5) <u>Law and justice are two entirely different concepts</u> that various governments unintentionally confuse in their efforts to persuade their people that their laws are 'justice.' The position is made worse because lawyers worldwide claim that they administer not only the law but also justice. Consequently many people believe that the law is synonymous with justice.

어휘리콜 •unintentionally: 무심코; •position: 여기서는 '형세'; '상황'이라는 뜻; •lawyers worldwide: 세계의 변호사들.
주제확인 문장을 따라 독해하여 다른 문장의 내용을 포섭하는 문장을 유도하면 첫 절이 된다.
전문국역 법과 정의는 다양한 정부 통치기관이자 국민에게 자신들의 법은 "공정"하다고 납득시키려 할 때에 무심코 혼동하는 두 가지의 전혀 다른 개념이다. 세계의 변호사들이 자신들은 법 뿐만 아니라 정의도 다스린다고 주장하기 때문에 형세는 점점 더 악화되고 있다. 그 결과 많은 사람들이 법과 정의가 같은 뜻이라고 믿고 있다.

(6) <u>Every year we promise ourselves the same things</u>: this year we will stop smoking or lose weight or eat less, or be nicer to our friends, and every year we gets the same mixed results: we start doing pretty good and then more often than not, we slowly slip back into our old ways of living.

어휘리콜 •the same mixed results: 똑 같은 뒤 섞인.
주제확인 문장을 따라 독해하여 다른 문장의 내용을 포섭하는 문장을 유도하면 첫 절이 된다.
전문국역 매년 우리들은 똑 같은 것을 우리 자신에게 약속 한다: 금년에는 담배를 끊고, 체중을 줄이고, 또는 식사량을 줄이고, 친구들에게 더 상냥하게 대하겠다고 약속한다. 그리고 똑 같은 뒤 썩힌 결과를 얻게 된다. 처음에는 아주 훌륭히 시작한다. 그러고 나서 대개는 옛날 습관으로 다시 돌아간다.

(7) <u>New features at this year's Polish Fest focus on family activities and the Polish culture</u>, which has played a major role in the history of New York City. One of

the first ethnic festivals of the season, Polish Fest will fill Elm Street Park with color, sounds, and activities from July 3-5.

> 어휘리콜 • feature: 특징; • ethnic: 인종의, 민족의.
> 주제확인 문장을 따라 독해하여 다른 문장의 내용을 포섭하는 문장을 유도하면 첫 절이 된다.
> 전문국역 올해 폴란드 축제의 새로운 특징은 가족 활동과 폴란드 문화에 두고 있다는 것입니다. 폴란드 축제는 뉴욕시의 역사에 중요한 역할을 해 오고 있습니다. 민족의 시즌 첫 축제의 하나인 폴란드 축제는 7월 3-5일부터 색깔, 음, 활동으로 Elm Street Park를 메울 것이다.

(8) As with every year, dancing and music will be seen and heard throughout the festival grounds. Dancers will whirl in their brightly colored costumes and solo musicians and bands will offer a variety of musical choices on five different stages.

> 어휘리콜 • whirl: 빙글빙글 돌다.
> 주제확인 문장을 따라 독해하여 다른 문장의 내용을 포섭하는 문장을 유도하면 첫 문이 된다.
> 전문국역 매년처럼, 춤과 음악이 축제의 장에서 보고 듣게 될 것이다. 무용수들이 밝게 채색된 의상을 입고 빙글 빙글 돌며, 솔로가수들과 악단들이 5개의 무대에서 다양한 음악을 들려줄 것이다.

(9) Hours of the festival are 3 p.m. to midnight, Friday, July 3; noon to midnight Saturday, July 4; and noon to 10 p.m. Sunday, July 5, Gate tickets are $8, but can be purchased in advance for $6. Children 14 and younger are admitted free when accompanied by an adult.

> 어휘리콜 • admit: 인정하다; • accompany: 동반하다.
> 주제확인 다른 문장의 내용을 포섭하는 밑줄 친 부분이 주제이다.
> 전문국역 많은 시간의 축제가 7월 3일 오후 3시에서 밤중까지, 7월 4일은 정오에서 밤중까지, 7월 5일은 정오에서 오후 10시까지 있었다. 출구에서의 표 가격은 8달러이지만, 미리 구매하시면 6달러에 이용 가능합니다. 14세 이하 어린이는 어른 동반일 경우 무료입니다.

(10) Thank you for meeting with me on Monday to discuss the financial consultant position at Arlington Financial Group. I hope the level of my interest in the job

came through in the interview; I am very excited about the possibility of working for Arlington.

> 어휘리콜 •financial consultant: 재무 상담.
> 주제확인 다른 문장의 내용을 포섭하는 밑줄 친 부분이 주제이다.
> 전문국역 월요일에 Arlington Financial Group사의 컨설턴트 직에 대해 논의하기 위해 저와 만나주셔서 고맙습니다. 그 직에 대한 저 관심의 정도가 인터뷰를 통해서 표현되어졌기를 기대합니다. 저는 Arlington을 위해서 근무할 가능성에 대해 매우 흥분됩니다.

(11) It has been proven by experiment conducted by some scientists that <u>colors of green and blue have a calming and relaxing effect, while dark gray and black create a depressing effect</u>. For example, a black bridge over the Thames River in London used to be the place of more suicide than some other bridges in the area.

> 어휘리콜 •relax: 이완시키다.
> 주제확인 다른 문장의 내용을 포섭하는 밑줄 친 부분이 주제이다.
> 전문국역 '초록색과 푸른색은 사람들에게 안정감과 긴장완화 효과를 준다'는 것은 일부 과학자들에 의한 실험결과로 밝혀졌고, 한편 진한 회색과 검은 색은 우울한 영향력을 행사한다. 예를 들면, 런던 템즈 강의 검은 다리는 이 지역의 다른 다리보다 더 많은 자살이 일어나는 장소였다.

(12) One early theory likened human memory to a muscle that had to be exercised regularly in order to function properly. This theory was eventually replaced by the idea that remembering was like writing, with experience as the pen and the mind as the blank page. But eventually this idea was also rejected. In its place came another theory that human memory functioned like a complex and well stocked library catalog. With a key wore, you could look up any piece of stored or cataloged information. Over time, that theory has also been discarded. <u>Human memory may, in fact, be too sophisticated and too complex to be explained through any one simile or metaphor.</u>

어휘리콜   •liken: ~에 비유하다; •stock: 비축하다, 갖추다; •wore(wear의 과거분사): 지닌; • sophisticated: 현학적인.

주제확인   다른 문장의 내용을 포섭하는 밑줄 친 부분이 주제이다.

전문국역   근육이란 적절히 기능하기 위하여 규칙적으로 운동이 이루어져야 하는 것인데, 초기 한 이론은 인간의 메모리를 이 근육에 비유하였다. 이 이론은 결국 기억하기라는 것은 쓰기라는 개념으로 대치되었는데, 쓰기는 펜과 마인드(즉 공백 페이지)로서 기억되는 경험인 것이다. 그러나 결국 이 개념 또한 거절되었다. 이 개념 자리에 또 한 이론이 들어오게 되었는데, 인간의 메모리는 복잡하면서도 잘 갖추어진 도서관 카탈로그와 같이 기능한다는 개념이다. 지니고 다니는 열쇠로, 여러분은 저장되어 있는 정보 중에서 어떤 정보를 찾아볼 수 있었다. 시간이 흘러 그 이론 또한 무시되었다. 인간의 메모리는, 사실, 너무 현학적이고, 너무 복잡하여 한 비유나 은유로 설명될 수 없을지도 모른다.

(13) Survey show that <u>about three out of four U. S. corporations have ethics codes.</u> The purpose of these codes is to provide guidance to managers and employees when they encounter an ethical dilemma. A typical code discusses conflicts of interest that can harm the company (for example, guidelines for accepting or refusing gifts from suppliers, hiring relatives, or having an interest in a competitor's firm). Rules for complying with various laws, such as antitrust, environmental, and consumer protection laws, also are popular code provisions. The most effective codes are those drawn up with the cooperation and widespread participation of employees. An internal enforcement mechanism, including penalties for violating the code, puts teeth into the code. A shortcoming of many codes is that they tend to provide more protection for the company than for employees and the general public. They do so by emphasizing narrow legal compliance rather than taking a positive and broad view of ethical responsibility toward all company stockholders and by focusing on conflicts of interest that will harm the company.

어휘리콜   •code: 규약, 규칙; •comply with: 승낙하다, 따르다; •put teeth into: 무기력하게 하다; •shortcoming: 결점, 부족; •stockholder: 주주.

주제확인   다른 문장의 내용을 포섭하는 밑줄 친 부분이 주제이다.

전문국역   조사가 보여 주는 바에 의하면 미국의 법인들 4개 중에서 3개 정도가 윤리 규칙을 가지고 있다. 이 윤리 규칙의 목적은 관리자들과 근로자들이 윤리적 문제에 직면할 때 그들에게 가이드를 제공하는 것이다. 한 전형적인 윤리 규칙은 회사에 손해를 보일 수 있는 이해관계(예를 들면, 업자들로부터의 선물을 받느냐 거절하느냐에 관한 가이드라인 혹은 경쟁사에 대한 이권에 관한 가이드라인)에 대한 갈등에 관해 쓰고 있다. 독점금지법, 환경보호법, 소비자보호법과 같은 여러 법규들 또한 대중적인 법 규정들이다. 가장 효과 있는 법규는 근로자들의 협력과 폭 넓은 참여를 끌어낸 법규들이다. 법규 위반에 대하여 벌금을 물리는 것을 포함하는 내적 강압장치는 법규를 무기력하게 한다. 많은 법규의 결점은 근로자와 일반대중보다도 회사를 더 많이 보호한다는 것이다. 이런 법규들은 회사 주주들의 적극적이고도 폭 넓은 윤리적 책임보다도 협의의 법적 승낙을 강조하기 때문이고, 회사에 해를 입힐 이해관계에 대한 갈등에 초점을 맞추고 있기 때문이다.

(14) <u>People have many different reasons for wanting children.</u> Some really like children and want an opportunity to be involved with their care. Some women strongly desire the experience of pregnancy and childbirth. Many young adults see parenthood as a way to demonstrate their adult status. For people coming from happy families, having children is a means of recreating their earlier happiness. For those from unhappy families, it can be a means of doing better than their parents did. Some people have children simply because it's expected of them. Because society places so much emphasis on the fulfillment motherhood is supposed to bring, some women who are unsure of what they want to do with their lives use having a child as a way to create an identity.

어휘리콜 •fulfillment: 이행, 성취, 실행; •motherhood: 모성, 모성애, 어머니임, 어머니 구실.
주제확인 다른 문장의 내용을 포섭하는 밑줄 친 부분이 주제이다.
전문국역 사람들은 아이를 가지는 데에 여러 이유들을 갖고 있다. 어떤 사람들은 진정으로 아이를 좋아하고 아이 돌봄이 관련되는 기회를 원한다. 어떤 사람들은 임신과 아이출산의 경험을 강력하게 원한다. 많은 젊은 성인들은 부모임을 성인신분을 나타내는 방법으로 본다. 행복한 가정의 사람들에게 아이를 갖는다는 것은 자기들 초기 행복의 재창조의 수단이다. 불행한 가정의 사람들에게 아이를 갖는다는 것은 그들의 부모들이 초기 행복의 재창조의 수단으로 삼았던 것보다 더 많은 행복의 재창조 수단이 될 수 있다. 어떤 사람들은 단순하게 자기들이 아이를 갖게 되는 것으로 기대되기 때문에 아이를 갖는다. 사회가 모성이 가져다주는 성취를 많이 강조하기 때문에, 자기들의 생활에서 원하는 것이 무엇인지에 대하여 잘 모르는 어떤 여성들은 아이 갖는 것을 정체성 창조의 수단으로 사용한다.

(15) Beavers, North America's largest rodents (they grow to more than two feet long), are delightful to watch for their industry and their family affection. Yet <u>few animals have been so relentlessly exploited as the beaver.</u> In the eighteenth and nineteenth centuries, beaver pelts were worth their weight in gold. As a result, by 1896, at least fourteen American states - Massachusetts, Vermont, New Hampshire, New York, Rhode Island, Connecticut, Pennsylvania, New Jersey, Delaware, Maryland, Illinois, Indiana, West Virginia, and Ohio - had announced that all of their beavers had been killed. By the beginning of the twentieth century, it looked as if the beaver was about to disappear from the face of the earth. But thanks to a beaver recovery program, which included trapping and relocating to protected areas, beavers have made an impressive comeback throughout the country.

> 어휘리콜 •worth one's weight in gold: 대단히 귀중한; •relentlessly: 잔인하게, 혹독하게; •pelt: 생가죽, 모피.
>
> 주제확인 첫 문장은 머리말이다. 대부분의 다른 문장들 내용을 포섭하는 밑줄 친 부분이 주제가 된다. 끝 문장은 주제문의 내용과 대조적이기는 하지만 그렇다고 첫 문장의 내용(근면성과 가족애)과 관련된 것은 아니다.
>
> 전문국역 비버, 북미의 최대 설치류(2피트 이상 길이로 자란다)인데, 기꺼이 그들의 근면함과 가족애를 보인다. 그러나 비버만큼 잔인하게 이용되는 동물은 없었다. 18,9세기에, 비버 가죽은 대단히 귀중했다. 그 결과 1896년까지는 적어도 미 14개주-Massachusetts, Vermont, New Hampshire, New York, Rhode Island, Connecticut, Pennsylvania, New Jersey, Delaware, Maryland, Illinois, Indiana, West Virginia, and Ohio-는 모든 비버를 잡도록 발표를 했다. 20세기 초에는 비버는 지구 표면에서 사라질 것처럼 보였다. 그러나 올가미로 포획해서 보호 구역으로 재방사하는 것을 포함하는 비버 복원 프로그램 덕택에 비버는 전국적으로 인상적인 회복을 했다.

(16) <u>The term bilingual education refers to programs designed to instruct nonnative speakers of English who have not yet mastered English as their second language.</u> For the most part, bilingual programs are considered purely transitional, providing support to students in their native language until they can speak English well enough to function in classrooms where only English is spoken. A typical bilingual program begins by teaching kindergarten students in their primary language and

translating key words into English. However, by the end of first or second grade, English is the primary language, with words only occasionally being translated into the students' native tongue. For a while now, bilingual education has been a controversial topic, with critics arguing that the native language should be eliminated from the classroom as early as possible because it interferes with the language of English. But research does not support this claim. On the contrary, bilingualism seems to improve the thinking abilities of children.

어휘리콜 •bilingualism: 2개 국어 병용; •controversial: 논쟁적인; •eliminate: 제거하다.

주제확인 다른 문장들 내용을 포섭하는 밑줄 친 부분이 주제가 된다.

전문국역 '2중 언어 교육'이라는 용어는 제2언어로서의 영어를 아직 숙달하지 못한 비모국어 영어화자에게 영어를 가르치는 프로그램을 말한다. 대개 2중 언어 프로그램은 전적으로 과도 기적인 것으로 간주되고 있고, 그리고 영어만 사용되는 교실에서 충분히 잘 역할을 할 수 있을 정도로 영어를 사용할 때까지 학생들에게 모국어로 지원을 제공한다(즉 도와준다). 전형적인 2중 언어 프로그램은 유치원생들에게 그들의 제1언어로 가르치면서 주요 어휘들을 영어로 번역해준다. 그러나 1학년이나 2학년 말에는, 영어가 제1언어이며, 단지 경우에 따라서만 학생들의 모국어로 번역이 된다. 이제 2중 언어 교육은 논쟁의 토픽이 되었는데, 비평가들은 모국어가 영어교육에 간섭한다는 이유로 가능한 일찍 교실에서 모국어가 제거되어야 한다고 주장한다. 그러나 연구들은 이 주장을 지지하지 않는다. 반대로 2중 언어 사용은 어린이들의 사고능력을 증진시키는 것 같다.

(17) A wild boar was standing against a tree and whetting his tusks. A fox asked why he sharpened them when no huntsman was pursuing him and no danger threatened. "I have a reason for doing so," he replied. "If danger overtakes me, I shall not have time then to sharpen them, but they will be all ready for use."

어휘리콜 •whet: (칼) 갈다, (식욕) 자극하다; •tusk: 엄니; •overtake: 덮치다.

주제확인 이솝의 우화이다. 주제는 표면에 나타나 있지는 않지만, 사전대비(ready for action) 즉 위험이 닥칠 때까지 준비를 미루지 말라(Do not wait till danger is at hand to make your preparations)가 주제이다.

전문국역 멧돼지가 나무에다 대고 그의 엄니를 갈고 있었다. 사냥꾼도 그를 쫓아 오지 않고, 아무런 위험도 없는데 왜 엄니를 갈고 있느냐고 여우가 물었다. "내게는 이럴만한 이유가 있다네," 멧돼지가 대답했다. "만약 위험이 들이닥친 그때에는 엄니를 날카롭게 갈 여유가 없을 것이네, 따라서 엄니는 항상 사용할 수 있도록 만반의 준비가 되어 있어야 한다네."

제4장
본문 독해

문들이 연결되어 단락이 형성되는 것과 같은 원리로 단락들이 연결되면 절(section)이 형성되고, 이 절들이 연결되면 장(chapter)이 형성된다. 더 나아가서 장 상위의 계층이 있을 수도 있다. 절(section)에서부터 위로 여러 계층들을 포함하는 넓은 영역을 본문이라고 부른다.[1] 본문영역에서 어떤 계층이든 독해의 방법은 1)직접구성단위의 마디(예: 본문이 절/section인 경우 단락의 마디)에서 관계를 확인하고, 2)내용의 흐름, 즉 직접구성단위(예: 본문이 절/section인 경우 단락)들의 주제문들(예: 본문이 절/section인 경우 단락의 주제문들)을 확인하고 3)본문 전체의 주제(본문이 절/section인 경우 주제단락의 주제문)를 확인하는 것이다.[2]

제1절 단위 마디의 관계식별

본문 독해에서도 단락 독해에서와 마찬가지로 첫 처리작업은 직접구성단위 마디(가령, 본문이 절/section)인 경우 단락 사이)의 관계를 이해하는 것이다. 즉 단락의

---

1) 원래는 단락 층에서부터 본문으로 간주하는데 이 책에서는 학습이해 편의상 임시로 분리되었다.
2) 본문에 속하는 층들 중에서 이 4장에서는 절 층만 대표적으로 다룬다.

주제문과 단락의 주제문 사이의 관계를 이해하는 것이다. 아래 (1)에서 둘째 단락을 읽은 후 이 단락의 주제문을 첫째 단락의 주제문과의 관계를 확인하는 것이다. 이 관계이해는 단락독해에서 이용된 절/clause마다 관계방식들이 재이용된다.3)

(1)

1 It is probably intuitively clear to anyone who knows a few languages <u>that some languages are closer to one another than are others.</u> For instance, English and German are closer to one another than either is to Russian, while Russian and Polish are closer to one another than either to English, This notion of similarity can be made more precise, as is done for instance in the chapter on the Indo-European languages below, but for the moment the relatively informal notion will suffice. Starting in the late eighteenth century, a specific hypothesis was proposed to account for such similarities, a hypothesis which still forms the foundation of research into the history and relatedness of languages. This hypothesis is that where languages share some set of features in common, theses features are to be attributed to their common ancestor. Let us take some examples from English and German.

2 In English and German we find a number of basic vocabulary items <u>that have the same or almost the same form,</u> e.g. English *man* and German *Mann*. Likewise, we find a number of bound morphemes (prefixes and suffixes) that have the same or almost the same form, such as the genitive suffix, as in English *man's* and German *Mann(e)s*. Although English and German are now clearly different languages, we may hypothesise that at an earlier period in history they had a common ancestor, in which the word for 'man' was something like *man* and the genitive suffix was something like -*s*. Thus English and German belong to the same language family, which is the same as saying that they share a common ancestor. We can readily add other languages to his family, since a word like *man* and a genitive suffix like -*s* are also found in Dutch, Frisian, and the

---

3) 논리/수사적 관계에 속하지 않는 명사성분관계와 명사한정관계는 이용에서 제외한다(3장 참조).

Scandinavian languages. The family to which these languages belong has been given the name Germanic, and the ancestor language is Proto-Germanic. It should be emphasised that the proto-language is not an attested language __ although if written records had gone back far enough, we might well have had attestations of his language __ but its postulation is the most plausible hypothesis explaining the remarkable similarities among the various Germanic languages.

어휘리콜 •attest: 증명하다, 입증하다; •postulation: 가정.

마디관계 첫 단락은 첫 문이 단락의 주제문(보다 핵심부분은 some ...are others)으로 확인되고, 둘째 단락도 첫 문이 주제문{보다 핵심부분은 that(=a number of basic vocabulary items) ... the same form}으로 확인된다. 첫 단락의 주제문과 둘째 단락의 주제문은 주장과 예증의 관계로 확인된다.

전문국역 **1** 몇몇 언어를 아는 사람들 누구에게나 직관적으로 아마도 분명한 것은 언어들 중 일부는 다른 언어들 보다 더 서로 친근하다는 것이다. 예를 들면, 영어와 독일어는 이들 중 어느 하나가 러시아어에 가까운 정도보다도 서로 더 가깝고, 반면에 러시아어와 폴란드어는 이들 중 어느 하나가 영어에 가까운 정도보다도 서로 더 가깝다. 이 친밀도 개념은 보다 더 정확하게 기술될 수 있는데, 예를 들면, 아래 인도유럽에 관한 장(chapter)과 같으나, 현재로는 비공식적인 이 정도의 비교만으로 충분할 것이다. 18세기 후반에 들어서면서 이러한 친밀도를 설명하려는 한 특수적인 가설이 제안되었는데, 이 가설은 아직도 언어들의 역사와 친밀도에 관한 연구의 근거를 형성하고 있다. 이 가설은 언어들이 어떤 자질들을 공유한다는 것이고, 이 자질들은 그 언어들의 공통 조상언어 탓으로 돌려진다는 것이다. 영어와 독일어로부터 몇 가지 예를 본다. **2** 영어와 독일어에서 우리는 많은 기본 어휘항목을 발견하게 되는데, 이 어휘항목들은 같은 형태 혹은 거의 같은 형태를 가진다.(영어 *man*과 독일어 *Mann*). 마찬가지로, 우리는 동일하거나 거의 동일한 형태를 가지는 많은 구속형태소(접두사와 접미사)를 발견하게 되는데, 예를 들면 영어 *man's*와 독일어 *Mann(e)s*에서 볼 수 있는 속격접미사이다. 비록 영어와 독일어가 지금은 분명하게 다른 언어이지만, 역사상 초기에서는 두 언어가 공통 조상을 가지고 있어서, 'man'에 해당하는 단어는 *man* 같은 것이었고, 그 속격접미사는 -s 같은 것이라는 가설을 말할 수 있다. 그러므로 영어와 독일어는 동일 어족에 속하고, 이 말은 두 언어가 공통조상을 공유한다고 말하는 것 같다. 우리는 다른 언어들을 그 어족에 쉽게 보탤 수 있는데, 이유는 *man*과 같은 단어와 -*s*와 같은 속격접미사가 Dutch, Frisian, Scandinavian어에서도 발견되기 때문이다. 이 언어들이 속하는 어족에게 Germanic 이라는 이름이 주어졌고, 조상언어가 원시게르만어(Proto-Germanic)이다. 원시언어가 입증된 언어가 아니라는 점이 강조되어져야 한다. 즉 만약 원시 언어와 관련 아주 오래 전까지 거슬러 올라가지는 기록이 있다면 그 원시언어에 대한 입증이 있었을지도 모르지만, 그래도 그 가정은 여러 게르만어 언어들 사이에 있는 유사성을 설명하는 가장 그럴듯한 가설일 뿐이다.

(2)

1 A recent report on the country's immigration policy should draw attention from the public as well as government policymakers as a catalyst for their far-sighted views on how to secure long-term sustainable growth and social vitality.

2 The report, submitted by the Migration Research and, Training Center to the Justice Ministry, proposed increasing the number of foreign nationals here, which stood at 1.44 million last year, to 3 million by 2030. If not, the paper predicted, the nation would begin to suffer from a severe workforce shortage, which would further decelerates its economic growth. There have been a series of warning of a possible demographic disaster.

> **어휘리콜** •catalyst: 촉매, 기폭제; •far-sighted view: 멀리 보는 눈(안목); •sustainable: 지속적인; •submit: 제출하다; •workforce shortage: 노동력 부족; •decelerate: 늦추다, 감속하다.
>
> **마디관계** 첫 단락은 밑줄 친 부분이 주제로 확인되고, 둘째 단락도 밑줄 친 부분이 주제문으로 확인된다. 두 밑줄 친 부분은 일반 개념과 구체 개념의 관계로 확인된다.
>
> **전문국역** **1** 우리나라 이민정책에 관한 최근 보고서는 장기적 지속 가능한 성장과 사회적 활력을 확보하는 방안에 관한 선견지명인 견해의 기폭제로서 정부 정책 관리들은 물론 국민들로부터 관심을 끌고 있다. **2** 인구정책연구원이 법무부에 제출한 이 보고서는 지난해 144만 명이었던 국내 외국인 수를 2030년까지 3백만 명으로 늘릴 것을 제안했다. 그렇지 않으면 우리나라는 경제성장을 더욱 둔화시킬 심각한 인력부족을 겪기 시작할 것으로 이 보고서는 전망했다. 인구 재앙 가능성에 대해 잇따른 경고가 나오고 있다.

(3)   **Five Approaches to Dealing with Conflict**

1 People react differently in dealing with conflict. Some people pull back, some attack, and others take responsibility for themselves and their needs. Most of us use a primary style for confronting conflict. Knowing your style and its ramifications can be helpful in determining whether you are pleased with your conflict style. If you are not, you may need to acquire the skills to make a change in your habitual pattern. The styles of conflict management are (1) avoidance, (2) accommodation/ smoothing over, (3) compromise, (4) competition/aggression, and (5) integration.

2 Some people choose to confront conflict by engaging in conflict avoidance-not confronting the conflict. They sidestep, postpone or ignore the issue. They simply put up with the status quo, no mater how unpleasant, While seemingly unproductive, avoidance may actually be a good style if the situation is a short-term one or of minor importance. If, however, the problem is really bothering you or is persistent, then it should be dealt with. Avoiding the issue often uses up a great deal of energy without resolving the aggravating situation. Very seldom do avoiders feel that they have been in a win-win situation. Avoiders usually lose a chunk of their self-respect since they so clearly downplay their own concerns in favor of the other person's. Avoiders frequently were brought up in environments in which they were told to be nice and not to argue, and eventually bad things would go away. Or they were brought up in homes where verbal or physical abuse was present, and to avoid these types of reactions, they hid from conflict.

3 People who attempt to manage conflict through conflict accommodation put the needs of others ahead of their own, thereby giving in. Accommodators meet the needs of others and don't assert their own. In this situation, the accommodator often feels like the "good person" for having given the other person his own way. This is perfectly acceptable if the other person's needs really are more important. But unfortunately, accommodators tend to follow the pattern no matter what the situation. Thus, they often are taken advantage of, and they seldom get their needs met. Accommodators commonly come from backgrounds where they were exposed to a martyr who gave and gave and got little but put on a happy face. They also tend to be people who have little self-respect and try to earn praise by being nice to everyone.

4 A form of accommodation known as conflict smoothing over seeks above all else to preserve the image that everything is okay. Through smoothing over, people sometimes get what they want, but just as often they do not. Usually they feel they have more to say and have not totally satisfied themselves.

5 As with avoidance and accommodation, smoothing over occasionally can be useful.

If, for example, the relationship between two people is more important than the subject they happen to be disagreeing about, then smoothing over may be the best approach. Keep in mind, however, that smoothing over does not solve the conflict; it just pushes it aside. It may very well recur in the future.

6 Those who use this technique as their normal means of confronting conflict often come from backgrounds in which the idea was stressed that being nice was the best way to be liked and popular. And being liked and popular was more important than satisfying their needs.

7 Conflict compromise brings concerns out into the open in an attempt to satisfy the needs of both parties. It usually means "trading some of what you want for some of what I want. It's meeting each other half way." The definition of the word compromise, however, indicates the potential weakness of this approach, for it means that both individuals give in at least to some degree to reach a solution. As a result, neither usually completely achieves what she or he wants. This is not to say that compromise is an inherently poor method of conflict management. It is not, but it can lead to frustration unless both participants are wiling to continue to work until both of their needs are being met. Those who are effective compromisers normally have had experience with negotiations and know that you have to give to get, but you don't have to give until it hurts. Those who tend to be weak in working toward a fair and equitable compromise believe that getting something is better than getting noting at all. Therefore, they are willing to settle for anything, no matter how little.

8 The main element in conflict competition is power. Its purpose is to "get another person to comply with or accept your point of view, or to do something that person may not want to do." Someone has to win, and someone has to lose. This forcing mode, unfortunately, has been the European-American way of operation in many situations-in athletic events, business deals, and interpersonal relations. Indeed, many people do not seem to be happy unless they are clear winners. Realize that if someone wins, someone else must lose. The overaggressive driver must force the other car off the road.

9 The value of winning at all costs is debatable. Sometimes, even though we win, we lose in the long run. The hatred of a child for a parent caused by continuous losing, or the negative work environment resulting from a supervisor who must always be on top, may be much worse than the occasional loss of a battle. In dealing with persons from other cultures, European Americans sometimes are perceived as being pushy and aggressive. Many sales, friendships, and relationships have been lost based on the win-at-all-costs philosophy. Many of the aggressive behaviors in the personal lives of professional athletes are directly credited to their not being able to leave their win-at-all-costs attitude on the athletic field.

10 Communicators who handle their conflicts through conflict integration are concerned about their own needs as well as those of the other person. But unlike compromisers, they will not settle for only a partially satisfying solution. Integrators keep in mind that both parties can participate in a win-win resolution and are willing to collaborate. Thus, the most important aspect of integration is the realization that the relationship, the value of self-worth, and the issue are important. For this reason, integrative solutions often take a good deal of time and energy.

11 People who are competitive, who are communication-apprehensive, or who are nonassertive find it nearly impossible to use an integrative style of negotiation. They feel that they must win, or that they cannot stand up for their rights, or that they have no right to negotiate. In contrast, people who tend to have assertiveness skills and value the nature of relationships usually attempt to work toward integration. (주제 분산)

12 Avoidance, accommodation, and smoothing over are all nonassertive acts; the person's needs are not met. Competition is an aggressive act in that the person gets his needs met at the expense of another person. Integration is assertive since the objective is to get one's needs met without taking away the rights of someone else. Compromise, depending on how it is acted out, can be either nonassertive or assertive. (주제 분산)

어휘리콜 •pull back: 물러가다, 삼가다; •confront: 직면하다, 마주하다; •ramification: 가지, 분파; •avoidance: 회피, 도피; •accommodation: 적응, 조정, 순응; •smoothing over: 숨기기; •preserve: 보존하다, 유지하다; •compromise: 타협, 협상; •competition: 경쟁; •aggression: 공격, 침략; •integration: 통합; •engage in: 착수하다, 시작하다; •put up with: 참다; •status quo: 현상; •aggravate: 악화시키다, 괴롭히다; •chunk: 덩어리, 조각; •downplay: 경시하다; •give in: 굴복하다, 양보하다; •come from: 생기다; •martyr: 순교자, 희생자; •equitable: 공정한, 정당한.

마디관계 각 단락의 주제는 밑줄 친 부분과 같다. 끝 11 번 단락과 12 번 단락은 주제가 분산되어 있다. 단락 2 는 1 의 주장에 대해 사례, 3 은 1 의 주장에 대한 사례, 4 는 3 의 일반에 대한 구체, 5 는 4 의 일반에 대한 구체, 6 은 5 에 대해 나열, 7 은 1 의 주장에 대해 사례, 8 은 1 의 주장에 대해 사례, 9 는 8 의 일반에 대해 구체, 10 은 1 의 주장에 대해 사례, 11 과 12 는 요약관계이다.

전문국역 1 사람들은 갈등을 다룰 때 대응이 다르다. 어떤 사람은 물러서고, 어떤 사람은 공격하고, 그리고 또 다른 사람들은 자기 자신과 자신의 요구를 위해서 책임을 진다. 우리 대부분은 갈등에 직면하기 위해 자기 본래의 스타일을 사용한다. 자기의 해결스타일과 그 하위 방식을 안다는 것은 자신이 자신의 해결스타일에 만족하는지 여부를 결정하는 데에 도움이 될 수 있다. 갈등관리의 스타일에는 1)도피(avoidance), 2)순응/숨기기(accommodation/smoothing over), 3)타협(compromise), 4)경쟁/공격(competition/aggression), 그리고 5)통합(integration)이 있다. 2 어떤 사람들은 갈등에 직면할 때 갈등을 도피 한다-갈등에 대적하지 않는다. 그들은 이 문제를 비켜서거나 지연시키거나 혹은 무시한다. 그들은, 비록 불쾌하더라도, 그 현상을 단순히 참는다. 도피가, 한편으로는 비생산적이면서도, 실제로는 그 상황이 단기적 상황이거나 중요성이 낮을 경우 좋은 스타일 일수도 있다. 그러나 만약 그 문제가 실제로 당신을 괴롭히거나 지속적이면, 그 때는 그 문제는 다루어져야 한다. 악화시키는 상황을 해결하지 않고 문제를 회피한다는 것은 많은 에너지를 고갈시킨다. 도피자들은 자기들이 윈-윈 상황에 처해 있어왔다는 것을 좀처럼 느끼지 못한다. 도피자들은 남의 관심사를 생각해주다가 자신의 관심사를 경시하기 때문에 종종 자존심을 상당히 잃게 된다. 도피자들은 자주 좋은 사람이 되려고 하고 다투려고 하지 말라, 나쁜 상황은 나쁜 상황은 사라진다고 하는 상황 속에서 성장해왔다. 혹은 언어적 혹은 신체적 비난이 있는 가정에서 성장을 했으며, 이러한 유형의 반응(다르게 되는 상황)을 피하기 위하여 그들은 갈등으로부터 숨어버렸다. 3 갈등에 순응함으로서 갈등을 다루려고 시도하는 사람들은 자신의 욕구를 앞서서 남의 욕구를 생각하고, 그리하여 자신의 욕구를 양보한다. 순응자들은 남의 욕구를 충족시키고 자신의 욕구를 주장하지 않는다. 이런 상황에서 순응자는 종종 남에게 자신의 입장을 양보했기 때문에 '좋은 사람'으로 느낀다. 만약 타인의 욕구가 정말로 중요하다면 완전히 입정할 수 있다. 그러나 불행하게도, 순응자들은, 상황이 어떠하든, 이 패턴을 따르는 경향이 있다. 그러므로 순응자들은 종종 이용당하며, 그래서 자신의 욕구가 충족되게 하지 않는다. 순응자들은 보통 남에게 주고 또 주면서도 행복한 표정을 짓는 순교자에 노출된 배경으로부터 나온다. 그들은 또한 자존심을 가지지 않으며, 남들에게 좋은 사람이 되는 것으로 칭찬을 받으려고 노력하는 사람들인 경향이 있다. 4 순응의 한 형태인 갈등숨기기는 무엇보다도 모든 것이 ok라는 이미지를 유지하기를 추구한다. 갈등숨기기를 통해서 사람들이 때때로는 자기들이 원하는 바를 얻지만, 종종은 얻지 못하는 그대로이다. 보통은 그들이 할 말이 많다고 느끼며 자신에게서 완전히 만족하지 못했다고 느낀다. **5** 도피와 순응에서처럼, 갈등숨기기는 경우에 따라서는 유용할 수 있다. 예를 들면, 만약 두 사람이 일치하지 않게 된 주제보다 두 사람 사이가 더 중요하다면, 그때는 갈등숨기기가 최선의 접근방법이 될 수도 있다. 그러나 갈등숨기기는 갈등을 해결하는 것이 아니고 갈등은 한 쪽으로 밀쳐놓는 것임을 명심해야 한다. 갈등이 향후 다시 쉽게 생겨날 수도 있다. **6** 이 테크닉(갈등숨기기)을 갈등에 직면하는 보통의 수단으로 이용하는 사람들은 '좋은 사람'이 선호되고 인기 있게 되는 최선의 방법이라는 마인드의 압박을 받았던 배경으로부터 나온다. 그리고 선호되고 인기 있게 되는 것이 자신의 욕구충족보다 더 중요했다. **7** 갈등타협은 관심사를 노출시켜서 쌍방의 욕구를 만족시키려고 시도한다. 갈등타협은 보통 '상대방이 원하는 것과 자신이 원하는 것 일부를 거래하고, 그것이 절반씩 충족시키는 것'을 의미한다. 그러나 타협이라는 단어의 정의는 (갈등)접근방법의 잠재적 약점을 나타낸다. 왜냐하면 타협이란 쌍방이 해결에 이르기 위해 적어도 어느 정도씩 내주기 때문이다. 그 결과 어느 쪽도 보통은 자기가 원하는 것을 완전히는 성취하지 못한다. 이 말은 타협이 갈등관리에서 본질적으로 나쁜 방법이라고 말하는 것은 아니다. 타협이 나쁘지는 않다. 그러나 참여자들이 쌍방의 욕구가 충족될 때까지 기꺼이 계속해서 타협작업을 해 나가지 않으면, 타협은 좌절로 이어질 수 있다. 효과적인 타협자들은 보통 협상의 경험을 가지고 있으며, 자신이 얻기 위해서는 주어야 한다는 것을 알고 있지만, 그렇다고 최후의 순간까지(상처를 입을 정도가 될 때까지는) 줄 필요가 없다. 공정하고 적당한 타협을 하는 데에 약한 경향이 있는 사람들은 뭔가 얻는 쪽이 아무것도 얻지 못하는 쪽 보다 더 낫다고 믿는다. 그러므로 그들은 아무리 작은 것이라도 뭔가를 위해서 기꺼이 해결하려고 한다. **8** 갈등경쟁에서 주요 요소는 파워(힘)이다. 힘의 목적은 '타인으로 하여금 자신의 견해를 따르게 하거나 받아들이게 하거나 그 사람이 원하지 않는 것을 하도록 하는 것'이다. 누군가는 이겨야하고, 누군가는 져야한다. 이 힘 양식은 불행하게도 많은 상황에서-즉 운동경기, 상업거래, 개인적인 관계에서-유럽과 미국식의 방식이었다. 실제로, 많은 사람들은 자기들이 진정한 승자가 아니면 행복한 것 같지가 않다. 만약 누군가 이기고, 누군가 패해야만 한다는 것을 깨달아라. 지나친 공격드라이브는 상대방의 차를 도로 밖으로 밀어 내버린다. **9** 모든 비용을 드린 승리의 값은 문제의 여지가 있다. 때때로 이긴다 하더라도 결국은 지게 되는 경우가 있다. 계속적인 패배를 하는 부모로서 아이에 대한 증오, 혹은 항상 상위 직에 있는 상급자로부터 초래되는 부정적인 작업환경은 싸움에서 이따금 패하는 경우보다 훨씬 더 나쁠 수도 있다. 다른 문화권 출신의 사람들을 다룰 때, 유럽 쪽 미국인들은 때때로 밀어붙이고 공격적인 성향으로 인식된다. 많은 경우의 거래, 우정, 그리고 관계는 모든 비용을 치른 승리를 바탕으로 해서는 패한 것이 되어버렸다. 직업 운동선수들의 개인 생활에서 공격적인 운동선수들 상당수는 경기장에서 전력투구하는 태도를 보여 줄 수 없는 것으로 생각된다. **10** 자신의 갈등을 갈등통합을 통해서 다루는 소통자들은 타인의 욕구뿐만 아니라 자신의 욕구에도 관여한다. 그러나 타협자들과는 달리, 의사소통자들은 부분적으로만 만족시키는 해결책으로는 해결하지 않으려 한다. 통합자들은 쌍방이 상생 해결방안에 참여할 수 있고 기꺼이 협력하는 것을 명심한다. 그러므로 통합의 가장 중요한 측면은 관계, 자존의 가치, 그리고 이슈 중요성의 실현이다. 이런 이유 때문에 통합적 해결방안은 많은 시간과 에너지를 요구한다. ⑪ 경쟁적인 사람들, 소통-종합적인 사람들, 혹은 비주장적인 사람들은 통합적인 협상스타일을 사용한다는 것은 불가능한 것으로 본다. 그들은 이겨야만 한다고, 혹은 그들의 권리를 참을 수 없다고, 혹은 협상할 권리가 없다고 느낀다. 대조적으로, 주장능력과 가치를 관계의 본질로 보는 경향이 있는 사람들은 보통 통합 방향으로 처리하려고 시도한다. ⑫ 도피, 적응, 그리고 갈등숨기기는 모두 비 주장적인 행동들이다. 자기의 욕구는 충족되지 않는다. 경쟁은 타인의 비용을 치르고 자신의 요구를 충족시킨다는 점에서 경쟁적이다. 통합은 그 목적이 타인의 권리를 멀리하지 않고 자신의 요구를 충족시킨다는 점에서 주장적이다. 타협은 행동의 방법에 의거, 비주장적일 수도 있고, 주장적일 수도 있다.

(4)
Editorial
Dispute Over noise

① Recent neighbor disputes over noise traveling between floors left two people dead and several others injured. The incidents, which took place in Seoul during the Lunar New Year holidays, raised the need for fundamental and institutional measures to solve the deteriorating problem. Also shown by them, as noted by some psychological experts, was Koreans' hot-tempered personality.

② In a country where more than 65 percent of its population lives in apartments, the combination of the noisy living environment and short-tempered residents would cause more fatal neighbor disputes in the days to come, if not properly addressed.

③ In an apartment complex on Saturday, two brothers in their 30s were stabbed to death by a 45-year-old man after they engaged in a squabble over the noise coming from the home of their parents' house. The murderer was staying at his girlfriend's home on floor directly below them.

④ In another incident the following day, a 49-year-old man set fire to the home above his in a multifamily dwelling after a long dispute over noise. Six people including the home-owner and his grandchildren were severely burned.

⑤ In recent years, similar cases occurred in Daegu, Gwangju and other provincial cities as well as Seoul. An office set up by the Environment Ministry to help solve disputes over noise received a total of 7.021 complaints last year.

6 It would be ideal for neighbors to settle feuds over noise through mutual dialogue and concessions. Unless one lives at the bottom or top floor of an apartment building, it is possible that he or she is annoyed by noise from above and at the same time makes noise bothering those below.

7 But it may be too much to expect apartment residents, who rarely communicate with one another in the anonymous living environment, to resolve the problem in a smooth and reasonable manner. What complicates the dispute is the lack of clear and effective rules for regulating noise between neighbors and compensating for distress with it.

8 There is no specific legal ground for curbing noise coming from neighboring houses while sounds and vibrations from vehicles and construction sites are subject to regulatory measures. A process for coordinating environmental disputes refers to excessive noise levels, but these are so high that no compensation has been actually made so far. It should be taken into account that residents causing noise that annoys neighbors can face considerable fines or even eviction from their homes in Britain, Germany, the U.S. and other nations.

9 In a belated move, the Land Ministry announced this week a plan to impose stricter building regulations to reduce sound traveling between floors of an apartment building. But the measure needs to be supplemented with provisions for specific penalties for violations, if its effectiveness is to be ensured. It may also be helpful to encourage apartment complexes across the country to include procedures for solving noise disputes in their management rules.

10 Concerted and continuous efforts should be made by residents, construction companies and relevant government agencies to prevent the problem from resulting in more tragic incidents.

11 Koreans also need to be more adroit in controlling their temper to live secure and harmonious lives in multiplex housing. The number of people diagnosed as having impulse control disorders increased from 1,660 in 2007 to 3,015 in 2011, according to the National Health Insurance Service.

12 The combination of impatient individuals with growing conflicts in society has increased crimes out of anger. Figures from the police showed the number of people who committed murder or arson from sudden outrage rose from 306 and 347 in 2000 to 465 and 583 in 2010, respectively.

13 Cramped housing conditions may be one of the factors that have made Koreans more short-tempered. Under these circumstances, Koreans are all the more required to be more considerate and accommodating toward their neighbors.

어휘리콜 •travel: 여행하다, 전해지다; •deteriorate: 나빠지게 하다, 악화시키다; •hot-tempered personality: 다혈질 성격; •short-tempered: 성마른, 불끈거리는; •address: 역점을 두어 다루다; •apartment complex: 아파트단지; •stab: 찌르다; •squabble: 언쟁, 말다툼; •multifamily dwelling: 다가구 거주; •settle feud: 불화를 해결하다; •annoy: 고통스럽게 하다; •anonymous: 익명의; •distress: 고통; •curb: 억제하다; •construction sites: 건설현장; •eviction: 추방; •belated: 뒤 늦은; •Land Ministry: 국토부; •impose: 과하다; •building regulation: 건축규제; •provision: 규정, 조항; •concerted: 협조적; •adroit: 교묘한, 솜씨 좋은, 기민한; •secure: 안전한; •diagnosed: 진단된; •impulse control disorders: 충동절제혼란; •impatient: 성급한; •murder or arson: 살인 혹은 방화; •cramp: 속박하다, 제한하다, 가두다; •accommodate: 편의를 도모하다.

마디관계 각 단락의 주제 부분은 밑줄 친 부분과 같다. **1**에 대하여 **2**는 원인 관계, **3**은 **1**에 대하여 일반구체관계, **4**는 **1**에 대하여 나열관계, **5**는 **4**에 대하여 나열관계, **6**은 **5**에 대하여 문제해결의 관계, **7**은 **6**에 대하여 대조의 관계, **8**은 **7**에 대하여 일반구체의 관계, **9**는 **8**에 대한 문제해결의 관계, **10**은 **8**에 대한 문제해결의 관계, **11**은 **8**에 대한 문제해결의 관계, **12**는 **11**에 대한 이유관계, **13**은 **12**에 대한 원인 관계이다.

전문국역 **1** 층간에 전해지는 소음 때문에 최근 이웃사이 다툼으로 두 사람이 사망하고 여러 사람이 부상을 입었다. 사건은 설 명절 휴일 동안에 서울에서 일어났는데, 악화시키는 문제를 해결하기 위하여 기본적이고도 제도적 대책의 필요성을 불러일으킨다. 또한 몇몇 심리전문가들에게서 주목된 바대로 사건들에서 한국인의 다혈질 성격이 보여 졌다. **2** 인구 65% 이상이 아파트에서 사는 나라에서 소음 주거 환경과 성마른 주민의 결합은, 만약 적절하게 역점을 두어 다루지 않는다면, 다가올 앞날에 더 치명적인 이웃 다툼을 유발시킬 것이다. **3** 토요일 아파트단지에서, 30대의 두 형제가 그들 부모님 집 가정 밖으로 나가는 소음 때문에 언쟁에 개입한 후 45세 남자에 의하여 찔러 사망했다. 그 살인자는 그들 부모 집 바로 아래층 거실 사기 여자 친구의 집에 머물고 있었다. **4** 그 다음날 또 한 사건에서 49세 남자가 소음으로 오랜 싸움 끝에 다세대 주거의 자기 위층 집에 불을 질렀다. 집주인 및 그의 손자를 포함 6명이 심한 화상을 입었다. **5** 최근에 유사한 사건들이 서울은 말할 것도 없고 대구, 광주, 기타 도시들에서 일어났다. 소음으로 인한 싸움을 해결하는 것을 돕기 위해 환경부에 의해 설치된 행정부서는 지난해 총 7,021건의 불평사항을 접수했다. **6** 이웃사람들이 상호 대화와 양보를 통해 소음에 대한 불화를 해결하는 것이 이상적이다. 만약 어느 누구든 아파트빌딩 맨 아래층 아니면 맨 위층에 살지 않는다면, 그는 위층으로부터의 소음에 고통스럽고 동시에 아래층 사람을 고통스럽게 하는 소음을 내게 되는 것은 어쩔 수 없다. [7] 그러나 이웃을 서로 모르는 생활환경에서 서로 의사소통 없는 아파트 주민들에게 원활하고도 합리적으로 문제를 해결하기를 기대하는 것은 지나치다. 다툼을 복잡하게 하는 것은 이웃 사이의 소음을 규제하고 소음으로 인한 고통을 보상해주는 분명하고도 효과적인 규칙의 결핍이다. [8] 자동차와 건설 현장으로부터 나오는 소음과 진동은 규제대책을 따르고 있는 반면에 이웃집으로부터 나오는 소음을 억제하는 구체적 법적 근거가 없다. 환경적 다툼 조정 절차는 지나친 소음 수준을 가리킨다. 그러나 이 소음 수준은 높기 때문에 실제로 지금까지 있어온 보상은 없었다. 영국, 독일, 미국 및 그 외 다른 나라에서는 이웃을 고통스럽게 하는 소음을 유발시키는 거주인이 상당한 벌금에 직면하거나 혹은 심지어는 추방까지 직면해야 하는 것이 당연하게 고려되고 있다. [9] 뒤 늦은 움직임으로 국토부는 아파트 빌딩의 층간 소음전달을 줄이기 위한 보다 엄한 건물규제책을 이번 주 발표했다. 그러나 그 대책은, 그 효과가 확실하다면, 위반 시 특정 벌금 부과 조항으로 보완되어질 필요가 있다. 소음 분쟁을 관리규칙으로 해결하기 위한 절차를 포함하기 위하여 전국 아파트단지를 격려하는 것도 도움이 될 수도 있다. [10] 문제로 인하여 더 비극적인 사건이 일어나지 않도록 협조적이고도 지속적인 노력이 주민, 건설회사, 관련 정부기관에 의해서 있어야 한다. [11] 한국 사람들은 또한 복합적 주거에서 안전하고 조화로운 생활을 영위할 수 있도록 자신들의 성질을 통제하는 솜씨를 더욱 발휘해야 할 필요가 있다. 한국건강보험공단에 따르면, 충동절제 문제가 있는 것으로 진단된 사람의 수가 2007년도 1,660명으로부터 2011년도 3,015명으로 증가했다. [12] 성급한 개개인과 증가하는 사회적 갈등의 결합이 분노로부터의 범죄를 증가시켰다. 경찰당국으로부터의 수치에 따르면 갑작스런 분노폭발로 살인 혹은 방화를 저지른 사람의 수가 2000년도 306명과 347명으로부터 2010년도 465명과 583명으로 각각 증가했다. [13] 가두어진 주거환경이 한국 사람들로 하여금 더욱 성마르게 만드는 요소들 중의 하나인지도 모른다. 이런 환경에서 한국인들은 자기들 이웃에 대하여 더욱 사려 깊게 하고 편의를 도모해주는 것이 요구된다.

제2절 본문의 내용흐름 파악

직접구성단위 마디(가령, 본문이 절/section)인 경우 단락 사이)의 관계를 이해하면서 진행하는 독자의 다음 절차는 무엇인가? 직접구성의 단위가 보태어져 가는 본문내용의 흐름을 파악하는 것이다. 본문내용의 흐름을 파악하는 하나의 효과적인 방법은 본문의 직접구성단위의 주제문 연속을 구성하는 것이다. 아래 (1)에서처럼 밑줄 쳐진 부분만을 연속적으로 구성하는 것이다. 가능한 적은 분량으로 처리되게 하는 것이 좋다.

(1)

1 For a long time scholars have tried to associate the Korean language to one of the major language families but have not been successful in this venture. There have been many theories proposed on the origin of Korean. <u>Based on the views as to where the Korean language first originated, two prominent views, which are called the Southern theory and the Northern theory, have been advocated by some scholars.</u> According to the Southern theory, the Korean people and language originated in the south, namely the South Pacific region. There are two versions of this theory. <u>One is that the Korean language is related to the Dravidian languages of India.</u> This view is not taken seriously by contemporary linguists, but it was strongly advocated by the British scholar Homer B. Hulbert at the end of nineteenth century. Hulbert's argument was based on the syntactic similarities of Korean and the Dravidian languages. For instance, both languages have the same syntactic characteristics: the word order subject-object-verb, postpositions instead of prepositions, no relative pronouns, modifiers in front of the head noun, copula and existential as two distinct grammatical parts of speech etc.

2 <u>The other version of the Southern theory is the view that Korean may be related to the Austronesian languages.</u> There are some linguistic as well as anthropological and archeological findings which may support this view. The linguistic features of Korean which are shared by some Polynesian languages include the phonological structure of open syllables, the honorific system, numerals and the names of various body parts. The anthropological and archeological elements shared by Koreans and the people in other regions of the South Pacific are rice cultivation, tattooing, a matrilineal family system, the myth of an egg as the birth place of royalty and other recent discoveries in paleolithic or preceramic cultures. Although this Southern theory has been brought to the attention of many linguists, it is not accepted as convincing by linguists.

3 The Northern theory is the view that Korean is related to the Altaic family. Although this view is not wholly accepted by the linguistic community, the majority of Korean linguists and some western scholars seem inclined towards believing this view. The major language branches which belong to the Altaic family are Turkic, Mongolian and Tungusic. The area in which the Altaic languages are spoken runs from the Balkans to the Kamchatka Peninsula in the North Pacific. The Northern theory stipulates that the Tungusic branch of Altaic tribesmen migrated towards the south and reached the Korean peninsula. The Tungusic languages would include two major languages: Korean and Manchu. The view that Korean is a branch of the Altaic family is supported by anthro-archeological evidence such as comb ceramics (pottery with comb-surface design), bronze-ware, dolmens, menhirs and shamanism. All these findings are similar to those found in Central Asia, Siberia and northern Manchuria. Korean is similar to the Altaic languages with respect to the absence of grammatical elements such as number, genders, articles, fusional morphology, voice, relative pronouns and conjunctions. vowel harmony and agglutination are also found in Korean as well as in the Altaic languages. Comparing the two theories, it is apparent that the Northern influence in the Korean language is more dominant than the Southern.

4 It has been discovered in recent archeological excavations that the early race called Paleosiberians lived in the Korean peninsula and Manchuria before the Altaic race migrated to these areas. The Paleosiberians, who include the Chukchi, Koryaks, Kamchadals, Ainu, Eskimos etc., were either driven away to the farther north by the newly arrived race or assimilated by the conquerors when they came to the Korean peninsula. It is believed that the migration of the new race towards the Korean peninsula took place around 4000 BC. Nothing is known about the languages of the earliest settlers. After migration, some ancient Koreans settled down in the regions of Manchuria and northern Korea while others moved farther to the south. Many small tribal states were established in the general region of

Manchuria and the Korean peninsula from the first century BC to the first century AD. The ancient Korean language is divided into two dialects: the Puyŏ language and the Han language. The Puyŏ language was spoken by the people of tribal states such as Puyŏ, Kokuryŏ, Okchŏ and Yemaek in Manchuria and northern Korea. The Han language was spoken by the people of the three Han tribal states of Mahan, Chinhan and Byŏnhan which were created in southern Korea.

5 Around the fourth century AD the small tribal states were vanquished and three kingdoms with strong central governments appeared in Manchuria and the Korean peninsula. Of these three kingdoms, the biggest kingdom, Kokuryŏ, occupied the territory of Manchuria and the northern portion of the Korean peninsula. The other two kingdoms, Paekche and Silla, established states in the southwestern and the southeastern regions of the Korean peninsula respectively. It is believed that the Kokuryŏ people spoke the Puyŏ language and the Silla people spoke the Han language; however, it is not certain what language the Paekche people spoke because the ruling class of the Paekche kingdom consisted of Puyŏ tribesmen who spoke the Puyŏ language. When the Korea peninsula was unified by Silla in the seventh century, the Han language became the dominant dialect paving the way for the emergence of a homogeneous language. The Han language finally became the sole Korean language through the two succeeding dynasties of Koryŏ(936-1392) and Chosŏn(1392-1910).

6 Since Silla's unification of the Korean peninsula in the seventh century, it appears that the language spoken in the capital has been the standard dialect. Thus, the Silla capital, Kyŏngju, dialect was the standard dialect during the unified Silla period from the seventh century to the tenth century. When Silla was succeeded by Koryŏ in the tenth century, the capital was moved from Kyŏngju, which was located in the southeastern region of the Korean peninsula, to Kaegyŏng in the central region of Korea and subsequently the dialect spoken in this new capital became the standard language in Koryo from the tenth century to the end of the fourteenth century. When the Yi (or Chosŏn) Dynasty succeeded Koryŏ at the end of the fourteenth century, the capital was established at Seoul, the present

capital of South Korea, and the language spoken in this area became the standard dialect and has continued as a standard dialect to the present time. Thus, it is obvious that the formation of the standard dialect has been dominated by political decisions. We can find this even in the twentieth century. There are officially two standard dialects existing in Korea; one is the Seoul dialect in South Korea and the other the p^hyŏng'yang dialect in North Korea. Each government has established prescriptive criteria for its own standard dialect and made separate policies on language.

7 Though the dialect distinction of one region from the other is not drastic owing to the relatively small size of the Korean peninsula, each region has its own characteristic dialects. For instance, in the Hamgyŏng dialect of northern Korea the final p. of verb bases ending in p is pronounced as [b] before suffixed morphemes starting in a vowel, while in the standard Seoul dialect this final p is pronounced as [w] before a vowel; $təp$- 'hot' is pronounced [təbə] in the Hamgyŏng dialect but [təwə] in the standard dialect. As another example, in the standard dialect palatalisation is normal but in the p^hyŏng'yang dialect palatalisation does not take place: kat^hi 'together' is pronounced as [kac^hi] in the standard dialect but as [kat^hi] in the p^hyŏng'yang dialect. Historically, both Hamgyŏng and p^hyŏng'yang dialects reflect archaic forms. That is, in the nineteenth-century Yi Dynasty language the words $təp$- and kat^hi were pronounced as they ~re pronounced in the. Hamyŏng and p^hyŏng'yang dialects; and the pronunciation of these words in the standard dialect reflects this historical change.

8 The Korean language spoken before the fifteenth century is not well known because there are not many records or documents revealing how the language was used before the fifteenth century. It was in the fifteenth century that the alphabetic script (Han'gŭl) for writing Korean was invented by King Sejong. Before the Korean script was invented, only Chinese characters were used for the purpose of writing. But Chinese characters could not depict the living language spoken by Korean people, since Chinese characters were meaning-based and the grammar of classical Chinese did not have any connection with Korean grammar. Even after

the Korean script was invented, Chinese characters were continuously used as the main means of writing until the twentieth century. In traditional Korean society, the learning and study of Chinese characters and classical Chinese were entirely monopolised by a small class of elite aristocrats. For average commoners, the time-consuming learning of Chinese characters was not only a luxury but also useless, because they were busy making a living and knowledge of Chinese characters did not help in improving their lives.

9 The use of Chinese characters imported a massive quantity of loanwords into the Korean lexicon. More than half of Korean words are Chinese-originated loanwords. Although Chinese loanwords and Korean-originated words have always coexisted, the Chinese loanwords came to dominate the original Korean words and subsequently many native Korean words completely vanished from use. A movement by people who wanted to restore native culture at the end of the nineteenth century tried to stimulate mass interest in the study of the Korean language. When the government proclaimed that the official governmental documents would be written both in Korean script and Chinese characters, the first newspapers and magazines were published in Korean script and the use of the Korean alphabet expanded. In the early twentieth century, more systematic studies on the Korean language were started and a few scholars published Korean grammar books. However, the active study of Korean grammar was discontinued owing to the Japanese colonial policy suppressing the study of Korean.

10 The study of the Korean language resumed after the end of World War II, but Korea was divided into two countries by the Big Powers. The language policies proposed and implemented by the two governments in the South and the North were different from each other. While both the Korean alphabet and Chinese characters were used in the South, only the Korean alphabet was used in the North. In the North the policy on the use of Chinese characters has been firm; that is, no instruction in Chinese characters has been given to students and Chinese characters are not used in newspapers, magazines or books. This policy has never been changed in the North. Contrary to this, in the South the policy on the instruction of Chinese characters has been inconsistent; whenever a new regime has come to power, both proponents and opponents of the use of Chinese characters have tried to persuade the government to adopt their views. Though the instruction of Chinese characters was abolished a couple of times by the government in the past, this abolition never lasted more than a few years. At ,he present lime in the South, the government has adopted a policy which forces students in secondary schools to learn 1,800 basic Chinese characters.

11 The South and the North also have different policies on the so-called 'purification' of Korean. The purification of Korean means the sole use of native Korean words in everyday life by discontinuing the use of foreign-originated words, The main targets of this campaign are Sino-Korean words. In the North, the government has been actively involved in this campaign, mobilizing newspaper and magazines to spread the newly translated or discovered pure Korean words to a wide audience of readers. In the South, some interested scholars and language study organizations have tried to advocated the purification of Korean through the media and academic journal, but the government has never officially participated in this kind of involvement. It will be interesting to see what course each of the two governments will take in future with respect to language policy.

어휘리콜　•venture: 모험, 모험적 사업; •originate: 기원하다; •advocate: 옹호하다; •anthropological: 인구학적; •archeological: 고고학적; •open syllables: 개방음절; •honorific system: 경어체계; •tattooing: 북치기; •matrilineal family system: 모계가족체계; •paleolithic: 구석기 시대의; •preceramic: 요업(도기) 이전의; •linguistic community: 언어학계; •stipulate: 규정하다; •anthro-archeological: 인류-고고학적; •comb: (산마루의) 볏; •bronze-ware: 청동제품; •dolmens: 고인돌; •menhirs: 선돌; •shamanism: 샤머니즘; •Manchuria: 만주; •fusional: morphology: 용해(연합) 형태론; •agglutination: 교착어형; •excavation:발굴; •Paleosiberian: 구석기시베리아인; •Chukchi: 추치인; •Koryaks: 코랴스인; •Kamchadals: 캄차카인; •Ainu: 아이누인; •Eskimos: 에스키모인; •migration: 이민; •small tribal state: 소 종족국가; •Puyŏ: 부여; •Kokuryŏ: 고려; •Okchŏ: 옥저; •Yemaek: 예맥; •vanquish: 이기다, 정복하다; •Dynasty: 왕조; •palatalisation: 구개음화; •Korean script: 한글자체; •monopolise: 독점하다; •elite aristocrat: 엘리트 귀족; •mobilize: 발휘하다, 유통시키다.

내용흐름　11개의 단락으로 구성되어 있는 본문에서 각 단락의 주제문을 확인하면 밑줄로 표시된 것과 같다. 이 밑줄로 표시된 주제문들의 연속이 내용의 흐름이다.

전문국역 **1** 오랫동안 학자들은 한국어를 대 어족 중의 한 어족에 관련시키려고 노력해 왔지만 이 모험적 노력에서 성공하지 못했다. 한국어의 기원에 관해 제안된 여러 이론이 있어왔다. 한국어가 처음 어디에서 기원했는가에 관한 견해에 기초한 두드러진 두 견해, 남방이론과 북방이론이라고 불리는 이론이 여러 학자들에 의하여 옹호되어 왔다. 남방이론에 따르면, 한국민족과 한국어는 남쪽, 즉 남태평양에서 기원했다. 이 남방이론에는 2 버전(견해)이 있다. 한 버전은 한국어가 인도의 드라비다 사람의 언어들과 관련이 있다. 이 견해는 오늘날 언어학자들에 의해서는 진지하게 받아들이지 않고 있지만, 17세기 말 영국 학자 Homer B. Hulbert에 의해 강력하게 옹호되었다. Hulbert의 주장은 한국어와 드라비다 언어들과의 통사적 유사성에 기초했다. 예를 들면, 두 언어는 다음과 같은 통사적 특징을 지니고 있다: 주어-목적어-동사의 어순, 전치사 대신 후치사 사용, 관계대명사 없음, 머리어 명사 앞에 수식어 사용, 뚜렷이 구별되는 문법적 품사로서의 계사와 존재사 등. **2** 남방이론의 나머지 한 버전은 오스트로네시아 언어들에 관련되어 있을 수 있다는 견해이다. 이 견해를 지지하는 인류학적 및 고고학적 발견내용 뿐만 아니라 언어학적 발견내용이 좀 있다. 일부 폴리네시아 언어들과 공유하는 한국어의 언어적 특징에는 개음절의 음운론적 구조, 경어체계, 수 및 신체부위의 여러 이름들이 포함된다. 한국 사람들과 남태평양 다른 지역 민족들과 공유하는 인류학적 및 고고학적 요소는 벼 재배, 북치기, 모계가족제도, 왕족 출생으로서의 알 신화, 그리고 구석기시대 혹은 요업시대 문화의 최근 발견들이다. 비록 남방이론이 많은 언어학자들의 관심을 끌었지만, 언어학자들에 의하여 확신적인 이론으로는 받아들여지지 않는다. **3** 북방이론은 한국어가 알타이어족과 관련이 있다는 견해이다. 비록 이 견해가 언어학계에서 전적으로는 받아들여지지 못하지만, 한국 언어학자 대다수와 일부 서방 학자들은 이 견해를 믿는 쪽으로 기울고 있는 것 같다. 알타이 어족에 속하는 주요 어계는 튀르크어계, 몽골리어계, 퉁구스어계이다. 알타이 어족의 언어들이 사용되는 지역은 발칸반도에서 북태평양 캄자카 반도에 이르는 지역이다. 북방이론은 알타이 종족의 퉁구스어계가 남쪽으로 이동해서 한 반도에 이르렀다고 규정한다. 퉁구스어계 언어에는 주요 두 언어, 즉 한국어와 만주어를 포함할 것이다. 한국어가 알타이 어족의 한 어계이라는 견해는 볏 도자기(볏-표면 디자인이 있는 도자기), 청동 제품, 고인돌, 선돌 및 샤머니즘과 같은 인류-고고학적 증거의 지지를 받는다. 이 모든 증거들은 중앙아시아, 시베리아, 그리고 북 만주에서 발견된 것들과 유사하다. 한국어는 수(number), 성(gender), 관사(article), 융합 형태(fusional morphology), 태(voice), 관계대명사(relative pronoun), 접속사(conjunction)와 같은 문법적 요소가 없다는 점에서 알타이 언어들과 유사하다. 모음조화와 교착어형(agglutination)이 또한 알타이어에서 뿐만 아니라 한국어에서 발견된다. 두 이론을 비교하면, 분명한 것은 한국어에 미친 북방의 영향이 남방의 영향보다 더 지배적이다. **4** 최근 고고학적 발굴에서 발견된 바에 따르면, 구석기시베리아인이라고 불리는 초기 종족은 알타이 종족이 한반도와 만주에 이주하기 이전에 이들 지역에서 살았다. 구석기시베리아인들에는 추키인, 고략인, 캄자달인, 아이누인 등이 포함되는데, 이 구석기시베리아인들은 새로 침입해 온 종족에 의해서 보다 먼 북쪽으로 쫓겨나거나 아니면 한반도로 침입해 종족에 동화되었다. 새로운 종족의 한반도 방향 이민은 B.C. 4,000년경에 일어났다고 믿어지고 있다. 최초 정착자들의 언어에 관해서는 알려진 것이 아무것도 없다. 이민이후, 일부 고대 한족은 만주와 북한지역에 정착했고, 다른 일부는 남쪽으로 더 이동했다. 많은 작은 종족의 국가가 BC 1세기로 부터 AD 1세기까지 만주와 한반도에 확립되었다. 고대

한국어는 두 방언으로 나누어졌는데, 부여 언어와 한 언어이다. 부여 언어는 만주와 북한 지역의 부여, 고구려, 옥저, 그리고 예맥과 같은 부족 국가의 종족에 의해 사용되었다. 한 언어는 남한에서 생성된 마한, 진한, 변한의 세 종족 국가에서 사용되었다. **5** AD 4세기경, 소국가들이 경쟁에서 지고 강력한 중앙정부를 가진 세 왕국이 만주와 한반도에 나타났다. 이 세 왕국 중에서 가장 큰 왕국이 고구려인데 만주 영토와 한반도 북반부를 차지했다. 나머지 두 왕국은 백제와 신라인데, 한반도 서남지역과 동남지역에서 각각 국가를 세웠다. 고구려 민족은 부여 언어를 사용하고 신라 민족은 한 언어를 사용한 것으로 믿어진다. 그러나 백제 민족은 어떤 언어를 사용했는지 확인되지 않는데, 그것은 백제 왕국의 지배 계급이 부여 언어를 사용하는 부여 종족으로 구성되어 있었기 때문이다. 한반도가 7세기에 신라에 의해 통일되었을 때, 한 언어가 지배언어가 되어 동질적 언어의 출현을 향한 길로 접어들었다. 한 언어는 마침내 한국의 언어가 되어 후속 고려와 조선 왕조의 언어로 이어졌다. **6** 7세기에 한반도의 통일이 있은 후, 수도에서 사용된 언어가 표준방언이 되었던 것으로 보인다. 그러므로 신라의 수도 경주의 방언이 7세기부터 10세기까지 통일신라시대의 표준방언이었다. 신라가 10세기에 고려로 넘어갈 때 수도가 한반도 동남 지방에 위치한 경주로부터 한국의 중앙지점인 개성으로 이동했고, 따라서 이 새 수도에서 사용된 방언이 10세기부터 14세기 말까지 고려의 표준방언이 되었다. 14세기 말 이씨(즉 조선) 왕조가 고려를 이어받게 되었을 때 수도는 현재 남한의 수도인 서울에서 확립되었고, 이 지역에서 사용되는 방언이 표준방언이 되었고 현재까지 표준방언으로 계속되고 있다. 그러므로 표준방언의 형성이 정치적 결정에 의해 지배를 받았다는 것은 분명하다. 우리는 이것을 20세기에서 발견하게 된다. 공식적으로는 한반도에 두 개의 표준방언이 현존하고 있다. 하나는 남한의 서울방언이고 다른 하나는 북한의 평양방언이다. 각 정부는 자신의 표준방언에 대하여 기술적 기준을 만들어 놓고 있으며 독립된 언어정책을 펼치고 있다. **7** 비록 두 지역의 방언 차이가 한반도의 비교적 작은 크기이기 때문에 극적이지는 않지만, 각 정권이 그 나름의 특징적 방언을 가지고 있다. 예를 들면, 북한의 함경방언에서는 p로 끝나는 동사어근의 끝 p는 모음으로 시작하는 접미사형태소 앞에서 [b]로 발음된다. 반면에 서울방언에서는 이 끝 음 p는 모음 앞에서 [w]로 발음된다. $təp$-'hot'는 함경방언에서는 [təbə]로 발음되지만 서울방언에서는 [təwə]로 발음된다. 또 한 예로, 표준방언에서는 구개음화가 정상이지만 평양방언에서는 구개음화가 일어나지 않는다. kat^hi 'together'는 표준방언에서 [kac^hi]로 발음되지만 평양방언에서는 [kat^hi]로 발음된다. 역사적으로, 함경방언과 평양방언은 고어형태를 반영한다. 즉 19세기 이씨 왕조 언어에서 $təp$-와 kat^hi는 지금 함경방언과 평양방언에서 발음되는 것처럼 발음되었고, 이 단어들의 표준방언에서의 발음은 역사적으로 변했음을 반영해준다. **8** 15세기 이전에 사용한 한국어는 잘 알려져 있지 않는데, 그 이유는 15세기 이전에 사용된 기록이나 문헌이 많이 남아 있지 않기 때문이다. 한국어 쓰기를 위한 알파벳(Han'gŭl)이 세종에 의하여 창제된 것은 15세기에 와서다. 한국어 문자가 발명되기 이전에는, 중국어 글자만이 쓰기목적으로 사용되었다. 그러나 중국어 글자는 한국민족에 의해서 사용되는 생생한 언어를 나타낼 수 없었다. 왜냐하면 중국어 글자는 의미에 기초하고 있으며, 고전 중국어의 문법이 한국어 문법하고 어떤 연결을 갖지 못했기 때문이다. 한국어 문자가 발명된 이후조차도 중국어 글자가 계속해서 20세기 까지 주요 쓰기수단으로 사용되었다. 전통적인 한국 사회에서는 중국어 글자와 고전 중국어의 학습과 연구는 전적으로 엘리트 귀족사회에 의해서 독점되었다. 보통의 사람들에는 중국어 글자의 시간이 많이 들어가는 학습이 사치일 뿐만 아니라 쓸모가 없었다. 왜냐하면 그 보통사람들은 생계를 유지하는데 바빴으며, 중국어 글자에 대한 지식은 그들의 생활을 향상시키는데 도움이 되지 못했다. ⑨ 중국어 글자의 사용은 대량의 어휘를 한국어 어휘에 차용하게 되었다. 한국어 어휘의 절반 이상이 중국어에 기원하는 차용어이다. 비록 중국어 차용어와 한국어에 기원하는 어휘들이 항상 공존하지만, 중국어 차용어가 한국어 기원 어휘를 지배하게 되었고 따라서 많은 본래의 한국어 어휘들이 완전히 사용되지 않게 되었다. 19세기 말 순수 한국어를 복원시키고 싶어 하는 한국민의 운동이 한국어 연구에 많은 관심을 자극시키려고 했다. 한국정부가 공식적인 정부 문서는 한국어 문자와 중국어 두 문자로 써야야 한다고 선언을 했을 때, 첫 신문과 잡지는 한국어로 발행되었고 한국어 철자의 사용이 확대되었다. 20세기 초에, 한국어에 대한 많은 체계적인 연구가 시작되었고 일부 학자들은 한국어 문법책을 발행했다. 그러나 적극적인 한국어문법의 연구는 한국어 연구를 압박하는 일본 식민 정책 때문에 지속되지 못했다. ⑩ 한국어 연구는 제2차 세계대전 말 이후 회복되었다. 그러나 한국은 강대국들에 의해서 둘로 나누어졌다. 남과 북의 정권에 의해서 제안되고 시행되는 언어정책은 서로 달랐다. 한국어 문자와 중국어 문자가 남한에서는 사용되었지만, 북한에서는 한국어 문자만 사용되었다. 북한에서는 중국어 글자에 대한 정책이 굳어 있어 왔다. 즉 중국어 글자에 대한 교육이 학생들에게 이루어지지 않았고 중국어 글자가 신문, 잡지, 혹은 책에 사용되지 않았다. 이 정책은 지금까지 북한에서는 변하지 않았다. 이와는 반대로 남한에서는 중국어에 대한 교육정책이 일관되지는 않았다. 새로운 정권이 들어설 때는 언제나, 중국어 글자의 사용에 관한 찬성론자와 반대론자가 그들의 입장을 채용해주기를 설득하려고 했다. 비록 중국어 글자의 교육이 과거 두 정부에서 폐지되기는 했지만, 이 폐지는 2-3년 이상은 지속되지 않았다. 현재 남한에서 정부는 중등학교 학생들에게 1,800 한자를 배우도록 강요하는 정책을 채용하고 있다. ⑪ 남한과 북한은 둘 다 소위 한국어의 '순수화'에 관한 다른 정책을 갖고 있다. 한국어의 순수화는 일상생활에서 외래어 기원의 어휘의 사용을 끊고 순수 한국어 어휘만의 사용을 의미한다. 이 운동의 주요 목표는 중국어-한국어 어휘이다. 북한에서는 정부가 적극적으로 이 운동에 관여하고, 신문과 잡지로 하여금 새로이 번역되거나 발견된 순수 한국어 어휘가 폭 넓은 독자층으로 널리 퍼지게 해왔다. 남한에서는 일부 관심 있는 학자들과 언어연구 기관들이 미디어 및 학술 저널지를 통한 한국어 순수화를 옹호해 왔지만, 정부는 공식적으로는 이런 류의 운동에 참여하지 않았다. 두 정부 각각이 언어정책과 관점에서 향후 취할 방향이 무엇인지 지켜보는 것은 흥미 있을 것이다.

(2) **KINDS OF DISCIPLINE**

<u>1</u> A child, in growing up, may meet and learn from three different kinds of disciplines. The first and most important is what we might call the Discipline of Nature or of Reality. When he is trying to do something real, if he does the wrong thing or doesn't do the right one, he doesn't get the result he wants. If he doesn't

pile one block right on top of another, or tries to build on a slanting surface, his tower falls down. If he hits the wrong key, he hears the wrong note. If he doesn't hit the nail squarely on the head, it bends, and he has to pull it out and start with another. If he doesn't measure properly what he is trying to build, it won't open, close, fit, stand up, fly, float, whistle, or do whatever he wants it to do. If he closes his eyes when he swings, he doesn't hit the ball. A child meets this kind of discipline every time he tries to *do* something, which is why it is so important in school to give children more chances to do things, instead of just reading or listening to someone talk (or pretending to). This discipline is a great teacher. The learner never has to wait long for his answer; it usually comes quickly, often instantly. Also it is clear, and very often points toward the needed correction; from what happened he can not only see that what he did was wrong, but also why, and what he needs to do instead. Finally, and most important, the giver of the answer, call it Nature, is impersonal, impartial, and indifferent. She does not give opinion, or make judgments; she cannot be wheedled, bullied, or fooled; she does not get angry or disappointed; she does not praise or blame; she does not remember past failures or hold grudges; with her one always gets a fresh start, this time is the one that counts.

2 The next discipline we might call the Discipline of Culture, of Society, of What People Really Do. Man is a social, a cultural animal. Children sense around them this culture, this network of agreements, customs, habits, and rules binding the adults together. They want to understand it and be a part of it. They watch very carefully what people around them are doing and want to do the same. They want to do right, unless they become convinced they can't do right. Thus children rarely misbehave seriously in church, but sit as quietly as they can. The example of all those grownups is contagious. Some mysterious ritual is going on, and children, who like rituals, want to be part of it. In the same way, the little children that I see at concerts or operas, though they may fidget a little, or perhaps take a nap now and then, rarely make any disturbance. With all those grownups sitting there, neither moving nor talking, it is the most natural thing in the world to imitate them. Children who live among adults who are habitually courteous to each other, and to them, will soon learn to be courteous. Children who live surrounded by people who speak a certain way will speak that way, however much we may try to tell them that speaking that way is bad or wrong.

3 The third discipline is the one most people mean when they speak of discipline-the Discipline of Superior Force, of sergeant to private, of "you do what I tell you or I'll make you wish you had." There is bound to be some of this in a child's life. Living as we do surrounded by things that can hurt children, or that children can hurt, we cannot avoid it. We can't afford to let a small child find out from experience the danger of playing in a busy street, or of fooling with the pots on the top of a stove, or of eating up the pills in the medicine cabinet. So, along with other precautions, we say to him, "Don't play in the street, or touch things on the stove, or go into the medicine cabinet, or I'll punish you." Between him and the danger too great for him to imagine we put a lesser danger, but one he can imagine and maybe therefore want to avoid. He can have no idea of what it would be like to be hit by a car, but he can imagine being shouted at, or spanked, or sent to his room. He avoids these substitutes for the greater danger until he can understand it and avoid it for its own sake. But we ought to use this discipline only when it is necessary to protect the life, health, safety, or well-being of people or other living creatures, or to prevent destruction of things that people care about. We ought not to assume too long, as we usually do, that a child cannot understand the real nature of the danger from which we want to protect him. The sooner he avoids the danger, not to escape our punishment, but as a matter of good sense, the better. He can learn that faster than we think. In Mexico, for example, where people drive their cars with a good deal of spirit, I saw many children no older than five or four walking unattended on the streets. They understood about cars, they knew what to do. A child whose life is full of the threat and fear of punishment is locked into babyhood. There is no way for him to grow up, to learn to take responsibility for his life and acts. Most important of all, we should not assume that having to yield to the threat of our superior force is good for the child's character. It is never good for *anyone's* character. To bow to superior force makes us feel importantly and cowardly for not having had the strength or courage to resist. Worse, it makes us resentful and vengeful. We can hardly wait to make someone pay for our humiliation, yield to us as we were once made to yield. No, if we cannot always avoiding using the Discipline of Superior Force, we should at least use it as seldom as we can.

4 There are places where all three disciplines overlap. Any very demanding human activity combines in it the disciplines of Superior Force, of Culture, and of Nature. The novice will be told, "Do it this way, never mind asking why, just do it that way, that is the way we always do it." But it probably *is* just the way they always do it, and usually for the very good reason that it is a way that has been found to work. Think, for example, of ballet training. The student in a class is told to do this exercise, or that; to stand so; to do this or that with his head, arms, shoulders, abdomen, hips, legs, feet. He is constantly corrected. There is no argument. But behind these seemingly autocratic demands by the teacher lie many decades of custom and tradition, and behind that, the necessities of dancing itself. You cannot make the moves of classical ballet unless over many years you have acquired, and renewed every day, the needed strength and suppleness in scores of muscles and joints. Nor can you do the difficult motions, making them look easy, unless you have learned hundreds of easier ones first. Dance teachers may not always agree on all the details of teaching these strengths and skills. But no novice could learn them all by himself. You could not go for a night or two to watch the ballet and then, without any other knowledge at all, teach yourself how to do it. In the same way, you would be unlikely to learn any complicated and difficult human activity without drawing heavily on the experience of those who know it better. But the point is that the authority of these experts or teachers stems from, grows out of their greater competence and experience, the fact that what they do *works*, not the fact that they happen to be the teacher and as such have the power to kick a student out of the class. And the further point is that children are always and everywhere attracted to that competence, and ready and eager to submit themselves to a discipline that grows out of it. We hear constantly that children will never do anything unless compelled to by bribes or threats. But in their private lives, or in extracurricular activities in school, in sports, music, drama, art, running a newspaper, and so on, they often submit themselves willingly and wholeheartedly to very intense disciplines, simply because they want to learn to do a given thing well. Our Little-Napoleon football coaches, of whom we have too many and hear far too much, blind us to the fact that millions of children work hard every year getting better at sports and games without coaches barking and yelling at them.

(John Halt(2001), in ed Gerald Levin, *Prose Models*, 135-138)

어휘리콜 •discipline: 학습, 훈련; •slant: 기울다; •squarely: 정면으로; •bend: 굽다, 휘다; •whistle: 휘 바람을 내다; •swing: 겨누어 때리다; •pretend to: ~인체 하다; •point toward: ~을 향하다; •impersonal: 비인간적인, 냉정한; •impartial: 냉정한; •indifferent: 공평한; •wheedle: 속다, 속이다; •bully: 협박하다; •grudge: 악의; •convince: 국한하다, 한정하다; •contagious: 전염성의; •fidget: 초조해하다; •disturbance: 소란; •sergeant: 하사관; •precaution: 사전주의; •spank: 찰싹 때리다; •unattended: 집중하지 않은; •resentful: 화를 잘 내는; •vengeful: 복수심에 불타는; •humiliation: 체면손상; •novice: 초심자; •abdomen: 복부; •autocratic: 전제적인; •suppleness: 유연성.

내용흐름 4개의 단락으로 구성되어 있는 본문에서 각 단락의 주제문을 확인하면 밑줄로 표시된 것과 같다. 이 밑줄로 표시된 주제문들의 연속이 내용의 흐름이다.

전문국역 학습 분야의 종류 **1** 어린이는 자라나면서 세 가지 다른 종류의 학습 분야를 만나며 그들로부터 배우게 된다. 그 첫째이면서 가장 중요한 학습 분야는 소위 말하는 자연 분야, 즉 실제 분야이다. 어린이가 실제의 무엇을 하려고 할 때, 만약 틀린 것을 한다든지 혹은 옳은 것을 해 내지 못한다면, 원하는 결과를 얻지 못한다. 만약 어린이가 다른 블록 위에 한 블록을 바르게 쌓아올리지 못하거나 혹은 경사진 표면 위에 올리려고 한다면, 그의 탑은 넘어진다. 만약 어린이가 틀린 키를 꽂으면 틀린 말을 듣게 된다. 만약 어린이가 못 머리 부분을 정면으로 때리지 않으면 그 못은 휘어지며, 그러면 어린이는 그 휘어진 못을 뽑고 다른 못으로 다시 시작해야 한다. 만약 어린이가 만들려고 하는 것을 정확하게 재지 않으면, 자기가 원하는 그 것이 기능해주기를 바라는 대로 열려지지 않거나, 닫혀 지지 않거나, 꼭 맞지 않거나, 바로 서지 않거나, 날지 않거나, 물 위에 뜨지 않거나, 소리가 나지 않거나, 혹은 작동을 하지 않을 것이다. 만약 어린이가 공을 강타하려고 할 때 자기의 눈을 감는다면, 어린이는 그 공을 때리지 못한다. 어린이는 자신이 무언가를 하려고 하는 때는 매번 이런 학습 분야를 만나며, 이점이 학교에서 어린이들에게 단지 읽게만 하거나 누군가가 말하는 것을 단지 듣게만 하는 것 (혹은 ~인체 하는 것)보다는 어린이로 하여금 무언가를 하도록 노력하게 하는 것이 매우 중요한 이유이다. 이런 학습 분야가 훌륭한 교사이다. 학습자는 결코 해답을 오래시간 기다리고만 있어서는 안 된다. 해답은 대개 빨리 오고, 종종 즉시 온다. 또한 그 해답은 분명하며, 매우 자주 필요한 수정을 요구한다. 과거에 일어났던 것으로부터 어린이는 자기가 행한 것이 틀렸음을 볼 수 있을 뿐만 아니라, 또한 대신에 자기가 해야 할 이유와 할 필요가 있는 것을 알게 될 수 있다. 마지막으로, 그리고 매우 중요한 것은 대답을 주는 자는, 그것은 자연(Nature)인데, 냉정하고, 공정하며, 공평하다. 자연은 견해를 주지 않고, 판단을 하지 않는다. 자연은 그럴듯한 말로 속거나, 협박당하거나, 혹은 놀림을 당하지 않는다. 자연은 화를 내거나 실망하지 않는다. 자연은 칭찬하거나 나무라지 않는다. 자연은 과거의 실수를 기억하거나 악의를 가지지 않는다. 자연에서 사람은 항상 새로운 시작을 얻으며, 이번이 바로 중요한 때이다.

2 다음 학습 분야는 소위 말해 문화 분야, 사회 분야, 사람들이 실제로 행하는 것의 분야들이다. 인간은 사회적인 동물, 문화적인 동물이다. 어린이는 자기 주위로부터 이 문화를 감지하고, 이 합의의 망을 감지하고, 관습, 습관, 그리고 어른들을 함께 결속시키는 규칙을 감지한다. 어린이들은 그 분야를 이해하고 싶어 하고, 그 분야의 일부이고 싶어 한다. 어린이들은 자기들 주위에 있는 사람들이 하고 있는 것을 매우 주의 깊게 관찰하고, 동일한 것을 하고 싶어 한다. 어린이들은 자기가 옳게 할 수 없다는 것에 국한하지 않는다면, 옳게 하고 싶어 한다. 그러므로 어린이들은 교회에서 좀처럼 버릇없이 굴지 않고, 가능한 한 조용히 자리에 앉는다. 성인들의 한 전형은 전염성이다. 어떤 신비스러운 의식이 진행되고, 그러면 의식을 좋아하는 어린이들은 그 의식의 일부가 되고 싶어 한다. 마찬가지로 필자가 콘서트나 오페라에서 보는 꼬마 어린이들은, 비록 조금 초조해하거나 가끔 졸기는 하지만, 불안해하지는 않는다. 움직이지도 않고 떠들지도 않으면서, 그기에 앉아 있는 모든 어른들과 함께, 어른들을 모방하는 것은 세계에서 가장 자연스러운 것이다. 습관적으로 어른들 서로서로 예의바른, 그리고 어린이에게도 예의바른 어른들 속에서 살고 있는 어린이들은 곧 예의바르게 되는 것을 배운다. 어떤 발화 방식으로 말하는 어른들에 둘러싸여 사는 어린이들은, 그런 식으로 말하는 것은 나쁘다 혹은 틀렸다고 그들에게 아무리 말을 해도, 그런 식으로 말을 하게 된다.

3 셋째 학습 분야는 대부분의 사람들이 학습 분야에 대해 이야기할 때 의미하는 그 분야 - 상위 힘, 사병에 대한 하사관, "내가 너에게 말하는 것을 너가 이행해야 하는 분야 혹은 너가 바라도록 내가 해주는 분야"이다. 어린이 생활에서도 이 어떤 힘의 분야가 꼭 있다. 어린이들에게 상처 줄 수 있는 것들, 혹은 어린이들이 상처 줄 수 있는 것들에 에워싸여 우리가 살아가는 우리는 그것을 피할 수는 없다. 우리는 복잡한 길거리에서 하는 놀이의 위험을, 혹은 스토브 위 항아리에 대해서 바보짓을 하는 위험을, 혹은 가정상비약 통에 있는 알약을 먹어버리는 위험을 어린아이가 경험으로부터 발견하도록 할 여유가 없다. 그러므로 다른 주의사항을 따라, 우리는 어린이에게 '거리에서 놀지 마라, 스토브 위에 있는 것 손대지 마라, 혹은 약통 케비넷으로 가지마라, 그렇지 않으면 혼내줄 거야'라고 말한다. 어린이와 그 어린이가 상상하기에 너무 큰 위험 사이에, 우리 어른은 보다 작은 위험을 놓기는 하지만, 위험을 어린이는 상상을 하고 아마 그 위험을 피하고 싶어 할 것이다. 어린이는 자동차에 부딪히는 것 같은 것이 어떤 것인지에 대해 모른다. 그러나 어린이는 소리 지르게 될 것을 상상하거나, 혹은 찰싹 얻어맞거나, 자기 방으로 보내질 것으로 상상한다. 어린이는 보다 큰 위험을 피하기 위해 다른 것을 대신 생각하며, 마침내 어린이는 그 본래의 위험을 이해하게 되고 그것을

피하게 된다. 그러나 우리는 사람들 혹은 살아있는 다른 피조물의 생활, 건강, 안전을 보호할 필요가 있을 때, 혹은 사람들이 돌 보아야할 것들에 대한 파괴현상을 막아야 할 때만 이 학습 분야를 사용해야 한다. 우리가 보호해 주기를 바라는 그 위험의 실제 본질을 어린이가 이해하지 못한다고 해서, 우리가 보통 그러는 것처럼, 우리는 그 이해 못함을 너무 오래 떠맡고 있어서는 안 된다. 우리 어른의 벌을 피하기 위해서가 아니라 상식의 문제로서 어린이는 위험을 보다 빨리 피하면 피할수록 더 좋다. 어린이는 그것을 우리가 생각하는 것보다 더 빨리 학습한다. 예를 들면, 사람들이 승용차를 집중하여 운전하고 있는 멕시코에서 필자는 다섯 혹은 여섯 살도 안 된 많은 어린이들이 길거리를 보호자도 없이 걷고 있는 것을 보았다. 그 어린이들은 승용차에 대해 이해를 하고 있었고, 어떻게 해야 하는지 알고 있었다. 자기 생활이 처벌의 위협이나 공포로 가득 차 있는 어린이는 맘마보이 안에 갇혀있다. 그 어린이를 성장하게 하거나, 자기의 생활과 행동에 대해 책임지는 것을 배우게 하는 방법이 없다. 모든 것 중에서도 가장 중요한 것은 상위 힘의 위협에 굴복해야 하는 것이 어린이 인격에 좋은 것이라고 우리가 가정해서는 안 된다. 그것은 누구의 인격에도 결코 좋지 않다. 상위 힘에 대하여 인사하는 것은 그 힘을 가지지 못했었기 때문에, 혹은 저항할 용기가 없기 때문에 우리로 하여금 중요하게 그리고 비급하게 느끼게 한다. 더욱 나쁜 것은, 그것은 우리로 하여금 후회스럽게 하고 복수심을 가지게 한다. 우리는 누군가가 우리의 체면손상에 대해 보상해 주기를, 혹은 우리가 한때 굴복하게 되었던 대로 우리에게 굴복하기를 거의 기다릴 수 없다. 아니다, 만약 우리가 상위 힘의 영역 이용을 피할 수 없다면, 우리는 적어도 그것을 가능한 한 드물게라도 이용해야 한다.

4 앞에 말한 세 학습 분야가 겹치는 곳들이 있다. 아주 엄격한 인간의 활동은 상위 힘의 분야, 문화의 분야, 그리고 자연의 분야를 그것 안에 결합시킨다. 이 새 것은 "그것을 이런 방식으로 해라, 이유 묻는 것을 꺼려하지 말라, 그것은 그런 식으로 하라, 그것이 우리가 항상 그렇게 하는 방식이다."라고 말해진다. 그러나 그것은 아마도 사람들이 항상 그렇게 하는 바로 그 방식이고, 그리고 그것이 작용하는 것으로 발견되어온 방식인 바로 그 정당한 이유 때문이다. 예를 들면, 발레 연습을 생각해보라. 수업을 받는 학생은 이렇게 하라, 혹은 저렇게 하라, 그렇게 서기, 머리, 팔, 어깨, 복부, 엉덩이, 다리, 발을 이렇게 혹은 저렇게 하라는 말을 듣는다. 학생은 계속 교정이 된다. 반론이 없다. 그러나 선생님의 독제적인 요구 이면에 수십 년의 관습과 전통이 있고, 그것 뒤에 댄싱 자체의 필요가 있다. 여러분은 만약 수년에 걸쳐 근육과 관절부위에서 필요한 힘과 유연함을 매일매일 가지게 되고, 새롭게 해 오지 않았었다면, 고전 발레의 동작을 할 필요가 없다. 그리고 또한 만약 여러분이 먼저 보다 쉬운 동작을 수백 번 학습하지 않았다면, 여러분은 어려운 동작을 할 수 없고, 어려운 동작을 쉽게 보이려고 할 필요도 없다. 댄스교사는 이 힘과 기술을 가르치는 세세한 내용에 대해서는 항상 동의하는 것이 아닐 수도 있다. 그러나 신참자는 자기 혼자서 그 모든 것들을 배울 수는 없다. 여러분은 발레를 보기 위하여 한 두 밤만 보고, 그 다음에 어떤 다른 지식도 없이 혼자 발레 하는 것을 연습할 수 없다. 마찬가지로, 여러분은 보다 더 잘 아는 사람의 경험에 대해 잘 얻어내지 않고는 복잡하고도 어려운 인간 활동에 대하여 배울 수 있을 것 같지가 않다. 그러나 요점은 이런 것이다: 이런 전문가 혹은 교사의 권위는 보다 큰 능력과 경험에서 유래하고 성장한다는 것이다. 요지는 그들이 행하는 것이 기능을 한다는 것이지, 그들이 어쩌다 우연히 교사가 되었다는 사실이 아니고, 그리고 또한 그들이 학생을 교실 밖으로 아낼

> 힘을 가졌다는 사실이 아니다. 그리고 한 걸음 더 나아가 요지는 이렇다: 어린이들은 항상 그리고 어떤 곳에서나 그런 능력에 매혹된다는 것이고, 그리고 준비되어 있고 열심히 그 능력으로부터 성장하는 분야를 따른다는 것이다. 어린이들은 유혹물이나 위협에 강요당하지 않는다면 결코 어떤 것도 하지 않는다는 것을 우리는 끊임없이 듣고 있다. 그러나 사적인 생활에서, 혹은 학교, 스포츠, 음악, 드라마, 예술, 신문읽기 등 교과 외 어린이들의 활동에서, 그들은 주어진 것을 잘 하기 위해서 배우고 싶어 하기 때문에, 종종 스스로 복종하여 집중하는 분야에 기꺼이 전심으로 임한다. 우리가 너무 많이 보아왔고, 너무 많은 말을 들어왔던 우리의 Little-Napoleon 축구 감독들 때문에, 우리는 수백만의 어린이들이 자기들에게 꾸지람하고 고함치는 감독이 없는데도, 스포츠와 게임에서 더 좋은 성적을 내기 위하여 매년 열심히 한다는 사실을 보지 못하고 있다.

제3절 본문의 주제 확인

진행하는 독해가 본문의 끝에 이르면 문장이나 단락 차원에서와 마찬가지로 본문 전체 차원의 주제(즉 주제문장)를 확인해야 한다. 확인하는 방법은 문장이나 단락에서와 본질적으로 동일하다. 확인 방법은 하위 직접구성단위 주제문들로 구성되는 내용흐름을 일반화하는 것이다. 이 내용흐름을 일반화하는 방법은 주제문들 중에서 나머지 주제문들의 내용을 포괄하는 최상위 주제문을 찾아내거나 없으면 구성해 내는 것이다.

(1)

1 <u>Linguists are typically very hesitant to answer the first question posed above, namely: how many languages are spoken in the world today?</u> Probably the best that one can say, with any hope of not being contradicted, is that at a very conservative estimate some 4,000 languages are spoken today. Laymen are often surprised that the figure should be so high, but I would emphasize that this is a conservative estimate. But why is it that linguists are not able to give a more accurate figure? There are several different reasons conspiring to prevent them from doing so, and these will be outlined below.

2 One is that many parts of the world are insufficiently studied from a linguistic viewpoint, so that we simply do not know precisely what languages are spoken there. Our knowledge of the linguistic situation in remote parts of the world has improved dramatically in recent years — New Guinea, for instance, has changed from being almost a blank linguistic map to the stage where most (though still not all) of the languages can be pinpointed with accuracy: since perhaps as many as one fifth of the world's languages are spoken in New Guinea, this has radically changed any estimate of the total number of languages. But there are still some areas where uncertainty remains, so that even the most detailed recent index of the world's languages, Voegelin and Voegelin (1977), lists several languages with accompanying question marks, or queries whether one listed language might in fact be the same as some other language but under a different name.

3 A second problem is that it is difficult or impossible in many cases to decide whether two related speech varieties should be considered different languages or merely different dialects of the same language. With the languages of Europe, there are in general established traditions of whether two speech varieties should be considered different languages or merely dialect variants, but these decisions have often been made more on political and social grounds rather than strictly linguistic grounds.

4 One criterion that is often advanced as a purely linguistic criterion is mutual intelligibility: if two speech varieties are mutually intelligible, they are different dialects of the same language, but if they are mutually unintelligible, they are different languages. But if applied to the languages of Europe, this criterion would radically alter our assessment of what the different languages of Europe are: the most northern dialects and the most southern dialects (in the traditional sense) of German are mutually unintelligible, while dialects of German spoken close to the Dutch border are mutually intelligible with dialects of Dutch spoken just across the border. In fact, our criterion for whether a dialect is Dutch or German relates in large measure to social factors — is the dialect spoken in an area where Dutch is the standard language or where German is the standard language? By the same criterion, the three nuclear Scandinavian languages(in the traditional sense), Danish, Norwegian and Swedish, would turn out to be dialects of one language, given their mutual intelligibility. While this criterion is often applied to non-European languages (so that nowadays linguists often talk of the Chinese languages rather than the Chinese dialects, given the mutual unintelligibility of, for instance, Mandarin and Cantonese), it seems unfair that it should not be applied consistently to European languages as well.

5 While native speakers of English are often surprised that there should be problems in delimiting languages from dialects — since present-day dialects of English are in general mutually intelligible (at least with some familiarisation), and even the language most closely related genetically to English, Frisian, is mutually unintelligible with English — the native speaker of English would be hard put to interpret a sentence in Tok Pisin, the English-based pidgin of much of Papua New Guinea, like *sapos ol i karamapim bokis bilong yumi, orait bai yumi paitim as bilong ol* 'if they cover our box, then we'll spank them', although each word, except perhaps *i*, is of English origin ('suppose all the cover-up-him box belong you-me, all-right by you-me fight-him arse belong all').

6 In some cases, the intelligibility criterion actually leads to contradictory results, namely when we have a dialect chain, i.e. a string of dialects such that adjacent dialects are readily mutually intelligible, but dialects from the far ends of the chain are not mutually intelligible. A good illustration of this is the Dutch-German dialect complex. One could start from the far south of the German-speaking area and move to the far west of the Dutch-speaking area without encountering any sharp boundary across which mutual intelligibility is broken; but the two end points of this chain are speech varieties so different from one another that there is no mutual intelligibility possible. If one takes a simplified dialect chain A - B - C, where A and B are mutually intelligible, as are B and C, but A and C are mutually unintelligible, then one arrives at the contradictory result that A and B are dialects of the same language, B and C are dialects of the same language, but A and C are different languages. There is in fact no way of resolving this contradiction if we maintain the traditional strict difference between language and dialects, and what such examples show is that this is not an all-or-nothing distinction, but rather a continuum. In this sense, it is impossible to answer the question how many languages are spoken in the world.

7. <u>A further problem with the mutual intelligibility criterion is that mutual intelligibility itself is a matter of degree rather than a clearcut opposition between intelligibility and unintelligibility.</u> If mutual intelligibility were to mean 100 per cent mutual intelligibility of all utterances, then perhaps no two speech varieties would be classified as mere dialect variants; for instance, although speakers of British and American English can understand most of one another's speech, there are areas where intelligibility is likely to be minimal unless one speaker happens to have learned the linguistic forms used by the other, as with car (or auto) terms like British *boot, bonnet, mudguard* and their American equivalents *trunk, hood, fender*. Conversely, although speakers of different Slavonic languages are often unable to make full sense of a text in another Slavonic language, they can usually make good sense of parts. of the text, because of the high percentage of shared vocabulary and forms.

8. <u>Two further factors enter into the degree of mutual intelligibility between two speech varieties.</u> One is that intelligibility can rise rapidly with increased familiarisation: those who remember the first introduction of American films into Britain often recall that they were initially considered difficult to understand, but increased exposure to American English has virtually removed this problem. Speakers of different dialects of Arabic often experience difficulty in understanding each other at first meeting, but soon adjust to the major differences between their respective dialects, and Egyptian Arabic, as the most widely diffused modern Arabic dialect, has rapidly gained in intelligibility throughout the Arab world. This can lead to 'one-way intelligibility', as when speakers of, say, Tunisian Arabic are more likely to understand Egyptian Arabic than vice versa, because Tunisian Arabic speaker are more often exposed to Egyptian Arabic than vice

versa. The second factor is that intelligibility is to certain extent a social and psychological phenomenon: it is easier to understand when you want to understand. A good example of this is the conflicting assessments different speakers of the same Slavonic language will often give about the intelligibility of some other Slavonic language, correlating in large measure with whether or not they feel well-disposed to speakers of the other language.

9 <u>The same problems as exist in delimiting dialects from languages arise, incidentally, on the historical plane too, where the question arises: at what point has a language changed sufficiently to be considered a different language?</u> Again, traditional answer are often contradictory: Latin is considered to have died out, although its descendants, the Romance languages, live on, so at some time Latin must have changed sufficiently to be deemed no longer the same language, but a qualitatively different language. On the other hand, Greek is referred to in the same way throughout its attested history (which is longer than that of Latin and the Romance languages combined), with merely the addition of different adjectives to identify different stages of its development (e.g. Ancient Greek, Byzantine Greek, Modern Greek). In the case of the history of the English language, there is even conflicting terminology: the oldest attested stages of English can be referred to either as Old English (which suggests an earlier stage of Modern English) or as Anglo-Saxon (which suggests a different language that is the ancestor of English, perhaps justifiably so given the mutual unintelligibility of Old and Modern English).

10 <u>A further reason why it is difficult to assess the number of languages spoken in the world today is that many languages are on the verge of extinction.</u> While it has probably been the case throughout mankind's history that languages have died out, the historically recent expansion of European population to the Americas and Australia has resulted in a greatly accelerated rate of language death among the indigenous languages of these areas. Perusal of Voegelin and Voegelin (1977) will show a number of languages as 'possibly extinct' or 'possibly still spoken', plus an even greater number of languages with only a handful of speakers — usually of advanced age — so that a language may well be dying out somewhere in the world as I am writing these words. When a language dies, this is sometimes an abrupt process, such as the death of a fluent speaker who happened to have outlived all other speakers of the language; more typically, however, the community's facility with the language decreases, as more and more functions are taken over by some other language, so that what they speak, in terms of the original language of the community, is only a part of that language. Many linguists working on Australian Aboriginal languages have been forced, in some case, to do what has come to be called 'salvage linguistics', i.e. to elicit portions of a language from someone who has neither spoken nor heard the language for decades and has perhaps only a vague recollection of what the language was like.

어휘리콜 •hesitant: 머뭇거리는; •contradict: 부정하다, 모순되다; •conservative estimate: 조심스러운 평가; •layman: 보통사람; •conspire: 음모를 꾸미다, 작당하다; •delimit: -범위(경계)를 정하다; •intelligibility: 명료함; 가해성; •genetically: 유전적으로; •pinpoint: 정확히 지적하다; •well-disposed: 호의를 가지는; •attest: 입증하다, 증명하다; •verge: 경계, 구역; •indigenous: 토착의; •perusal: 정독, 정사, 읽음; •a handful of: 적은; •abrupt: 갑작스런; •outlive: 보다 오래 살다; •facility: 재주, 능숙함; •aboriginal: 원주민의; •recollection: 회상, 추억.

주제확인 본문은 10단락으로 구성되어 있다. 각 단락에서 밑줄로 표시된 부분이 단락의 주제이다. 이 10개 주제문들 중에서 나머지 문장들을 포괄하는 한 문장을 찾아내면, 첫 문은 문제를 제기하고, 나머지 문장들은 제기된 문제에 대한 대답(머뭇거리게 하는 이유, 즉 정확한 수치를 말 못하는 이유)을 말한다. 이유는 크게 4가지(문2번, 3번, 9번, 10번)이고, 문4-8번은 문2에 포괄되는 내용이다. 따라서 나머지 문들을 포괄하는 주제적 문은 **1** 의 밑줄 부분이다.

전문국역 **1** 언어학자들은 위에 제시된 첫 질문, 즉 오늘날 이 지구상에 몇 개의 언어가 사용되고 있는가에 대해 대답하기에 주저한다. 모순되지 않는다는 바람을 가지고, 우리가 말할 수 있는 최선의 대답은 매우 신중한 평가로 대략 4,000개가 오늘날 사용되고 있다는 것이다. 보통 사람들은 종종 그 수치가 너무 높다는 것에 놀란다. 그러나 저자는 이 숫자는 조심스러운 수치라는 점을 강조하고 싶다. 그러나 언어학자들이 보다 정확한 수치를 내 놓을 수 없는 이유는 무엇인가? 언어학자들이 그렇게 하지 못하게 하는 서로 관련된 여러 가지 이유가 있는데, 이것들이 아래에 개괄적으로 제시된다. **2** 하나는 세계의 여러 지역들이 언어 관점에서 충분하게 연구되어 있지 않고 있어서, 우리는 어떤 언어들이 그 지역들에서 사용되고 있는지를 정확하게 알고 있지 않다는 것이다. 지구상의 먼 지역 언어 상황에 대한 우리의 지식이 최근 수년 동안에 극적으로 증가하고 있다. 즉 예를 들면, 뉴기아나는 언어지도상 거의 공백상태에서 대부분의 언어들이(비록 전부는 아니지만) 정확하게 말할 수 있는 단계까

지 변했다는 것이다: 아마도 세계 언어의 5분의 1의 언어 개수가 뉴기니아에서 사용되고 있기 때문에, 이것이 세계 전체 언어의 수를 근본적으로 변화시켰을 것이다. 그러나 아직도 불확실성이 남아있는 지역들이 있다. 그래서 최근의 가장 구체적인 세계 언어 색인인 Voegelin and Voegelin(1977) 조차도 수반되는 질문표시 혹은 질문이 있는 여러 언어를 목록으로 나타내고 있다-목록에 들어 있는 한 언어가 실제로는 다른 언어와 동일한 언어일수도 있는데도 다른 이름으로 올라 있는지의 질문. **3** 또 한 문제는 두 관련 변이가 다른 언어로 간주되어야 하는지 혹은 동일 언어의 단순히 다른 방언인지를 결정하는 것이 많은 경우에 어렵거나 불가능하다는 것이다. 유럽의 언어들에게는, 일반적으로 두 언어 변이가 다른 언어로 간주되어야 하는지 혹은 단순한 방언 변이로 간주되어야 하는지에 대한 확립된 전통이 있지만, 이 결정은 엄격한 언어적 기준 보다는 오히려 정치 및 사회적 기준에 따라 종종 내려져 왔다. **4** 순수한 언어적 기준으로 진전되어 온 한 기준은 다음의 상호 인지가능성 (mutual intelligibility)이다: 만약 두 언어 변이가 상호 인지 가능하면, 그 두 언어는 동일 언어에 속하는 다른 방언이고, 그러나 만약 두 언어가 상호 인지가능하지 않으면 두 언어변이는 다른 언어이다. 그러나 만약 유럽의 언어들에 적용되면, 이 기준은 유럽 언어들의 정체성에 대한 우리의 평가를 근본적으로 바꿀 것이다: (전통적인 의미에서) 독일어에서 가장 북쪽의 방언들과 가장 남쪽의 방언들은 상호 인지가능하다. 반면에 네덜란드 국경 가까이에서 사용되는 독일어 방언들은 국경 가까이에서 사용되는 네덜란드 방언들과 상호 인지가능하다. 사실, 한 방언이 네덜란드어냐 독일어냐에 대한 우리의 기준은 크게는 사회적 요소들에 관련된다. - 네덜란드어가 표준어인 지역에서 사용되는 언어이냐 독일어가 표준어인 지역에서 사용되는 언어이냐? 동일한 기준에서, (전통적인 의미에서) 스칸디나반도 중심 세 언어인 덴마크어, 노르웨이어, 그리고 스웨덴어는, 상호 인지가능성 기준이 주어지면, 한 언어에 속하는 방언들로 판단될 것이다. 이 기준이 비 유럽어들에 종종 적용(그래서, 예를 들어, 만주어와 켄턴어에 대해, 상호 인지가능성 기준이 주어지면, 오늘날 언어학자들은 종종 중국어 방언들이라는 말 보다는 오히려 중국어들이라는 말을 한다)할 때, 그 기준이 유럽 언어들에 일관되게 적용되지 말아야 하는 것은 불공평한 것 같다. **5** 방언이 아니고 서로 다른 언어들이라고 경계를 구분 짓는 데에 문제가 있다는 것에 영어화자들은 종종 놀란다. - 왜냐하면 오늘날의 영어 방언들은 일반적으로 상호 인지가능하며(적어도 어느 정도 친밀함을 가지고 있어), 심지어 생성적으로는 영어와 프리시안어에 매우 가까운 언어조차도 영어와 상호 인지가능하지 못하다 - 영어 화자는 영어에 기초를 많이 두고 있는 파푸아 뉴기니아의 Tok Pisin어의 문장, 예컨대 *sapos ol i karamapim bokis bilong yumi, orait bai yumi paitim as bilong ol* 'if they cover our box, then we'll spank them'을 이해하지 못한다. 비록 각 단어가, 아마 *i*를 제외하고, 영어 어원이다('suppose all the cover-up-him box belong you-me, all-right by you-me fight-him arse belong all'). **6** 어떤 경우들에는, 이해가능성 기준이 모순적 결과를 초래한다. 즉 방언의 연쇄현상, 즉 방언들의 연쇄현상이 있게 될 때, 인접하는 방언들은 쉽게 상호 인지 가능하지만, 연쇄의 먼 끝에 있는 방언끼리는 상호 인지가능하지 않다. 이 경우의 좋은 한 사례가 네덜란드-독일어 복합이다. 한 방언이 독일어사용 지역 최남단으로부터 출발하여 네덜란드 사용 지역 최 서쪽으로 상호 이해가능성을 차단하는 어떤 경계의 개입 없이 이동할 수 있다. 그러나 이 연쇄의 두 끝 지점은 언어변이형이 되는데, 서로 매우 달라서 상호 이해가능하지 않다. 만약 방언연쇄를 간단하게 A-B-C로 나타낸다면, 여기에서 A와

B는 상호 인지가능하고, B와 C가 상호 인지 가능하지만, A와 C가 상호 인지가능하지 않는다면, 우리는 모순적인 결과에 도달하게 되는데, A와 B는 동일 언어에 속하는 방언들이고, B와 C가 동일 언어에 속하는 방언들이지만, A와 C는 서로 다른 언어가 된다는 것이다. 사실 이 모순을 해결할 방법은 없다, 만약 우리가 언어와 방언들 사이를 구별하는 전통적 엄격한 차이점을 견지하지 않는다면. 그래서 이러한 예들이 보여주는 바가 전부 아니면 하나도 아니다가 아니고 오히려 일직선상에서의 현상이다. 이런 의미에서 얼마나 많은 언어가 이 지구상에서 사용되고 있는가 하는 질문에 대답하는 것은 불가능하다. **7** 상호 인지가능성 기준에게 있어 또 한 문제는 상호 인지가능성 자체는 인지가능성과 상호 인지불가능성 사이의 깔끔한 대립보다는 오히려 정도 문제이다. 만약 상호 인지가능성이 모든 발화에 대해 100%의 인지가능성을 의미한다면, 아마도 어느 두 언어 변이도 순수 방언으로 분류되지 않을 것이다. 예를 들면, 비록 영국영어 화자와 미국영어 화자가 서로의 말을 대부분 이해한다고 하더라도, 만약 한 화자가 다른 화자에 의해 사용된 언어 형태를 학습하지 않았더라면, 예를 들어 자동차 용어로 영국영어의 *boot, bonnet, mudguard*와 그기에 해당하는 미국영어의 *trunk, hood, fender*와 같이, 인지가능성이 최소인 지역이 있을 것이다. 반대로, 비록 슬라브계 한 언어의 화자가 슬라브계 다른 언어에서의 텍스트에 대해 의미를 충분히 읽지 못하지만, 그들은 보통 공유하는 어휘 및 형태들의 높은 백분율 때문에, 텍스트에 대해 혹은 텍스트의 일부분에 대해 의미를 잘 읽을 수 있다. **8** 두 다른 요소가 두 언어변이 사이 상호 인지가능성의 정도에 개입된다. 하나는 다음과 같다: 인지가능성은 익숙함이 증가함으로써 급속히 올라간다: 미국 영화를 영국에 처음 수입했던 것을 기억하는 사람들은 자기들이 처음에는 이해하기에 어려웠었다고 회상한다. 그러나 미국영어에 노출이 증가함으로서 이 문제는 제거된다. 아랍어의 여러 방언의 화자들은 종종 처음 만날 때 서로서로 이해하는데 어려움을 경험하지만 곧 방언들 사이 큰 차이점들에 적응하며, 이집트의 아랍어는, 가장 널리 분산되어 있는 현대 아랍어 방언인데, 아랍계 전체에 인지가능성을 빠르게 획득했다. 이것은, 말하자면 화자들이 말할 때처럼의, 일방통행의 인지가능성을 초래한다. 투니시안 아랍어는 이비티언 아랍어를 더 잘 이해할 것이다, 그 반대 방향보다도. 둘째 요소는 다음과 같다: 인지가능성은, 어느 정도, 사회 심리적 현상이다: 당신이 이해하고 싶을 때 이해하는 것이 더 쉽다. 이에 대한 좋은 예는 동일 슬래브 언어 사용 다른 화자들이 슬래브 언어에 속하는 다른 언어에 대한 인지가능성에 대하여 종종 내리는 상반된 평가인데, 크게는 상대 언어의 화자에 대하여 호의를 가지고 있는 것으로 느끼느냐 아니냐에 관련된다. **9** 경우에 따라서는, 역사적인 국면에서도, 방언과 언어를 구별하는 경계문제에 존재하는 것과 동일한 문제들이 발생한다. 이 경우에는 다음과 같은 질문이 제기 된다: 한 언어가 어느 시점에서 다른 언어라고 생각될 수 있을 정도로 충분히 변하는가? 다시 전통적인 대답은 종종 모순된다: 라틴어는 사어가 된 것으로 고려된다, 비록 그 후계자들, 즉 로만스 언어들이 살아 있지만, 그러므로 어느 시점에서 라틴어는 충분히 이미 동일한 언어(즉 라틴어)가 아니라 질적으로 다른 언어로 생각되는 정도로 변했음에 틀림이 없다. 다른 한편으로, 그리스어는 마찬가지 관점에서 입증되는 역사(라틴어와 로망스어들의 역사가 합쳐진 것 보다 더 긴)에서, 발달사에서 시대구분하기 위해 별개의 형용사를 부가(고대 그리스어, 비잔틴 그리스어, 현대 그리스어)함으로서 언급된다. 영어발달사의 경우, 모순적인 용어가 있다: 영어에서 입증되는 가장 오래된 단계는 Old English(이것은 Modern English 보다 더 이른 단계를 암시한다) 혹은 Anglo-Saxon(이것은 영어의 조상과

다른 언어를 암시하며, 아마도 당연히 Old and Modern English와 상호 인지가능하지 않는 것으로 됨)라고 부른다. ⑩ 오늘날 지구상에서 사용되는 언어의 수를 말하는데 어려운 또 하나의 이유는 많은 언어들이 사멸의 경계에 있다는 것이다. 인류 역사상에서 언어들이 죽어가고 있는 한편, 역사적으로 최근 유럽인들이 아메리카와 오스트레일리아로 진출한 사실은 그 지역 토착 언어의 죽음을 가속화 시키는 결과를 가져왔다는 것은 인류 역사를 통해서 아마 사실일 것이다. Voegelin and Voegelin (1977)을 정독하면 많은 언어들이, 화자의 수가 적은 많은 언어들 특히 선진시대인 언어들에 대해서까지, 사어가 될 것이거나 혹은 계속해서 사용될 것임을 보게 될 것이다. 그리하여 한 언어가 세계 어느 곳에서 죽어가고 있을지도 모른다, 내가 이 단어를 쓰고 있는 이 순간에도. 한 언어가 죽을 때, 이 죽는 것은 갑작스런 과정인데, 마치 다른 모든 화자들 보다 오래 살 것으로 생각되었던 유창한 화자가 죽는 경우와 같다. 그러나 더 전형적으로 말하면, 그 언어에 대해 그 지역사회의 그 언어사용이 감소하는 것이다, 그 언어의 역들이 다른 어떤 언어에게 더욱 넘어감으로써, 그 결과 그 지역사회 사람들이 사용하는 것은, 그 지역사회 원래의 언어 관점에서 그 언어의 일부가 되어버리는 것이다. 오스트레일리아 원주민 언어들을 연구하는 많은 언어학자들은, 어떤 경우에는, 'salvage linguistics(구출 언어학)'이라고 불리게 된 것을 하도록, 즉 수십 년 동안 말해보지도 들어보지도 못해서 그 언어가 어떤 것인지에 대해 희미한 기억만 가지는 사람으로부터 언어의 일부를 유도하도록 강요 받아왔다.

(2)

1 Ron has known for months that his research paper is due on Monday, but he didn't start working on it until the Friday before. Sherrie never begins to study for even major exams until the night before the test. Michael has a great idea for a novel, but he always has a reason for not sitting down to write it. Juanita never finishes her tax return until minutes before the midnight deadline on April 15. Tyrone checks his e-mail frequently but rarely replies to his friends' messages. **2** <u>These people are among the one in five individuals who are chronic procrastinators.</u> They habitually postpone doing something until it's difficult or impossible to get it done; meanwhile, they are overwhelmed with guilt and they worry about the consequences of putting off important tasks. The problem is especially widespread among college students; about 70 percent have admitted to submitting papers late or having to cram for an exam. As a result, students tend to smoke and drink more, and they suffer from more insomnia, stomach problems, colds, and flu. Why do so many people make life harder for themselves by putting things off? Psychologists say that a problem with procrastination arises from an individual's anxieties and misconceptions about productivity.

3 According to procrastination expert Neil Fiore, Ph. D., <u>fear of failure is the main reason why people postpone the inevitable.</u> Thus, Procrastinators delay because of their anxiety about not having the required talent, skills, or knowledge to complete the task at hand. They would rather fail to try than be exposed as stupid or incapable. So when they flunk tests, procrastinators can blame their failure on inadequate study time rather than on lack of intellect. When they force themselves to write entire research papers in one weekend, they can attribute their papers' low grades to time pressures rather than lack of writing ability.

4 <u>Another type of anxiety that causes procrastination is perfectionism.</u> If perfectionists can't do something flawlessly, they don't want to do it at all. So they put off a task when they feel anxious about producing something imperfect. It is for this reason that many people keep postponing work on projects-from novels to quilts to home renovations- that they'd like to finish.

5 <u>It is also quite common to put off those tasks that cause anxiety because they are unpleasant or painful.</u> Even people who don't usually procrastinate will delay dental appointments and physical exams simply because of the discomfort involved.

6 In addition to one or more of these anxieties, <u>false beliefs about productivity could be at the root of a procrastination problem.</u> Many procrastinators are convinced that the pressure of an impending deadline causes them to work faster and better. This idea, however, is a myth because work quality usually suffers if a task is completed at the last minute. Papers ate core poorly written, and tax returns are often filled with errors if done in a hurry while trying to beat a deadline. Nor does the adrenaline rush that results from being forced to finish a last-minute task improve one's performance. Again, the finished product usually suffers. People who enjoy feeling this rush are often thrill seekers who are not doing themselves any favors by putting things off.

어휘리콜 •due: 마감인; •chronic: 만성의, 상습적인; •procrastinator: 질질 끄는 자; •overwhelm: 압도하다; •submit: 제출하다; •insomnia: 불면증; •cram: 주입시키다; •flawlessly: 흠 없이, 완벽하게; •impending: 절박한, 임박한; •adrenaline: 자극제, 아드레날린.

주제확인 6단락으로 구성되어 있는 본문 (2)에서 단락 **1** 에는 주제(자신의 일을 미루는 사람들이 있다.)가 분산되어 있다고 할 수도 있다. 둘째 단락부터는 주제가 명시적으로 나타나 있는데, 밑줄 친 부분이 그 단락의 주제이다. 단락들 주제 중에서 둘째 단락의 주제가 글 전체의 주제로 기여한다.

전문국역 **1** 론(Ron)은 자신의 텀 페이퍼가 월요일이 마감이라는 것을 여러 달 동안 알고 있었지만, 직전 금요일까지 착수하지 않았다. 쉐리(Sherrie)는 결코 시험 전날 밤까지는 큰 시험조차 시험공부를 시작하지 않는다. 마이클(Michael)은 소설에 대해 생각은 갖고 있으면서 항상 앉아서 소설을 쓰지 않는 이유는 갖고 있다. 주아니타(Juanita)는 4월15일 자정 마감시간까지 (납세를 위한) 소득신고를 하지 않는다. 티로니(Tyrone)는 자기의 전자 멜을 자주 체크는 하지만 자기 친구의 메시지에 좀처럼 응답을 하지 않는다. **2** 이런 사람은 상습적으로 질질 끄는 5명 중 한 사람에 속한다. 이들은 그 일이 이루어지기에 어렵거나 불가능하게 될 때까지 무엇 하는 것을 습관적으로 지연 시킨다; 그러면서 그들은 죄의식에 압도당하고 중요한 일을 지연시킨 결과를 걱정한다. 이 문제는 특히 대학생들 사이에 널리 퍼져있다; 약 70%가 페이퍼를 늦게 제출하고 시험을 위해 주입식으로 하는 것으로 되어 있다. 그 결과 학생들은 담배를 피우고 술을 더 많이 마시는 경향이고, 그리하여 그들은 더 많은 불면증, 위장장애, 감기, 독감을 겪는다. 왜 그리 많은 사람들이 일을 지연시킴으로서 스스로 생활을 힘들게 하는가? 심리학자들은 말하기를 미루는 문제는 개인의 분노와 생산성에 대한 그릇된 생각에서 비롯된다. **3** 미루기 문제 전문가인 Neil Fiore 박사에 따르면, 실패에 대한 공포가 사람들이 불가피한 일을 미루는 주요 이유이다. 그러므로 미루는 사람들은 당면한 일을 완성시키는데 요구되는 재능, 능력, 혹은 지식을 갖지 못함에 관한 그들의 분노 때문에 지연시킨다. 그들은 오히려 어리석거나 능력이 없어 보이기보다는 노력에 실패하려고 한다. 그러므로 미루는 자들은 시험에 실패할 때, 자기들이 지적 부족 때문이 아니라 부족한 공부 시간으로 그들의 실패를 탓할 수 있다. 그들이 주말에 연구 페이퍼 전부를 억지로 앉자 작성할 때, 자기들은 자기들의 페이퍼의 낮은 학점을 쓰기 능력 부족 보다는 시간 압박으로 돌린다. **4** 미루기를 유발시키는 또 한 분노 유형은 완벽주의다. 만약 완벽주의자들이 무엇을 완벽하게 할 수 없다면, 그것을 전혀 하고 싶어 하지 않는다. 그러므로 그들은 무엇이 불완전하게 생산되는 것에 대해 분노를 느낄 때, 일을 미루어버린다. 많은 사람들이 프로젝트에 관한 일 – 소설 작업에서부터 가사 누비이불 작업에 이르기까지 – 자기들이 끝내고 싶은 일을 계속해서 미루어버리는 것은 이런 이유 때문이다. **5** 또한 그들이 즐겁지 아니하거나 고통스러울 때 분노를 유발하는 그런 작업을 미루는 것은 아주 흔하다. 평소 미루지 아니하는 사람조차도 치과치료 예약과 물리학 시험을 단순히 관련 불편함 때문에 미루어버리곤 한다. **6** 이러한 분노들 외에도, 생산성에 대한 잘못된 믿음이 미루기 문제의 근저에 있을 수 있다. 많은 미루는 상습자들은 임박한 마감일의 압박이 자기들로 하여금 보다 빨리 그리고 보다 더 잘 하도록 강요한다고 확신하고 있다. 그러나 이 생각은 미신이다. 왜냐하면 작업이 마지막 순간에 완성이 되면, 작업의 질이 보통 상처를 입는다. 페이퍼는 어설프게 쓰진 핵심을 먹어버린다. 만약 납세신고는 마감일을 맞추려고 노력하는 동안에 서두르게 되면, 종종 오류로 채워진다. 그리고 마지막 작업을 끝내라고 독촉되는 결과는 수행력을 향상시킨다는 자극제는 좋지 않다. 또한 완성된 생산물은 보통 상처받는다. 이렇게 서두르는 것을 느끼기 좋아하는 사람들은 종종 스릴 추구자이지만, 그들 스스로는 일들이 미루어진 후 그 일을 하는 것은 좋아하지는 않는다.

제5장

독해사후 처리

본문의 독해가 이루어진 다음에는 독자가 어떻게 해야 하는가? 독해수행을 마무리하는 것이다. 독해수행 마무리는 1)독해 첫 단계에서 예측했던 작자의 의도를 본문에 의거 확인하고, 2)본문을 구성패턴으로 압축하고, 3)마무리 정리하는 것이다.

제1절 글의 의도 확인

마지막 5단계에서의 글 의도 확인은 제1단계 윤곽확인에서 예측했던 작자의 의도를 앞 단계에서 읽었던 본문의 내용에 기초하여 확인하는 것이다. 본문의 내용에 기초하여 글의 의도를 확인하는 방법은 본문 최상위 주제문을 대상으로 작자의 의도를 확인하는 것이다. 최상위 주제문을 유도하는 방법은 3-4장에서 제시되었다. 이 확인된 최상위 주제문을 직접화행문으로 하여, 만약 직접화행이 아니면 직접화행으로 전환하여, 수행동사의 의미를 글의 의도로 확인하는 것이다. 직접화행의 구조는 1인칭 주어(I/We)+수행동사+상대방(to you)+전달내용(that절/to root/-ing)이다. 이 구조에서 1인칭은 작자, 수행동사는 작자의 의도가 담긴 말 행위 동사이다.

(1) Dear Sir/Madam

1 We understand from Knowles Hardware Ltd of Glasgow that you are looking for a reliable firm with good connections in the textile trade to represent you in Scotland.

2 For some years we have acted as Scottish agents for one of your competitors, Jarvis & Sons of Preston. They have recently registered as a limited company and in the reorganization decided to establish their own branch in Edinburgh. As they no longer need our services we are now free to offer them to you.

3 As we have had experience in marketing products similar to your own, we are familiar with customers' needs and are confident that we could develop a good market for you in Scotland. We have spacious and well equipped showrooms not only at our Glasgow headquarters but also in Edinburgh and Perth, plus many experienced sales representatives who would energetically promote your business.

4 We hope you will be interested in our proposal and will let us know on what terms you would be willing to conclude an agreement. I will be visiting your town in 2 weeks' time and hope it will be possible to discuss details with you then.

5 We can provide first-class references if required, but for general information concerning our standing in the trade we suggest you refer to Knowles Hardware Ltd.

We hope to hear from you soon.

Yours faithfully

어휘리콜 •textile: 직물; •limited company: 유한회사; •showroom: 전시실; •headquarters: 본

부, 본사, 사령부.

의도확인 (1)은 본문만으로 구성된 지면서신이다. 허두와 끝 인사말을 실마리로 하면 의도는 '업무내용 전달'일 것으로 1단계에서 예측되었을 것이다. 지금 5단계에서 의도 파악에 접근하면, 앞 4단계에서 정직한 문장으로 되어 있는 5단락의 본문을 독해했었다면 4번째 단락(We hope...with you then)이 주제단락이고, 이 단락 내 첫 문장이 주제문이다. 이 주제문 중에서도 둘째-셋째 절(We hope you will let us know on what terms you would be willing to conclude an agreement.)이 핵이다. 직접화행 구조(*you* 앞에 수신자를 의미하는 *to you*는 생략됨)이고, 이 구조에서 hope(기대)가 수행동사이고, 그래서 작자가 '합의서에 포함될 조건 알려주기 기대'가 이 글의 의도이다.

전문국역 **1** 저희는 Glasgow에 있는 Knowles Hardware Ltd로부터 스코틀랜드에서 귀 회사를 대표해주기 위해 섬유업계에서 좋은 관계망을 가지고 있는 믿을만한 회사를 찾고 있다는 소식을 들었습니다. **2** 여러 해 동안 저희 회사는 귀 회사의 경쟁사들 중의 하나인 Jarvis & Sons of Preston 쪽에서 스코틀랜드 대리점으로서 활동을 해왔습니다. 최근에 Jarvis & Sons of Preston이 유한회사로 등록을 하고 에든버러에서 그들의 지사를 세우기로 결정된 조직을 가지게 되었습니다. 이 회사는 더 이상 저희 회사의 서비스를 필요로 하지 않기 때문에, 저희 회사는 이제 귀 회사에 서비스를 드릴 수 있게 되었습니다. **3** 저희 회사는 귀 회사의 제품과 유사한 제품을 마켓팅 하는데 경험을 가지고 있기 때문에 저희는 고객들의 요구를 잘 알고 있으며, 스코틀랜드에서 귀 회사를 위해서 좋은 마켓팅을 할 수 있다고 자신합니다. 저희는 글라스고우 본사에 뿐만 아니라 에든버러와 퍼스에 공간이 넓고 내부 설비가 잘된 쇼룸을 가지고 있고, 더불어 귀 회사 영업을 열성적으로 향상시켜 줄 수 있는 영업 팀장들을 확보하고 있습니다. **4** 저희는 귀 회사가 저의 제안에 관심을 가져주시기를 바라며, 귀하가 합의서에 포함시키고 싶은 기간에 대해 알려주시기 바랍니다. 저는 2주 후에 귀 도시를 방문하기로 되어 있으며 세세한 내용을 논의할 수 있기를 희망합니다. **5** 필요하시면 일급 참고자료를 제공해드릴 수 있습니다만, 업계에서의 저희 회사 관련 일반정보에 관해서는 Knowles Hardware Ltd에 알아보시기를 제안 드립니다. 소식 있기를 기대합니다. Yours faithfully.

(2) Dear Mrs Matthews

1 Thank you for your letter of 10 September. We are very interested <u>to discuss further your proposal</u> for an agency in Scotland.

2 Your work with Jarvis & Co is <u>well-known to us</u> and in view of your connections throughout the trade in Scotland we feel there is much you could do to extend our business there.

3 Our final decision would depend upon the terms and conditions. As you will be visiting our town soon it would be better to discuss these in person rather than to enter upon what may become lengthy correspondence.

4 Please let me know when we may expect you to call.

Yours sincerely

어휘리콜 •terms and conditions: 계약 조건.

의도확인 허두, 끝 인사말을 포함하는 본문만으로 구성되어 있다. 작자의 의도가 명시적으로 나타나 있다 '전화 시점 알려주기 요청'이다.

전문국역 **1** 귀하의 9월 10일의 서신 감사합니다. 스코틀랜드에서의 지점을 위한 귀하의 제안을 더 논의하자는데 저희는 매우 관심이 많습니다. **2** 귀하가 Jarvis & Co 쪽에서 일을 하셨다는 것은 저희는 잘 알고 있으며, 스코틀랜드 지역 거래에서 귀하의 거래처를 이용하여 그 지역에서 우리 회사를 확장시키기 위하여 귀하가 하실 일이 많이 있을 것으로 느낍니다. **3** 저희의 최종 결정은 계약조건에 달려 있을 것이다. 긴 글을 쓰는 것 보다 오히려 귀하가 금명간 저희 도시를 방문하게 될 때, 이것들을 개인적으로 의논하는 것이 더 좋을 것입니다. **4** 귀하가 언제 전화 주실 수 있는지를 알려주시기 바랍니다. Yours sincerely

---

(3)

Dal
Taste of India

The taste of India, "Dal"
The exclusive authentic Indian restaurant

- Experience truly traditional Indian dishes at Dal, serving a wide range of curry, tandoori, naan and drinks.

- Prepared by a native veteran chef from India, offering fresh **vegetarian dishes** and

halal food.

**We at Dal invite you to the finest Indian cuisine
with our delicious delicacies served with a warm,
welcoming atmosphere.**

- head shop   Artsonje Center 1F, 144-2, Sokyuk-dong, Jongro-gu, Seoul, Korea
Samcheong   **Tel.**01-736-4627 **Fax.**02-736-4628

- Branch   Gangnam Finance Center B1, 737, Yeoksam-dong,
Yeoksam   Seoul, Korea **Tel.**02-2112-3888 **Fax.**02-2112-3889

www.dalindia.com

어휘리콜   •exclusive: 유일한, 전문적인; •authentic: 믿을만한, 진정한; •dishes: 요리; •curry: 카레요리; •vegetarian dishes: 야채요리; •cuisine: 요리(법); •delicacies: 진미.

의도확인   상호, 상호소개 등을 포함하는 광고이다. '초대' 의도를 명시적으로 나타내고 있다.

전문국역   믿을만한 유일한 인도 식당, Dal에서 진짜 전통적인 인도 요리를 경험해보십시오. 카레, 탄두리, 난, 음료의 여러 요리를 제공합니다. 인도에서 온 토착의 베테랑 쉐프가 요리하고, 신선한 야채 요리와 하랄 푸드를 제공합니다. Dal의 저희들이 아늑하고 환영하는 분위기에서 서빙 되는 맛있는 진미의 최고 인도 요리에 귀하를 초대합니다.

---

(4) It's not that speed and size aren't important. <u>The economy is in a death spiral</u>: businesses are shedding workers at a record pace, which saps consumer spending, which leads to more layoffs. The public sector needs to get an awful lot of unemployed workers and equipment back to work.

어휘리콜   •spiral: 나선모양, 악순환; •shed: 뿌리다, 흘리다, 버리다; •sap: 점차로 악화시키다; •layoff: 해고.

의도확인   첫 문은 머리말이고, 밑줄 친 부분이 주제이고 나머지 문들은 주제에 관한 내용이다. 주제부분을 머리말에서 설명한 화행기저구조(1인칭 주어+수행동사+독자+메시지) 관점에서 보면 작자의 '전달'이 의도이다.

전문국역   속도와 그 규모가 중요하지 않은 것은 아니다. 경제가 완전히 악순환을 맞이하고 있다. 기업체들은 기록적인 속도로 근로자들을 잘라내고 있고, 이것이 소비를 위축시키고 있으며, 더 많은 해고를 야기하고 있다. 공공 부분은 많은 실업자들과 장비를 다시 일자리로 복귀시켜야 한다.

(5) Many health experts say that <u>Africa's poverty and politics are to blame for diseases</u> that in most developed countries are easily preventable. International health agencies set out more than two years ago on a $2 billion campaign to stamp out the global threat of polio.

> 어휘리콜 •be to blame for something: -에 대한 원인이 되다; •set out on: -에 착수하다; •polio: 척수성 소아마비; •stamp out: 박멸하다.
>
> 의도확인 두 문장 중에서 첫 문장이, 그 중에서도 밑줄 친 절이 핵정보절이 되고 있다. 둘째 문장은 이 핵정보절에 관한 내용이다. 따라서 밑줄 친 절이 주제부분이다. 이 주제부분에 대한 보건전문가의 견해에 동의하고 있음을 함축한다. 따라서 이 글의 의도는 '전달'이다.
>
> 전문국역 많은 보건전문가들은 아프리카의 가난과 정치가 대부분의 선진국에서 쉽게 예방될 수 있는 질병의 원인이라고 한다. 국제보건기구들은 2년 보다 훨씬 전에 척수성 소아마비 퇴치를 위한 20억불 규모의 운동에 착수했다.

(6) We Americans are taught that <u>everyone is equal</u>. Because of this, we have to wait our turn. We have to wait in line at bus stops, wait for food at the table, wait at meetings until questions are raised, wait at stop sign when driving. To wait one's turn is related to the concept of "first come, first served."

> 어휘리콜 •first come, first served: 선착순이다.
>
> 의도확인 첫 문의 밑줄 친 부분이 주제이고, 그 다음 문들은 이 주제에 관한 내용이다. 이 주제문에 대해 화행기저구조 관점에서 보면 글의 의도는 '전달'이다.
>
> 전문국역 우리 미국 사람들은 모두 사람이 동등하다는 것을 배웠다. 이것 때문에 우리는 우리의 차례를 기다려야 한다. 우리는 버스정류장에서 줄을 서서 기다려야 하고, 테이블에서 식사를 기다려야 하고, 회의에서 질문이 나올 때까지 기다려야 하고, 운전을 할 때 정지신호에서 기다려야 한다. 우리의 차례를 기다리는 것은 '먼저 온 사람은 먼저 서비스 받는다'는 개념과 관련이 있다.

(7) <u>IWK, the International Women in Korea, invite all English-speaking women</u> to our monthly Coffee Morning Saturday, Jan. 26, 10:30 am to 1:30 pm. Presentation on

similarities/differences between Italy and Korea, light lunch, discussion. Call Lucilla 010-3242-6325.

> 어휘리콜 • Presentation: 발표.
> 의도확인 밑줄 친 부분에서 1인칭을 주어로 하여 화행동사 invite가 의도를 나타내고 있다.
> 전문국역 국제한국여성회(the International Women in Korea: IWK)는 모든 영어사용여성을 1월 26일 오전 10:30-오후 1:30에 있는 저희 월 커피모닝 토요 행사에 초대합니다. 이태리와 한국 사이 유사점/차이점에 관한 발표회, 토의가 있습니다. 전화 010-3242-6325번 Lucilla에게 전화 주세요.

(8) We are opening Ping-pong(table tennis) fellow-ship and English worship service at Sinchon area on every Sat. and Sunday. Even though you are not in Christianity, it doesn't matter. If you wanna join us, <u>feel free to contact us</u>. 010-6282-3945, hi.matrls@gmail.com or http://cafe.daum.net/cef05

> 어휘리콜 • worship service: 예배.
> 의도확인 밑줄 친 부분에서 의도 '참여'를 명시적으로 나타내고 있다.
> 전문국역 우리는 매주 토요일과 일요일 신촌에서 탁구 친목 및 영어 예배 모임을 갖고 있습니다. 비록 여러분이 기독교인이 아닐지라도, 문제가 되지 않습니다. 우리와 함께 하고 싶으면, 연락주시기 바랍니다. 연락처는 다음과 같습니다.

(9) WAYTA (We Are Youths Travelling Around) is looking for interested in walking or running. We gather every other Saturday (3-5 p.m) in Seoul or other places. If interested, <u>please contact John</u> on jungkuka@naver.com or find us (WAYTA) on football page. ON! ON!

> 어휘리콜 • gather: (여기서는 자동사) 모이다.
> 의도확인 밑줄 친 곳에서 의도 '참여 희망'을 명시적으로 나타내고 있다.
> 전문국역 WAYTA는 걷고 달리기를 좋아하는 모임입니다. 우리는 격주 토요일 서울 혹은 기타 지역에서 모입니다. 관심 있으시면, John에게 연락주시거나 football 페이지에서 우리를 찾으세요.

(10) Any newly arrived expats to Seoul area interested in playing football (soccer) on Sundays? Contact damardo@yahoo.caexp preferred

> 어휘리콜 • expats는 expatriate(외국인, 이주인)의 약어.
> 의도확인 밑줄 친 곳에서 의도 '참여 희망'을 명시적으로 나타내고 있다.
> 전문국역 서울 지역에 새로 도착한 외국인들의 축구동호회로 일요일에 축구함. 뜻이 있으면 다음으로 연락바람.

(11) <u>Hanwoori Taekwondo is looking for new members</u>! Foreigners and Koreans can break a sweat together learning taekwondo while sharing one another's cultures, languages. If you're interested, or have questions, visit www.hanwooritaekwondo.com or call us at 02-707-1711.

> 어휘리콜 • sweat: 땀.
> 의도확인 밑줄 친 곳에서 글의 의도 '회원 모집'을 명시적으로 나타내고 있다.
> 전문국역 한우리태권도는 신입 회원을 모집합니다. 외국인 및 한국인은 서로의 문화와 언어를 공유하는 동안 태권도를 배우면서 함께 땀을 흘릴 수 있습니다. 관심이 있거나 물어보고 싶은 점이 있으시면, 다음으로 방문을 하시거나 전화를 주세요.

(12) Bangladesh male in his 40's, living in Seoul. <u>I'm looking for a nice, kind and warm-hearted female</u> for friendship, maybe more. I love reading and exploring new things. Write me or call me. mostafa.uddin@yahoo.com 0119602122.

> 어휘리콜 • explore: 탐험하다.
> 의도확인 밑줄 친 곳에서 글의 의도 '여성 구함'을 명시적으로 나타내고 있다.
> 전문국역 서울에 살고 있는 40대 방글라데시 남성. 친절하고, 마음이 따뜻한, 좋은 여성을 친구로, 아마 더 많은 것을 목적으로 찾고 있습니다. 저는 책을 많이 읽으면서 새로운 것을 탐구하고 있습니다. 다음으로 글 또는 전화 주세요.

(13) Hey guys! I am a 16 year old Korean/New Zealand male. I am living in Seoul at the moment, and <u>am looking for friends</u> to talk with! Message me on Facebook: Julian Jung Looking forward to hearing from you guys!

어휘리콜	•'look forward to' 다음에는 명사류가 온다.
의도확인	밑줄 친 곳에서 글의 의도 '친구 구함'을 명시적으로 나타내고 있다.
전문국역	안녕 친구들, 나는 16세 한/뉴질랜드 남성, 지금은 서울에 살고 있는 중으로 같이 대화할 친구들을 찾고 있습니다. 다음 페이스 북으로 연락 주세요.

(14) Shinu can help you with English-Korean translation and interpretation or even become your personal tour guide. Lived in the US and the UK for 14 years. Taught TOEFL on EBS and Suwon University. A bilingual. Unsurpassed understanding of Korean psyche and its culture. 070-7796-8356

어휘리콜	•psyche: 정신, 심리; •Unsurpassed: 능가할 자 없는, 탁월한.
의도확인	밑줄 친 곳에서 글의 의도 '도움 줄 의사'를 명시적으로 나타내고 있다.
전문국역	신우가 영-한 번역 및 해석을 도와 줄 수 있으며, 더 나아가서 개인적 여행가이드가 될 수 있습니다. 14년 동안 미국과 영국에서 살았습니다. EBS와 수원대학교에서 토플을 가르쳤습니다. 이중 언어사용자입니다. 한국의 정신과 문화에 탁월한 이해자입니다.

(15) I'm an American looking to tutor students in English conversation. You must live in Seoul and be at least a university student. Tutoring rates and days of the week (except Sundays) are flexible. Contact Peter for more information at 010-7185-6394.

어휘리콜	•tutor: 가정교사로 가르치다.
의도확인	밑줄 친 곳에서 글의 의도 '가정교사 대상 학생 찾음'을 명시적으로 나타내고 있다.
전문국역	저는 영어회화 가르칠 학생을 찾고 있는 미국인입니다. 학생은 서울 거주하고 적어도 대학생이여야 합니다. 주 단위 지도비 및 날 수(일요일 제외)는 조정될 수 있습니다. 더 정보가 필요하면 다음 전화로 연락주시기 바랍니다.

(16) Volunteering free Korean class for foreigners in Cheongju. Please send me an e-mail: geminicjk@hanmail.net

어휘리콜	•volunteer: 자원하다.

| 의도확인 | 밑줄 친 곳에서 글의 의도 '외국인 지원 희망'을 명시적으로 나타내고 있다. |
| 전문국역 | 청주 외국인을 위한 무료 한국어 공부 신청하십시오. 다음 메일로 연락 주십시오. |

(17) Free Korean lessons for cat lovers! A cat cafe where you can befriend with adorable cats and learn Korean on weekends! It's a cozy little place located at Moran station, Line #8, or Bundang Line. For more information, email at ashleysandol@gmail.com.

어휘리콜	•adorable: 사랑스러운, 귀여운; •cozy: 아늑한.
의도확인	밑줄 친 곳에 글의 의도 '무료 한국어 수강자 모집'을 명시적으로 나타내고 있다.
전문국역	고양이 애호가들을 위한 무료 한국어 교육! 귀하가 귀여운 고양이와 친구가 될 수 있고 주말에 한국어를 배울 수 있는 고양이 카페! Moran역에 위치한 아늑하고 자그마한 장소입니다. 정보가 더 필요하면 다음 전자 메일로 들어오세요.

(18) **Vatican plans big send-off for pope**

1 VATICAN CITY (Reuters) - Cardinals around the world began informal contacts to discuss who should next lead the Church through a period of major crisis and the Vatican said it planned a big send-off for Pope Benedict before he becomes the first pontiff in centuries to resign.

2 At a Tuesday news conference on how the pope plans to spend the next two weeks before he steps out of the limelight, the Vatican also disclosed that the 85-year-old Benedict has been wearing a pacemaker since before he was elected pope in 2005.

3 It said no specific illness led him to resign, merely old age and diminishing mental and physical strength.

4 It also said he would not play any role in the running of the Church after his Feb. 28 resignation.

5 "The pope has said in his declaration that he will use his time for prayer and reflection and will not have any responsibility for guidance of the Church or any administrative or government responsibility," said Vatican spokesman Father

Federico Lombarcli.

6 "This is absolutely clear and this is the sense of the resignation," Lombardi said, adding that he "will not intervene in any way" in trying to influence the choice of his successor.

7 The shock announcement sent the Vatican scrambling to change venues of some papal activities so that more people can see him before the resignation.

8 On Wednesday, the pope was to have led a traditional Ash Wednesday service at a small church in Rome but the event has been moved to St. Peter's Basilica for what will likely be his last Mass in public.

9 His last general audience, scheduled for the day before his resignation, has been moved from the Vatican's audience hall, which has a capacity of some 10,000 people, to St. Peter's Square, which can hold hundreds of thousands.

어휘리콜 •cardinal: 추기경; •pontiff: 로마교황, 주교; •limelight: 주목의 대상; •diminish: 줄이다, 감소시키다; •scramble: 다투다; •venue: 개최지, 논거, 입장; •papal: 로마 교황의, 교회 제도의.

의도확인 '바티칸 시티로부터의 로이터 통신'이라는 말이 글의 목적은 '뉴스전달'임을 말해준다.

전문국역 •바티칸이 로마교황 대 환송을 계획하다. **1** 바티칸 시티(로이터통신)-전 세계 추기경들이 대 위기를 뚫고 교회를 이끌 다음 교황에 관해 논의하기 위해 비 공식접촉을 시작했으며, 바티칸은 수세기 동안 베네딕트 교황이 사직하는 첫 교황이 되기 이전에 베네딕트 교황 대 환송을 계획했다고 발표했다. **2** 교황이 주목의 대상으로부터 벗어나기 이전인 다음 2주간을 어떻게 보내려고 하는가에 관한 화요일 뉴스 협의에서, 바티칸은 85세의 베네딕트 교황은 2005년 교황으로 선출되기 이전부터 평화조정자의 지위에 있어왔다고 또한 밝혔다. **3** 바티칸은 특별한 질병이 그로 하여금 은퇴하도록 한 것이 아니며, 단지 고령에 허약해져가는 정신적 육체적 힘이라고 말했다. **4** 바티칸은 또한 베네딕트 교황은 2월 28일 은퇴 이후는 교회의 운영에 어떤 역할도 하지 않을 것이라고 밝혔다. **5** "교황은 자기 발표문에서 자기는 여생을 기도하고 회고할 것이라고 말했으며, 교회의 어떤 안내 책임이나 행정 혹은 정부의 직책을 맡지 않을 것이라고 말했다."고 바티칸 대변인 Father Federico Lombarcli가 말했다. **6** "이것은 절대적으로 분명하며 이것이 은퇴의 의미이다."라고 Lombarcli는 말하고, 덧붙여 Lombarcli는 교황은 자기 후임자 결정에 영향을 미치는 일에는 "어떤 방식으로든 관여하지 않을 것이다"라고 말했다. **7** 그 충격 발표는 바티칸으로 하여금 보다 더 많은 사람들이 은퇴 이전에 교황을 볼 수 있도록 하기 위하여 교황활동의 개최지를 변경하는 데에 논의를 하게 했다. **8** 수요일에 교황은 로마 내 한 작은 교회에서 전통적인 Ash Wednesday 예배를 인도하기로 되어 있었지만, 그 행사는 그의 마지막 대중미사가 될 것을 위해 St. Peter's

> Basilica로 옮겨졌다. ⑨ 그의 은퇴 직전 날로 예정된 그의 마지막 일반 대중은 바티칸 대중 홀로부터, 이 홀은 약 1만 명의 수용 능력을 가지고 있는 홀인데, 수백만 명 수용 능력인 St. Peter's Square로 옮겼다.

(19) **MEMORANDUM**

To Departmental Heads

From Steven Broom, Administration Manager

Ref SB/ST

Date 2 July 19-

OPERATIONS MEETING - 14 JULY

Please note that the next Operations Meeting will be held in the Conference Room at 1000 hours on Monday 14 July.

Follow-up items from our last meeting which will be included under Matters Arising are:

- New brochure (Suzanne Sutcliffe)
- Annual Dinner and Dance (Mandy Lim)

If you wish to add any further items to the agenda please let me know before 8 July.

어휘리콜	•Operations Meeting: 운영회의; •Follow-up: 속행.
의도확인	회의 관련 사항 전달
전문국역	다음 운영 회의는 7월 14일 월요일 컨퍼런스 룸에서 개최됨을 주목해 주십시오. 제기

> 되는 문제들에 지난 회의로부터의 다음 문제들이 포함될 것이다. 만약 안건에 더 포함할 항목이 있으면 7월8일 전에 저에게 알려 주세요.

(20) 123 York St. Kingston, Ontario, Canada.

www.abccompany.org

Email: admin@abccompany.org   Tel: 1-800-222-3333

The Fire Chief

Fire Department, Station – 222
123 Street Address,
Kingston, Ontario, Canada

INVITATION TO ATTEND OUR FAMILY DAY EVENT

ABC is a community development center. There are a total 250 households in the Kingston north end most of which are members of ABC. As part of its annual activities, ABC is planning to hold a Family Barbecue on Saturday, 25th January, 2014 at 11:00 am at the John McDonald Park. The main purpose of this Barbecue is to foster community sprit amongst the residents of the community.

As part of the activities of the day, we would be honored to have the Community Fire Development with a Fire Engine at the event, so that the children can interact with the firemen and the fire engine. If possible, we would also appreciate a short speech about fire prevention and what to do in the event of a fire. We have scheduled this presentation for 1:00pm on that day.

We are expecting a total of about 200 – 400 people at the event. Kindly let us know as soon as possible if you would be available to attend our event and any other question you may have.

SUSAN MILLER

CHIEF COORDINNER

> 어휘리콜 •household: 세대, 가구, 가정; •foster: 육성하다, 촉진하다, 기르다.
> 의도확인 본문의 의도가 초청임을 나타내 주고 있다.
> 일부국역 ABC는 지역 발전 센터입니다. Kingston 북쪽 끝에 총 250가구가 있는데, 대부분 ABC의 회원입니다. ABC는 연중 활동의 일부로서 2014년 1월 25일 토요일 John McDonald Park에서 11시 가족 바비큐 행사를 계획하고 있습니다.

(21) This is certify that mr/ms ooo a malaysian, bearer of identity Card No 8585555 has declared under oath on 13/12/2012 that she/he is 28 years of age and single by virtue of a sworn statement in the files of this office and based on the computerized records available in this department there is no record of any marriage being registered under the law reform(marriage and divorce) act 1976.

I further certify that, based on documents submitted to this department, mr/ms. ooo intends to marry mr/ms ooo korea national and holder of identity card / passport no oooooo.

This certificate of marital status shall be valid for 150 days after issuance thereof and shall be deemed invalid at the expiration of said period.

This certificate is issued by national registration department of malaysia for the purpose of marriage with foreigner.

> 어휘리콜 •oath: 서약, 선서; •swear: 명세하다, 선서하다.
> 의도확인 본문의 의도가 증명서 서식임을 나타내 주고 있다.
> 부분국역 이것은 남/여 ooo 말레이시아인, 신분증 번호 8585555의 소유자가 2012년 12월 13일 자신이 28세이고 미혼임을 … 선언했음을 확인합니다.

제2절 본문구성의 패턴 요약

5단계 독해사후 처리에서 글의 의도를 확인한 다음에 독자가 어떻게 해야 하는가? 본문의 내용흐름을 구성패턴으로 요약하는 것이다. 구성패턴으로 요약하는 것은 2단 구성패턴(가령, 주장-증거), 3단 구성패턴(가령, 서론-본론-결론), 5단 구성패턴(가령, 머리말-주제-계획-주장-끝맺음), 혹은 기타 패턴으로 압축하는 것이다.

(1)   **EDITORIAL**
                        Rows over child care

1 In recent years, <u>many countries have increased investment in early childhood education and care (ECEC) as it brings a wide range of benefits</u>, including better child well-being and learning outcomes, poverty reduction, increased fertility rates and higher female labor market participation.

2 <u>The Korean government has also started to expand investment in ECEC</u> to reap its benefits. The first thing it did was to assume more responsibility for education of children at age 5.

3 <u>In 2011, the government developed a common preschool curriculum for 5-year-olds for use by both kindergartens and child-care centers.</u> Previously, the two institutions taught different curricula. Kindergartens used the National Kindergarten Curriculum, while child-care centers used the Standard Child Care Curriculum.

4 <u>The common preschool curriculum, dubbed the Nuri Curriculum, began to be taught from March this year.</u> To make it universally available, the government expanded its subsidy scheme. Previously, the subsidies were offered to children from families in the bottom 70 percent of the income ladder. From March this year, they were provided to all 5-year-olds attending a kindergarten or a daycare facility.

5 In an unexpected move, the government also expanded its subsidy scheme for toddlers under 24 months old. Previously, the benefits were given to the bottom 70 percent of Korean families. Now, they are provided to all families that send their children to a day-care facility.

6 The government's ECEC initiatives were a step in the right direction. However, the problem was that they were implemented without due preparation. The government should have considered beforehand the funding capabilities of local governments and the accommodation capacities of existing child-care institutions.

7 As a result, local governments have had a hard time this year meeting their share of the financing burden for ECEC. Kindergartens and child-care centers also had difficulties due to the abrupt surge in enrollment.

8 Next year, the problem is expected to worsen as the government will expand its ECEC program for children aged 3 and 4. It has already developed the Nuri Curricula for these children and plans to offer day care subsidies to all families that enroll their 3 and 4-year- olds at a kindergarten or a day-care facility. Currently, the subsidies are provided to those in the bottom 70 percent of the income scale.

9 According to reports, local councils of several big cities and provinces, including Seoul and Gyeonggi Province, have recently refused to pass budget bills for next year, saying that the spending proposals related to ECEC are simply beyond their financing abilities.

10 These councils argue that the central government should shoulder the additional funding burden as their financial resources have been already depleted due to the universal free school-lunch scheme as well as the expanded ECEC schemes for children aged 0-2 and 5.

11 The central government and local governments need to resolve the funding problem through dialogue as they can neither scale down the ECEC program nor delay its planned expansion. The power to do so is in the hands of the main political parties, which have already pledged to increase investment in ECEC.

12 Instead of engaging in unseemly wrangling, they need to speed up the construction of kindergartens and state-run day-care centers. Recently, kindergartens and day-care centers in Seoul and Gyeonggi Province were crowded with parents who sought slots for their children. Due to the limited capacities of these institutions, many parents could not register their children.

어휘리콜 •dub: -라고 칭하다; •fertility rate: 출산율; •subsidy: 보조금, 장려금; •unseemly wrangling: 꼴사나운 논쟁.

패턴요약 윤곽관점에서는 제목을 포함하는 본문만으로 구성되어 있다. 첫 부분의 **EDITORIAL**이라는 단어가 (1)은 신문사설 장르라는 것을 가리켜 주고 있다(2012.12.10).1) 각 단락의 주제적 내용은 밑줄 친 부분이다. 논설에 속하는 신문사설은 크게 3단 구성(1.사실, 2.분석 혹은 평가를 통한 장점 혹은 문제점, 3.작자의 견해, 주장, 혹은 해결방안)이라는 것을 리콜하면 좋을 것이다. 12 단락(즉 주제문)으로 되어 있는 (1)은 ①-⑤는 사실, 즉 데이터를 제시하고, ⑥-⑩은 문제점을 제시하고, ⑪-⑫는 작자의 견해를 제시하고 있다. 따라서 독자는 1)영유아 교육과정의 확대(사실), 2)예산 부족문제 발생(문제점), 3)중앙정부/지자체의 대화를 통한 예산확보와 유치원과 보육원의 건설(해결방안) 등으로 압축된다.

전문국역 영유아 보육 논쟁 ① 최근에 많은 국가들이 유아보육(ECEC)에 투자를 증가했는데, 그것은 더 나은 어린이 복지, 학습 결과, 가난 축소, 출산율 증가, 그리고 고급여성 노동시장참여를 포함하여 광범위한 이익을 가져오기 때문이다. ② 한국정부 또한 그 이익을 높이기 위해서 ECEC에 투자를 확대하기 시작했다. 정부가 하는 첫 번째 일은 5세 어린이의 교육에 더 많은 책임을 떠맡는 것이다. ③ 2011년에, 정부는 유치원과 보육센터에 의해서 사용될 5세 어린이 용 취학 전 공통 커리큘럼을 개발했다. 이전에는 두 교육기관이 다른 교과과정을 가르쳤다. 유치원은 국가 재정 유치원 교과과정을 가르쳤고, 반면에 보육센터는 표준 보육 교과과정을 사용했다. ④ 누리 교과과정이라고 명명된 취학 전 공통 커리큘럼은 금년 3월부터 가르치기 시작했다. 이 커리큘럼을 보편적으로 적용하기 위하여 정부는 장려금 계획을 확대했다. 이전에는 지원금이 소득계층의 하위 70%에 있는 가정의 어린이에게 주어졌다. 금년 3월부터 장려금은 유치원 혹은 낮 보호시설에 참여하는 5세 어린이에게 제공되었다. ⑤ 기대하지 않았던 방법으로, 정부는 또한 생후 24개월 이하 유아에게로 지원금을 확대하였다. 이제 지원금이 어린이를 낮 동안의 보호시설에 보내는 모든 가정에 지원된다. ⑥ 정부의 ECEC 출발은 올바른 방향으로의 첫 단계이다. 그러나 문제는 사전 준비 없이 시행이 되었다는 것이다. 정부는 미리 지방정부의 재원 능력과 기존 보육시설의 수용 능력을 고려했어야만 했다. ⑦ 그 결과, 지방정부는 금년 ECEC를 위한 재정부담의 몫을 충당하는 어려운 때를 만났다. 유치원과 보육센터 또한 급격한 등록 증가 때문에 어려움을 가졌다. ⑧ 내년에는 정부가 ECEC 프로그램을 3-4세 어린이에게로 확대할 것이기 때문에 그 문제가 나빠질 것으로 예상된다. ECEC 프로그램은 이 어린이들 용 교과과정을 개발해서 유치원과 낮 보육시설

---

1) 논설은 논하는 글, 즉 주장하는 글이다. 주장하는 글이란 어떤 사실(가령: 일, 사건, 남의 견해나 주장)에 대하여 자신의 주장을 논리적으로 서술하는 글이다. 이런 논설의 한 종류인 사설은 신문, 잡지 등에서 그 회사의 주장을 실어 펼친다.

의 3-4세 나이를 등록하는 모든 가정에 낮 보육 지원금을 계획한다. 현재로는 지원금이 소득 하위 70%에 있는 어린이에게 지원되고 있다. ❾ 보고에 따르면, 대 도시 및 지방들의 의회들은, 서울과 경기를 포함해서, 최근에 금년 예산통과를 거부하면서 ECEC 관련 소비성 제안들은 단순히 재정능력을 넘어선다고 말했다. ❿ 이 의회들은 0-2세와 5세 어린이 용 확대 ECEC계획과 전체 무료 학교급식 제도로 자기들의 재원이 이미 고갈되었기 때문에 중앙정부가 추가 재정 부담을 짊어져야 한다고 주장한다. ⓫ 중앙정부와 지방정부는 ECEC프로그램을 축소하거나 기존 계획된 확대를 지연시킬 수 없기 때문에 대화를 통해서 재원문제를 해결할 필요가 있다. 그렇게 하는 힘은 주요 정당들의 수중에 있는데, 그들 정당들은 ECEC에 투자를 증대하기로 이미 공약을 했었다. ⓬ 꼴사나운 논쟁에 개입하는 것 대신에, 그들은 유치원과 국가 운영 낮 보육센터의 건립에 속도를 내야 할 필요가 있다. 최근에, 서울과 경기 지방의 유치원과 낮 보육센터는 자기 아이들 자리를 찾는 부모님들로 북적였다. 이 교육기관들의 제한된 수용능력 때문에, 많은 부모들은 자기 아이들을 등록시킬 수가 없었다.

(2) Food security still a major issue in SE Asia

Joel Brinkley

LUANG PRABANG, Laos -

1 Travel through Southeast Asia, and wherever you go <u>you'll find statues of Buddha</u> - meditating, cogitating, calling for peace or for rain. The multiple poses are varied, and each one has its own meaning.

2 But <u>only one pose shows the Buddha actually grinning</u>. That's the Buddha who is fat, sitting in a chair, his belly so big it looks like he'll be unable to stand up.

3 <u>This might seem odd</u>, given that Budhism is generally an ascetic faith. To reach enlightenment, you're supposed to temper your craving for wealth and physical things. Be satisfied with who you are and what you have.

4 But then, <u>Buddhists, like everyone, must eat</u>. And in this part of the world, that's a constant challenge for most people. So the fat Buddha is smiling because he has reached the state where he no longer has to worry about getting enough to eat. He's finally content - and oh-so happy.

5 <u>Vietnam, according to Central Intelligence Agency figures, has a lower obesity rate than any nation on earth</u>. Just above Vietnam at the bottom of the list is Laos. And that's not because Vietnamese and Laotians are devotees of Weight

Watchers diet plans. No, too many of these people generally cannot get enough to eat.

6 Some Vietnamese like to say they envy fat people. And here in Laos, I watched a middle-aged Laotian man affectionately pat the belly of an overweight American tourist and smile, his voice laced with envy, as he bowed his head and said: "Good, Good!"

7 The CIA was able to get obesity figures for fewer than half the world's nations. Otherwise, Cambodia and Myamar would certainly be near the bottom, too. While Myanmar is changing, slowly, it, like these other states, has been governed by uncaring, obdurate leaders for ages.

8 Five years ago, the United Nations' World Food Program conducted a comprehensive study of Laotian children and found that half of them were severely malnourished in the first years of life - setting them up for physical and mental stunting, which of course means they will grow up short and not terribly smart.

9 Well, here we are five years later, and UNICEF puts Laos's stunting rate at 48 percent. No change. In Cambodia, it's 40 percent, Vietnam 31 percent and 35 percent Burma. By comparison, in Mexico, hardly a wealthy state, the figure is 16 percent.

10 Laos calls itself a Communist society, which means it's supposed to bring workers into the larger economy. But the government totally ignores most of its people and provides almost nothing for them. Aid agencies here say their projects are "program based," meaning that the program will die if the aid agency stops what it's doing. The government just doesn't care.

11 The most glaring example today: Laos is building a hydroelectric dam on the Mekong River, bringing howls of complaint from countries downstream, including Cambodia and Vietnam. You might think the needs of the Laotian people outweigh the complaints from the south. After all, only a handful of states, most of them in sub-Saharan Africa, provide less electric power to its population than Laos. This country's total, on average: only 39 watt per person each year.

12 Laotian officials, explaining the dam project at the groundbreaking ceremony late last year, told journalists they wanted to vault their nation from its status as one of the world's poorest. But since then, the government has instead made a contract with its neighbor, Thailand. The Thai will buy most, if not all, of the power that the new dam generates.

13 So the dam will almost certainly benefit the Lao people not at all. The money earned from the Thai will go where most money here goes - into the pockets of the Lao leaders. Laos ranks 160th out of 174 nations in Transparency International's 2012 corruption index.

14 As a result, "there's been a shift among donors; they're moving away from supporting dam projects" here, Karen Stewart, U.S. ambassador to Laos, told me.

15 Around the world, religion is often a refuge, a salve for the poor. And many of the Buddhist nations are extremely poor. Buddha's Four Noble Truths tell his followers they can reach Nirvana by abandoning sensual cravings and self-indulgence - attaining dispassion toward physical things.

16 But when Buddhist pagodas all over this region so proudly display ancient images of the Buddha, their role model, when he is most joyful - displaying the broadest imaginable grin because he's obese - you know that, through the ages, the people's greatest concern has been getting enough to eat.

Joel Brinkley, a professor of journalism at Stanford University, is a Pulitzer Prize-winning former foreign correspondent for the New York Times. -Ed.

(Tribune Media Services)

어휘리콜   •grin: 씩 웃다, 히죽거리다; •ascetic: 금욕주의의, 고행의; •odd: 뜻밖의, 기묘한; •enlightenment: 계몽, 교화, 깨달음; •crave: 열망하다; •temper: 진정시키다, 경감시키다; •devotee: 열성가; •weight watcher: 체중에 신경을 쓰는 사람; •lace with: -로 혼합하다, 가미하다; •uncaring: 부주의한, 멍한; •obdurate: 완고한, 고집 센; •malnourished: 영양실조의; •stunt: 성장을 방해하다; •glaring: 빛나는, 눈에 띄는; •howl: 큰 소리, 불평; •outweigh: 보다 무겁다, 보다 중요하다, 보다 가치가 있다; •sub-Saharan: 사하라 사막 이남의; •groundbreaking ceremony: 기공식; •vault: 도약하다.

패턴요약   양식 관점에서 제목, 저자명, 본문, 저자소개, 출처 등으로 구성되어 있으며, 그 중 본문은 16단락으로 구성되어 있다. 단락들의 내용은 다음과 같다: **1** 은 도처에 부처의 상이 있음, ② 는 배부른 부처의 웃는 모습, ③ 은 고행의 신앙에 안 어울림, ④ 는 신자들 식사 필요성, ⑤ 는 베트남은 최하 비만 국임, ⑥ 은 베트남인이 살찐 사람 부러워함, ⑦ 은 세계에서 비만 국은 절반이하임, ⑧ 은 라오스 어린이 영양실조, ⑨ 는 라오스는 성장 장애 국, ⑩ 은 라오스의 공산주의 정치이념과 실제의 모순, ⑪ 은 라오스의 수력발전 댐 수익의 부패, ⑫ 라오스 전기 외국 판매, ⑬ 은 댐이 국민에 공헌 못함, ⑭ 는 그 결과 라오스 기부자 이탈, ⑮ 는 종교는 가난한 자의 도피처, ⑯ 은 사람들 관심사는 먹는 것을 획득하는 것. 이 16단락의 내용은 지역의 문화적 배경(단락1-4), 식량부족 실태(단락5-10), 식량부족 실태의 이유(단락11-14), 그 결과(단락15-16)로 구성되어 있다.

전문국역   식량안보가 동남아시아에서 아직도 큰 이슈임. ① 동남아시아를 여행해보십시오. 그러면 여러분은 어디를 가든지 간에, 명상하는, 숙고하는, 평화나 비를 기원하는, 부처(Buddha)의 조상을 발견하게 될 것입니다. 많은 자세들은 다양하며, 각 자세는 그 나름의 의미를 지니고 있습니다. ② 그러나 오직 한 자세는 부처가 실제로 씩 웃고 있음을 보여줍니다. 그 모습은 살이 찐 모습으로 의자에 앉아 있으며, 배가 불룩해서 마치 일어설 수 없을 것 같은 자세입니다. ③ 이 모습은, 부처가 일반적으로 고행의 신앙이라고 할 때, 뜻밖인 것일 지도 모릅니다. 깨달음에 이르기 위해서 여러분은 부와 물질적인 것을 열망하는 것을 누그러뜨려야 할 것으로 기대됩니다. 현재의 자신과 가진 것에 만족하십시오. ④ 그런데, 부처주의자들은, 모든 사람처럼, 먹지 않으면 안 됩니다. 그리고 이 불교계에서는 그것이 대부분의 사람들에게 지속적인 도전입니다. 그래서 살찐 부처는, 먹을 것을 많이 얻는 것과 관련하여 걱정 할 필요가 없는 상태에 도달했기 때문에, 미소 짓고 있습니다. 부처는 결국 만족하고 있으며, 그리고 매우 행복합니다. ⑤ 중앙정보기관의 계수에 따르면, 베트남은 지구상에서 어떤 나라보다도 낮은 비만 율을 갖고 있습니다. 하위에서부터의 비만 율 리스트에서 베트남 바로 위는 라오스입니다. 그리고 그것은 베트남 사람과 라오스 사람들이 체중에 신경을 쓰는 사람, 다이어트 계획의 열성가이기 때문이 아닙니다. 아니, 이들 나라에 너무나 많은 사람들은 먹을 것을 충분히 얻을 수가 없습니다. ⑥ 일부 베트남사람들은 살찐 사람을 부러워한다고 말하기를 좋아합니다. 그리고 라오스 여기서, 나는 중년의 라오스 남자가 과체중의 미국 여행자의 배를 애정스럽게 뚝뚝 치면서, 목소리에는 부러움이 가미되어 미소 지으면서 머리 숙여 인사하고, 굿, 굿, 이라고 말하는 것을 보았습니다. ⑦ CIA는 세계의 국가들 중 절반이 못되는 국가에서만 비만 수치를 얻을 수 있었습니다. 캄보디아와 미얀마 역시 확실히 최저 가까이 있을 것입니다. 미얀마가 변하고 있는 동안에, 그것도 천천히, 이런 다른 나라들과 같이, 미얀마는 여러 시대 동안 부주의하고, 고집 센 지도자들에 의해 통치되어 왔습니다. ⑧ 5년 전에, 유엔 세계 식량프로그램이 라오스 어린이들에 대해 종합적인 연구를 수행했는데, 어린이 절반이 생후 초기에 심각한 영양실조에 있었고 - 어린이들로 하여금 신체적 및 정신적 성장장애를 가져오게 하고 있음을 발견했는데, 이것은 물론 어린이들이 키가 작게 자라게 하고 무섭게도 영리하지 못하게 할 것입니다. ⑨ 그런데, 여기서 우리는 5년이 늦습니다. 그리고 UNICEF는 라오스의 성장장해 율을 48%로 봅니다. 변화가 없음입니다. 캄보디아에서는 그것이 40%, 베트남에서는 31%, 그리고 버마에서는 35%입니다. 비교컨대, 멕시코에서는, 부의 나라가 아닌데, 그 수치는 16%입니다. ⑩ 라오스는 스스로를 공산주의 사회라고 말하는데, 공산주의 사회는 사회가 노동자들로 하여금 더 큰 경제 속으로 들어가게 하는 것으로 예정되어 있다는 것을 의미합니다. 그런데 정부는 전적으로 대부분의 국민을 무시하고 그들에게 거의 아무것도 제공하지 않습니다. 여기 원조기관들은 자기들의 프로젝트는 "프로그램에 근거한다."고하는데, 프로그램에 근거한다는 말은 만약 원조기관이 자기가 하고 있는 것을 멈춘다면 프로그램은 죽는다는 것을 의미합니다. 정부는 관심을 갖지 않습니다. ⑪ 오늘날 가장 눈에 띄는 예는 다음과 같습니다. 라오스가 메콩 강에 수력발전 댐을 건설하고 있으며, 캄보디아와 베트남을 포함하여 하류에 있는 국가들로부터 불평을 듣고 있는 것입니다. 독자 여러분은 라오스 사람들이 필요한 것은 남쪽으로부터 오는 불평을 보다 중요하게 여기는 것이라고 생각할지도 모릅니다. 결국, 단지 적은 국가들, 사하라 사막 이남의 국가들 대부분은 자기 국민들에게 라오스보다도 전기를 덜 공급하고 있습니다. 이 나라 총 전력은 평균하여 년 1인당 단지 39와트 입니다. ⑫ 라오스 공무원들은, 지난해 말 기공식에서 댐 프로젝트를 설명하면서, 저널리스트들에게 자기들은 세계에서 가장 가난한 국가 중의 한 위상으로부터 도약시키고 싶다고 말했습니다. 그러나 그때 이후, 이 정부는 대신에 이웃, 태국과 계약을 했습니다. 태국은, 전부는 아니지만, 새 댐이 생산하는 전력 대부분을 살 것입니다. ⑬ 그러므로 그 댐은 거의 확실히 라오스 국민들에게 전혀 이익이 되지 않을 것입니다. 태국으로부터 번 돈은, 여기서 오는 대부분의 돈은 라오스 지도자들의 주머니 속으로 들어갈 것입니다. 라오스는 Transparency International's 2012 corruption index에서 174개국 중 160 순위입니다. ⑭ 그 결과, "기부자들 사이에 변화가 있어 왔습니다. 기부자들은 댐 프로젝트를 지지하는 것으로부터 떨어져 나가고 있는 중이다."라고 여기 Karen Stewart 주 라오스 미국 대사가 내게 말했습니다. ⑮ 전 세계에서 종교가 종종 피난처, 가난한 사람들을 위한 위안처입니다. 그리고 불교국가들 중 많은 국가들이 극히 가난합니다. 부처의 4가지 유명한 진리는 추종자들에게 물질적인 것을 향한 감각적 열망, 자기 탐닉을 포기함으로써, 즉 물질적인 것을 향한 냉정함을 유지함으로서 열반(해탈)에 이를 수 있다고 합니다. ⑯ 그러나 이 전 지역에 있는 불교 탑들이 매우 자랑스럽게 부다의 고전적 이미지를, 탑들의 역할 모델을 드러내 줄 때, 부처가 기뻐할 때 - 부다 자기가 살이 찌기 때문에 가장 폭넓은 상상할 수 있는 웃음을 드러낼 때 - 독자 여러분은, 시대를 꿰뚫어서, 사람들의 최대 관심사가 먹을 것을 충분히 얻는 것이었음을 알고 있습니다.

(3)

1. As was indicated in the Preface, the notion of 'major language' is defined in social terms, so it is now time to look somewhat more consistently at some notions relating to the social side of language, in particular the social interaction of languages. Whether a language is a major language or not has nothing to do with its structure or with its genetic affiliation, and the fact that so many of the world's major languages are Indo-European is a mere accident of history.

2. First, we may look in more detail at the criteria that serve to define a language as being major. One of the most obvious criteria is the number of speakers, and

certainly in making my choice of languages to be given individual chapters in this volume number of speakers was one of my main criteria. However, number of speakers is equally clearly not the sole criterion.

3 An interesting comparison to make here is between Chinese (or even more specifically, Mandarin) and English. Mandarin has far more native sneakers than English, yet still English is generally considered a more useful language in the world at large than is Mandarin, as seen in the much larger number of people studying English as a second language than studying Mandarin as a second language. One of the reasons for this is that English is an international language, understood by a large number of people in many different parts of the world; Mandarin, by contrast, is by and large confined to China, and even taking all Chinese dialects (or languages) together, the extension of Chinese goes little beyond China and overseas Chinese communities. English is not only the native language of sizable populations in different parts of the world (especially the British Isles, North America, Australia and New Zealand) but is also spoken as a second language in even more countries, as is discussed in more detail in the chapter on English. English happens also to be the language of some of the technologically most advanced countries (in particular of the USA), so that English is the basic medium for access to current technological developments. Thus factors other than mere number of speakers are relevant in determining the social importance of a language.

4 Indeed, some of the languages given individual chapters in this volume have relatively few native speakers. Some of them are important not so much by virtue of the number of native speakers but rather because of the extent to which they are used as lingua franca, as a second language among people who do not share a common first language. Good examples here are Swahili and Malay. Swahili is the native language of a relatively small population, primarily on the coast of East Africa, but its use as a lingua franca has spread through much of East Africa, (especially Kenya and Tanzania), and even stretches into parts of Zaire. Malay too is the native language of relatively few people in western Malaysia and even smaller number in Indonesia, but its adoption as the lingua franca and official language of both countries has raised the combined first and second language speakers to well over a hundred million. In many instances, in my choice of languages I have been guided by this factor rather than by raw statistics. Among the Philippine languages, for instance, Cebuano has more native speakers than Tagalog, but I selected Tagalog because it is both the national language of the Philippines and used as a linga franca across much of the country. Among the Indonesian languages, Javanese has more native speakers than Malay and is also the bearer of an old culture, but in terms of the current social situation Malay is clearly the dominant language of this branch of Austronesian. A number of other Indo-Aryan languages would surely have qualified for inclusion in terms of number of speakers, such as Marathi, Rajasthani, Panjabi, Gujarati, but they have not been assigned individual chapters because in social terms the major languages of the northern part of South Asia are clearly Hindi-Urdu and Bengali.

5. Another important criterion is the cultural importance of a language, in terms of the age and influence of its cultural heritage. An example in point is provided by the Dravidian languages, where Telugu actually has more speakers than Tamil; Tamil, however, is the more ancient literary language, and for this reason my choice rested with Tamil. I am aware that many of these decisions are in part subjective, and in part dangerous: as I emphasised in the Preface, the thing furthest from my mind is to intend any slight to speakers of languages that are not considered major in the contents of this volume.

6. Certain languages are major even despite the absence of native speakers, as with Latin and Sanskrit. Latin has provided a major contribution to all European languages, as can be seen most superficially in the extent to which words of Latin origin are used in European languages. Even those languages that have tried to avoid the appearance of Latinity by creating their own vocabulary have often fallen back on Latin models: German *Gewissen* 'conscience', for instance, contains the prefix *ge-*, meaning 'with', the stem *wiss-*, meaning 'know', and the suffix *-en* to form an abstract noun – an exact copy of the Latin *con-sci-entia*; borrowings

that follow the structure rather than the form in this way are known as calques or loan translations. Sanskrit has played a similar role in relation to the languages of India, including Hindi. Hebrew is included not because of the number of its speakers - as noted in the chapter on Hebrew, this has never been larger - but because of the contribution of Hebrew and its culture to European and Middle Eastern society.

7 A language can thus have influence beyond the areas where it is the native or second language. A good example to illustrate this is Arabic. Arabic loans form a large part of the vocabulary of many languages spoken by Islamic peoples, even of languages that are genetically only distantly related to Arabic (e.g. Hausa) or that are genetically totally unrelated (e.g. Turkish, Persian and Urdu). The influence of Arabic can also be seen in the adoption of the Arabic writing system by many Islamic peoples. Similarly, Chinese loan words form an important part of the vocabulary of some East Asian languages, in particular Vietnamese, Japanese and Korean; the use of written Chinese characters has also spread to Japan and Korea, and in earlier times also to Vietnam.

8 It is important to note also that the status of a language as a major language is far from immutable. Indeed, as we go back into history we find many significant changes. For instance, the possibility of characterising English as the world's major language is an innovation of the twentieth century. One of the most important shifts in the distribution of major languages resulted from the expansion of European languages, especially English, Spanish, Portuguese, and to a lesser extent French as a result of the colonisation of the Americas: English, Spanish and Portuguese all now have far more native speakers in the New World than in Britain, Spain or Portugal. Indeed, in the Middle Ages one would hardly have imagined that English, confined to an island off the coast of Europe, would have become a major international language.

9 In medieval Europe, Latin was clearly the major language, since, despite the lack of native speakers, it was the lingua franca of those who needed to communicate across linguistic boundaries. Yet the rise of Latin to such preeminence – which includes the fact that Latin and its descendants have ousted virtually all other languages from southwestern Europe - could hardly have been foreseen from its inauspicious beginnings confined to the area around Rome. Equally spectacular has been the spread of Arabic, in the wake of Islamic religious zeal, from being confined to the Arabian peninsula to being the dominant language of the Middle East and North Africa.

10 In addition to languages that have become major languages, there are equally languages that have lost this status. The earliest records from Mesopotamia, often considered the cradle of civilisation, are in two languages: Sumerian and Akkadian (the latter the language of the Assyrian and Babylonian empires); Akkadian belongs to the Semitic branch of Afroasiatic, while Sumerian is as far as we can tell unrelated to any other known language. Even at the time of attested Sumerian inscriptions, the language was probably already approaching extinction, and it continued to be used in deference to tradition (as with Latin in medieval Europe). The dominant language of the period was to become Akkadian, but in the intervening period this too has died out, leaving no direct descendants. Gone too is Ancient Egyptian, the language of the Pharaohs. The linguistic picture of the Mediterranean and Middle East in the year nought was very different from that which we observe today.

11 Social factors and social attitudes can even bring about apparent reversals in the family-tree model of language relatedness. At the time of the earliest texts from Germany, two distinct Germanic languages are recognised: Old Saxon and Old High German. Old Saxon is the ancestor of the modern Low German (Plattdeutsch) dialects, while Old High German is the ancestor of the modern High German dialects and of the standard language. Because of social changes - such as the decline of the Hanseatic League, the economic mainstay of northern Germany - High German gained social ascendancy over Low German. Since the standard language, based on High German, is now recognised as the standard in both northern and southern Germany, both Low and High German dialects are now considered dialects of a single German language, and the social relations between a given Low German dialect and standard German are in practice no different from those between any High German dialect and standard German.

12 One of the most interesting developments to have arisen from language contact is the development of pidgin and creole languages. A pidgin language arises from a very practical situation: speakers of different languages need to communicate with one another to carry out some practical task, but do not speak any language in common and moreover do not have the opportunity to learn each other's languages properly. What arises in such a situation is, initially, an unstable pidgin, or jargon, with highly variable structure - considerably simplified relative to the native languages of the people involved in its creation - and just enough vocabulary to permit practical tasks to be carried out reasonably successfully. The clearest examples of the development of such pidgins arose from European colonisation, in particular from the Atlantic slave trade and from indenturing labourers in the South Pacific. These pidgins take most of their vocabulary from the colonising language, although their structures are often very different from those of the colonising language.

13 At a later stage, the jargon may expand, particularly when its usefulness as a lingua franca is recognised among the speakers of non-European origin, leading to a stabilised pidgin, such as Tok Pisin, the major lingua franca of Papua New Guinea. This expansion is on several planes: the range of functions is expanded, since the pidgin is no longer restricted to uses of language essential to practical tasks; the vocabulary is expanded as a result of this greater range of functions, new words often being created internally to the pidgin rather than borroewd from some other language (as with Tok Pisin *maus gras* 'moustache', literally 'mouth grass'); the structural becomes stabilised, i.e. the language has a well defined grammar.

14 Throughout all of this development, the pidgin has no native speakers. The next possible stage (or this may take place even before stabilisation) is for the pidgin to 'acquire native speakers'. For instance, if native speakers of different languages marry and have the pidgin as their only common language, then this will be the language of their household and will become the first language of their children.

Once a pidgin has acquired native speakers, it is referred to as a creole. The native languages of many inhabitants of the Caribbean islands are creoles, for instance the English-based creale of Jamaica, the French-based creole of Haiti, and the Spanish-and/or Portuguese-based creole Papiamentu (Papiamento) of the Netherlands Antilles (Aruba, Bonaire and Curaçao). At an even later stage, social improvements and education may bring the creole back into close contact with the European language that originally contributed much of its vocabulary. In this situation, the two languages may interact and the creole, or some of its varieties, may start approaching the standard language. This gives rise to the so-called post-creole continuum, in which one finds a continuous scale of varieties of speech from forms close to the original creole (basilect) through intermediate forms (mesolect) up to a slightly regionally coloured version of the standard language. Jamaican English is a good example of a post-creole continuum.

15 <u>No pidgin or creole language has succeeded in gaining sufficient status or number of speakers to become one of the world's major languages, but pidgin and creole languages provide important insights into the processes that arise from natural language contact</u>. And while it would probably be an exaggeration to consider any of the world's major languages a creole, it is not unlikely that some of the processes that go to create a pidgin or a creole have been active in the history of some of these languages- witness, for instance, the morphological simplification that has attended the development from Old English to Modern English or from Latin to the modern Romance languages.

16 A few centuries ago, as we saw above, it would have been difficult to predict the present-day distribution of major languages in the world. It is equally impossible to predict the future. In terms of number of native speakers, <u>it is clear that a major shift is underway in favour of non-European languages</u>: the rate of population increase is much higher outside Europe than in Europe, and while some Europeian languages draw some benefit from this (such as Spanish and Portuguese in Latin America), the main beneficiaries are the indigenous languages of southern Asia and Africa. It might well be that a later version of this volume would include fewer of the European languages that are restricted to a single country, and devote more space to non-European languages. Another factor is the increase in the range of functions of many non-European languages: during the colonial period European languages (primarily English and French) were used for most official purposes and also for education in much of Asia and Africa. but the winning of independence has meant that many countries have turned more to their own languages, using these as official language and medium of education. The extent to which this will lead to increase in their status as major languages is difficult to predict - at present, access to the frontiers of scholarship and technology is still primarily through European languages, especially English; but one should not forget that the use of English, French and German as vehicles for science was gained only through a prolonged struggle against what then seemed the obvious language for such writing: Latin. (The process may go back indefinitely: Cicero was criticised for writing philosophical treatises in Latin by those who thought he should have used Greek.) But at least I hope to have shown the reader that the social interaction of languages is a dynamic process, one that is moreover excitig to follow. The most comprehensive and up-to-date index of the world's languages, with genetic classification, is Voegelin and Voegelin (1977); while some of their individual assignments are no doubt questionable, this is certainly the most reliable such index available. For sources that also give information on the structure of at least some of the languages and language families included, reference may be made to Meillet and Cohen (1926; 1952). The latter is now out of print, and is being replaced by a completely new series of volumes under the general editorship of Perrot (1981-). Another series of volumes each dealing with a particular language family or geographical area is the Cambridge Language Surveys series, in which so far volumes have appeared on Australia (Dixon 1980), the Soviet Union (Comrie 1981a), and Meso-America (Suarez 1983); further volumes are in preparation.

17 Readers wanting to delve deeper into problems of genetic classification should consult a good introduction to historical and comparative linguistics, such as

Bynon(1977). For discussions of language universals and typology, reference may be made to Comrie (1981b) and Foley and Van Valin (1984).

18 The standard reference on language contact is Weinreich (1953), while Todd (1984) is a useful introduction to pidgins and creoles.

어휘리콜 •affiliation: 동맹, 유대, 관계; •criteria: 기준; •overseas Chinese communities: 해외 중국인 공동체; •slight: 경시; •Latinity: 라틴어 사용(어법, 말투); •calque: 어의 차용, 번역 차용; •immutable: 변경할 수 없는, 불변의; •oust: 내 다, 탈취하다; •inauspicious: 불길한; •in the wake of: ~의 결과로, ~을 따라서; •attest: 증명하다, 입증하다; •deference: 복종, 존경, 경의; •Hanseatic League: 한자동맹; •mainstay: 대들보; •ascendancy: 우세, 우월; •indenture: 도제살이(노예살이)로 보내다; •language contact: 언어접촉; •exaggeration: 과장, 과대; •beneficiary: 수익자; •indigenous: 토착의; •devote: 바치다, 배당하다; •delve: 탐구하다, 정사하다, 찾다; •by and large: 대체로.

패턴요약 18단락으로 된 본문에서 **1**은 대 언어의 개념 정의, **2**는 개념정의 첫 기준, **3**은 첫 기준 사례로서 중국어와 영어의 비교, **4**는 개념 정의 기준으로서 링구아 프랑카, 제2언어로서의 사용범위, **5**는 또 한 기준으로 언어의 문화적 중요성, **6**은 문화의 중요성 기준에 해당하는 사례, **7**은 언어가 모국어 및 제2언어 사용 지역 넘어 영향 미침, **8**은 언어의 위상이 불변일 수는 없음, **9**는 위상 불변일 수 없음에 대한 사례, **10**은 대 언어의 위상을 상실한 경우 있음, **11**은 사회적 요소들과 사회적 태도들이 언어 관련성 수지도 모델을 뒤집는 경우 있음, **12**는 언어접촉으로부터 발전인 경우(피진어와 크레올), **13**은 그 다음 진행 단계에서 특수 용어의 확대, **14**는 다음 단계는 피진어가 화자 갖는 것, **15**는 대 언어가 된 피진어와 크레올은 없음, **16**은 미래 예측은 불가능 하나 사람 수 관점에서는 비 유럽어 선호 쪽, **17**은 참고자료 소개, **18**은 참고자료 소개 등에 관한 내용. 따라서 머리말(**1**), 대 언어 개념 정의의 기준과 사례(**2**-**16**), 끝맺는 말(**17**-**18**)로 압축 요약된다.

전문국역 **1** 머리말에서 나타난 대로 '대 언어(major language)'의 개념은 사회적 관점에서 정의된다. 그러므로 이제 언어의 사회적 측면과 관련시켜, 특히 언어의 사회적 상호작용의 관점에서 몇 가지 개념을 좀 더 일관성 있게 보아야할 때이다. 어떤 언어가 대 언어인지 혹은 아닌지는 그 언어 구조와 혹은 유전적 관계와 관련이 없으며, 세계에 그렇게 많은 대 언어들이 인도유럽어라는 사실은 단순히 역사적 사건일 뿐이다. **2** 첫째, 우리는 언어를 대 언어로 정의하는데 기여하는 기준을 더 상세하게 살펴볼 수 있다. 가장 분명한 기준들 중의 하나는 화자의 수인데, 이 책 특정 장(chapters)에서 필자가 언어들 중에서 선택할 때, 화자의 수가 필자의 주요 기준들 준의 하 이었다. 그러나 최지의 수기 마친가지로 분명히 유일한 기준은 아니다. **3** 여기서 흥미 있는 한 비교는 중국어(혹은 좀 더 구체적으로 만다린, 즉 표준 중국어)와 영어 사이다. 만다린은 영어보다도 더 많은 모국어 화자를 가지고 있지만, 만다린을 제2언어로 배우는 것보다도 영어를 제2언어로 배우는 사람의 수가 훨씬 더 많음을 보는 것처럼. 아직도 영어가 세계에서 일반적으로 만다린보다 더 유용한 언어로 간주되고 있다. 이에 대한 이유들 중의 하나는 영어가 국제적인 언어이고, 세계의 많은 지역에서 많은 사람들에 의하여 사용되고 있다는 것이다. 대조적으로 만다린은 대체로 중국에 국한되어 있고, 중국어 방언들(혹은 언어들)을 모두 함께 포함하고, 중국어의 확장은 중국과 해외 중국인 커뮤니티를 넘어서지 않는다. 영어는 세계의 여러 다른 지역에서 꽤 큰 인구집단의 모국어(특히, 영국의 제도, 북아메리카, 호주 및 뉴질랜드)일뿐만 아니라 '영어'라는 장(chapter)에서 상세하게 논의된 대로 훨씬 더 많은 나라에서 제2언어로 사용되고 있다, 영어는 또한 과학기술적으로 대부분의 선진국들(특히 미국)의 언어이므로, 영어가 오늘날 과학기술 발달의 접근을 위한 기본 미디어이다. 그러므로 단순한 화자수가 아닌 다른 요소들이 언어의 사회적 중요성을 결정하는데 관련된다. ❹ 실로, 이 책에서 개개의 장들에서 부여된 일부 언어는 비교적 모국어 화자가 적다. 일부 언어는 중요한데, 그것은 모국어 화자의 수 때문이 아니라, 오히려 공통 제1언어가 없는 사람들에서 링구아 프랑카로서, 제2언어로서의 사용되는 범위 때문이다. 좋은 사례가 스와힐리어와 말레이어이다. 스와힐리어는 일차적으로는 동 아프리카 해안에 있는 비교적 적은 사람 수의 모국어이지만, 링구아 프랑카로서의 사용은 동 아프리카(특히 케냐와 탄자니아에까지, 자이레의 여러 지역에까지 뻗어 있다. 말레이어 역시 서 말레이시아 지역과 인도네시아에서 사용되는 비교적 적은 사람의 모국어이지만, 두 나라에서 링구아 프랑카 및 공용어로서의 채용은 1억이 족히 넘는 제1 및 제2 언어 위상을 야기 시켰다. 필자가 선택한 언어에서 많은 경우, 필자는 순수 통계에 의해서보다는 오히려 이 요소(링구아 프랑카, 공용어 위상)에 의해서 안내 받았다. 예를 들면, 필리핀 언어들 중에서 타갈로그어 보다는 체부아노어가 더 많은 화자를 가지고 있지만, 필자는 타갈로그어를 선택했는데, 이유는 타갈로그어가 필리핀의 국립 언어이고, 필리핀의 많은 지역에서 링구아 프랑카로 사용되고 있기 때문이다. 인도네시아 언어들 중에서 자바언어가 말레이어보다 많은 화자를 가지고 있고 그리고 또한 옛 문화의 생산지이지만, 현재의 사회적 상황 관점에서는 말레이어가 분명히 오스트로네시언 계파 중에서 지배적인 언어이다. 다른 많은 인도-아리안 언어들이, 예를 들면 Marathi, Rajasthani, Panjabi, Gujarati가 확실히 화자의 수 관점에서는 장(chapter)에 포함되는 데에 자격이 있었을 것이다, 그러나 이들 언어에게는 개개의 장이 배정되지 않았는데, 이유는 사회적 관점에서 남아시아 북쪽 지역의 주요 언어는 분명히 Hindi-Urdu와 Bengali이다. ❺ 또 하나의 중요한 기준은 문화적 유산의 시대 및 영향 관점에서 언어의 문화적 중요성이다. 주요한 한 사례가 드라비디언 언어들에 의해서 제공된다. 이들 중에서 Telugu어가 실제로 Tamil어보다 많은 화자를 가지고 있다. 그러나 Tamil어는 보다 더 고대 문학적 언어이고, 이런 이유 때문에 필자의 선택은 Tamil어에 주어졌다. 많은 결정들이 부분적으로는 주관적이고, 그래서 부분적으로는 위험하다는 점을 필자가 알고 있다: 서문에서 필자가 강조한 대로, 필자의 마음으로부터 최적의 것은, 이 책의 목차에서 대 언어로 간주하지 아니하는 대로, 화자의 수를 경시하는 것이다. ❻ 어떤 언어들은 모국어 화자가 없는데도 불구하고, 라틴어와 산스크리트에서처럼, 대 언어이다. 라틴어는 모든 유럽 언어들에게 큰 공헌을 했다, 라틴어 기원의 단어들이 가장 표면적으로 유럽 언어들에서 사용되고 있는 정도 면에서 보이는 바대로. 자신들의 어휘를 창조함으로써 라틴어 어법의 출현을 피하려고 노력해왔던 언어들조차도 종종 라틴어모델로 되돌아 가버렸다: 독일어 *Gewissen* '양심'은, 예를 들어, 'with'를 의미하는 접두사 *Ge-*, 'know'를 의미하는 어간 *wiss-*, 추상명사화 접미사 *-en*을 포함하는데, 라틴어 *con-sci-entia*를 정확하게 복사한 것이다. 이런 식으로 형태

보다도 오히려 구조를 따르는 차용어들은 calque(외국어축자역) 또는 차용번역어(loan translation) 이라고 알려져 있다. 산스크리트어가 힌디어를 포함하여 인디아 언어들과 관련하여 유사한 역할을 했다. 히브리어는, 히브리어 장에서 주목된 대로, 화자의 수 때문에 대 언어에 포함되는 것이 아니라 유럽 및 중동 사회에 대한 히브리어의 기여 및 그 문화의 기여 때문에 포함된다. ７ 그러므로 언어는 그 언어가 모국어 혹은 제2언어로 사용되는 지역을 넘어 영향을 미칠 수 있다. 이것을 예증해 주는 좋은 사례가 아랍어이다. 아랍어 차용어가 이슬람 민족들에 의하여 사용되는 많은 언어들 어휘에서 많은 부분을 형성하고 있으며, 심지어는 유전적으로 아랍어와 거리가 먼 언어들(예: Hausa)의 어휘를 형성하고 있으며, 혹은 유전적으로 전혀 관련이 없는 언어(예: Turkish, Persian, Urdu)의 어휘를 형성하고 있다. 또한 아랍어의 영향은 많은 이슬람 민족들이 채용하고 있는 아랍어 쓰기 체계에서 보여 질 수 있다. 중국어 차용어들은 동아시아 언어들, 특히 베트남어, 일본어와 한국어의 어휘에서 중요한 부분을 차지하고 있다. 마찬가지로, 중국어 문자의 사용이 또한 일본어와 한국어에, 그리고 초기 베트남어에 역시 널리 퍼졌다. ８ 대 언어로서의 한 언어의 위상이 불변일 수 없음을 주목하는 것이 중요하다. 진실로, 우리가 역사를 거슬러 올라가볼 때, 우리는 많은 변화를 발견하게 된다. 예를 들면, 영어를 세계의 대 언어로 특정 지우는 가능성은 20세기의 혁신이다. 대 언어들의 분포에서 가장 중요한 변화 중의 하나는 아메리카의 식민지화로 유럽 언어들, 특히 영어, 스페인어, 포르투갈어, 좀 덜 하지만 불어 등의 확장으로부터 왔다: 영어, 스페인어, 포르투갈어는 이제 영국, 스페인, 포르투칼에서 보다도 신세계에서 더 많은 모국어 화자를 가지고 있다. 실로 중세 시대에 유럽의 해안으로부터 떨어져 있던 섬에 국한된 영어가 대 국제 언어가 될 것이라고는 거의 상상도 못했었다. ９ 중세 유럽에서, 라틴어가 분명히 대 언어였다, 왜냐하면 모국어 화자의 부족에도 불구하고, 언어적 경계를 넘어 소통할 필요가 있는 사람들의 링구아 프랑카였기 때문이다. 그러나 라틴어가 그렇게 탁월하게 등장한 것은, 라틴어와 그 후계자가 남서 유럽의 모든 언어들을 내   았다는 사실을 포함하는데, 로마 주위 지역에 국한된 불길한 발족으로부터 거의 예측되지 않았었다. 마찬가지로 장관인 것은 아랍어의 확장인데, 이슬람 종교의 열성의 결과로서, 아라비아 반도에 국한된 것으로부터 중동 및 북 아프리카의 지배 언어가 되었다. １０ 대 언어가 된 언어들 외에도, 마찬가지로 대 언어의 지위를 상실한 언어들이 있다. 종종 문명의 요람으로 간주되는 메소포타미아의 초기 기록은 두 언어로 쓰여 있다; 그것은 수메리아어와 아카디언어(후자는 아시리아와 바빌로니아 제국의 언어)이다. 아카디언어는 아프리카아시아계 셈어의 갈래이고, 반면에 수메리아어는 현재 알려져 있는 어떤 언어와도 관련이 없는 먼 언어라고 말할 수 있다. 증명된 수메리아어 비문의 때에서 조차, 수메리아어는 이미 아마도 멸종에 접근하고 있었을 것이고, 그리고 그 언어는 전통(중세 유럽에서 라틴어 경우처럼)에 종속되어 계속해서 사용되었다. 당시의 지배적 언어는 아카디언어가 될 것이었지만, 과도기에 이 언어 역시 사멸했고, 직접적인 후계자를 남기지 못했다. 역시 사멸한 언어가 고대 이집트 언어, 즉 파라오의 언어이다. 지중해와 중동 언어의 모습은 오늘날 우리가 관찰하는 모습과 크게 다르지 않았다. １１ 사회적 요소들과 사회적 태도들이 언어 관련성 수지도 모델에서 뒤집는 모습을 생성시키기까지 한다. 독일어의 초기 텍스트(문헌) 시대에, 뚜렷한 두 게르만어가 인지되었는데, Old Saxon어와 Old High German어이다. Old Saxon어는 현대 Low German(plattdeutsch) 방언들의 조상이다. 반면에 Old High German어는 현대 High German 방언들과 표준어의 조상이다. 사회적 변화들 – 한자 동맹의 쇠퇴, 복독일의 경제적 대들보의 쇠퇴처럼 - 때문에 High German은 Low German에 대해 사회적 우세를 얻었다. High German을 바탕으로 한 표준어가 지금 남북독일의 표준어로 인식되고 있기 때문에, Low German과 High german의 방언들 양쪽 단일 독일어로부터의 방언들로 인식되고 있고, 그리고 특정 Low German 방언과 표준 독일어 사이의 사회적 관계가 High German의 방언과 표준 독일어 사이의 사회적 관계와 실제로 다르지 않다. ⑫ 언어 접촉으로부터 일어났던 가장 흥미 있는 발전들 중의 하나는 피진어와 크레올어이다. 피진어는 매우 실제적 다음 상황으로부터 생겨난다: 서로 다른 언어의 화자들이 어떤 실제적 일을 수행하기 위해서 서로서로 소통을 할 필요가 있지만, 공통의 어떤 언어를 사용할 수가 없고, 상대방의 언어를 적당히 배울 기회가 없는 상황에서 생겨난다. 이러한 상황에서 생겨나는 것은, 처음에는, 매우 다양한 구조를 가지는, 불안정한 피진어, 즉 특수 용어(jargon)인데, – 생성에 관련된 사람들의 모국어와 비교적 단순하게 관련된 매우 단순한 모습- 실제적 일이 적당한 수준에서 성공적으로 수행이 되게 해줄 정도로 충분할 정도의 단지 어휘 차원이다. 이러한 피진어 발달의 가장 분명한 사례는 유럽의 식민지화에서, 특히 대서양 노예무역으로부터 그리고 남태평양에서의 도제살이로 보내는 노동력으로부터 발생했다. 이 피진어들은, 비록 그 언어들의 구조가 종종 식민지 언어로부터 매우 다르다 하더라도, 식민지화 하는 언어로부터의 어휘를 가장 많이 이용한다. ⑬ 그 뒤 진행 단계에서 특수 용어(jargon)는, 특히 비 유럽어 기원인 화자들 사이에서 링구아 프랑카로서 그 유용성이 인정될 때, 확대되어서 파푸아 뉴기아나의 대 링구아 프랑카인 Tok Pisin과 같은 안정된 피진어로 진행될 지도 모른다, 이러한 확장은 다음과 같은 여러 면에서 일어난다: 기능들의 범위가 확장된다. 이유는 피진어가 이미 더 이상 실제적 일 처리에 필수적인 언어의 사용에 국한되지 않기 때문이다; 어휘가 이런 기능의 결과로 확장된다. 새로운 단어들이 종종 다른 어떤 언어로부터 차용하기 보다는 내부적으로 만들어지기 때문이다(Tok Pisin의 *maus gras* 'moustache'에서처럼, 문자적으로 'mouth grass'); 구조가 안정적으로 된다. 즉 언어가 잘 정의되는 문법을 가진다. ⑭ 이 모든 발전을 통해서 시종 피진어는 모국어 화자를 가지지 않는다. 다음 가능한 단계는 (혹은 이 단계는 안정화 단계 이전에 조차 일어날 수도 있다) 피진어가 '모국어 화자를 얻는 것'이다, 예를 들면, 만약 서로 다른 언어의 모국어 화자들이 결혼을 해서 피진어를 그들의 유일한 공통언어로 갖는다면, 그럴 때는 이 언어가 그들 가정의 언어가 될 것이고, 그들 아이들의 첫 언어가 될 것이다. 피진어가 모국어 화자를 얻게 된다면 그 언어는 크레올이라고 불린다. 카리비안 섬들의 많은 주민들의 모국어들은 크레올인데, 예를 들면, 영어에 기초한 자마이카의 크레올이고, 불어에 기초한 하이티의 크레올이고, 그리고 스페인어와/혹은 포르투칼어에 기초한 네덜란드 안틸레(아루바, 보나이레, 그리고 쿠아라카오)의 크레올 파피아멘투이다. 좀 더 진행된 단계에서는, 사회적 발전과 교육이 크레올로 하여금 원래 많은 어휘로 기여했던 유럽 언어와 밀접한 접촉을 가져오게 할 수도 있다. 이런 상황에서 두 언어는 상호작용하고 크레올은 혹은 그 변이형의 언어들은 표준 언어로 접근해 갈 수도 있다. 이것은 소위 후속 크레올 연속을 낳게 되는데, 여기서 한 언어는 원래의 크레올(basilect)에 가까운 형태로부터 중간적인 형태를 거쳐 다소 지역적 색깔이 들어간 형태의 표준어로 조금씩 정도를 달리하는 변이형들을 보게 된다. 자마이카 영어가 포스트 크레올 연속상에서의 좋은 예이다. ⑮ 충분한 위상을 얻거나 많은 화자를 획득하여 세계 대 언어 중의 하나가 되는데 성공한 피진어나 크리올어는 없다. 그러나 피진어나 크레올어는 자연언어 접촉으로부터 일어나는 과정에 대하여 중요한 통찰을 제공해준다. 그리고 한편으로는 어느 세계 언어든 그 세계 언어를 크레올로 생각하는 것은 아마도 과장일지도 모르겠지만, 피진어나 크레올어를 창조하는 과정들이 어떤 언어들의 역사에서는 적극적 이였다-증거로서 예를 들면, 고대영어로부터 중세영어로 혹은 라틴어로부터 현대 로망스 언어로의 형태 단순화이다. **16** 2-3세기 전에는, 위에서 보았던 대로, 세계 대 언어들의 오늘날 분포를 예측하기 어려웠을 것이다. 마찬가지로 미래를 예측하는 것은 불가능하다. 모국어 화자의 수 관점에서 분명한 것은 큰 변화는 비유럽 언어들을 선호하는 쪽으로 겪는다는 것이다: 인구 증가율이 유럽에서 보다 유럽 밖의 지역에서 훨씬 높다. 그리고 일부 유럽 언어들이 이것(예를 들면 라틴 아메리카에서 스페인어와 포르투칼어)으로부터 장점들을 끌어 낼 수 있는 반면에, 주요 수익자들은 남아시아와 아프리카의 토착 언어들이다. 당연히 이 책의 다음 버전은 한 나라에 국한된 유럽 언어들을 더 적게 포함 할 것이고, 그리고 비유럽의 많은 언어들에 더 많은 공간을 배려할 것이다. 또 한 요소는 많은 비유럽어들의 역할 범위의 증가이다: 식민지 시대에 유럽 언어들(우선 영어와 불어)은 대부분 공적인 목적으로 사용되었으며, 또한 아시아와 아프리카에서 교육으로 많이 사용되었다. 그러나 독립의 성공은 많은 나라들이 그들 나라의 언어로 돌아섰으며, 그들의 언어를 공식 언어와 교육의 매체로 사용했다는 것을 의미했다. 이것이 대 언어로서의 위상 증가로 이어질지는 예측하기 어렵고, 현재로서는 학문과 기술의 개척자로서의 접근은 아직도 일차적으로 유럽의 언어들, 특히 영어를 통해서다; 그러나 우리가 잊지 말아야 할 것은 영어, 불어, 독일어를 과학의 수레로 이용하는 것은 당시 문어로서 분명했던 언어인 라틴어에 반대하여 오랜 기간의 투쟁을 통해서 얻어졌다는 것이다. (그 과정은 애매하지만 다음과 같이 거슬러 올라갈 수 있을지도 모른다; 키케로는 철학적인 논문을 라틴어로 쓴 이유 때문에 그리스어로 써야만 한다고 생각한 사람들에 의하여 비평을 받았다.) 그러나 적어도 나는 독자에게 언어들의 상호교류가 다이내믹한 과정, 즉 더구나 따르기에 흥분되는 과정이라는 것을 보여주었기를 기대한다. 가장 종합적이고 업데이트된 세계 언어의 목록표(index)는, 유전적 분류가 들어있는 Voegelin and Voegelin(1977)이다; 언어 개개의 지정에 대해서는 일부 언어에 문제가 있지만, 이 목록표는 확실히 가장 믿을만한 이용 가능한 목록표이다. 또한 포함되어 있는 일부 언어들과 언어그룹들의 구조에 관한 정보를 제공하는 소스에 대해서는 Meillet and Cohen(1926; 1952)이 참고문헌이 될 수도 있다. Meillet and Cohen(1926; 1952)이 지금 현재 인쇄가 되어 있고, 완전히 새로운 권시리즈로 총편집자 Perrot(1981-)에 의하여 대치되고 있다. 각 권에서 특정 어족 혹은 지리적 영역을 다루는 또 한 권시리즈는 케임브리즈 언어 조사 시리즈인데, 지금까지의 권은 오스트레일리아(Dixon 1980), 소비엣트 유니온(Comrie 1981a), 그리고 메소-아메리카(Suarez 1983)에 관한 내용이고, 더 많은 권이 준비 중에 있다. **17** 유전적 분류의 문제점들에 대해 더 깊이 탐구하고 싶어 하는 독자들은 역사언어학 및 비교언어학의 좋은 개론서, 예를 들면 Bynon(1977)을 보아야 하다, 언어보편석과 유형론에 대한 논의로는 Comrie(1981b)와 Foley and Van Valin(1984)가 참고가 된다. **18** 언어접촉에 대한 표준 참고는 Weireich(1953)이고, 반면에 Todd(1984)는 피진어와 크레올에 대한 유용한 개론서이다.

제3절 마무리 수행

독해 마지막 절차인 마무리 수행은 독해재료와 관련하여 독자가 마지막으로 처리하는 것이다. 이 마지막 처리는 발신자(즉 작자)가 수신자 자신에게 요구한 의도를 이행(가령: 세금납부통지서의 세금납부, 새로운 과학적 발견 에세이의 내용 이해)하거나, 독해 내용을 독자 자신의 독해목적에 이용(가령: 독자의 문서에 내용을 인용)하거나, 독해자료를 없애버리거나, 혹은 정리보관 하는 것과 같은 행위이다.

(1) Time waits for no man.

> 마무리 수행 '기억' 차원의 수행이 요구됨.
> 전문국역 때는 사람을 기다리지 않는다.

(2) A bad carpenter quarrels with his tools.

> 어휘리콜 •carpenter: 목수.
> 마무리 수행 '기억' 차원의 수행이 요구됨.
> 전문국역 서투른 목수가 자기 연장 탓만 한다.

(3)

International Import Company
100 East Houston St.
New York, NY 10053

Farmers Fruit Ltd.
Aghia Paraskevi 19081
Athens, Greece

Dear Sirs

In reply to your letter dated May 3rd, we thank you for allowing us a special discount. This makes it possible for us to place an order and to expect quite good sales. We have pleasure of enclosing our Order No. 813/BS, and would ask you to return the duplicate to us, duly signed, as an acknowledgement.

Yours faithfully
Paul Hogen
Enc. Order No. 813/BS

어휘리콜 •place an order: 주문을 하다; •duplicate: 이중의, 사본의; •duly: 정식으로, 적당하게.

마무리 수행 발신자(작자)의 목적은 수신자(독자)가 승인된 주문서 사본을 보내달라는 것이다. 따라서 이 서한문의 수신자(Farmers Fruit Ltd.)는 이 행동(승인된 주문서 사본 보내기)을 취하는 것이다.

전문국역 5월 3일자 귀하의 편지에 대한 회신입니다. 귀하가 우리에게 특별 할인을 해 주신데 대하여 귀하에게 감사를 드립니다. 이것은 저희가 주문이 가능하도록 하고, 그리고 매우 많은 새 일을 기대하게 합니다. 저희는 기꺼이 주문서 번호 813/BS를 첨부하면서 저희에게 인정서로 사인을 하셔서 복사 본을 보내 주실 것을 부탁드립니다.

---

(4) **Readers' voice**

To have your views on next week's question or any other issue appear in "voice," contact voice @heraldcorp.com or call 02 727 0213

Reducing suicide ...

1 Within the past few weeks I have read various articles concerning the increasing suicide rate here and the need for greater attention in developing suicide prevention measures. For example, I read about the installation of cameras along the bridges by the Han River to catch those who appear at risk of suicide. I am sure there are many more great measures being made but I believe that Korea's government, or whoever is in charge of leading this serious project, needs to look into the underlying causes of suicide.

2 Instead of asking "where is one likely to kill themselves?" or "With what or how will they kill themselves?" we should ask "why do so many individuals seek death over life?" and "why do so many individuals solve hopelessness with death?"

3 I feel that a greater amount attention is needed in researching the backgrounds of those who have already committed suicide. Finding the common areas in their education, family background, and social environment for the majority of the underlying causes of suicide is from these areas.

4 One commits suicide mostly because one sees no other way out from their problems. We need to find out what exactly these problems are and why they exist; instead of trying to prevent the action, trying to prevent the thought. I believe that this is the first and most important measure that needs to be taken in reducing suicide in Korea.
- Jonathan Yoo, Seoul

5 I believe that if you cut the number of hours that Korean men have to work then the rate of suicide will decrease. Men work way too much and have little time with their families. If they had more time to spend with their families, or to do a hobby that they like, they would be happier, therefore not wanting to commit suicide.
- Christina Ross, Oklahoma City, USA

6 When you read or watch the news, you will sometimes find out that someone died by or tried to commit suicide. With the high unemployment rate, pressure for students to do well in school, get into a great college and find a great job after graduation, the suicide rate has increased over the past few years. There are so many reasons why someone who is living today will decide to commit suicide, and the rationale that I have mentioned above are just a few.

7 In today's tough economy, people are living to paycheck trying to provide food on the table, to have clothes on their backs, and to pay for their month's rent and utilities. Finding a job is really tough these days, especially one in which you went to school for and spent countless hours and money on.

8. Just recently, South Korea elected and made history by making Park Geun-hye the first female president and the people of South Korea are expecting a lot from her. One of them is jobs - jobs to be created so the people can find employment as well as earn well. There are thousands of people who are struggling to find a job and some that have been looking for a long time and have not found what they are looking for are turning to suicide and ending their life.

9. The people who cannot find work are not the only ones committing suicide; students who attend school face enormous pressure to do well in school and to prepare for exams. Students spend lots of hours preparing for bar exams and to do well in their classes which can impact a student if he/she fails. With all the time spent by going to night classes and studying until 3:00 a.m., students do everything possible to be the best student in the class and to attend a great college in the future.

10. So, what can the country of South Korea do to reduce suicide? The answer to this question is to make sure that the president creates more jobs so that people can find work that they desire and to have places where people can go and talk to someone about their problems.

11. For parents of students who attend college, make sure that you talk to them and ask how they are feeling. It is good to talk to your son or daughter because they are getting stressed in school, and having someone to talk to will make them feel better.

12. Another is to probably have a suicide hotline in case someone you know is planning to commit suicide and that you can call someone and tell about your friend and the problems he or she is facing because it is better to save your friend's life. So, to reiterate on how to reduce suicide in South Korea is to create jobs, establish a place or phone number that someone can talk or call about their problems, and to have friends and family who will always make you happy in times of trouble.

~ *James Buhain, Reno, USA*

어휘리콜 •suicide: 자살; •installation: 설치; •in charge of: ~에 책임이 있는; •paycheck: 월급;
•hotline: 핫라인; •reiterate: 반복하다.

마무리 수행 '서재보관' 차원의 수행이 요구되고, 이 기사 란의 다음 주제에 대하여 투고의 생각이 가능하다.

전문국역 독자의 소리//"보이스"에 다음 주의 문제에 대하여 당신의 견해를 나타내고 싶거나, 혹은 다른 이슈를 나타내고 싶으면, 소리 주소에 접촉 하세요//자살을 줄이기... **1** 지난 몇 주 동안에 필자는 국내 자살률 증가와 자살 방지 대책 개발에 보다 큰 관심의 필요성 관련하여 여러 기사를 읽었다. 예를 들면, 필자는 자살 위험으로 보이는 사람들을 포착하기 위하여 한강 다리를 따라 카메라 설치 관련 기사를 읽었다. 필자는 보다 더 큰 대책이 강구되어야 한다고 확신하지만 필자가 믿기로는 한국 정부 혹은 누구든 간에 이 중요한 프로젝트 주도에 책임이 있으며, 자살의 기저 원인을 깊이 들여다 볼 필요가 있다고 본다. **2** "사람들이 어디서 자살할 것 같은가?" 혹은 "무엇으로 혹은 어떤 방법으로 자살 할 것인가?"라고 물어보는 것 대신에 "그렇게 많은 개인들이 왜 삶을 버리고 죽음을 택하는가?, 그리고 '왜 그렇게 많은 개개인들이 죽음으로 절망을 해결하는가?"라고 질문해야 한다. **3** 이미 자살을 했던 사람들의 배경을 연구하는 데에 많은 관심이 필요하다고 필자는 느낀다. 자살의 사회적 환경에서 공통의 분야를 찾기 위하여 그들의 교육, 가족 배경, 그리고 사회적 환경에서 공통 분야를 찾는 것은 이 분야로부터다. **4** 사람이 자살을 하는 이유는 대개 자기의 문제로부터 다른 방법은 보지 못하기 때문이다. 우리는 이 문제들이 무엇인지 그리고 그 문제들이 왜 존재하는지를 정확하게 발견할 필요가 있다; 그 행동을 막으려고 노력하기 보다는 그런 생각을 막으려고 하는 것. 필자가 믿는 바로는 이것이 한국에서 자살을 줄이는 데 취해져야 할 필요가 있는 첫째로서 그리고 가장 중요한 대책이다. **5** 만약 우리가 한국남자들이 일해야 하는 근로 시간을 줄인다면 자살률이 낮아질 것이라고 필자는 믿는다. 남자들은 너무 많이 일을 하고 가족과 함께 보내는 시간이 거의 없다. 만약 자기 가족과 보내는 시간이 보다 많다면, 혹은 자가가 좋아하는 취미생활을 할 시간이 보다 많다면, 그들은 더 행복할 것이고 그러면 자살을 범하고 싶어 하지 않을 것이다. **6** 여러분이 뉴스를 읽거나 볼 때, 여러분은 때때로 누군가가 죽었다거나 자살했다는 것을 발견하게 될 것이다. 높은 실업률에, 학교에서 학생이 공부를 잘해서, 좋은 대학 들어가서 졸업 후 좋은 직장에 들어가야 하는 압박으로 자살률이 지난 몇 년 동안에 증가했다. 오늘날 살아가고 있는 어떤 사람이 자살을 감행할 여러 가지 이유가 있고, 필자가 위에서 말한 합리적 이유는 단지 몇 가지뿐이다. **7** 오늘날 어려운 경제에서 사람들은 급여로 식비, 옷값, 월세 및 자동차세를 치르면서 살아가고 있다. 직장을 찾는 일은 실로 오늘날 어렵다, 특히 학교에 가고, 많은 시간과 돈을 소비하는 직장은 찾기가 어렵다. **8** 아주 최근에 한국은 박근혜를 첫 여성대통령으로 뽑는 역사를 만들었으며, 한국 사람들은 그녀로부터 많은 것을 기대하고 있다. 그것들 중의 하나는 직업이다 – 사람들이 직업을 발견할 수 있고 뿐만 아니라 많이 벌 수 있는 창조된 직업이다. 직업을 찾으려고 애써 노력을 하는 수천 명이 있으며, 직업을 찾아왔지만 발견하지 못하는 일부 사람은 자살 쪽으로 돌아서서 자기들의 생명을 끊는다. **9** 일을 발견하지 못하는 사람들이 자살을 범하는 유일한 사람은 아니다. 학교에 다니는 학생들은 학교에서 잘하고 시험 준비를 하기 위해 많은 압박에 직면한다. 자기들이 실패하는 경우 그들에게 영향을 미칠 수 있는 정기시험 및 수업시간에 잘해내기 위해 준비하는 데에 많은 시간을 학생들은 소비한다. 밤 학원으로 가서 오전 3시까지 공부하느라고 보내는 모든 시간으로 모든 학생들은 학급에서 최상의 학생이 되고 향후 좋은 대학에 가기 위해 가능한 모든 것을 한다. ⑩ 그러므로, 대한민국은 자살을 줄이기 위해 할 수 있는 것은 무엇인가? 이 질문에 대한 그 대답은 대통령이 보다 많은 일자리를 확실히 만들어서 자기가 바라는 일자리를 찾아가도록 하는 것이고, 그리고 그들이 가서 그들의 문제에 대해 누구에게 이야기 할 수 있는 곳을 찾게 하는 것이다. ⑪ 대학에 다니는 학생들의 부모들로서는, 학생들 하고 대화하고 어떻게 느끼는기를 물어보는 것을 해야 한다. 여러분들의 아들 혹은 딸에게 대화하는 것이 좋은데, 그 이유는 자녀들이 학교에서 스트레스를 받기 때문이고, 그리고 학생으로 하여금 대화를 하도록 하는 것은 그들로 하여금 더 좋은 느낌을 갖게 하기 때문이다. ⑫ 또 하나는 아마 자살 하트 라인을 가지는 것인데, 여러분이 알고 있는 어떤 사람이 자살을 계획하는 경우, 여러분이 누군가에 전화를 해서 여러분의 그 친구와 그 친구가 직면해 있는 문제를 알리는 것이다. 왜냐하면 여러분 친구의 생명을 구하는 것은 좋은 일이기 때문이다. 그러므로 한국에서 자살을 줄이는 방법에 대해 말을 반복한다면 일자리를 만드는 것이다. 그리고 어려울 때 여러분을 행복하게 해주는 친구와 가족을 가지는 것이다.

(5)

1 Active listening is one of the most important communication skills you can learn (Gordon 1975). Consider the following brief comment and some possible responses:

> Aphrodite: That creep gave me a C on the paper. I really worked on that project, and all I got is a lousy C.
>
> Apollo: That's not so bad; most people got around the same grade. I got a C, too.
>
> Athena: So what? This is Your last semester. "Who cares about grades anyway?"
>
> Achilles: You should be pleased with a C. Peggy and Michael both failed, and John and Judy got Ds.
>
> Diana: you got a C on that paper you were working on for the last three weeks? You sound really angry and hurt.

2 All four listeners are probably eager to make Aphrodite feel better, but they go about it in very different ways and, you can be sure, with very different outcomes. The first three listeners give fairly typical responses. Apollo and Athena both try to minimize the significance of a C grade, a common response to someone who has expressed displeasure or disappointment. Usually, it's also inappropriate. Although well-intentioned, this response does little to promote meaningful communication and understanding. Achilles tries to give the C grade a more positive meaning. Note, however, that all three listeners also say a great deal more; that Aphrodite should not be feeling unhappy, that these feelings are not legitimate. These responses deny the validity of these feelings and put Aphrodite in the position of having to defend them.

3 Diana, however, is different, Diana uses active listening, a process of sending back to the speaker what the listener thinks the speaker meant, both literally and emotionally. Active listening does not meant, simply repeating the speaker's exact words. It's rather a process of putting into some meaningful whole your understanding of the speaker's total message- the verbal and the nonverbal, the content and the feelings.

4 Active listening serves a number of important purposes. First, it shows that you're listening, and often that is the only thing the speaker really wants-to know that someone cares enough to listen.

5 Second, it helps you check how accurately you have understood what the speaker said and meant. By reflecting back what you perceive to be the speaker's meaning, you give the speaker an opportunity to confirm, clarify, or amend your perceptions. In this way future messages have a better chance of being relevant and purposeful.

6 Third, through active listening, you express acceptance of the speaker's feelings. Note that in the sample responses given, the first three listeners challenge the speaker; they refuse to give the expressed feelings legitimacy. The active listener accepts the speaker. The speaker's feelings are not challenged; rather, they're echoed in a sympathetic and empathic manner. {Not surprisingly, training in active listening helps to increase a person's empathy (Ikemi and Kubota 1996.)} Note, too, that in the first three responses, the feelings of the speaker are denied without ever actually being identified. Diana, however, not only accepts these feelings but also identifies them explicitly, again allowing the opportunity for correction.

7 Fourth, in active listening you prompt the speaker to further explore his or her feelings and thoughts. The active listening response gives the speaker the opportunity to elaborate on these feelings without having to defend them. Active listening sets the stage for meaningful dialogue, a dialogue of mutual understanding. In stimulating this further exploration, active listening also encourages the speaker to resolve his or her own conflicts.

어휘리콜 •creep: 녀석; •minimize: 최소화 한다; •well-intentioned: 의도가 잘된; •validity: 타당성; •sympathetic: 동정적인; •prompt: 자극한다.

마무리 수행 서재보관 차원의 수행이 요구된다.

전문 국역 **1** 능동적인 청취는 여러분이 학습할 수 있는 가장 중요한 소통능력 중의 하나이다. 다음의 간결한 코멘트와 몇 가지 가능한 응답을 보자.

Aphrodite: 저 녀석은 나에게 페이퍼에 C를 주었다. 나는 정말로 저 프로젝트에서 연구를 했는데, 내가 받은 것은 인색한 C이다

Apollo: 그것은 그렇게 나쁜 것은 아니다; 대부분 사람들은 그 정도의 학점을 받았다. 나도 C 받았다.

Athena: 그래서 어쨌다는 것이냐? 이번 학기는 너의 마지막 학기이다. "누가 학점에 신경 쓰나?"

Achilles: 너는 C에 만족해야 한다. Peggy와 Michael 둘은 실패했고, John과 Judy는 D받았다.

Diana: 너는 지난 3주 동안 연구 해온 페이퍼에 C를 받았다고? 너는 실로 화나고 상처 받은 것으로 들린다.

2 4명의 청자 모두 아마 Aphrodite로 하여금 보다 더 기분이 나아지게 하려는 것 같다. 그러나 그들은 기분 좋게 하는 것을 매우 다른 방식으로 한다. 첫 3명의 청자는 상당히 전형적인 응답이다. Apollo와 Athena 둘은 C학점의 의미를 최소화, 즉 불쾌 혹은 실망을 표현하는 사람에게 하는 보통의 응답을 하려고 한다. 보통은 그것은 또한 적절하지 못하다. 비록 의도는 좋았다고 하더라도, 이 응답은 의미 있는 소통과 이해를 향상시키지는 못한다. Achilles는 C학점에 보다 더 적극적인 의미를 준다. 그러나 주목할 것은 세 청자 모두 또한 말을 많이 한다는 것이다; Aphrodite는 행복하지 않게 느끼지 말아야 한다는 것이고, 이 느낌들은 합법적인 것이 아니라는 것이다. 이 응답들은 이 느낌들의 적절성을 부정하고, Aphrodite를 방어해야만 하는 입장에 놓는다. **3** 그러나 Diana는 다르다. Diana는 적극적인 청취를 하고, 화자가 의미한 것을 청자가 생각하는 것을 화자에게 문자적 의미 그대로 그리고 감정적으로 되돌려 주는 과정을 이용한다. 적극적인 청취는 화자의 말 그대로를 단순히 반복하는 것을 의미하지 않는다. 그것은 오히려 화자의 전체 메시지에 대한 여러분의 이해를 - 언어적 및 비언어적 내용 및 느낌을- 의미 있는 전체 속으로 놓는 과정이다. **4** 적극적인 청취는 여러 중요한

목적에 기여한다. 첫째, 적극적인 청취는 여러분이 듣고 있음을 보여주고, 그리고 종종 그것은 화자가 진실로 원하는 유일한 것-누군가가 듣기 위해서 충분히 주의 하고 있다는 것-을 아는 것이다. 5 둘째, 적극적인 청취는 화자가 말하고 의미한 것을 여러분이 얼마나 정확하게 이해했는가를 체크하는 것을 도와준다. 여러분이 화자의 의미 일 것이라고 인지한 것을 다시 반응함으로서, 여러분은 화자에게 여러분의 인지내용을 확인하고, 분명히 하고, 수정하는 기회를 준다. 이런 방식이면 다음에 나올 메시지는 관련되면서 의미 있게 되는 더 나은 기회를 가지게 된다. 6 셋째, 적극적인 청취를 통해서, 여러분은 화자의 느낌에 대한 수용을 표현한다. 주목할 것은 위에 주어진 간단한 응답에서, 첫 세 청자가 화자에 도전하고 있다는 것이다; 그들은 표현된 느낌에게 합법성 주기를 거부한다. 적극적인 청자는 화자를 수용한다. 화자의 느낌은 변하지 않는다; 오히려 화자의 느낌이 동정적이고 단호한 매너로 반향 된다. {(놀랄 것 없이, 적극적인 청취는 사람의 감정이입을 증가시키는데 도움을 준다(Ikemi and Kubota 1996.)}. 또한 주목할 것은 첫 세 사람의 응답에서는 화자의 느낌이 실제로 확인되지도 않고 부정된다는 것이다. 그러나 Diana는 이 느낌들을 수용할 뿐만 아니라 느낌들을 확인하고, 다시 수용할 기회를 허용한다. 7 넷째, 적극적인 청취에서는 여러분들이 화자로 하여금 화자 자신의 느낌과 생각을 더 탐구하도록 자극한다. 적극적인 청취 응답은 화자에게 이 느낌들에 대하여 방어해야 할 필요 없이 정교하게 할 기회를 준다. 적극적인 청취는 의미 있는 대화, 즉 상호 이해의 대화를 위한 무대를 놓는다. 이 탐구를 더 자극하면, 적극적인 청취는 또한 화자를 고무시켜서 자신의 갈등을 풀도록 한다.

(6) **FOOLS DIE FOR WANT OF WISDOM**

A monkey made a great impression by dancing before an assembly of animals, who elected him their king. The fox was jealous. Noticing a snare with a piece of meat in it, he took the monkey to it and said: "Here is a choice titbit that I have found. Instead of eating it myself I have kept it for you as a perquisite of your royal office. So take it." The monkey went at it carelessly and was caught in the snare. When he accused the fox of laying a trap for him, the fox replied: "Fancy a fool like you, friend monkey, being king of the animals!"

어휘리콜 •snare: 덫; •titbit: 한 입의 진미; •perquisite: 정표, 특권.
마무리 수행 본문만으로 구성. 독자에게 수행을 요구하는 것 없음. '서재보관' 차원의 수행 필요.
전문국역 지혜가 모자라 죽은 바보/많은 동물들 앞에서 춤을 추니 강렬한 인상을 남긴 원숭이가 그들에 의해 왕으로 추대되었다. 여우는 질투가 났다. 고기가 놓여 진 덫을 발견한 여우는 원숭이를 그 곳으로 데려가 "여기 제가 찾아 낸 맛있는 고기 한 덩어리가 있습니다. 제가 먹지 않고 전하께서 특별히 잡수시라고 보관해 왔습니다. 그러니 드십시오." 원숭이는 무심코 고기를 덥석 잡다가 덫에 걸리고 말았다. 원숭이가 여우에게 함정을 만들어 놓은 것을 비난하자 여우는 대답했다. "이봐 원숭이 친구, 너 같은 바보가 동물의 왕이라니, 상상이나 해 봐." (Lesson: 적절한 고려 없이 일을 행하는 사람들은 그로 인해 고통을 받게 되고 게다가 비웃음까지 사게 된다(People who attempt things without due consideration suffer for it and get laughed at into the bargain).

(7) **Deadline For Filling Taxes**

Today, April 15, is the last day to file income tax returns. To avoid penalties, all tax returns must be postmarked by midnight tonight.

To accommodate the expected rush of last-minute filers, dozens of post offices throughout the region will be open until midnight tonight - including the Robert J. Oakley Post Office at 10th Street and Sixth Avenue. Others will be open until 8 p.m. Call your local post office for further information.

People who have not completed their Federal returns can ask for an extension by filing internal Revenue Service Form 4868. Late payers are still expected to pay their estimated tax obligations and can face penalties and fines for underpayment.

어휘리콜 •fill: 채우다, 이행하다; •tax return: 소득신고, 납세신고; •postmark: 소인(을 찍다).
마무리 수행 (독자가 수신자인 경우) 세금납부 이행.
부분국역 (첫 단락)오늘 4월 15일은 소득세 납부 마지막 날입니다. 벌금을 피하기 위해서는 모든 납세가 오늘 밤 자정까지 소인이 찍혀져야 합니다.

(8) **JOB OPPORTUNITIES !!**

Language Studies International is looking for dynamic and experienced English and Japanese instructors. Our schools in Berlin., Paris, Taipei and Bangkok have openings for Senior Instructors (M.A. and at least 3 years exp. required) and Lecturers (B.A and 2 years exp. required). Send resume and salary history to L.S.I., 700 Bradway, Ste 913, New York 10010, Fax 212-967-8721. Please, no visits or calls.

> 어휘리콜 •dynamic: 동적인, 활동적인.
>
> 마무리 수행   구인 광고에 수행 여부 판단에 따라 수행.
>
> 부분국역   (첫 부분)취직 기회!!/국제 언어 연구(회사명)는 다이내믹하고 경험 있는 영어 및 일본어 교사를 찾고 있습니다.

(9)

John and Eve Grant

Invite you to celebrate the marriage of their daughter

Emily Rose

- TO -

Joseph Alan Robinson

Son oj Bruce ami Helen Robinson

On Friday, the Twentieth o/February. Two Thousand and Tw elve At Three O'Clock in the Afternoon St John' sCathedral.\'n\'York.NewYork

Please Reply To:

Eve Grant on 0421 123 234

> 어휘리콜 •celebrate: 축하하다.
>
> 마무리 수행   결혼(marriage) 축하 여부 판단에 따라 수행.
>
> 부분국역   (첫 부분)John과 Eve Grant가 자기들 딸 Emily Rose가 Brace와 Helen Robinson의 아들 Joseph Alan Robinson에게 결혼함을 축하해 주기 위해 귀하를 초대합니다.

제Ⅱ부
독해의 실제

다음의 영어를 독해하는 독자에게 '나름의 처리방법으로 접근합니까?' 혹은 '영어를 독해처리 할 때 보통 어떻게 합니까?' 라고 묻는다면, 대답이 쉽게 나오지 않을 것이다. 아마 많은 사람들에 있어서 독해는 순서대로 보태어져 나가는 문장들을 이해해 가는 정도의 방식일 것이다.

Fountainview Bakery has cakes for any occasion! Whether you are celebrating a birthday, an anniversary, or hosting a corporate party, we have the cake to suit your tastes and needs. All our products are made from the finest, organic ingredients, and are decorated by our staff of professional bakers. Cakes are offered in a variety of sizes and shapes. We also have more than twenty flavors to choose from including the following:

Southern Belle: A delicious combination of chocolate and cherries in a light cake with a smooth custard filling

Tropicana: A rich fruit cake that includes fresh mango and tangy lemon cream

Devil's Delight: A dark chocolate cake with a strawberry filling and a caramel frosting

For additional flavors and pictures of our cake designs, please visit our Web site at www.fountaincakes.com. We accept online orders and offer free delivery service to local residents.

FOUNTAINVIEW BAKERY   CAKES FOR ANY TASTE!

> **어휘리콜** •corporate: 단체, 조직체; •organic ingredient: 유기물 재료(성분); •light cake: 푸하게 부푼; •custard: 커스타스 소스; •tangy: 맛이 싸한, 코를 쏘는; •dark chocolate cake: 짙은 초클릿 케이크; •flavors: 향.

하나의 영어텍스트에 대하여 하나의 독해처리 절차만을 다룬 I부에이어 II부에서는 하나의 영어텍스트에 대하여 5단계 15절차를 통합적으로 다룬다. 통합적 독해는 언어 자체의 구성적 특성과 작자 쓰기 인지과정의 특성이 함께 고려된 인지적 독해방법이다. 언어 자체 구성과정 면에서 언어 자체는 철자로부터 단어로, 단어로부터 문장으로, 문장으로부터 텍스트가 형성된다. 작자 쓰기 인지과정 면에서 언어는 작자의 의도로부터 구성적 틀로, 구성적 틀로부터 구체적 의미로 실현된다. 독자 인지적 관점은 작자 인지적 관점의 역순 과정이다. 텍스트 구성적인 면과 독자 인지적인 면은 귀납적 과정이고, 작자 인지적인 면은 연역적 과정이다. 여기서의 통합적 독해에는 귀납적 과정과 연역적 과정이 반영된 것이다. 통합적 독해는 '무 원리적 독해' 개념에 대조하여 '원리적 독해'라고 할 수 있다.

두 인지과정이 고려된 통합적 독해는 구체적으로 다음 도표가 보여주는 <독해처리 모델>을 의미한다.

〈독해처리 모델〉

윤곽확인
(양식구성 확인 → 작자의도 확인 → 본문크기 확인)
↓
절독해
(구성성분 어휘의미 리콜→ 어휘의미들의 구성처리→ 주제어휘와 초점어휘 확인)
↓
단락독해
(절마디 관계 이해 → 단락의 내용흐름 파악 → 단락의 주제 확인)
↓
본문독해
(단위 마디의 관계식별 → 본문의 내용흐름 파악 → 본문의 주제 확인)
↓
독해사후처리
(글의 의도 확인 → 본문구성의 패턴 요약 → 마무리 처분)

이 <독해처리 모델>은 텍스트를 접하게 될 때부터 독해가 끝날 때까지 일어나는 일련의 처리과정(5단계 15절차)을 보여준다. 텍스트의 크기 등 상황에 따라 다소 변형될 수도 있다. 가령, 본문독해의 경우 단락들로 구성된 절(section)보다 위 층(즉 절들로 구성된 장/chapter)이 가정될 수 있는데, 여러 절(section)로 구성되는 장(chapter) 본문을 독해처리 할 이 경우는 여러 단락으로 된 절(section) 본문 독해처리 방식이 차원만 높여 한 번 더 적용된다.

II부에서 독해처리 모델을 적용하여 다루는 영어텍스트는 다양한 장르들이다. 이 다양한 장르들은 6요소(작자 writer: r/쓴 때 when: n/쓴 장소 where: e/내용 what: t/독자 to whom: m/전달방법 how: w) 중에서 상대적으로 더 중심에 있는 요소(들)는 어느 요소이냐 관점에서 구분된다. 이 구분기준에 의하여 4요소(r/n/t/m) 중심인 통신 영역, 3요소(r/n/t) 중심인 시사 영역, 또 다른 3요소(r/t/m) 중심인 홍보 영역, 2요소(t/m) 중심인 확인 영역, 또 다른 2요소(r/t) 중심인 주장 영역, 1요소(t)중심인 효과 영역의 텍스트로 구분된다. 여섯 영역(통신, 시사, 홍보, 확인, 주장, 효과)을 목차에서 장(chapter) 이름으로 하였다. 장 이름의 영역은 더 구체적으로 구분되는데, 구분된 결과는 실제의 텍스트 장르들이고, 이 장르들은 목차에서 절(section) 이름으로 하였다.

구분기준에 기초하여 여섯 영역은 다음과 같이 규정될 수 있다: 통신 영역은 작자와 독자(독자의 의무적 반응 필요) 사이 소통이 초점인 영역이다. 시사 영역은 작자가 불특정 독자 다수에게 의무적 반응을 요구하지 않는 시사성 정보전달이 초점인 영역이다. 홍보 영역은 작자가 독자에게 유/무형의 제품 구입 설득이 초점인 영역이다. 확인 영역은 독자(의 것)에 대한 작자의 확인이 초점인 영역이다. 주장 영역은 작자가 자신(의 것)에 대한 주장이 초점인 영역이다. 그리고 효과 영역은 독자에게 미치는 텍스트 자체의 효과가 초점인 영역이다.

제1장
통신 영역

제1절 대화

(1) A: Hey, Bill. Is that another new jacket you're wearing?
B: Yeah. Just got it the other day. Like it?
A: I sure do. But tell me — lately you've been spending like a madman. Where's all this money coming from?
B: No problem. I've been buying everything on credit.
A: Easy there, pal. Aren't you getting in over tour head? Remember: after the feast comes the reckoning.
B: I know I've been spending a lot, but so far I've been able to make my monthly payments.
A: Sure. But what happens if you get laid off? That construction job you have won't last forever, and you'll still have to pay for your excesses.
B: I know, but I'll cross that bridge when and if I get to it.

> 어휘리콜 •pal: 친구, 단짝; •over tour head: 돌아버린 머리; •feast: 축제, 잔치; •reckoning: 계산(서), 응보; •get laid off: 일을 그만두다, 해고되다.

(2) "Oh do hurry up, Jane! You're going to be late for work again!"

Mrs. Biggs went into her daughter's room Jane was sitting on the edge of the bed with head in her hands.

"Are you ill or something?"

"Just tired."

"You don't get a proper night's sleep. That's your trouble. You were out late again last night."

"I was only down at the club," Jane answered sleepily on her way to the door.

"That place! You're always down there these days."

Jane paused at the door. "You just imagine things! It's a social club, that's all. We sit around and talk. Or have a coke and play records."

"Is that all?"

Jane went into the bathroom without answering.

"This room's in a mess again," complained her mother. "Clothes and magazines all over the place." She started to tidy them up, still grumbling to herself.

Jane came back into the room with a wet face, combing her hair.

"Have you washed already?" her mother asked.

"Someone's invited me to a party in London on Saturday night," Jane said. "Can I go?"

"First the club, now parties...."

"But can I go, though?"

"I don't know. Ask your father." Mrs. Biggs went out of the room. "Is it the boy who rang last Saturday?" she called over her shoulder. "The one with the funny voice?"

"Funny voice!" muttered Jane to herself. "Well he's not my boyfriend!"

> 어휘리콜 •sleepily on her way: 가면서 잠 길에; •mess: 어지러운; •tidy: 정돈하다; •grumble: 불평하다; •mutter: 중얼거리다.

(3) Dear Pamela

I've been dating a very attractive, well-educated foreign student. I know he comes from a good family because in general his manners are perfect. However, there is one thing that bothers me. Thomas touches everyone he talks to. He puts his arm around other men and everytime he talks to a woman he takes her arm or just stands too close. It makes everybody uncomfortable. Why does he do this? Doesn't he understand it's rude?

Who Loves Thomas

Dear Who Loves Thomas

In many countries touching is more common than it is in the United States. People always shake hands when they see each other. Sometimes they put their arms around each other when they walk down the street. Often people from these countries think Americans are cold because they don't touch each other very much. Your boyfriend probably feels that touching is a way to show friendship. If this bothers you, you should explain to him that here two men will probably shake hands when they meet, but otherwise they don't usually touch each other. Men don't touch women very much either unless they're dating. When you talk to him, let him know you're trying to help, not criticize.

어휘리콜   •bother: 괴롭히다; •rude: 무례한.

(4) To: Mike Kim

When you were out, these people called:

1. Mr./Mrs.: Francisco
   From: Private
   Telephone number (724) 985-4231
   Message: Ms. Francisco wants to make an appointment for next week for a general checkup.
2. Mr./Mrs.: Smith
   From: Universal Pharmaceuticals

Telephone number 985-8628

   Message: Mr. Smith will drop by the clinic tomorrow morning with samples of several new drugs for you to try with patients. He also wants to know if you can play golf this Saturday morning.

3. Mr./Mrs.: Mantas

   From: Downtown Dental

   Telephone number 985-9997

   Message: Your gold crown is ready and will be fitted during your appointment this afternoon at 5:30 P.M.

4. Mr./Mrs.: Brown

   From: Private

   Telephone number 985-3420

   Message: Mr. Brown would like to know if his test results have been returned from the lab yet.

어휘리콜   •Pharmaceuticals: 약조제국; •clinic: 진료소.

---

(5) For: Kelly Davis

   Date: 14.7.08

   Time: 15:35

   From: Carmel J. Allison, Marketing director

   High Score Sports Shoes

   Phone: (551) 482-585

Telephoned	V	Please call	V
Wants to see you		Will call again	
Returned your call		Urgent	V

   Message: Ms. Allison called to discuss your interest in purchasing her company's new line of soccer shoes, the XSS 720 series. Ms. Allison said she will be available for the rest of the afternoon today and from 11:00 to 14:30 tomorrow. She gave her personal cell number in case you can't get through with the number above. Her cell is (033) 4823-348.

Taken by: Ami Thompson

어휘리콜 •Sports Shoe: 운동화; •soccer shoe: 축구화.

(6) **10 Questions**. As our TimeFrames issue reconsiders the recent past, we asked futurist **Ray Kurzweil** for his prediction of what's to come

Is it a mistake to use the events of the recent past as a method of predicting the future?

Our intuition about the future is linear. But the reality of information technology is exponential, and that makes a profound difference. If I take 30 steps linearly, I get to 30. If I take 30 steps exponentially, I get to a billion.

You predict we'll reach a point with artificial intelligence that you call the singularity. How will that affect us?

By the time we get to the 2040s, we'll be able to multiply human intelligence a billion-fold. That will be a profound change that's singular in nature. Computers are going to keep getting smaller and smaller. Ultimately, they will go inside our bodies and brains and make us healthier, make us smarter. We'll be online all the time. Search engines won't wait to be asked.

Will this make it more difficult for us to focus?

We've always been responsible for the triage of our time. I actually think these technologies enable us to focus better. My father was a musician, and he had to hire an orchestra and raise money just to hear his compositions. Now a kid in her dorm room can do that with her synthesizer and computer.

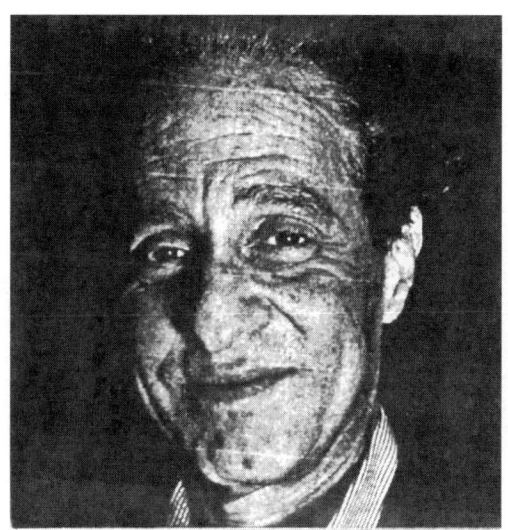

How exactly will technology make us healthier?

We will reprogram our biology. My cell phone's probably updating itself as we speak, but I'm walking around with 1,000-year-old software that was for a different era. One gene, the fat insulin receptor gene, says, "Hold on to every calorie, because the next hunting season may not work out so well." I'd like to be able to tell my fat insulin receptor gene, "You don't need to do that. I'm confident I'll have food tomorrow."

Will we be eating differently?

We'll grow in vitro cloned meats in factories that are computerized and run by artificial intelligence. You can just grow the part of the animal that you're eating. Some people say, "Oh, that sounds yucky." I say, "Well, why don't you go visit a factory-farming installation? You'll find that getting meat from living animals is yucky." But we'll need a marketing genius to sell the idea.

Speaking of marketing, what idea about the future do you have the hardest time selling?

People are most resistant to the idea of dramatic extensions to life expectancy, because it affects every decision they make. They have this cycle of life in mind. People sort of wax philosophical - "Oh, I don't want to live past 100." I'd like to see them say that when they're 100.

Do you think we'll find intelligent life elsewhere in the universe?

The consensus in the field is that there's somewhere between a thousand and a million technologically advanced civilizations just in our own galaxy. But once you get to a point where we are, within a few centuries at most, these civilizations would be doing galaxy-wide engineering. It's impossible we wouldn't be noticing that. So my conclusion is that we may be the first.

What are the dangers of technological innovation?

Technology is a double-edged sword. New technologies can be used for destructive purposes. The answer is to develop rapid-response systems for new dangers like a bio-terrorist creating a new biological virus. We don't have to just sit back and wait.

How will science affect the religious and ethnic differences in the world?

I think we are evolving rapidly into one world culture. It's certainly one world economy. With billions of people online, I think we'll appreciate the wisdom in many different traditions as we learn more about them. People were very isolated and didn't know anything about other religions 100 years ago.

How will our technological progress make us feel about God?

I believe our civilization is going to be vastly more intelligent and more spiritual in the decades ahead. You can argue how we got here, but we are the species that goes beyond our limitations. We didn't stay on the ground. We didn't stay on the planet. Our species always transcends.

(video at Time.com. To watch interviews with Ray Kurzwell and other newsmakers, go to time.com/10 questions)　　(Time December 6, 2010)

> 어휘리콜　•TimeFrames: 잡지이름; •exponential: 지수적인; •artificial intelligence: 인공지능; •singularity: 특이한 것; •billion-fold: 10억배; •Search engine: 검색엔진; •triage: 자원의 선별적 문제; •synthesizer: 소리 합성 악기; •fat insulin receptor gene: 지방 인슐린 흡입 인자; •vitro cloned meats: 유리관에서 복제된 고기; •yucky: 시원스러운; •factory-farming installation: 공장형 농업시설; •life expectancy: 기대수명; •cycle of life: 생의 주기; •wax: 물건; •double-edged sword: 양날의 칼; •ethnic: 민족적; •transcend: 탁월하다.

(7) Situation: Getting Up in the Morning.

(The alarm clock rings.)

Catherine: Honey, it's seven o'clock. Time to get up.

James: Okay, just a few more minutes.

Catherine: No. You told me to make sure you were up by seven.

James: I know but I can sleep till seven—thirty if I don't take a shower.

Catherine: James, you know that's impossible. You have a meeting with your boss and later with an important client.

James: Christ, I almost forgot. That's what happens when I don't get enough sleep.

Catherine: Enough sleep? You went to bed at ten. That's nine hours.

James: Do you have to be right all the time? But you are right ; I'm getting up.

Catherine: Jump in the shower, that will make you feel better. And I'll make a pot of strong coffee, but what do you want for breakfast?

James: Something simple. How about a bagel and cream cheese?

Catherine: No problem. It'll be ready before you are.

James: Don't be so sure.

Catherine: Why wouldn't I be? You haven't beaten me yet.

James: True. But there's a first time for everything.

> 어휘리콜　•clint: 고객.

제2절 편지

(1) **Bradley Art Museum**

John Fleming
564 Leafy Lane
Small Ville, Texas
April 19

Dear Mr. Fleming

I would like to sincerely thank you for your very generous art donation to the Bradley art Museum. As a small gesture of thanks, the Museum board would like to offer you a V.I.P. pass for you and any guests you choose to accompany you to our new and exciting exhibition in Scotland starting on May 28. This exhibition has been in the making now for 10 years and we are sure that you and yours will truly enjoy the event.

This V.I.P. pass also includes complimentary meals at our newly refurbished restaurant in addition to a champagne reception when you first arrive. We also have at your disposal a museum store where you can purchase many special gifts for your family and friends back home. Products consist of high quality books, eyewear, and perfumes.

On May 29, we are going to start the special series on several kinds of topics. In particular, on the evening of May 30, there will be a talk given by Ralf Simmons concerning "The Art Behind the Art." This will take place in Carney Hall and next day, visitors will be offered a guided tour of the museum grounds. Details of the show itself will be sent to you in our April 25 newsletter in which you'll find plenty of information to get you started.

Kindest Regards

Jane Chapel

Jane Chapel
Museum Director

어휘리콜 •generous art donation: 관대한 미술품 기부; •Museum board: 미술관 위원회; •V.I.P. pass: V.I.P 회원권; •accompany: 동반하다; •you and yours: 당신과 당신의 가족들; • complimentary meals: 무료식사; •refurbished: 단장된; •at your disposal: 편하신 대로; • eyewear: 안경류; •perfumes: 향수.

---

(2) **20 November 2001**

Consular/Visa Section
4 Jeong-dong
Jung-ku
Seoul 100-120
Republic of Korea

Tel: (822) 3210 5500
Direct: (822) 3210 5500
Fax: (822) 3210 5653
E-mail: consular.seoul@fco.gov.uk
www.britishembassy.or.kr
www.britain.or.kr

The British Government is committed to providing a fair and fast visa service.

In order to aid travellers, it has changed the way that visas are used to allow travellers to enter the UK.

The visa you have just received will enable you to enter the UK as often as you wish. You will note that the grant of a visa also gives leave to enter the United Kingdom. Such leave will no longer be granted on arrival in the UK, but an Immigration Officer will still check your passport.

Please note that you may not remain in the UK after the date of expiry of

your visa. The date of expiry is clearly given on the visa: please note this carefully.

If the visa has been issued prior to your expected date of travel, you should be aware that you cannot enter the UK before the 'valid' from date given on the visa.

어휘리콜 • commit: (의무를) 지우다; • fair and fast: 공정하고 빠른; • grant: 수여; • give leave: 허락하다; • Immigration Officer: 이민국.

---

(3) **Scaper Phones**

January 15
Diana Price
252 77th Street
Aurora, IL 60504

Dear Ms. Price

We have received the wireless telephone kit that you shipped to us for replacement. The apparatus has been forwarded to the technical support department for a diagnostic test and the results will be released in three days.

Our warranty guarantees replacement of defective handsets returned to us within three weeks of purchase. Should we find the product you purchased defective, we will immediately send you a new telephone kit of the same model.

Thank you for your patience.

Respectfully yours

Ted Patel
Customer service representative
Scaper Phones

> 어휘리콜 •kit: 짝, 벌; •ship: 배, 선적하다; •replacement: 교환(품); •technical support department: 전문지원부서; •diagnostic test: 진단검사; •release: 해결하다; •warranty: 보증(서); •defective handsets: 결함이 있는 핸드셋.

(4)

26 Windsor Road
CHINGFORD
CH4 6PY

15 May 19–
Mrs W R Jenkinson
Personnel Manager
Leyland & Bailey Ltd
Nelson Works
CLAPTON
CHS 8HA

Dear Mrs Jenkinson

PRIVATE SECRETARY TO MANAGING DIRECTOR

I was interested to see your advertisement in today's Daily Telegraph and would like to be considered for this post.

I am presently working as Private Secretary to the General Manager at a manufacturing company and have a wide range of responsibilities. These include attending and taking minutes of meetings and interviews, dealing with callers and correspondence in my employer's absence, and supervising junior staff, as well as the usual secretarial duties.

The kind of work in which your company is engaged particularly interests me, and I would welcome the opportunity it would afford to use my language abilities which are not utilised in my present post.

A copy of my curriculum vitae is enclosed with copies of previous testimonials. I hope to hear from you soon and to be given the opportunity to present myself at an interview.

Yours sincerely
Jean Careon
JEAN CARSON (Miss)
Encs

> 어휘리콜 •this post: 이 자리; •minutes of meetings: 미팅 의사록; •callers and correspondence: 전화와 우편; •curriculum vitae: 이력서.

(5)

FINANCIAL TIMES Financial Times Management
PITMAN PUBLISHING 128 Long Acre
 London WC2E 9AN
ST/PJ Telephone +44(0)171 447 2240
 Facsimile +44(0)171 240 5771

12 November 19—

Mr Christopher Long
General Manager
Long Printing Co Ltd
34 Wood Lane
London WC1 8TJ

Dear Christopher

FULLY BLOCKED LETTER LAYOUT

This layout has become firmly established as the most popular way of setting out letters, fax messages, memos, reports - in fact all business communications. The main feature of fully blocked style is that all lines begin at the left-hand margin.

Open punctuation is usually used with the fully-blocked layout. This means that no punctuation marks are necessary in the reference, date, inside address, salutation and closing section. Of course essential punctuation must still be used in the text of the message itself. However, remember to use commas minimally today; they should only be used when their omission would make the sense of the message unclear.

Consistency is important in layout and spacing of all documents. It is usual to leave just one clear line space between each section.

I enclose some other examples of fully blocked layout as used in fax messages and memoranda.

Most people agree that this layout is very attractive, easy to produce as well as businesslike.

Yours sincerely

Shirley Taylor

SHIRLEY TAYLOR
Secretarial Consultant

Enc

Copy   Pradeep Jethi, Publisher
       Amelia Lakin, Publishing Coordinator

> 어휘리를 •BLOCKED LETTER LAYOUT: 영역을 구분하는 편지 구성; •business communications: 업무수행 소통방법; •salutation: 인사말; •consistency: 일관성.

(6) CONTACT FORM:

In order to receive the quickest response from our customer service representatives, please fill out the form below.

NAME: Yoo Jin Lee   PHONE: (509)555-4332

E-MAIL: yoojin@axl.com

MESSAGE:

I recently purchased an air conditioner from your company. I have been using it for several days now, and the fan is not operating properly. Please let me know what steps I need to take in getting it repaired, or whether you would be willing to send me a replacement. Thanks for your time, and please contact me as soon as possible.

TO: Yoo Jin Lee <yoojin@axl.com>

FROM: Alex Mann <Alma@clielectronics.net>

DATE: June 9

SUBJECT: Your air conditioner

Dear Ms. Lee

Thank you for contacting Clientele Electronics' customer service department about the problem with your air conditioner. We apologize for any inconvenience this may have caused. Our production plant has contacted us with a list of defects discovered in our most recent line of products:

MODEL	MALFUNCTION
CX-290	Temperature button nonfunctional
CP-145	Cooling unit overheats
CR-92	Fan system malfunction
CB-51	Auto-cooling system nonfunctional

Clientele Electronics is currently working on ways to solve these problems. In the meantime, your purchase will be replaced free of charge. Simply visit the location of your purchase with your original receipt. Again, I apologize for your trouble.

Alex Mann

> 어휘리콜   •replacement: 교환 품; •Thanks for your time: 읽어 주셔서 감사합니다; •production plant: 생산 공장; •malfunction: 결함; •free of charge: 무료로.

제3절 email

(1) Subject: Model Business Letters
   Date: Mon, 22 Sept 1997 15:17:59+0000
   From: shirley.taylor@northern.net
   To: pradeep.jethi@ftmanagement.com

Hi Pradeep

Thanks for your email today. I'm glad you had a good holiday.

I've been able to progress well with revisions to Model Business Letters. Help from my friends Nan Harper and Barrie Mort has been so valuable.

You'll be glad to know that I'll be able to meet the deadline and should be able to finalise things within the next week or so. Can we arrange to meet early October so that I can hand over my manuscript and discuss the amendments and new page design etc?

Talk to you soon. All the best...

Shirley

> 어휘리콜　•with revisions: 수정작업으로; •deadline: 마감일; •finalise: 끝내다; •Talk to you soon: 빠른 시간 내에 이야기 하고 싶다; •All the best...: 그대에게 행복을....

(2) From: Elise Mendez <mendez@innovatctech.com>
　　To: Nolan Smith <director@floalexchange.com>
　　Subject: Request for floral arrangements
　　Date: October 1

　　Attachment: floor_plan.jpg: Products.jpg

　　Dear Mr. Nolan

　　I was very impressed with your company after attending my sister's wedding last month. Your beautiful arrangements of flowers have made me decide to make your business a part of a company event this month. My company will have a product launch for new mobile phones and computers, and we need your flower arrangements to add character to the event.
　　I have attached the layout and color scheme of the event and the images of our product line to be launched.
　　E-mail me if you have any questions.

　　Thank you

　　Elise Mendez
　　Product Manager, Innovate Technologies

> 어휘리콜　•Attachment: 첨부; •arrangements of flowers: 꽃 장식; •product launch: 제품 발매 (개시, 발표, 출판).

(3) From: Nolan Smith <director@floralexchange.com>

To: Elise Mendez <mendez@innovatetech.com>
Subject: The revised arrangement
Date: October 10

Attachment : floor_plan_revision.jpg

Dear Ms. Mendez

Thank you for choosing Floral Exchange for your important event. We have studied the set design of your location and have come up with the necessary displays to fit your particular requests.

Attached is the new layout for the floral arrangements for the product launch on October 20.

May we also suggest using bright flowers to complement the new product colors you are displaying? Using pale colored flowers for your floral backdrop might not work very well in highlighting the company's design efforts.

Please reply to this e-mail to confirm the new arrangement. Your utmost satisfaction is our primary concern, so please do not hesitate to coordinate with us to make your event a success.

Again, thank you for your business.

Regards

Nolan Smith (212-555 9119)
Proprietor, Floral Exchange

어휘리콜 •Floral Exchange: 업체이름; •location: 위치; •come up with: 떠크디, •necessary •displays: 필요한 배치; •pale colored: 옅은 색상의; •backdrop: 배경; •Proprietor: 사업주.

---

(4) From: Karl Brandt <ktxandt@billingsnet.com>

To: All Staff Members
Subject: Anniversary party
Date: June 19

Hello everyone

This is just a reminder that the company's 25th anniversary party will be held on Saturday, August 5th. It will be at the Mandalay Hotel and begin at 7 P.M. but wine will be served an hour before dinner. So, we expect to see you all there early to enjoy a wonderful opportunity to meet your associates and get to know one another better. For seating arrangements, RSVP with me as soon as possible.

Regards

Karl

Date: Saturday August 5th
Time: 7:00 P.M.
Place: Mandalay Hotel

> 어휘리콜　•reminder: 독촉장; •RSVP: Please reply 의미의 불어.

(5) From: Matthias Kleine <mkleine@deutchhosting.com>
　　To: Subscriptions manager <subscrib@zapcomix.net>
　　Subject: Acc. #2856465234236
　　Date: March 16

Dear Subscriptions manager

I was on business trip for the last 3 months, and while I was away I suspended my subscription to your magazine. The problem is that I haven't gotten my magazine for this month.

From my experience in the past, you have never missed an issue and been always on time. Could you check what might have caused this problem?

If there is a problem with my subscription, please e-mail me so we can work out what to do.

Thank you very much

Regards
Matthias Kleine

> 어휘리콜 •suspend: 중지하다.

(6) Please Renew Your MLA Membership

Rosemary G. Feal<membership@mla.org>
2011. 5.17 오전 12:31:40
ydkim@pufs.ac.kr
To view an online version of this message click here.

Dear Professor Kim

I want to thank you for your past support of the Modem Language Association and to encourage you to renew your MLA membership for 2011. If this message crosses with your renewal, I thank you. If you're still deciding whether to renew, I'd like to take a moment to let you know how much your support matters and to ask you to stay with the MLA community.

In these tough economic times, we are all facing difficult budget choices. But I hope that, in making your decision, you will consider the ways in which the association serves its members and the field. Your support enables the association to stand up for core principles of higher education: that tenured faculty members are integral to student learning; that part-time, adjunct, and non-tenure-track faculty members deserve fair pay and equitable treatment; and that language study is a critical component of education in a global era. Your support funds the gathering and analysis of data on the job market, the development of tools for teachers and students, the advocacy of the study and teaching of languages, the maintenance of the MLA Language Map, the association's distinguished publishing program, the revamped annual convention, and our ongoing efforts to enhance the public's understanding of our day-to-daywork. More information about the MLA's current activities appears in the president's column and editors column of the Summer Newsletter.

The significant individual benefits of MLA membership include priority online convention registration and reduced registration fees, discounts on more than three hundred books and pamphlets published by the MLA, and five issues of PMLA. With the humanities under attack, every single member matters. The MLA needs your involvement, and I hope that you will renew your membership today. If you have any questions, please call the membership office at 646 576-5151 or e-mail membership@mla.org. Cordially,

Rosemary G. Feal
Executive Director

Please do not reply to this automatically generated message. To contact the MLA staff, please see here; to contact members, please use the directory here.

Constant Contact

Try for yourself

This emil was sent to ydkim@pufs.ac.kr by membership@mla.org

Instant removal with SafeUnsubscribe™ Privacy Policy.

Modem Language Association 26 Broadway, 3rd floor New York NY 10004

> 어휘리콜　•cross: 교차하다; •tough economic times: 경제가 어려운 때; •stand up: 나타내다; •tenured: 종신 재직 자격이 있는; •integral: 필수의; •adjunct: 조교수; •advocacy: 고취; •revamped: 개편된; •attack: 개시, 착수.

(7) 보낸 사람 Ravi Kumar, Indian Translators Association
　　받는 사람 XXXX
　　숨은 참조
　　제목 New Book on Translation Studies
　　날짜 2013-06-21 16:54:36
　　Dear ML Member and Language Colleague,

Greetings from Indian Translators Association, New Delhi.

Recently, we launched the book "**Role of Translation in Nation Building**". It has been jointly published by modlingua and Indian Translators Association. You may like to refer it to your library and colleagues.

The mentioned book talks about how translators have always played a pivotal role in social and cultural change in society and how they continue to play a major role in dissemination of the ever expanding knowledge and information available today. In this globalized world the demand for translation and language related services has increased many times and that translation is not only needed for the creation of national identity but it has also become an essential tool for keeping pace with the processes of globalization and localization. Many times we take for granted the translator's crucial role at the (intra) national level and we are less aware of their equally pivotal place as mediators at the international level and, potentially, in the creation of the even larger and comprehensive global supra national identities which seem destined to follow in the future.

It also covers "how translation has played crucial role in shaping up nations not only in Indian/Asian context but also in the context of Europe, Canada, Africa, Australia and Arab world". Hence, in a way, the extent/range of thoughts/issues discussed in the book, encompass the entire globe. The book is also an attempt to find answers to issues like:

- What role has translation played in Nation Building in the Indian as well as global context?
- How easy or difficult is it to view Translation and Nation Building as a well-gelling couple?
- Did translation play a role in Turkish modernism movements and its accession to European Union?
- What about Translation and Nation Building in the African, Arabian and Australian contexts?
- Do national conflicts and language politics actually impact literary works and translations?
- How can media play an effective part in bringing social changes by means of translations?
- How has translation impacted the discourse on nationalism and globalization in the Arab World?

The book can be utilized as a guiding base/reference tool/textbook by:

1. Students of language learning and its theory; translation studies; literature.
2. Research scholars working in areas related to translation, nationalism, globalization, international studies, etc.
3. Professors, teachers involved in teaching the above mentioned subjects/topics.

Digital as well as print version available at Modlingua. K-5B, Lower Ground Floor, Kalkaji, New Delhi -110019, India SMS: +91-8287636881
E-mail: sales@modlinuua.com

ISBN Printed Version: 978-81-926798-0-8;
ISBN Digital Version: 978-81-926798-1-5.

Price outside India US $ 24.95 + Postal Charges

Payment option available through Paypal.

Preface and chapter details available at link below

http:/www.alliedmodlingua.com/Book Review R Translation Nation Building.pdf
Best regards

Ravi Kumar (Editor)
President
Indian Translators Association, New Delhi

어휘리콜 •launch: 내보내다, 출판하다; •jointly published: 공동 출판되다; •pivotal: 중요한, 중추적인; •dissemination: 보급, 전파; •national identity: 국가 정체성; •entire globe: 지구 전체; •modernism movements: 현대화 운동; •nationalism and globalization: 국수주의와 세계화.

제4절 통지

(1)

SS/PAT

25 March 2003

THE UNIVERSITY
OF BIRMINGHAM
Hospitality and Accommodation
Services
Student Accommodation

Edgbaston
Birmingham B15 2TT

United Kingdom

General Manager
Student Accommodation
Lesley Stewart

The Occupier(s)
Flat 2, 53 Anderton Park Road
Moseley
Birmingham B13 9DU

Dear Occupier(s)

RE: Portable Appliance Testing

The University is obliged to provide an annual safety check on all portable electrical items it provides to tenants.

As such, an appointment has been arranged for an Electrical Contractor to visit your flat on Wednesday 2 April 2003, during the morning.

The person carrying out the checks is Mr Colin Penny. He is appointed by the University and has carried out these checks on a regular basis.

Our records indicate that the portable electrical equipment provided to you is a vacuum cleaner. (The fridge and cooker fall under a different category due to their size and as such are only required to be tested once every 3 years).

Please ensure that the said vacuum cleaner is emptied and left in a prominent position in the lounge or other suitable area.

If you are unable to be at home during the time of the visit, keys to your flat will be released to Mr Penny to let himself in.

Please further note that tenants are advised to have their own electrical equipment tested at regular intervals.

Should you have any questions, please do not hesitate to contact me directly.

Yours sincerely

Satnam

Satnam Singh, LL.B., BA (Hons)
Housing Officer
Tel: 0121 414 6438 / Fax: 0121 414 6443
Email: s.singh.l@bham.ac.uk

INVESTOR IN PEOPLE

Enquiries: Private Sector 0121 414 6434/6236   Undergraduate Accommodation 0121 414 6441/7469
           Properly Management 0121 414 6438/6236   Postgraduate Accommodation 0121 414 6237
Fax: 0121 414 6443

어휘리콜 •SS/PAT: 작성자 이니셜; •Occupier: 거주자; •Portable Appliance Testing: 이동 전열기 점검; •is obliged to: ~할 의무가 있다; •tenant: 거주자; •vacuum cleaner: 진공청소기; •fridge and cooker: 냉장고와 주방기구; •regular basis: 정해진 기존사항; •prominent position: 눈에 띄는 장소; •lounge: 거실.

(2)

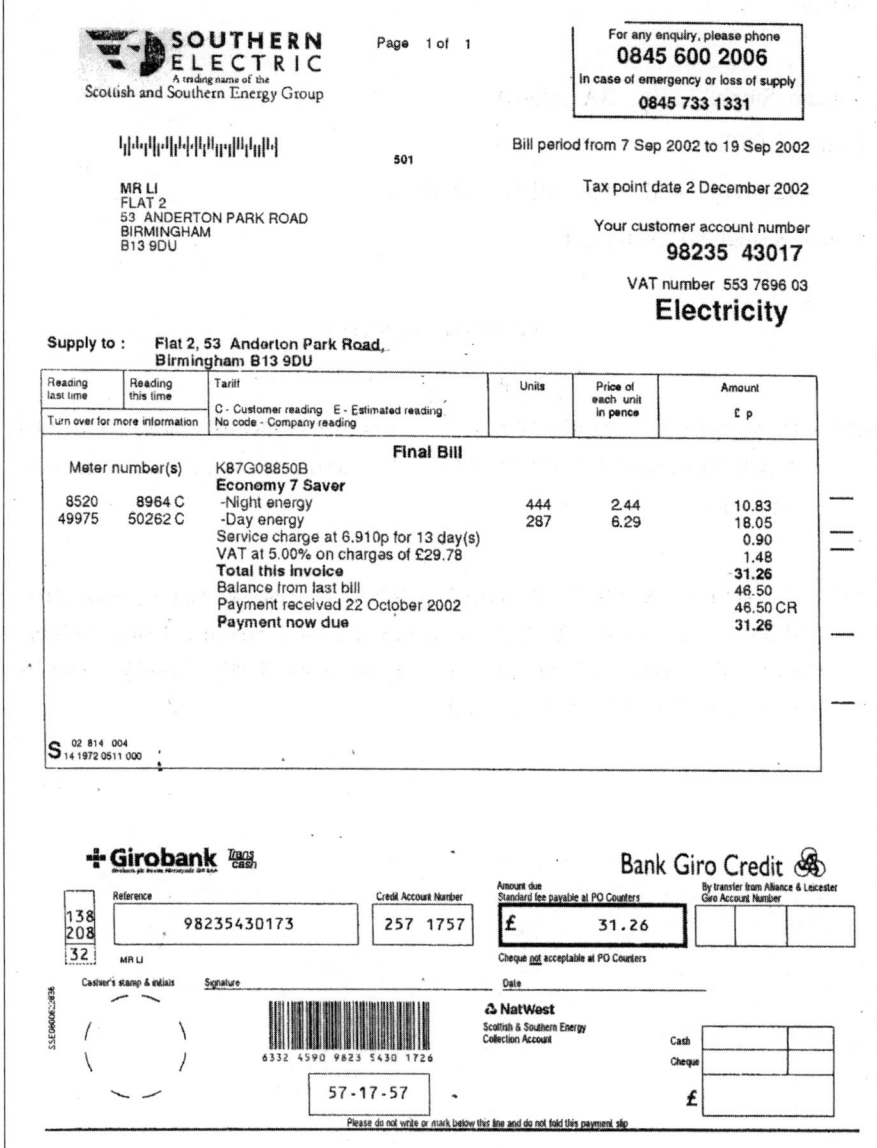

어휘리콜 •flat: (연립식)공동주택; •supply to: 수급자; •VAT: Value Added Tax(부가가치세); •customer account number: 고객번호.

(3)

Post Office Ltd.
Your Receipt

Moseley
149 Alcester Road
Birmingham
West Midlands
B13 8LH

VAT REG No. 243 1700 02
FI 14 Mar 2003   16: 58
SESSION : 2-1143246-1

Transcash   2571757
1   94.11   84.11
T'csh fee
1   1.30   1.30
TOTAL DUE TO POST OFFICE 85,41
Cash   FROM CUSTOMER   85.41
BALANCE   0.00

Thank You

> 어휘리콜 •due: 요금; •balance: 잔액.

(4) **ATTENTION ALL CONFERENCE PARTICIPANTS**

There have been some last-minute schedule changes due to the large number of participants this year. The workshop "Digital Marketing" has been moved from room 21 to room 145 and will now start at 10:30 instead of 10:15. Also, the seminar entitled "Advantages of Consumer Surveys" will be held in basement room 14B, which offers more seating space than its original location in room 55. This seminar will begin at 9:30 as scheduled, Thank you for your attention, and welcome to the conference.
Staff.

> 어휘리콜 •last-minute schedule: 마지막 스케줄; •basement room: 지하실; •original location: 원래 위치.

(5)

More connections. More possibilities.

Your account and bill number
CM 6264 0350 Q002 C2

MISS Y.K KIM
FLAT 2
53 ANDERTON PARK RD
BIRMINGHAM
B13 9DU   50153 012

BT

Date
10 November 2002

If you have a query
please see reverse for
our contact details.

BT Standard

Bill for 0121 442 6250

Cost of calls	£ 34.75
Your benefits	- £ 3.38
Service charges	£ 26.80
VAT	£ 10.17
Total now due	**£ 68.34**

Please make sure we receive the total now due by
24 November 2002

Save Money!
Switch to Monthly Payment Plan

- Save £12 a year – it's easy to do
- Call us now on 0800 150111 or
  visit www.bt.com/billing-payments
- It's one less thing to worry about.
  Remember,
  you can choose the date for payments
  and spread them evenly over the year.
  It couldn't be simpler.

Make sure you're getting the
most value for money from BT.
Just phone 150 or visit
www.bt.com/valueformoney
for your free booklet of
money-saving tips.

0009934

BT

- You can find details of how to pay overleaf.
- If appropriate, fill in the details on this payment slip.
- Please don't send cash by post.
- Please quote 'Your account number' below on correspondence or remittance advices.

bank giro credit

Cashier's stamp and initials

Your account number
CM62640350

Signature   Date

8944 0190 6264 0350 0021 7006

Bank details
44-70-34   HSBC Bank plc
            Head Office Collection Account

Total now due
£ 68.34

Cash

Cheques

£

No. cheques   Fee

Please do not fold, pin or staple this slip or write below this line.

03 CM 62640350 Q002   C2   68.34

<3CM62640350Q002< 447034+< 73   X

Date: 10 November 2002
Your account and bill number: CM 6264 0350 Q002 C2
Your phone number: 0121 442 6250

Summary

This section shows a summary of your bill. To see the detail behind this summary, go to the Detail section.

Cost of calls £ 34.75 *see page 4*

These are the totals for all your calls. See the Detail section for further details of your calls.

Type of call	Total number of calls	Total duration	Total cost	
Local	19	00:26:28	£ 0.878	see page 4
National	4	00:11:55	£ 0.800	see page 4
International	19	00:33:01	£ 30.127	see page 4
To a mobile	13	00:14:18	£ 1.726	see page 4
National rate	16	00:05:56	£ 0.689	see page 4
Lo-call	1	00:25:46	£ 0.325	see page 4
Other	5	00:01:33	£ 0.210	see page 4

Your benefits − £ 3.38 deducted from your bill *see page 5*

BT Standard
These are the benefits you've received. Any other discounts are also detailed.

Type of benefit	Total benefit	
Call Allowance	− £ 3.378	see page 5

Service charges £ 26.80 *see page 5*

This section includes your line rental and any packages, services and equipment you have selected.

Type of charge	Total cost	
Package fees/line rental	£ 26.80	see page 5

VAT £ 10.17

This is the summary of your VAT. If you require a tax invoice for VAT recovery purposes, please call us free on 0800 671 282.

VAT rate	Charge (ex VAT)	Total VAT
17.5%	£ 58.17	£ 10.17
0%	£ 0.00	£ 0.00
	Total £ 58.17	Total £ 10.17

어휘리콜 •account and bill number: 회원 및 계좌 번호.

(6)

 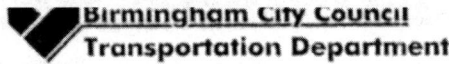

Penalty Charge Notice

(ROAD TRAFFIC ACT 1991 - Section 66 and Schedule 3 as amended)

Notice Number:
The Motor Vehicle with Registration Number:
Make: Colour:
was seen in:

on: at:

by Parking Attendant (number):

Signature: _____

Who had reasonable cause to believe that the following parking contravention had occurred:

You are therefore required to pay a penalty of £   within 28 days. The charge will be reduced to £   if payment is received within 14 days.

INSTRUCTIONS FOR PAYMENT

- If payment of the Penalty Charge Notice is received within 14 days of the date of issue(as shown overleaf), the reduced charge will be accepted as settlement. If payment is not received within 14 days, you will be required lo pay the full amount of this Notice.

If no payment is received within 28 days of the date of issue, a Notice to Owner may be sent to the registered keeper of the vehicle requesting payment. The Notice to Owner will also describe how to make formal representations regarding the issue of this Penalty Charge Notice.

PLEASE NOTE: If payment is made by post, please allow for postal delays.

HOW TO PAY

- By Post
  (a) Make your cheque or postal order payable to Birmingham City Council (Transportation) write the Penalty Charge Notice number on the back of you cheque/postal order (to avoid error), complete the slip below and attach it to your cheque or postal order.
  (b) For credit/debit card payments made by MASTERCARD, VISA, SWITCH, DELTA complete and return the slip below.

All postal payments must be sent to: Birmingham City Council
　　　　　　　　　　　　　　　　　Transportation Department
　　　　　　　　　　　　　　　　　POBOX77
　　　　　　　　　　　　　　　　　Birmingham B4 7WA

- Payments By Telephone
  Credit/Debit card payments only • call o121464 2100 between 9.30am and

5.30pm Monday to Saturday, giving details ol Card Number, Penalty Charge Notice number and amount.

ENQUIRIES

Enquiries concerning this Penalty Charge Notice should be made in writing within 14 days to the address shown below. Please quote the Notice number and the vehicle registration number as shown overleaf. PLEASE NOTE: your enquiry is received after 14 days you will lose the opportunity to pay the reduced charge.

All enquiries must be sent to: Birmingham City Council
Parking Section, Transportation Department.
PO Box 37
Birmingham B4 7DQ

> 어휘리콜 •postal delay: 우체국 지연.

(7) **(Letterhead)**

Sep.15, 1997

Mr. Mobert Krost
3660 Wilshire Blvd., Suite 1030
Los Angeles, CA 90010
U.S.A.

Dear Mr. Frost:

It is with extreme regret that I have to inform you that Executive Managing Director, Mr. Robin William, suddenly passed away because of the traffic accident last night in Korea Town.

As you may know, our company is deeply indebted to Mr. William for its present position in this market. Thanks to his insight our company has an efficiently excellent organization and a strong management and also, I'm sure, our company will be able to carry forward the company's progress under some major plans already done by him.

The farewell service will be held at St. Peter's Church on Sep.18 at 4:00 p.m.

Yours truly
(Signature)

어휘리콜 •pass away: 죽다; •farewell service: 장례식.

(8) March 1, 19--

Mr. Louis Ferron
First Security, Inc.
389 Queen Street West
Madison, WI 53711

Dear Mr. Ferron

Thank you for submitting specifications and a cost estimate for the security system work on the Tri-Oaks Building project. Your references and client list are impressive. We received over thirty bids for the office building work. Each bid was carefully reviewed against our budget and the qualifications of the bidder.

Your firm was among the five final contenders we considered. However, after careful deliberation, we chose Net Security, Inc. for the project. Their bid was closest to our budget and their experience was in an area that matched our needs.

We appreciate your interest in our project and the time and effort you went to in preparing your bid. We hope we will have other opportunities to work with you on a future project as your company has an exceptional reputation in the field.

Sincerely

OFFICE SPACE DESIGN, INC.

Margaret Plant

Project Supervisor

어휘리콜　•submit: 제출하다, 제안하다; •client: 고객; •bid: 입찰; •bidder: 입찰자; •contender: 경쟁자, 도전자.

---

(9) **TRANSPORT DEPARTMENT NOTICE**

Temporary Traffic Arrangements in Torrance

Notice is hereby given that the following temporary traffic arrangements in Torrance will be implemented to facilitate the erection of footbridge on the dates specified below:

(A) From 1:00 a.m. to 6:00 a.m. on 14 September, 1995.

  (1) The section of Sepulveda Blvd from its junction with 190th Street to its junction with the Maple Road will be temporarily closed to all vehicular traffic.

  (2) Vehicles on Sepulveda Blvd east-bound heading for I-95 will be diverted via Hawthorne Blvd.

(B) From 1:00 p.m. to 5:00 p.m. on 15 September, 1995.

  (1) The section of Pacific Coast Highway from its junction with Ravenspur Road to its junction with the Rolling Hills Street will be temporarily closed to all vehicular traffic.

  (2) Torrance green minibus no.50 on its journey to Center Mall will follow the route of Municipal bus no.39 along Western Avenue.

어휘리콜　•Traffic Arrangement: 교통 계획; •implement: 이행하다; •facilitate: 촉진하다, 돕다; •erection: 건설; •footbridge: 인도교, 육교; •junction: 교차점; •Blvd: boulevard, 대로, 가로수길; •vehicular: 운반용의, 탈것의.

제5절 메모

(1) **MEMORANDUM**

To   Mandy Lim, Administrative Assistant
From   Sally Thomas, PA to Chairman
Ref   ST/JJ
Date   14 August 19___

INHOUSE DOCUMENT FORMATS

Many congratulations on recently joining the staff in the Chairman's office. I hope you will be very happy here.

I am enclosing a booklet explaining the company's general rules regarding document formats. However, I thought it would be helpful if I summarised the rules for ease of reference.

1. DOCUMENT FORMATS

All documents should be presented in the fully-blocked format using open punctuation. Specimen letters, fax messages, memoranda and other documents are included in the booklet. These examples should guide you in our requirements.

2. SIGNATURE BLOCK (LETTERS)

In outgoing letters it is usual practice to display the sender's name in capitals and the title directly underneath in lower case with initial capitals.

3. NUMBERED ITEMS

In reports and other documents it is often necessary to number items. In such cases the numbers should be displayed alone with no full stops or brackets. Subsequent numbering should be decimal, ie 3.1, 3.2, etc.

I hope these guidelines will be useful and that you will study the layouts shown in your booklet. If you have any questions please do not hesitate to ask me.

Sally Thomas

Enc
Copy Personnel Department

어휘리콜 •Administrative Assistant: 행정보조원; •PA: private account(개인비서); •INHOUSE DOCUMENT FORMATS: 사내 서류양식; •booklet: 소책자, 팜플렛; •fully-blocked format: 영역이 구분되는 포맷; •open punctuation: 구속점이 없는; •Specimen: 사례; •outgoing: 외부로 나가는; •title: 직위; •lower case: 소문자; •initial capital: 첫 대문자.

---

(2) **Memorandum**

To: Marcus Sprotte
From: Belinda Mae
Date: May 14th
Subject: Good Restaurants

Hi Marcus

I thought you might like to have a copy of this news report since you are new in town. It might help you when it is time to entertain our clients.

Although we do sometimes take the top account executives to restaurants on the Fine

Dining list, most of the time we use the International Cuisine places. The Fine Dining restaurants take a long time to serve you and even our top clients usually do not want to spend quite that much time at a business dinner!

I would avoid the Family Fare places. By all means, take your own family there. They do offer good food and good prices, but will be too noisy and too casual for clients.

Belinda

> 어휘리콜 •entertain: 초대하다; •client: (상업거래상의) 고객; •account executive: 섭외부장; •business dinner: 업무상의 식사; •by all means: 반드시.

(3) **MEMORANDUM**

TO: Segment producers
FROM: Lawrence Bash. Kitchen Hub executive producer
SUBJECT: Partial viewers survey results

Below are the preliminary results from the viewers' survey conducted by the researchers of the show in April. A total of two thousand local respondents participated in the online survey. It has only been a week since the research team concluded data collection, so we still need to wait another month for the complete findings. In the meantime, I want you to look at some of the viewers' responses and draw inferences from them:

Question number 1: How often do you watch Kitchen Hub?

Results:		
	Every week	20 percent
	Twice a month	20 percent
	Three times a month	10 percent
	Once a month	50 percent

Question number 2: How would you rate Kitchen Hub?

Results:
	Excellent	10 percent
	Good	20 percent
	Satisfactory	20 percent
	Needs Improvement	50 percent

Question number 3: Please rate the difficulty of Kitchen Hub recipes.

Appetizers:	Easy	80 percent
	Moderate	15 percent
	Difficult	5 percent
Main courses:	Easy	30 percent
	Moderate	10 percent
	Difficult	60 percent
Desserts:	Easy	80 percent
	Moderate	17 percent
	Difficult	3 percent

Note: The majority of respondents said most main courses were difficult to cook because they required the use of unconventional cooking tools and equipment.

We will have a meeting tomorrow at 9 a.m. to discuss the partial results.

어휘리콜 •Segment producer: 부품생산자; •hub: 덮개; •partial viewers survey results: 부품검수자의 조사결과; •preliminary results: 예비결과; •the show in April: 4월의 전시; •local respondents: 지역 응답자들; •In the meantime: 현재로서는; •Please rate: 평가 하십시오; •Kitchen Hub recipes: 부엌덮개 다루기; •Main courses: 요리과정.

---

(4) Date: 8 Nov 2004
   To: Warehouse Personnel
   From: Meredith Glover, Supervisor
   Subject: Work Schedule for Winter Season

We are expecting orders for our products to peak this coming holiday season. Demand has already increased by 10 percent in the first week of November. We are not, at this time, planning to hire new packers and other warehouse personnel for the season, however. There fore, we would like to announce that it will be necessary for all warehouse personnel to increase their work hour load beginning November 11 until the first week of January. An additional break will be provided during the shift. Each warehouse staff must increase his total weekly work load by 12 hours. Management is asking that employees who work the morning shift turn in their schedule requests to their supervisors. Those who work the after noon shift must pick from the hours available on the sign up sheet located in the main office. Graveyard workers are expected to meet with their department heads individually to arrange their shifts. As usual, extra work will be remunerated with overtime wages, compensatory time off, or free products. Previously, we offered grocery coupon books, but that option has been discontinued.

어휘리콜 •Warehouse Personnel: 철물점 인사담당자; •Supervisor: 감독관; •Work Schedule: 작업스케줄; •orders: 주문서; •Demand: 수요; •additional break: 휴식시간; •packers: 포장자; •work hour load: 작업시간 부담; •shift turn: 변경시간; •pick: 적어 넣다; •remunerate: 보상하다.

---

(5)

To: Marketing managers

From: Wilfred Hayes, Associate Director of Marketing Communications

In keeping with the company's program to accelerate the professional development of its managers, I have invited James Olsen to host a series of workshops for our managerial staff.

All the workshops will be held on weekday afternoons and will last for a week. There will be a total of six workshops, and the first one is scheduled to begin on Monday, March 25, at 3 p.m.

By the end of today, Maureen O'Sullivan will be e-mailing a copy of the complete schedule of the seminars to all the managers. Please review the timetable and report any possible scheduling conflicts to me. We will do our best to make arrangements so that all managers can attend the seminars.

For those of you who are not familiar with Mr. Olsen, he has been a marketing professional for over thirty years and has previously worked on promotional campaigns for such diverse companies as the Huang-Xi Bicycle Company in Shanghai, China, Canard Outerwear in Montreal, Canada, and McGuinn's Brewery in Glasgow, Scotland. Mr. Olsen has now retired from the world of business, and teaches marketing courses, including effective promotion, advanced selling techniques, brand building, and contract negotiation, at Viscount University in Alberta, Maine. I hope you will give Mr. Olsen a warm welcome and I'm certain you will find his seminars both interesting and useful.

> 어휘리콜 •Marketing managers: 영업부장; •Associate Director: 차장; •Marketing Communications: 영업소통; •professional development: 전문성 개발; •to host: 주도하다; •promotional campaigns: 능력개발운동; •world of business: 업계; •brand building: 브랜드 개발; •contract negotiation: 계약협상.

(6) To: Employees of Anderson Furniture
   From: Richard K. Norse, Director of Building Security
   Date: April 15
   Re: Security System

Please be aware that beginning Thursday next week the security system for this building is going to be replaced. Instead of the code accessible doors currently in place, there will be audiovisual monitors and armed personnel present at every entryway. This change is taking place due to the fact that a few employees have given their codes to persons not authorized to be in this building. We feel that using maximum security measures will benefit both the corporation and the staff.

According to our new policy, all employees must display their ID badges on their shirt pockets or around their necks at all times. Starting Thursday, anyone without proper identification will not be allowed into the premises. Guests will be ushered to the front information desk to fill out a visitor's application and will be issued a temporary ID before entering secure areas of the building. If you forget your pass, you will have to be screened by the front office before being allowed into your workplace.

In the case that you don't yet have your ID, stop down in the records department in the basement floor. Bring a passport size photograph and your social security card, as well as a signed copy of your employment contract. These documents will be retained for two days while your badge is being processed and the identification card will be valid for one year as of the issue date. You will also find a copy of this information in the weekly agenda in your mailboxes. Thank you for your cooperation.

> 어휘리콜 •Building Security: 건물보안; •Security System: 보안시스템; •every entryway: 모든 통로; •arm: 대비하다; •badge: 뱃지; •premise: 구내; •usher: 안내하다; •secure area: 보안구역; •screen: 비치다; •basement floor: 지하실; •retain: 보관하다; •valid: 유효한; •issue date: 발행일.

(7) To: Design Team
    From: Donald Koran
    Date: June 14
    Subject: Lunch

    Hello everyone

I first would like to thank and congratulate you all on your hard work this season. The collection was a great critical success. Because we've been so busy, we haven't had time to sit down together and discuss some different ideas for next season.

I'd like to invite everyone to lunch tomorrow at Maharani's. We'll meet at 1 o'clock and this will also give everyone a chance to meet our team's newest member, Antonio Musco. Antonio will be developing a new line of accessories for our company, and

I'm sure he will become a valuable member of our team.

If you would like to attend this meeting, please call Eva Green sometime this afternoon, so that she can make a reservation at the restaurant. I look forward to seeing you all, and congratulations again, on a job well done.

> 어휘리콜 •collection: 전시; •Maharani's: 마하라니 식당.

제6절 기타

(1) **Turner Communications**　　　　　　Mobile Phone specialists
　　21 Ashton Drive　　　　　　　　　　Tel +44 114 2871122
　　Sheffield　　　　　　　　　　　　　　Fax +44 114 281123
　　S26 2ES　　　　　　　　　　　　　　Email TurnerComm@intl.uk

FAX MESSAGE

To	Janet Benson, General Manager
Company	Asia Communication (Singapore) Pte Ltd
Fax Number	65 6767677
From	Sally Turner, Managing Director
Ref	ST/DA
Date	6 June 19−
Number of Pages (including this page)	1

VISIT TO SINGAPORE

Thank you for calling this morning regarding my trip to Singapore next month. I am very grateful to you for offering to meet me at the airport and drive me to my hotel.

I will be arriving on flight SQ101 on Monday 8 July at 1830 hours. Accommodation has been arranged for me at the Supreme International Hotel, Scotts Road.

I will be travelling up to Kuala Lumpur on Sunday 14 July on MH989 which departs from Singapore Changi Airport Terminal 2 at 1545 hours.

I look forward to meeting you.

Sally Turner

> 어휘리콜 •Mobile Phone specialists: 모바일 폰 전문 업체; •Accommodation: 숙박; 1545: 15시 45분.

(2) **North Central**
packing slip

Ship to: Rasa Corporation
        3372 East Grace Street
        Tampa, Florida 33679

Cartons: 1

Older Number: EF37867

Packed by: Aline Kelly

Item Number	Quantity	Description	Comment
178-D	2		ink cartridge (black)
170-D	1 dozen		note-pads (weekly special)
120-A	2 boxes		file folders (500/box)

		→ out of stock, will ship on May 2
202-F	5 boxes	paper clips (1500/box)
100-B	2 boxes	white envelopes (100/box)

Our reports indicate that payment was received in full on May 24.

Please check contents of the shipment for missing or incorrect items.
Contact our office immediately for any **discrepancies**. Unfortunately, we cannot correct wrong **shipments** that are reported more than 24 hours after receipt of the package. Unavailable items will be shipped within 10 working days.

For return, contact Ellena Malasa at (767) 555-3849.

> 어휘리콜 • packing slip: 물표; •carton: 상자; •comment: 명세; •out of stock: 재고 없음; •ship: 선적하다; •discrepancy: 하자; •unavailable items: 재고가 없는 품목.

(3) **Confession Over First fruit**

I profess this day, unto my High Priest, Jesus Christ, that I come unto the promises, which the Lord swore unto our fathers (Abraham, Isaac, and Jacob) to give us. I was a sinner, on my way to hell - in bondage to sin and the flesh. I operated in the lust of the eyes, the lust of the flesh, and the pride of life. And when I cried unto the Lord God tn save me. He heard my cry and delivered me from tin, sickness, poverty; death, and hell. I was in a pit, and He delivered me out of the pit onto solid ground and put a new song in my heart. And because of the blood of Jesus, I am now redeemed, righteous, saved, satisfied. Holy Ghost-filled, and fire baptized. I am delivered, prosperous, and blessed. And now, behold, I have brought the first fruit of my increase, as my love, gratitude, and honor to my God. And I receive plenty instead of lack and breakthrough instead of failure. I am blessed.

> 어휘리콜 •confession: 고백; •profess: 공언하다, 인정하다, 고백하다; •bondage: 속박, 붙잡힌 몸, 노예임; •flesh: 육욕(의 몸); •lust: 정욕, 성욕, 욕망; •redeem: 구하다; •baptize: 세례를 베풀다, 정화하다.

4) (*ON OFFICE LETTERHEAD INCLUDING PROVIDER NAME AND ADDRESS*)
SAMPLE LETTER OF APPEAL: CLAIM DENIAL

<Date>
<Payer Name>
<Payer Address>

Attn: Appeals Department

Re: <Patient Name>
<Policy ID/Group Number>
<Date of Service>
<Disputed Amount>

To Whom It May Concern:

I am writing to request an appeal of the claim denial for <Patient Name> for the administration of Elaprase (idursulfase) for Hunter syndrome (Mucopolysaccharidosis II, MPS II). <Payer Name> has indicated that the reason for the denial, which was explained on the <Explanation of Benefits or Remittance Advice>, was <list reason(s) for denial>. I disagree with this decision and request that this claim be reversed.

My patient, who has been diagnosed with Hunter syndrome, received an infusion of ELAPRASE on <Date>. In my clinical judgment, treatment with ELAPRASE was medically necessary. <Provide clinical justification for treatment>.

ELAPRASE was approved by the US Food and Drug Administration on July 24, 2006 for patients with Hunter syndrome. It has been shown to improve walking capacity in these patients.

I have enclosed additional documentation that supports treatment with ELAPRASE. I would appreciate your reconsideration of this claim and ask that you consider reversing your decision. If you have any further questions, please feel free to call me at <Physician Telephone #> to discuss.

Thank you in advance for your immediate attention to this request.

Sincerely

<Physician Name>

Enclosures
<include original claim form, denial/EOB, patient medical history, additional supporting documents>

어휘리콜 •reverse: 역으로 하다, 뒤집다; •infusion: 주입(물).

제2장

시사 영역

제1절 일간

(1)

어휘리콜 •nerve: 신경소식; •notch: 단계; •Signs of currency tension resurface: 통화긴축 징후가 다시 떠오르다; •impose: 드러내다; •intrusive: 강압적인; •devaluation: 평가절하; •stage verbal intervention: 언어적 중재를 계획(행)하다; •greenback: 달러; •current account deficits or surpluses: 현 통화량 부족 혹은 초과; •rekindled: 다시 불붙은.

제2절 주간

(1)

Newsweek Table of Contents
July 18, 2011

The World off its axis Page 6

Columns
6 Connecting the Dots
Carl Bernstein
Murdoch's Watergate.
Finance
**Amar Bhide and
Edmund Phelps**
What's wrong with the IMF.
13 Tech
Dan Lyons
Twitter quitters.
43 Compass
Niall Ferguson
The global temper tantrum.

Prime Minister Yingluck Page 16

9 NewsBeast
Will and Kate do Canada;
America's shocking murder
trial; the DSK brouhaha.

Moussa's improbable rise Page 30

Features
22 Palin Plots Her Next Move
She hasn't jumped into the race, but she
believes the prize is there for the taking.
By Peter J. Boyer
30 Egypt's Rising Power Player
Why Amr Moussa is Egypt's
presidential frontrunner.
By Dan Ephron
33 The Next Space Race
As NASA's last shuttle takes flight,
private companies rush to fill the gap.
By Tony Dokoupil
36 Why Winners Win
The new science of triumph
in sports, business, and life.
By Nick Summers
PLUS: **Jack and Suzy Welch** on how to
build a winning team.
44 Bernard Arnault Rethinks Fashion
The LVMH chief shakes
up his empire after the fall of Dior's
star designer John Galliano.
By Robin Givhan

52 Omnivore
Harry Potter's villain speaks;
fathering a president;
Lionel Shriver on Belfast.

Life as Voldemort Page 52

THE DAILY BEAST

5 PERSPECTIVES
WHAT NEWSWEEK'S
WEB ANIMAL
TALKED ABOUT LAST WEEK

Plus
4 THE MAIL / 55 FOOD
56 THE CITY

ON THE COVER:
Sarah Palin at home in Alaska.
Photograph by
Emily Shur for NEWSWEEK.

어휘리콜 • 통신사(News Agency)-독자적인 취재조직을 가지고 신문사, 방송국, 기타 보도기관을 대신해서 뉴스와 기사자료를 수집 배포하는 기구.

TIME

VOL. 182, NO. 4 | 2013

Former members like Albert Einstein have made the Institute for Advanced Study an intellectual haven. Photograph by Jason Fulford for TIME

4 | Inbox

BRIEFING
7 | Verbatim

8 | LightBox
A massive Michigan mud bath

10 | World
A car bomb rattles Lebanon; devastation in a tiny Quebec town; Pakistan's bin Laden problem

12 | Milestones
Inventor Douglas Engelbart dies; Andy Murray wins Wimbledon

COMMENTARY
14 | The Curious Capitalist
Rana Foroohar on the economic benefits of immigration reform

16 | Viewpoint
Ayman Mohyeldin on how the Middle East is framing events in Egypt

ON THE COVER:
Photograph by Yuri Kozyrev—Noor for TIME; *color treated by* TIME

THE CULTURE
50 | Pop Chart
Coaching advice from Jane Lynch; Walker Evans at MOMA; farewell to *LOL?*

52 | Pets
Pit bulls shake their fearsome reputation

57 | Movies
Pacific Rim's arty Armageddon; a star arrives in *Fruitvale Station*

58 | Essay
Lisa Abend on Gelinaz—dinner and a show indeed

60 | 10 Questions
Musician and former French First Lady Carla Bruni

FEATURES

18 The Trouble With Tahrir
Protests in Egypt force out an elected President. Is this any way to run a country? *by Karl Vick*

Plus: Fareed Zakaria on the perils of illiberal democracy

28 Rana Plaza Stories
Retracing the steps of the victims of Bangladesh's garment-factory collapse *by Krista Mahr*

36 America's Brain Bank
The Institute for Advanced Study gives geniuses room to think *by Eliza Gray*

42 Full Kid Press
Second-graders may be too short to dunk a basketball, but they're old enough to shoot for a U.S. title *by Sean Gregory*

The softer side of pit bulls

TIME July 22, 2013

(3)

Bloomberg Businessweek
July 15-July 21, 2013

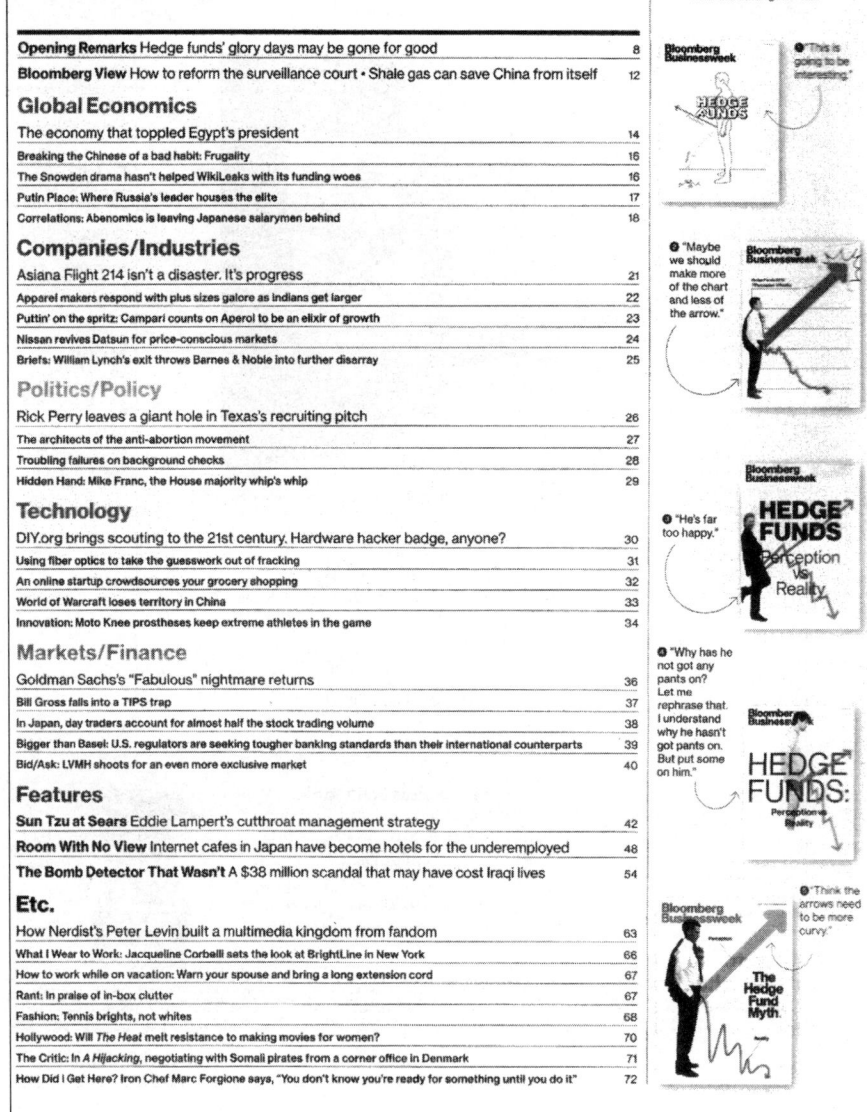

Cover Trail — How the cover gets made

Opening Remarks Hedge funds' glory days may be gone for good 8
Bloomberg View How to reform the surveillance court • Shale gas can save China from itself 12

Global Economics
The economy that toppled Egypt's president 14
Breaking the Chinese of a bad habit: Frugality 16
The Snowden drama hasn't helped WikiLeaks with its funding woes 16
Putin Place: Where Russia's leader houses the elite 17
Correlations: Abenomics is leaving Japanese salarymen behind 18

Companies/Industries
Asiana Flight 214 isn't a disaster. It's progress 21
Apparel makers respond with plus sizes galore as Indians get larger 22
Puttin' on the spritz: Campari counts on Aperol to be an elixir of growth 23
Nissan revives Datsun for price-conscious markets 24
Briefs: William Lynch's exit throws Barnes & Noble into further disarray 25

Politics/Policy
Rick Perry leaves a giant hole in Texas's recruiting pitch 26
The architects of the anti-abortion movement 27
Troubling failures on background checks 28
Hidden Hand: Mike Franc, the House majority whip's whip 29

Technology
DIY.org brings scouting to the 21st century. Hardware hacker badge, anyone? 30
Using fiber optics to take the guesswork out of fracking 31
An online startup crowdsources your grocery shopping 32
World of Warcraft loses territory in China 33
Innovation: Moto Knee prostheses keep extreme athletes in the game 34

Markets/Finance
Goldman Sachs's "Fabulous" nightmare returns 36
Bill Gross falls into a TIPS trap 37
In Japan, day traders account for almost half the stock trading volume 38
Bigger than Basel: U.S. regulators are seeking tougher banking standards than their international counterparts 39
Bid/Ask: LVMH shoots for an even more exclusive market 40

Features
Sun Tzu at Sears Eddie Lampert's cutthroat management strategy 42
Room With No View Internet cafes in Japan have become hotels for the underemployed 48
The Bomb Detector That Wasn't A $38 million scandal that may have cost Iraqi lives 54

Etc.
How Nerdist's Peter Levin built a multimedia kingdom from fandom 63
What I Wear to Work: Jacqueline Corbelli sets the look at BrightLine in New York 66
How to work while on vacation: Warn your spouse and bring a long extension cord 67
Rant: In praise of in-box clutter 67
Fashion: Tennis brights, not whites 68
Hollywood: Will *The Heat* melt resistance to making movies for women? 70
The Critic: In *A Hijacking*, negotiating with Somali pirates from a corner office in Denmark 71
How Did I Get Here? Iron Chef Marc Forgione says, "You don't know you're ready for something until you do it" 72

어휘리콜   •technology: 기술(개발).

제3절 월간

(1)

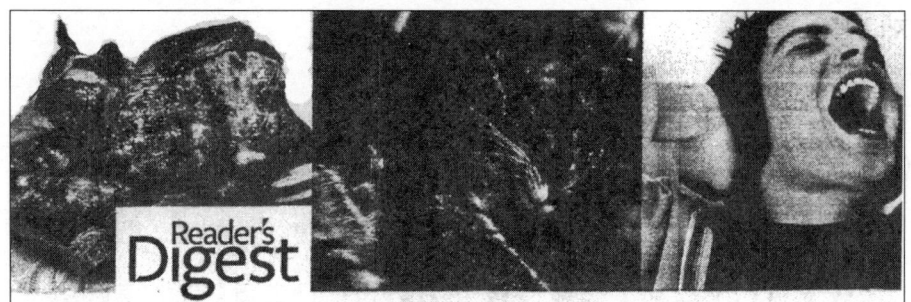

Reader's Digest

DEPARTMENTS

Letter From the Editor 05
Dora Cheok on devastating tsunamis

Click 07
What's on rdasia.com

Letters 08
Share your views

@Work 10

My Story 11
Irfana Qadri gets a lesson in trust

The Tech Guy 14
Stan Yee on the iPad 2's place in the tablet world

Health Smart 18
Health news you can use

Heroes 25
Galwalin Surakup is a champion to disabled dogs and cats

Word Power 27

Voice 29
Renata Cervankova talks about the meaning of worth

Kindness of Strangers 31
Random acts of kindness

Pet Tales 33

Unbelievable! 34
Nury Vittachi thinks accountants shouldn't write novels

Life 54
It's really like that

Quotes 69

What's Cooking? 85
allrecipes.asia

Unseen Asia 100
Celebrating the beauty of daily life

Service 132
Customer care

Ask Aunty 133
Advice from the heart

Money $avvy 135
Gabriel Yap wants to help you manage your money

The Guide 137
Rainforest World Music Festival, a blog for mums, new at the movies

Laugh 144
It's the best medicine

Puzzler 147

Last Laugh 148

어휘리콜   •victims of honour: 영예의 희생자들; •fight back: 반격하다; •pros and cons: 찬반; •puppetry: 가면극; •facial disfigurement: 얼굴손상; •diagnose: 진단하다; •legacy: 유산; • savvy: 알다, 이해하다; •technophile: 테크노 애호가; devastate: 황폐시키다; disabled: 장애의.

(2)

Editor **Dora Cheok** shares her thoughts on the devastation of tsunamis

Beacon of Hope

Titi, a former colleague, is a small spry woman with an inner peace that shines through. She's a survivor of the Indian Ocean Tsunami that hit Aceh in 2004. She was working at the United Nations office in the centre of Banda Aceh close to the beach, when the earthquake struck. The ground shook so hard that everything that wasn't bolted down fell. Titi ran outside to wait it out.

The mosque in Banda Aceh stands tall amidst the devastation

Barely 10 minutes later, word spread that the sea was receding along the beach. People got tense and nervous. Something was happening but they didn't know what. Suddenly Titi heard a sound she'd never heard before and the water came.

People ran in all directions; Titi too. At one point, she looked behind her and saw "a wall of black heading straight for me". She ran for her life. The water hit and she blacked out.

When she came to, the only thing she remembers was how eerily silent it was. She got up, found a tree, climbed up and stayed there. She doesn't remember how long she was there, just that it became dark and then it was light again before she came down.

When she came down, there was nothing left. Everything had been levelled. She wandered around for a while until she finally found a building that was standing. It was the city's mosque. It stood upright, like a beacon of hope.

Seven years later, the devastation repeats itself in Japan, only this time, we're flooded with images of the actual waves tearing through the coastline. I am reminded of Aceh and Titi's story.

It's hard to believe that this kind of devastation has happened twice in Asia, within the span of a decade. We grieve with the people of Japan and in this issue, we share with you their stories. We bear witness to their grace and resilience (p.70), and honour their memories. The rest is silence.

We love letters! Send in your thoughts – both the cheers and the flames. Write to rdaeditor@readersdigest.com

---

어휘리콜 •devastation: 재난; •tsunamis: 쓰나미; •Beacon: 햇불; •spry: 활발한; •bolt: 달아나다; •recede: 퇴각하다, 멀어지다; •eerily: 썸뜩하게; •mosque: 회교사원; •bear witness: 입증하다, 증인이 되다; •grace and resilience: 신의 은총과 회복(력); •honour: 경의를 표하다.

(3)

H&G | AUGUST

HOMES

90 **SLEEPING BEAUTY**
    How an abandoned country house in the Loire Valley has been painstakingly restored in 18th-century French style.

100 **INDUSTRIAL REVOLUTION**
    Concrete elements make a bold statement in this mid-century home, while natural wood adds a softening touch.

107 **WHITE MAGIC**
    Formerly made up of small, dark rooms, this Périgord barn is barely recognisable in its current light-filled incarnation.

120 **DRAWN BY THE SEA**
    A treasure trove of shells, white coral and starfish is used to surprising decorative effect in this striking French house.

126 **ALL CHANGE**
    Flea market finds and repurposed furniture have brought interest and character to a simple La Rochelle property.

GARDENS

114 **VISION IN GREEN**
    Surrounding a stone-built farmhouse in Provence, Isa de la Porte's verdant garden of vineyards, olive groves and slender cypress trees is a joy to behold.

132 **TERRACOTTA POTS**
    Whether rustic or contemporary, earthenware pots will introduce a Mediterranean flavour to the British garden.

136 **DESIGNER SECRETS**
    The first Englishman to hold the post of head gardener at Giverny, James Priest reveals how he has maintained and developed Claude Monet's horticultural masterpiece.

138 **HOW TO CREATE A LAVENDER BORDER**
    This wonderfully versatile plant can be used to add colour, scent and interest to a garden, attract bees and beneficial insects, decorate the home and even flavour food. ▶

SHOPPING

19 MODERN FRENCH
Furniture and accessories with Gallic charm.
27 WALLPAPER BORDERS
Quirky patterns to invigorate plain walls.
29 TAPS AND BASINS
Practical and attractive solutions for your bathroom.
32 REFECTORY TABLES
Smart designs evoking the camaraderie of the school canteen.

DESIGN IDEAS

51 LE STYLE MODERNE
Colourful geometric designs with a mid-century feel.
61 THE FRONT DOOR
How to make a stylish first impression.
65 OUTDOOR LIVING
Three looks for al fresco entertaining.
76 GO WITH THE GRAIN
Wood is a versatile and luxurious choice for the bathroom.

REGULARS

22 DECORATING AND DESIGN NEWS
The latest collections, names and events in the design world.
35 DESIGN SOLUTIONS: CLASSIC BEDROOMS
Elegant ideas for your sleeping quarters.
38 LIFESTYLE NEWS
Events, food, art, shopping, gardening and travel inspiration.
40 ON OUR BOOKSHELF
A peek inside cutting-edge chic Parisian properties.
44 HOW WE BECAME CERAMIC DESIGNERS
Astier de Villatte invites us inside its Paris workshop.
73 ESSENTIAL GUIDE TO GARDEN LIGHTING
How to make the most out of your outdoor space after dark.
81 BATHROOM NEWS
The latest looks to update your space.
82 DREAM KITCHEN
A rustic Scandinavian-style scheme by Katrin Cargill.
84 HOUSE CLINIC
Your decorating queries answered by Celia Rufey.
141 SPICE ISLAND
MasterChef's Shelina Permalloo shares her latest recipes.
148 WHERE TO BUY
Contact details for stockists in this issue.
170 WE LOVE
Hotel Verneuil in the historic heart of Paris.

SPECIAL OFFERS

48 HOW TO SUBSCRIBE TO HOMES & GARDENS
Get two years for the price of one when you pay by Direct Debit. Also buy digital editions at bit.ly/15MLa5p.
86 KITCHEN STORAGE OFFER
A larder cupboard and plate rack, from just £215.

COVER STORIES
■ The best of France
90, 100, 107, 114, 120, 126, 132
■ Inside style 19, 27, 29, 32
■ Lavender 138
■ Bedded bliss 35
■ Escape outdoors 65, 73, 136

COVER PHOTOGRAPH CAMERA PRESS

FOLLOW US ON TWITTER.COM/HOMESANDGARDENS AND FACEBOOK.COM/HOMESANDGARDENS

어휘리콜 •painstakingly: 애써서, 공들여; •trove: 귀중한 수집품; •shell: 껍질; •starfish: 불가사리; •verdant: 초록의, 식물로 뒤덮인; •vineyard: 포도원; •earthenware: 도기(의), 토기(의); •versatile: 용도가 많은, 만능의; •invigorate: 기운 나게 하다, 고무하다.

(4)

WELCOME

As I left the house this morning, I saw something that always annoys me: a pair of my shoes lying abandoned in the hallway. I left them there when I came in from the garden where I had been planting and watering and, since I thought they would be dirty, I had simply stepped out of them and walked away. Scattered shoes are one of the things I don't like to see in photographs of our houses either, along with flowers casually laid to one side, as if waiting to be placed in a vase, and clothes artfully hung on the outside of a wardrobe. Seeing my shoes did remind me that real life isn't always neat and tidy, but I feel there is a balance to be struck between an interior with plenty of character and one that is verging on the bland. When we photograph houses for the magazine, we show them as we find them, which is usually very tidy – but don't we all tidy up before visitors arrive? Each of the homes in this month's issue exudes a wonderfully lived-in feel. I particularly love the rich tones and beautifully displayed treasures in Thomas Boog's French country home on page 120. In contrast, the updated sixties house on page 100 is a successful mix of cool concrete with rustic accents, which only confirms my belief that welcoming interiors come in all shapes and sizes.

This summer, my family and I are off to France, so I have been enjoying everything this French themed issue has to offer. They are leaving before me and I'm flying out to meet them. The last time I tried to do this I flew to Milan, but my connecting flight was cancelled because of a thunderstorm and I eventually arrived by train at midnight to be met by a two-year-old who had resolutely stayed awake until I got there, then promptly fell asleep as soon as he saw me. If, like me, you enjoy a good read on holiday, but are put off by the thought of carrying a magazine with you, why not download *Homes & Gardens* onto your tablet? Present and past issues are available – to find out how to do this, simply visit bit.ly/15MLa5p. Happy holidays!

Deborah

DEBORAH BARKER, EDITOR-IN-CHIEF

This once dark barn (page 107) is now a vision in white thanks to careful renovation and a pale decorating palette.

Topiary, olive trees and vines all feature in this verdant Provençal garden full of striking vistas (page 114).

Bold graphic shapes and vibrant shades (page 51) that give room schemes a fresh mid-century flavour.

어휘리콜 • annoy: 괴롭히다; • hallway: 복도, 현관; • artfully: 교묘하게; • wardrobe: 옷장, 벽장; • tidy: 정돈된; • verge: -에 접해있다; • exude: 발산시키다; • cool concrete: 차가운 콘크리트; • rustic accents: 시골 분위기; • themed issue: 테마가 된 이슈; • connecting flight: 갈아타는 비행기; • palette: 팰리트; • topiary: 장식적 전정법; • vistas: 전망; • Bold: 대담; • room scheme: 방 구도; • mid-century: 세기 중엽.

제4절 시간

(1) **Cold spell breaks eight-year record**

By Robert Lee

A cold spell accompanied by strong winds plunged temperatures nearly 20 degrees Celsius over the past three days, bringing in the first frost over northern parts of the country and setting an eight-year temperature low, said the nation's weather service Tuesday.

According to the Korea Meteorological Administration, this was the first time in eight years Seoul experienced frost this early into the season. The first frost set in through most of Gyeonggi and Gangwon provinces.

In the past 10 years, the earliest recorded frost in Seoul, during the month of October, was on Oct. 22, 2002, with yesterday coming in second.

If today's weather drops below zero, it would be the first time in eight years, breaking another record, according to the KMA.

The current weather forecast in Seoul today is set to range from 0 degrees to 12 degrees Celsius. Partly cloudy skies are expected throughout the country, from today through to the end of the week.

A wind advisory has been issued over most coastal areas and other parts of the nation are expected to face strong wind as well.

The peak of the cold snap hit the nation yesterday and temperatures are expected to crawl back as the week goes on. (*rjmlee@heraldm.com*)

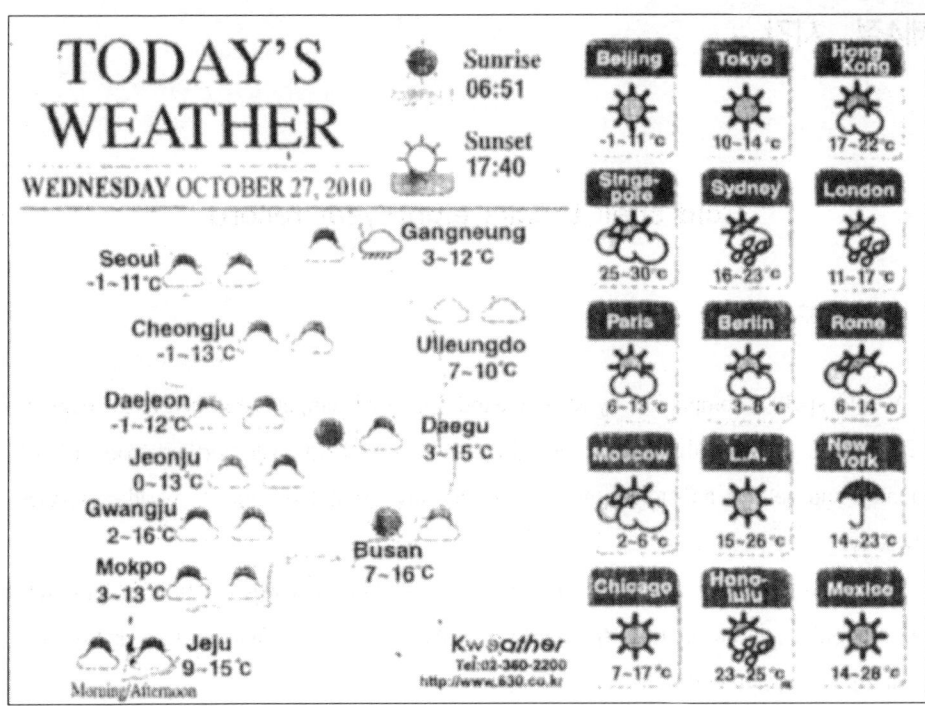

어휘리콜 •spell: 한 차례; •plung: 빠지게 하다; •nation's weather service: 국립기상대; • weather forecast: 날씨 예보; •wind advisory: 바람예보.

(2) After rainy weather during the first part of the week, the Northeast will be chilly with brisk winds Thursday through Saturday. Thursday will be cloudy with showers possible. Some sunshine is likely Friday and Saturday, but a gusty northwest breeze will keep a chill in the air. The weather will change very little in the South and West Thursday through Saturday, so people there can expect sunny and warm weather.

어휘리콜 •rainy weather: 비 오는 날씨; •brisk wind: 쾌적한 바람; •gusty: 돌풍의; •breeze: 미풍.

(3)

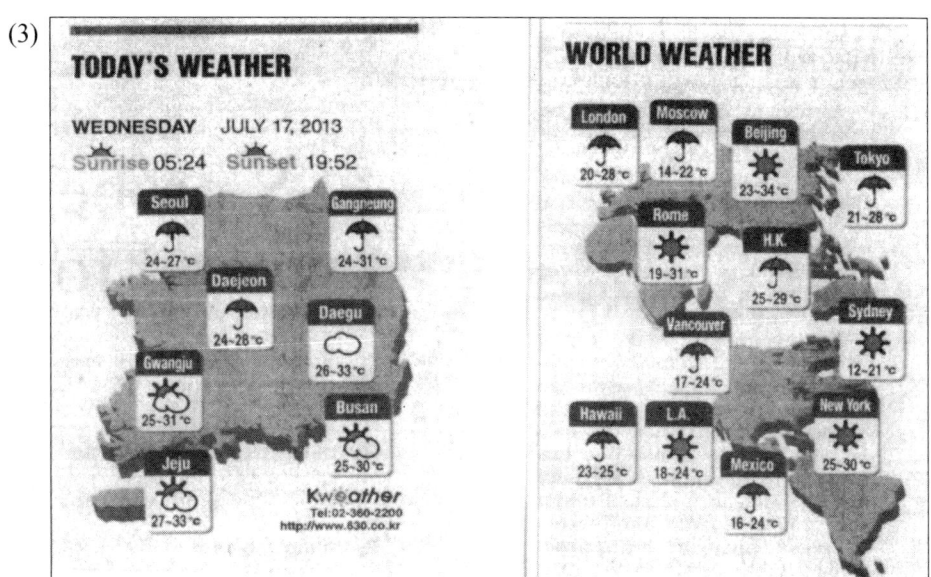

| 어휘리콜 | •sunrise: 일출;　•sunset: 일몰. |

제5절   부정기

(1)

Gyeongbokgung Palace

Address : 1-1, Sejongno, Jongno-gu, Seoul

Management Office : 02-734-2458

Description:

Gyeongbokgung Palace (Historic Site No. 117) was built as the primary residence for the royal family in 1395 by King Taejo, the founder of Joseon Dynasty. Among the five palaces in Seoul, Gyeongbokgung Palace has the largest and most beautiful architectural style. There are elegant pavilions such as Gyeonghoeru and Hyangwonjeong and refined wood and stone structures such as Geunjeongjeon Hall.

The palace's ten-story Stone Tower (Pagoda) of Gyeongcheonsa is presently kept in the National Culture Research Institute and will be moved to the National Museum of Korea when the museum is completed.

The National Folk Museum opened in 1975 is located near the palace and Gyeongbokgung admission ticket is available here as well.

◆ Free Guide for foreigners
   English   09:30, 12:00
   Japanese   10:00, 12:30, 15:00
   Chinese   11:00, 13:30, 14:30

어휘리콜 •royal family: 왕족, 왕가; •pavilion: 누각, 정자; •refined wood and stone structures: 정교하게 조각된 나무와 석조; •ten-story Stone Tower: 10층 석탑.

---

(2)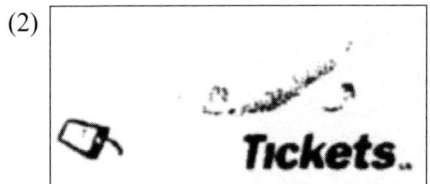

TERMS AND CONDITIONS

PRICES
1. Prices are valid from 31 March to 1 April.
2. Children's fares apply to those under 12 years of age on the date of departure.
3. Prices may be changed without notice.

TICKETING
Air tickets and hotel vouchers will be issued 7 days prior to departure. An alteration fee of $20.00 will be charged for each amendment to a booking once tickets and vouchers have been issued.

REFUNDS
1. Payments will be refunded in full only if cancellations are made 7 days prior to departure.
2. There will be no refund for any unused air tickets, accommodation, airport transfers, optional tours, breakfasts or other services noted in the brochure that were not used either in part or completely.

CANCELLATION FEE
1. More than 7 days prior to departure-none
2. 1-7 days prior to departure-10% of package price
3. No show or cancellation on departure date-50% of package price

> 어휘리콜 •TERMS AND CONDITIONS: 계약조건; •valid: 유효한; •hotel vouchers: 호텔숙박권; •alteration: 변경; •charge: 부과하다; •amendment: 수정; •booking: 예약; •accommodation: 숙박; •airport transfers: 공항변경; •optional: 선택이.

(3)

Dr. Saroj Adlakha
Dr. Abid A. Deiry

SHILPA MEDICAL CENTRE

0121-444 2668

1c Ashfield Avenue
Kings Heath
Birmingham
B14 7AT

PRACTICE AREA

B10
B11
B12
MOSELEY
B13
B14
KINGS HEATH

MINOR SURGERY

Our minor surgery procedures are as follows:

INJECTIONS
Periarticular
ASPIRATION
Joints, Cysts, Bursae and Hydroceles
INCISIONS
Abscesses, Thrombosed External Piles
OTHER
Removal of Splinters, Suturing Skin

Dr Saroj Adlakha (female) MB., BS. 1969
Registered Birmingham 1972

Dr Abid Deiry (male) M.B.B.Ch., 1945
Registered London 1947 (Full Time Assistant)

This is a very old established traditional practice which was started 120 years ago and it has kept growing very rapidly. We have to make an extra effort to keep it reasonably small to provide personal service.

SURGERY OPENING TIMES

Monday	09.00 - 11.00
	05.30 - 06.30
Tuesday	09.00 - 11.00
	05.30 - 06.30
Wednesday	09.00 - 11.00
	05.30 - 06.30
Thursday	09.00 - 11.00
	05.30 - 06.30
Friday	09.00 - 09.30
Saturday	09.00 - 11.00 Emergencies only

All surgeries are open – No appointment system.

THESE ARE THE SURGERY TIMES WHEN WE ARE OPEN, YOUR OWN G.P. MAY NOT BE AVAILABLE AT ALL THESE TIMES. CHILDREN UNDER 16 SHOULD ALWAYS BE ACCOMPANIED BY A RESPONSIBLE ADULT.

SPECIAL CLINICS

The following clinics are available at our surgery on various days. Please enquire at reception for details of the clinic you are interested in

Ante-Natal
Post-Natal
Family Planning
Cervical Smear and Well Woman
Stress Management
Childhood Immunisation
Elderly Screening
Cardiac Disease Prevention
Diabetic Clinic
Asthma Clinic
Lipid Clinic

DISABLED PERSONS

Our premises have suitable access for disabled persons and ample parking is available in the Car Park opposite the surgery. We have ground floor consulting rooms.

Additional languages spoken by:
Dr Saroj Adlakha – Hindi, Punjabi, Urdu
Dr Abid Deiry – Arabic

HOME VISITS

All non urgent visits to be requested before 10.00a.m. by ringing the surgery. These should only be requested by patients too ill to travel to the surgery. This lets the doctors plan the day more efficiently, enabling them to see more patients.

EMERGENCY CASES

In an emergency please phone the surgery. Outside of surgery hours a recorded message will give you the phone number of the Deputising Service.

REPEAT PRESCRIPTIONS

Please bring your repeat prescription request to the surgery allowing 24 HOURS NOTICE. Alternatively you may post your request to the surgery with a stamped addressed envelope. ONLY those drugs already agreed between you and your doctor can be provided on repeat prescription in between your regular check-ups.

PATIENTS COMMENTS

Comments on any aspect of the practice will be received with interest. We are keen to provide a high standard of service. Please help us to do so by passing any complaints or grievances directly to Doctor Adlakha.

NEW PATIENTS

All new patients are offered a check-up on joining the practice and this service is also offered to patients between 16-75 who have not seen the doctor in the past three years.

Over 75
We offer an annual check-up to all patients over the age of 75 (in their own homes if necessary).

COMPUTER

All our patient records are kept on computer. We can assure patients of complete confidentiality. Your rights are also protected by the Data Protection Act.

PRACTICE STAFF

Adequate modern medical care is not provided by doctors alone. We therefore work as a team to provide a comprehensive service.

As well as our two doctors our team comprises the following workers:
1 Practice Nurse
1 District Nurse
1 Health Visitor
1 Midwife

We also employ four secretary/receptionists who are there to help you as much as possible. They will arrange appointments, order prescriptions, order ambulances etc.

어휘리콜 • minor surgery: 일차 외과; • injection: 주사; • incision: 절개.

(4)

Home Insurance

up to 30% OFF

BRILLIANT INSURANCE

Cover your home for less

NatWest   another way

Up to 30% off your home insurance

If you're looking for quality home cover, you've got it with NatWest Home Insurance. It's great value even before you take your potential extra savings into account. And those savings could add up to 30% off the standard NatWest Home Insurance premium.*

So if you're looking to renew your home insurance in the next three months call us for a quote* now on **0800 051 51 00*** and find out how much you could save.

NatWest can also offer you a great deal on car insurance. Call us for a quote on **0800 051 51 05**.

If your home or car insurance renewal date is more than three months away, simply complete and return the attached coupon and we'll remind you nearer the time.

* Discounts may apply if you have or take out Annual Multi Trip Travel Insurance and/or Car Insurance, if you are a member of a Neighbourhood Watch Scheme and have approved burglar alarms, locks and bolts fitted, or if you are an Advantage Customer.

* Please note that there are certain circumstances where a quote and/or cover cannot be provided. Quotes are valid for three months.

* We are available to take your call Monday to Friday 8am to 8pm and Saturday 9am to 4pm (except Bank Holidays). Hearing or speech impaired customers can contact us on 0800 051 30 30. In order to maintain the highest levels of service we may record and monitor telephone communications.

NatWest Home and Car Insurance is underwritten by UK Insurance Limited and arranged through NatWest Insurance Services which act as an insurance intermediary. Both are members of The Royal Bank of Scotland Group. NatWest Insurance Services is a trading name of RBS Group Insurance Services Limited. Registered Office: Waterhouse Square 138-142 Holborn, London EC1N 2TH. Registered Number: 216870 England.

UK Insurance Limited is a member of the General Insurance Standards Council (GISC) and complies with the GISC Private Customer code. UK Insurance Limited, The Wharf, Neville Street, Leeds LS1 4AZ. Registered in England Number: 1179980 England.

National Westminster Bank Plc. Registered Office: 135 Bishopsgate, London EC2M 3UR. Registered Number: 929027, England.

February 2003

MOISTEN HERE

Your Information We are RBS Group Insurance Services and we are owned by The Royal Bank of Scotland Group Plc. We are also known as the data controller. The information you supply on this form will be used for the purpose of providing you with the information you have requested. It may also be used for keeping you informed of other products and services, unless you tell us not to.

Not yet ready to renew?

You still don't have to miss out on our great deals. If your home or car insurance renewal date is more than three months away, simply complete this form and we'll contact you at the appropriate time.

Personal details

Title   Mr   Mrs   Miss   Ms   Other
First name(s)
Surname
Address

                            Postcode
Tel. No.
E-mail

Bank details

NatWest account number
Sort code

FOLD HERE

Your insurance renewal dates
Please let us know when your home or car insurance is due for renewal.

Home

My buildings insurance is due for renewal on
My contents insurance is due for renewal on
                          or
My combined buildings and contents
insurance is due for renewal on

Car

My car insurance is due for renewal on

Thank you for taking the time to complete this coupon

Keeping you informed We would like to tell you by letter, phone or fax, including automatic dialling, e-mail or other electronic means, about products and services which we believe would be of interest to you and which are offered by us and other selected companies. If you do not want us to do this, please tick this box ☐. By supplying your address, telephone number, fax number or e-mail address, you are giving your consent for us to contact you in any of those ways in connection with this request.

Please sign here _____
RDCSI 02

BUSINESS REPLY SERVICE
Licence No. KE2355

NatWest Insurance Department
Marketing Services Solutions Ltd
LS12 4YY

Not yet ready to renew? Ask us to remind you

어휘리콜   •quality home cover: 고급 가족 커버; •renewal date: 갱신 일.

제6절 기타

(1) May Basket Cupcakes

To create captivating May baskets, wrap a wide strip of decorative paper around each cupcake, holding it in place with double-stick tape. Then attach narrow strips of plain paper for the basket handles.

Servings: 12 servings
Prep Time: 40 mins
Total Time: 58 mins
Ingredients on sale: 4

<Ingredients>

	Nonstick cooking spray	
1-2/3 cups	all-purpose flour	
1-1/2 teaspoons	finely shredded lime peel	
1-1/4 teaspoons	baking powder	
1/2 teaspoon	baking soda	
1/8 teaspoon	salt	
1/4 cup	butter, softened	see savings
3/4 cup	sugar or sugar substitute blend* equivalent to 3/4 cup sugar	
1/2 cup	refrigerated or frozen egg product, thawed, or 2 eggs	
2/3 cup	light sour cream	see savings
2 tablespoons	fat-free milk	see savings
1-1/2 cups	sliced or coarsely chopped fresh strawberries, kiwifruit, pineapple, and/or whole fresh raspberries or blueberries	see savings
1 cup	frozen light whipped dessert topping, thawed	
2 tablespoons	coconut chips, lightly toasted (optional)	

Directions

1.
Preheat oven to 350 degrees F. Line twelve 2-1/2-inch muffin cups with paper bake cups. Coat paper bake cups with cooking spray; set aside. In a medium bowl, combine flour, lime peel, <u>baking powder</u>, baking soda, and salt; set aside.

2.
In a large bowl, beat butter with an electric mixer on medium speed for 30 seconds. Gradually add sugar, beating until light and fluffy. Beat in eggs. In a small bowl, combine <u>sour cream</u> and milk. Alternately add flour mixture and sour cream mixture to egg mixture, beating on low speed after each addition just until

combined.

3.

Spoon batter evenly into prepared muffin cups, filling each 2/3 to 3/4 full. Bake for 18 to 20 minutes or until a toothpick inserted near the centers comes out clean. Cool in cups on a wire rack for 5 minutes. Remove cupcakes from pans. Cool completely on wire rack.

4.

Using a small knife, cut a shallow dip in the top of each cupcake. Save cut off cake tops for another use, such as for making fruit parfaits. Top cupcakes with fruit, whipped topping, and, if desired, coconut.

SUGAR SUBSTITUTES

Use Splenda Sugar Blend for Baking. Follow package directions to use product amount equivalent to 3/4 cup sugar. PER SERVING WITH SUGAR SUBSTITUTE: same as above, except 167 cal., 23 g carb. Exchanges: 1.5 other carb. Carb choices: 1.5.

Nutrition information

Per serving: Calories 186, Total Fat 6 g, Saturated Fat 4 g, Monounsaturated Fat 1 g, Polyunsaturated Fat 0 g, Cholesterol 14 mg, Sodium 157 mg, Carbohydrate 30 g, Total Sugar 14 g, Fiber 1 g, Protein 3 g. Daily Values: Vitamin A 0%, Vitamin C 18%, Calcium 4%, Iron 6%. Exchanges: Other Carbohydrate 2, Fat 1. Percent Daily Values are based on a 2,000 calorie diet

Recipe from Better Homes and Gardens

어휘리콜 •captivate: 현혹시키다; •wrap: 싸다; •strip: 조각; •basket handle: 바구니 손잡이; •ingredient: 성분, 재료, 원료.

(2)

The Garden Fields

Where dreams do come true!

Celebrate life's special moments at The Garden Fields. With our enchanting gardens and European-inspired courtyards, you can plan an occasion that will definitely be a unique experience for your clients and their guests. If you want to organize a formal garden wedding or birthday party, we can help you. The Garden Fields has different reception venues for anniversaries, corporate events, and other functions. In addition, we have affiliated catering companies ready to arrange grand feasts for different occasions. We provide tables, seating, service dishes, and floral arrangements. If you have any other requirements or additional requests for decorations, our expert event planners will do their best to make those arrangements for you! Contact us today and let us help you create the celebration of a lifetime!

The Garden

Fields

#20 Cluny Drive cor. Napier Road, Singapore

For inquiries and reservations, please contact
The Garden Fields office
at 555-4144
Or visit
www.thegardenfields.com.

어휘리콜   •enchanting: 매혹적인; •European-inspired: 유럽식에서 영감을 얻은; •unique: 독특한, 특별한; •client: 고객; •corporate event: 기업의 행사; •affiliate: 회원으로 하다; •catering: 케이터링(여객기 음식제공 업무).

제3장

홍보 영역

제1절 광고

(1)

> 어휘리콜 •weather: 뚫고나가다; •poise: 자세를 취하다; •innovative staffing and training: 개혁적인 직원직무 및 트레이닝; •HR: Human Relation(인사).

(2) *Marketing Representative Wanted*

PULL-TIME marketing representative needed for growing utility company. With the recent deregulation of the energy industry, there are numerous opportunities for creative, industrious individuals to market electricity to consumers. Marketing representatives must be self-starters, maintain a positive attitude, and be a team player. Prior experience in related fields is required.

Contact: Mary@Fueltime.com for further information.

> 어휘리콜 •growing utility company: 성장 일로에 있는 회사; •deregulation: 규제철폐; •self-starter: 자발적 실행가; •Prior experience: 유 경험.

(3) **FOR SALE (Advertisement)**

Two-Story Town house
(brand-new)

Location: 201-45th Street, San Diego, California
Lot Area: 950 square feet
Price: $220,000 (negotiable)

This beautiful, historic home includes three bedrooms, two bathrooms, and a separate laundry room. It also has a lovely backyard garden and a parking area. Perfect for a family!

For more information, please contact Elsie Boyle at 555-2263.

SERIOUS BUYERS ONLY. NO AGENTS.

어휘리콜 • Two-Story Town house: 2층짜리 시내 집; • brand-new: 새집; • historic: 고즈넉한; • separate laundry room: 별도 세탁 룸; • lovely backyard garden: 멋진 뒤 뜰 정원; • SERIOUS BUYERS ONLY: 구매자 직접; • AGENT: 대리인.

(4)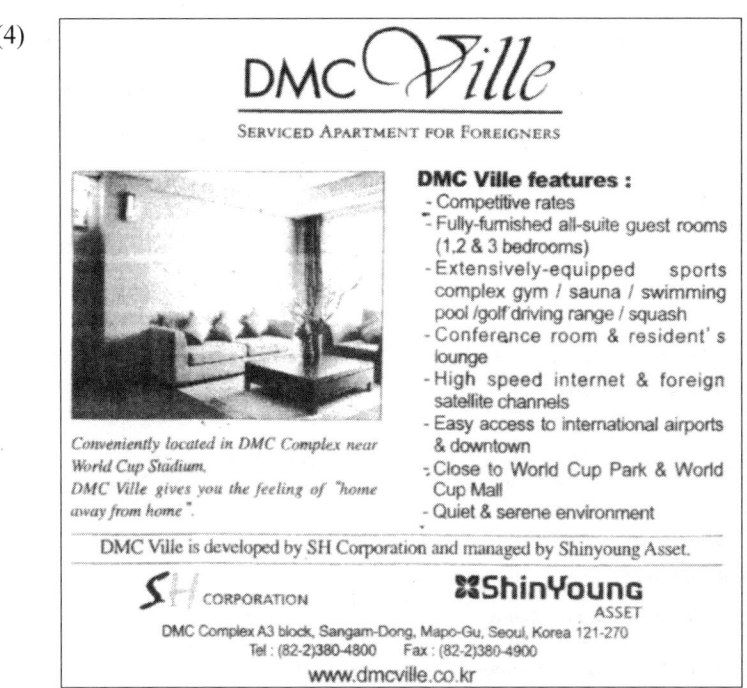

어휘리콜 • ville: 빌라; • competitive rate: 경쟁적 가격; • furnished: 설비된; • all-suite: 적합한, 완벽한; • complex gum: 종합체육관; • squash: 테니스 비슷한 구기; • serene: 평온한; • asset: 부동산.

(5) **SPECIAL OPPORTUNITY IN RETAIL SALES**

Gladstone's Men's Clothing Stores is seeking a talented and highly motived individual to run the Gladstone's store in Dover Center. The store in Dover Center is one of our largest and busiest. It offers a complete line of men's clothing including: suits, sports coats and blazers, dress shirts, causal clothing, overcoats accessories and an extensive selection of shoes, There are over 20 people working as sales clerks and assistants.

The manager's responsibilities are to supervise the staff, hire and train more people as needed, train an assistant manager who can run the store in the manager's absence and coordinate special sales events. The successful applicant will have: at least 10 years' experience in retail sales, at least 5 years' experience in managing employees, extensive knowledge of men's clothing, a through understanding of inventory procedures and a capacity for hard work. The store is open 7 days a week, so the routine will be challenging until an assistant manager is fully trained. Salary is negotiable. We are willing to pay the right price for the right person. Call our executive office at 833‐2442 for further information.

> 어휘리콜　•RETAIL SALES: 소매상; •extensive selection: 넓은 매장; •sales clerks and assistants: 판매점원과 보조원; •supervise: 감독하다; •coordinate: 돕다; •assistant manager: 부 매니저; •extensive knowledge: 많은 지식.

(6)

> 어휘리콜　•workforce: 인력.

(7)

어휘리콜　•clinic: 클리닉, 진료소; •skin & aesthetic: 피부 미용의; •venereal: 성(병, 교, 욕)의; •tattoo: 문신의; •packing & transit: 포장 이사.

(8)

어휘리콜　•alien: 외국인;　•real estate: 부동산.

(9)

Community Bulletin Board

To apply for a free ad, send your ad text to hapark@theviuim.com

All ads must be under 40 words in English and commercial ads are not acceptable.

Announcements

We are peace, prosperity and freedom? Join us at the Seoul Libertarian Party Meetup Group. We meet on the 2nd Friday night of each month. For information go to http://libertarian.meetup.com/330 or phone Georgia on 010-3604-9661.

Do you speak Spanish? Do you want to worship in Spanish? Join the Ministerio Hispano at Yeouido Full Gospel Church and participate. Sunday Service 3:30 p.m. Visit www.misterichispano.com or call (010) 6778-6211, (010) 8888-5942. Everybody welcome!

Seoul Environmental Group is looking for environmentally active people to take part in our urban home-based green projects. Whether it's a roof garden, a beehive or something even more exotic, we're interested. E-mail janjamesgordon@gmail.com

WAYPA, an English Club, is looking for people who want to practice English and meet new faces in Garaju, Seoul. For more information, visit our website cafe.daum.net/WAYPA. If you're interested, please text or call 010-2813-5157.

Personals

Friendly single American male, early 30s. Just moved to Sookdae and am looking for a female companion to show me around the city. If interested, please e-mail me at hophop1231@hotmail.com

I am a 31-year-old foreign male live in Seoul, looking for female and male friends. I am interested in exchanging cultures, languages and having fun also. Please feel free to call me on 010-4128-3466 or e-mail me at shehnim@gmail.com.

Korean girl, 29, looking for friends who speaks good English. We can have language exchange and also play together. I live in Bundang-On station. I'm ready to be a good friend. Call me on 010-8107-2210.

I'm a travel guide here in Korea. I can guide for you to a lot of beautiful places and nice restaurants. I go on trips once a week during weekdays. I'm a Korean female in my early 40s and can speak good English. If you need help, e-mail me: pehva@hanmail.net.

One free English class. Young entrepreneur, business man, and native English speaker from Canada looking for experience in teaching to help me decide my career. Focus will be on conversation: current events and culture exchange. E-mail kareinthreseoul@gmail.com.

I am a mixed male, Korean, my father is Arab and mother is Korean. I am living in Incheon and want to find good friends. E-mail me at my_sky_dream2000@yahoo.com.

I'm a Korean who lives in Seoul, Korea. If you want to have Korean friends, you should call me now. I like musicals, concerts and movies. You can enjoy your life in Seoul after we become friends. 010-3263-3936.

I'm looking for friends who speak English very well. Currently, I live in Byungjeom. Anyone who lives in Byungjeom, Suwon and Dongtan area is welcome. Age 20-40 is perfect. I'm 28yrs old. Then — feel free to e-mail me.

I taught English to professors and doctors as a native speaker. Looking for Japanese native speakers. Please e-mail me rlrj2000@hanmail.net

Gyeonggi. Want to have English-speaking friends who spend time going on an excursion on Sunday hope friend to stay in the nearby town. Contact: (016) 875-0454, E-mail: julia2362@naver.com.

Sports

A firing Taekwondo Club is looking for new members. We offer classes for beginner and advanced adults of all levels. For those interested in sports and martial arts, we can help you reach your goalism, whatever they may be. All nationalities are welcome. For more information, please contact at tm3ym@hotmail.com or call 010-3078-1433.

Seoul Flyers Running Club: Join us for health and socializing. We are foreigners and Koreans who get together to run every Saturday and Sunday mornings in Hangang Park. We also meet for social outings. It's fun! Go to www.seoulflyers.com for more information.

German Soccer Team is looking for teams to play for matches. We would like to play on Saturday 3:30 p.m. at our pitch or yours. If interested please contact kimchikickers@gmail.com.

We play touch (aka Touch footie or Touch rugby) every Saturday 9:30-11:30 a.m. on the Jamwon rugby pitch in Seoul, open to all, men and women, beginners and experienced are all very welcome. Contact korealtouch@gmail.com for more information or visit www.touchrugby.blogspot.com

The Seoul Survivors Rugby Football Club is looking for players, aged 14+ to join our senior and junior teams. All ability levels welcome. We train Saturdays at Jamwon rugby pitch, Seoul, from 10am. Contact info@survivorsrfc.com or go to www.survivorsrfc.com.

Any Korean amateur baseball team looking for an American baseball player for the upcoming league pitch and play centerfield contact 010-5784-1917

International badminton club is looking for new foreign members. Competitive (top class level) players preferred. We play on Saturday, Sunday near Jamsil, Lotte World 2-6 p.m. If interested, send me an e-mail for more information: helloj@hanmail.net

Wanted

Looking for a Korean female in male. A Korean female is looking for an English, Chinese, or Japanese speaking female roommate who can share 3-bed. Near. Gyobo Building in Kangnam. (3-600,000 won/mon + up to deposit). Full furnished. If you are interested, please e-mail me: realotteam@hanmail.net.

Apple computer tutor wanted. I have purchased a Mac Book Pro and I am looking for someone to help me get the most of it. I am flexible with times and place. Happy to exchange for language but I am no English teacher! E-mail naavi@hotmail.com.

Housemate wanted in Pyeongchang-dong. Female only. 010-4544-2377

Want an English teacher who help enjoy English Premier League broadcasting. train84@hanmail.net

Korean classes

Want to learn to read and write in Korean? I can help you with both English and Korean by drawing your true interest in the language. Call (010) 3052-2460

Are you looking for a teacher who is good at Korean language? Here is a Korean male who has a bachelor degree in Korean language, and is fluent in English, as well as knowing Japanese a little. If you would like to learn the language with fun, please contact me at Youbyun@gmaiil.com: 010-4784-2188

FREE Korean class. Right beside Sports Complex Station in Jamsil (line 2) near COEX exit 3. Saturday at 11 am-12:40 p.m. Beginner to Advanced. Please contact Daniel at daniel5vtpark@gmail.com or 010-2751-3498.

We invite you to take part in our Language Exchange Club. You can make many friends, learn various cultures and languages, enjoy outdoor activities as well as learn Korean. Please come to Starbucks in Myeongdong at 5 p.m. every Sunday. E-mail Song at discgok@naver.com

---

어휘리콜 • announcement: 공고, 고지, 발표, 공표; • personals: 교제, 연락; • wanted: 구인.

어휘리콜 • athlete: 운동선수, 스포츠맨.

제2절 전단

(1)

> 어휘리콜 • free consultation: 상담무료; • small-mid sized businesses: 중소 기업체들.

(2) Beginners Archery Class at Nomad Sports Center!

Sign up for our beginners archery class and learn the basics of the sport! All sessions are taught by licensed instructors and adhere to the policies instituted by the Moroccan National Archers Association.

SESSION	INSTRUCTOR	SCHEDULE
Establishing Eye Dominance	Ihsana Chadili	Tuesdays (4 P.M.)
Range Safety and Etiquette	Leron Sahere	Wednesdays (5 P.M.)
Basic Shooting Techniques	Zahra Tannous	Thursdays (3:30 P.M.)
Proper Use and Care of Equipment	Fadil Nyambek	Fridays (6 P.M.)

Sessions are conducted once a week and must be taken in sequence. Each session is limited to fifteen people; so, pre-registration via e-mail is required to ensure your slot. For more information, please contact the Nomad coordinator, Yazid Ouaili, at (212) 537-555-2709.

어휘리콜 •archery: 궁도, 궁술; •adhere to: 부착하다, 따르다; •use and care: 사용과 관리.

(3)

어휘리콜 •present: 공연하다.

제3절 표어

(1) 2014 FIFA World Cup Brazil의 공식 표어

> 어휘리콜 • All in one rhythm: 모두 한 리듬으로.

(2) "Ability first" is our motto in employing men.

> 어휘리콜 • Ability first: 능력 우선.

(3) 'My motto is "Be humble and learn",' he says.

> 어휘리콜 • humble: 겸손한.

(4) I have a motto, "Work is for work, not for the home."

> 어휘리콜 • motto: 좌우명, 표어.

(5) My motto is, "Never bring your work home with you."
(6) 'Live and let live.' That's my motto.

> 어휘리콜 • Live and let live: 자기 방식대로 살아라.

(7) "Always do my best" is my motto.
(8) "France, Love It or Leave It."
(9) War to end war was the catchword of the nation.

> 어휘리콜 • catchword: 표어, 슬로건.

(10) The catchword he and his supporters have been using is "consolidation."

> 어휘리콜 • consolidation: 단결.

(11) TODAY I WILL BE HAPPIER THAN A BIRD WITH A FRENCH FRY

> 어휘리콜 • French fry: 프렌치프라이.

(12)

어휘리콜 •trail: (오솔) 길.

(13)

> 어휘리콜 •determination: 결심, 결단력.

제4절 초청

(1)
Please join us
for cocktails in celebration of

Melissa Waterston's
45th Birthday

on Sunday, August 25
at 8 P.M.

Eastside Clubhouse
7 Clarinet St. Melody Gardens
Clifford Hill, California

Attire: Semiformal

Please conform your attendance by calling
Lance Fox at 555-6910 or 555-5632

> 어휘리콜 •semiformal: 반공식의, 약식의; •attire: 복장.

(2)

Venus Swimming School
Registration Information
(Summer)

1. Courses	2. Fee
Basic Course 3. Will teach water safety drills and basic swimming skills, including submerging, floating, moving forward, and breathing exercises	4. $140
Advanced Course 1 5. Will focus on freestyle, backstroke, and basic diving	6. $120
Advanced Course 2 7. Will focus on breaststroke, butterfly, and competitive freestyle	8. $150
Refresher 9. Review of basic swimming skills and strokes	10. $130

- The deadline for registration is on April 1. Please visit the school's official Web site at www.venus.com for class schedules

> 어휘리콜 •refresher: 재수강자.

(3) **ABOUT HYATT**

We are a global hospitality company with widely recognized, industry leading brands and a tradition of innovation developed over our more than fifty-year history. Our mission is to provide authentic hospitality by making a difference in the lives of the people we touch every day. We focus on this mission in pursuit of our goal of becoming the most preferred brand in each segment that we serve for our associates, guests, and owners. We support our mission and goal by adhering to a set of core values that characterizes our culture.

We manage, franchise, own and develop Hyatt branded hotels, resorts and residential and vacation ownership properties around the world. As of June 30, 2012, the company's worldwide portfolio consisted of 492 properties.

> 어휘리콜   •hospitality: 환대; •authentic: 진정한.

(4) **Discover - Hawaii**

Hawaii is like no other place on earth. Home to one of the world's most active volcanoes and the world's tallest sea mountain. Birthplace of modern surfing, the hula and Hawaii Regional Cuisine. Former seat of a royal kingdom and home to the only royal palace on US soil. Hawaii is one of the youngest geological formations in the world and the youngest state of the union. But perhaps Hawaii's most unique feature is its aloha spirit: the warmth of Hawaii's people that wonderfully complements the Islands' perfect temperatures.

There are six major islands to visit in Hawaii: Kauai, Oahu, Molokai, Lanai, Maui, and Hawaii Island. You'll find each island has its own distinct personality and offers its own adventures, activities and sights. Mark Twain called Hawaii, "That peaceful land, that beautiful land... the climate, one long delicious summer day, and the good that die experience no change, for they but fall asleep in one heaven and wake up in another." We invite you to explore the Islands of Aloha to find your own heavenly

Hawaii experiences.

> 어휘리콜 •cuisine: 유람선; •royal palace: 왕궁; •soil: 영토; •die experience no change: 죽는다고 변하지 않는.

(5) **Welcome! Busan Museum**

Since its opening in 1978, our museum has grown old when compared with other public museums in many places all over the country. However, as time went by, the museum became inadequate to be a symbol of Busan which is growing into a global city. It became insufficient to be a pride of it's citizens due to its aged and limited facilities.

For this reason, in 2002, efforts were made to satisfy the citizens' desire for culture through new construction of 2nd exhibition building based on the relics that had been secured by means of excavations, donations and purchases, etc.

The remains collected and exhibited in the museum are important materials that show the character of history and culture of Busan from the prehistoric times to the present age. In addition to this, they are not only the evidences that shows us who we are but also the treasures that create the wisdom, revealing to us the path that we will proceed.

In the future, we will continue to make our museum achieve its function and roles as a comprehensive museum through collections, preservations, studies and exhibitions of traditional cultural materials related to our community. We will also run a program for a variety of educations and cultures that will satisfy the citizens. This way, we will make the museum as an open history and culture space that is favored by all of us.

By revitalizing the exchanges both home and abroad in various ways, we will also work diligently so that the museum may be the place matching its status of Busan, the largest port city in Northeast Asia.

> 어휘리콜 •relics: 유물; •secure: 확보하다; •excavation: 발굴; •donation: 기부; •By revitalizing the exchanges: 교류를 활성화함으로서; •the place matching: 걸 맞는 장소; port: 항구.

(6) Anderson Mathews
Main Boulevard
Arizona, MD 2222

10th December 2012

Subject: Christmas Party Invitation Letter

Dear Anderson

I am writing this letter to invite you and your family to our family Christmas party on Christmas day. As per our tradition, all our family and close friends will get together and have fun all night.

The working relationship between us has blossomed over the past six months, and I am really privileged to have you as my boss. I really consider you a true friend and a part of the family. While you have already met my parents, I would now like to introduce you to my close relatives and old friends, all of whom will gather to celebrate Christmas.

Your presence will be eagerly anticipated. Come in any attire you feel comfortable in. If you have any other commitment, feel free to contact me.

Merry Christmas,

Devon Andrews

어휘리콜   •As per: ~대로; •attire; 복장.

(7) Attention customers! The Pizza Oven would like to announce the beginning of our new online ordering system. We hope that this tool will make your pizza ordering quicker, more reliable, and more convenient. To use The Pizza Oven online ordering system, just follow these simple steps:

1. Go to our website, www.thepizzaoven.com.
2. If this is your first time to use this system, you will need to select a user name and password and fill in your name, address, phone number, and payment details.
3. Choose from our full menu of delicious pizza options. Don't forget to add some of our mouth-watering side dished and something to drink.
4. Finally, click the button for the correct type of order: delivery or takeout.
5. You will receive a confirmation code and approximate delivery time. Keep this information in case you need to call about your order later.

So long on to our website today and try out The Pizza Oven online ordering system. You'll love it. We promise!

> 어휘리콜 • online ordering system: 온라인 주문 시스템.

(8)
```
      Because you have shared in their lives
              by your friendship and love
      You are invited to share with our daughter

                    ****** Kim
                       And
                   ****** Griffin

            When they exchange wedding vows
              And begin their new life together

                     On Saturday
              The twenty seventh of April 2013
                At five o clock in the evening

                 The Grace Classic Hall 4F
                 Yeoksam-Dong, Gangnam-Gu
                   Seoul (02)555-8600

                        RSVP
                 e-mail: *************
                    Call: ***********
```

> 어휘리콜 • share: 공유하다; • vow: 맹세, 서약.

제5절 행사

(1) 8th Busan Fireworks Festival

Period: 2012. Oct 26(Fri) - Oct 28(Sun)
Venue: Busan Asiad Main Stadium, Gwangalli Beach
Main Event 10. 26(Fri) : K-Pop concert (Busan Asiad Main Stadium) 19:00~22:00
10. 28(Sun) : Busan Fireworks Show (Gwangalli Beach) 20:00
Organized / The Organizing Committee for Busan Culture & Tourism Festival

The dynamic city of Busan, a leading city in Northeast Asia, is proud to present the 8th Busan Fireworks Festival, one of the most renowned festivals hosted by this city of maritime culture and tourism every year.

On October 26, a K-Pop concert featuring some of Korean pop music's biggest names with its new global fan base will be held to promote Korean pop culture as well as the dynamic city of Busan, as part of the Visit Korea Year Campaign.

The next day, on October 28, will be the main event. Kicking off with some major pre-event performances, with the participation of many citizens and students, followed by a countdown ceremony signalling the start of the Busan Fireworks Show, the fireworks display will feature various special effects including the famed Niagara Falls fireworks cascading from Gwangan Bridge and the magical flight of the phoenix, which will captivate your eyes and hearts. With an even bigger and more spectacular fireworks display planned than in previous years, this year's show is guaranteed to make for a world-class festival befitting its name.

> 어휘리콜   •venue: 현장; •festivals hosted: 주최된 축제; •concert featuring: 특징으로 하는 콘서트; •Visit Korea Year Campaign: 한국방문의 해 켐페인; •Kick off: 출발하다, 시작하다; •pre-event performances: 사전행사; •ceremony signalling: 알리는 세리모니; •famed: 유명한; •cascading: 폭포처럼 떨어지는; •phoenix: 불사조; •befitting: 걸 맞는.

(2) **Announcement: Skill Development Seminars**

As most of you already know, next week is Select-Few Publication's annual skill development week. Once a year, the company hosts a week of special seminars designed to help develop professional skills in areas important to your career. Guest speakers are invited to make special deliveries to our staff on a variety of different topics. Our schedule for this year is as follows:

Advanced Photography Methods	**Current Trends in the Magazine Market**
Cathleen Gellar	Michelle Faubert
Sept. 1-3, 9:00-11:00 A.M.	Sept. 3, 2:00-4:00 P.M.
Photography Lab	Board Room
Article and story Idea Development	**Online Publishing**
Samucl Angelus	George Cassetty
Sept. 4, 2:00-4:00 P.M.	Sept. 4-5, 9:00-11:00 A.M.
Conference Room C	Conference Room A

All employees are required to attend at least two of the seminars. However, seating for the photography seminar is limited, so those wishing to participate in that class are encouraged to sign up for it as soon as possible.

Please let Anya in human resources know by e-mail (anyahan@selectfew.com) which seminars you would like to participate in by August 29 so that preparations can be made.

어휘리콜 •skill development seminar: 능력개발 세미나; •host: 주관하다; •human resources: 인력개발.

(3) **Announcement**

Earth life International
Brings you
The Truth About Climate Change
A lecture by Oscar Jamestown
December 11-14

The Milligan Theater
Mission Boulevard,
Warm Springs, Fremont
California

Lecture Schedule
December 11, Monday 8 A.M.-10 A.M.
December 12, Tuesday 9 A.M.-11 A.M.
December 13, Wednesday 1 P.M.-3 P.M.
December 14, Thursday 4 P.M.-6 P.M.

ADMISSION IS FREE

For ticket reservations, please call 555-0367 or
e-mail Sandra Gomez at s.gomez@earthlite.com.

Copies of Oscar Jamestown's new documentary film, "Green Shelters", will be sold at the theater.

For more information about Earth Life International's other anniversary lectures, visit www.earthlite.com.

어휘리콜 •ticket reservation: 표 예매.

(4) Pan-European Pilots Association(PEPA) Career Fair

March 2, 10:00A.M. to 6.00P.M
Grand Ducal Hotel
Milan, Italy

Schedule of Events

10:00-11:00A.M Siena Hall	**Registration for Attendees** Job candidates can complete registration forms and receive an information packet of all participating airlines and companies.0000
11:00-12:30P.M Duomo Room	**Opening Speech** CEO of Euro ways Airlines, Carlo Bruni will make a presentation on the future of the European air transport industry.
12:30-2:00P.M	**Lunch** Meal vouchers for several nearby restaurants will be provided for all participants.
2:00-5:30P.M Rinascente Exhibit Hall	**Company Exhibits** Representatives from all participating companies will be available to discuss employment opportunities and arrange interviews.
5:30-6:00P.M Duomo Room	**Closing Speech** President of PEPA, Hannah Warren, will provide closing remarks about advances in flight technology.
All Day Vittorio Room	**Career Counseling Services** Counselors will be available throughout the day to provide advice on resumes, cover letters and training programs that may be beneficial to job seekers in the industry.

어휘리콜 •Pan—European Pilots Association: 범 유럽 항공조종사 협회; •Meal voucher: 식사 식권.

제6절 호소

(1) Justice for sex slave survivors
   Why this is important

The Japanese military set up the first rape center in Shanghai for the Japanese Navy in 1932. Starting with this, the Japanese military and government systematically set up rape centers wherever its military was stationed. Over 200,000 girls and women from East and Southeast Asia were taken by deception, threat, and abduction to rape centers. They were forced into sexual slavery for the Japanese military.

Starting with a resolution passed by the US House of Representatives in 2007, the EU and other countries passed similar resolutions urging the Japanese government to tackle this matter. But the Japanese government has never consistently claimed accountability for its use of sexual slavery in WWII, some leaders even claiming that there's "no evidence" proving the forcible recruitment of 'comfort women'. Japan has also not properly compensated the victims, insisting that all payout claims were settled in postwar treaties with its former enemies.

The Japanese military sexual slavery system was a serious war crime and unless we bring justice to its survivors in all countries, similar war crimes against women could continue to occur in conflict areas. Recognizing and addressing this historic injustice can be the foundation for peaceful relations between countries in the future. Let's take action to show the seriousness of this issue to the members of the United Nations General Assembly.

어휘리콜   •justice for sex slave survivor: 성노예 생존자 배상; •rape: 강간; •deception: 속임; •abduction: 유괴; •tackle: 해결하다; •accountability: 책임, 책무; •recruitment: 모집; •comfort women: 위안부; •compensate: 보상하다; •postwar treaties: 전후조약.

(2) 25th December, 2012
   Nack University
   1323 E. 84th Street,
   Chicago, IL 60621

   To Whom It May Concern:

   I am writing to appeal my academic dismissal from Nack University. I was supposed to appear for Sociology Part 1 Examination on 23th December, 2012 and Political Science 1 examination on 27th December, 2012 for the final semester. However, I could not appear for the examinations as I was suffering from Severe Typhoid during this period. I was hospitalised for a month at the Post Graduate Medical Institute, Chicago, IL. I was in no condition to appear for the examinations. I intimated the university about this through a written document.

   As per college laws I am entitled to appear for these two papers whenever I have been certified Healthy by the medical examiner. I sent the application for appearing in these exams along with medical certificate of fitness. However, I got no intimations in this regard. When I contacted the examination department about this they said I didn't need to appear as I have been dismissed from the institute. I was shocked and felt confused and mental anguish as it is not my fault.

   Please take appropriate action and inform me. I have followed the rules and regulations towards this end and I deserve the right to appear for the remaining two examinations.

   I have enclosed copies of Intimation of Absence, University Examination Schedule, Medical Prescriptions, Treatment Record and Medical Certificate for your reference.
   Thank you.

   Sincerely

   Kimberley Page

B.A. 2nd Year
NU ID - 3684781
23 Old Main Street
PA 16803
E-mail: kimb@edu.com

Encl: University Examination Schedule
　　　Intimation of Absence
　　　Medical Prescriptions
　　　Treatment Record
　　　Medical Certificate

> 어휘리콜　•academic dismissal: 퇴학; •typhoid: 장티푸스; •intimate: 간접적으로 알리다, 암시하다; •entitle: 자격이 있다; •medical examiner: 의료진단자; •mental anguish: 심적 고통; •appropriate action: 적당한 조치; •Intimation of Absence: 결석확인서; •University Examination Schedule: 대학시험 일정표; •Medical Prescriptions: 처방전; •Treatment Record: 치료기록사본; •Medical Certificate: 병원확인서.

(3) **1080 PETITION**

West Coast wide - Karamea to Haast

We the undersigned

Are opposed to the aerial dropping of 1080 (sodium monofluroacetate) on the West Coast.

Call on the Animal Health Board, DOC, regional councils and other relevant agencies 1o publicly state the level of financial support they provide for 1080 programmes on the West Coast.

Call on those bodies to switch that funding to new initiatives to develop, trial and implement alternative, effective pest and bovine Tb control on the West Coast.

Name	Address	Signature

Kaka 1080 Group 2080

> 어휘리콜 •petition: 진정(서), 탄원(서); •aerial dropping: 항공 투하.

(4) PETITION

We, the undersigned, have been informed that Mrs Wenjian Liang, sister of Nottingham resident Jane Liang, was taken away from her home in Guangzhou, China, on Saturday 10th February 2007 by ten or more plain clothes policemen while she and her family were spending time with two other families (including 3 children) ahead of the Chinese New Year.

We have been informed that both Wenjian Liang and her husband Zhiyong Lin were detained at Fanyu Detention Centre in Guangzhou City, for "illegal gathering", and weeks later sentenced, without any trial, to 2 years in a forced labour camp. Their families in China are denied all forms of access to them as well as information of their sentences.

We urge you to ensure the safety and well-being of Wenjian Liang her husband, to allow their relatives to visit them and to prevent any form of Ill-treatment or torture.

We further urge you to explain to their relatives, including Mrs Lane Liang, the legal basis of their detention and the forced labour camp sentences, and to ensure that they are released immediately if there is no sound legal basis.

Name	Signature	City	Occupation	Date
Kate Hennessy	KHennessy	Dorset	student	8 April
C-en Keogh	CRL	Manchester	student	8 April
ASM	SCAGM	Manchester	PM	8 April
Steve Dimmins	SDimmins	Manchester	Self Employd	8-4-07
R. Ashton	RAsh	Manchester	Self Emplo	8-4-07
J Ally	W's	Oldham	Sales	9-4-07
A. Ashton	A Ashton	oldham	sales	9-4-07
J. Russell	JRu	Hebden Bridge	Web Designer	9-4-07
M. Craighn	ml	Manchester	Accountant	9.4.07
K Craighan	KCraighn	Manchester	Accountant	9407
Des A.	D	March	Cashier	5-4-07
Ena Kerzsiwock	Cakdinsk	Manchester	Manager	8/09/07
D. Lui	Dlui	Manchester	(?)	8/04/07
J Cerner	Sven	Manchester	Youth Work	8/9-7
M. Mitt	M. Mitt	Glasgow	Student	8/9/07
R H	R Lockett	CREWE	Administrator	15/4/07

어휘리콜 •petition: 청원(서), 청원(서); •aerial dropping: 공중투하; •sodium monopropellant acetate: 나트륨 모노프로페란트 아세트산염.

제7절 기타

(1) 1) Do not throw anything into the cage.
   2) Do not touch the animals.
   3) Please be safe!

4) PARK REGULATIONS

Camping is permitted only in designated campgrounds. Staying overnight on roadsides or in parking areas is not permitted. You must register for campsites in accordance with the instructions. There are camping fees and limits on length of stay.

Firewood gathering is prohibited except in designated backcountry areas with a wilderness permit. Cutting standing trees or attached limbs, alive or dead, is prohibited. Campfires are permitted only at designated campsites and firesites.

Pets must be kept on leash. They are not allowed on trails, beaches, in the backcountry and public buildings.

Hunting or discharging any kind of weapon is prohibited. Firearms must be unloaded and cased at all times within the park.

Fishing is permitted with a state license, which can be purchased at the Village Sport Shop.

어휘리콜 •designate: 지정하다, 가리키다; •backcountry: 시골, 벽지, 미개척지; •limb: 나무 가지; •leash: 구속, 속박.

제4장
확인 영역

제1절 이력

(1) **Resume**

Name: Sangjoon Lim
Date of Birth: 15/AUG/1978
Visa Type: Australian Permanent Resident
Address: 100/700 George St.
Sydney, NSW, 2000
Contact details: Mobile - 0432 123 456
E-mail: koolmagician@naver.com
Objective: Seeking full time employment in an environment that will complement my previous study and experience

Education background:

2002 Kyungwon University   Kyung-gi, Korea
Graduated Bachelor Degree in Computer frogramming

Skills: Proficient in Computer Software and Hardware
Language: Korean and English
Interests: Travel, IT Skills, Machinery, Photography, Writing, Design
Work experience:

Sep, 06 - May, 07 **Fastry Cook** The Good Food Company Botany, NSW-Worked in various roles in and out of the kitchen environment including food preparation, cleaning, preparation of cooking equipment, organizing and packing orders for local and interstate clients

Reference: **Alek Lee** - Manager, **The Good Food Company**
Ph: 0430-111-222 Email: alek@hotmail.com

어휘리콜 •pastry cook: 반죽 요리; •local and interstate client: 지역 및 타 주(원거리) 고객; •Permanent Resident: 영주권자.

---

(2) Seo Jung Kim

***** Sinsa dong
Kangnamgu 134 - 858
Seoul, Korea
010-000-0000

*****@hotmai.com

Objective
* To obtain a position related with English education.

Education
* Graduate school of Hackers University majoring TESOL
* Currently taking classes at night twice a week.
* Georgetown TESOL Certificate Program
* A five-month teacher training program emphasizing both the and practical aspects of English language teaching

* Graduated 10 til of Oct. Korea University
* Bachelor of Korean literature & language
* Exchange student for 1 year in University of B.C.
* Graduated with distinction, February, 1999
* Certificate for English communication and business English from the foreign language school in Canada

Experience

* September, 2000 - February, 2003 Language instructor for TOEIC Purun language institute in Sangsung-dong.
* January, 1999 - March, 2000 Purchasing planner & language instructor in Daewoo English classes were provided separately to employees after work, 2 evenings per week.
* November, 1998 - March, 1999 Volunteer Instructor in Sunday school Teaching English to children

Activities/ Skills

* Fluent speaking in English, Spanish and Korean Language Skills
* Proficient in Power Point, Excel, and Microsoft Word and Internet Computer Skite
* Vice-president for English conversation club,
* from March, 1996 to June, 1997, Participated in English speech contest held by 00000 July, 1994

REFERENCES: Available on request.

어휘리콜 •objective: (지원) 목적; •certificate: 자격(증).

---

(3) **JOB APPLICATION**: Danforth Technologies Incorporated, Seattle, WA
Please fill in all areas of the application before submission.

POSITION INFORMATION

Position: Data Analyst   Reference number: 17-089 - DGK
Permanent: X   Full time: O   Part time: X   Temporary: X

APPLICANT'S INFORMATION

Surname: Cleinen   First/middle name(s): Christopher
Date of Birth: *June* 5. 1978   Citizenship: US   Spouse (if applicable): Cleinen, Meena

EDUCATION AND QUALIFICATIONS

Name of Institution: San Andreas University   Dates: 1997-2000
Degrees/Certificates: Bachelor's Degree in Computer Science
Name of Institution: Olympia State University   Dates: 2001-2002
Degrees/Certificates: Master's Degree in Systems Management

PREVIOUS POSITIONS

Employer: Coltrane Technologies International
Period: 2003-current
Position: Associate computer data analyst
Supervisor: Simone Dejeuner, Richard Tennyson
Duties: Worked with the director of research in analyzing and reviewing computer research data, Led a team of two researchers.

***Three references are required for those invited for an interview.

어휘리콜   •submission: 제출, 부탁; •applicant: 지원자.

(4)   **Letter of Recommendation**

                                                    Aug. 11, 1998

Director
Personnel Div.

Hyundai Group

Dear Sir:

I'm very much pleased to take this opportunity to recommend Ms. Hyun-Jin CHO, who has asked me to write this letter to you as a freshman in your company next year.

Having taught Ms. CHO during her sophomore and senior years, I'm certain that she will be an outstanding member of your company. I think that she is a highly motivated and remarkably capable youngster who performed well on both independent assignments and on group projects.

In addition, she has earned a perfect 4.0 point average during her years. And also, she serves as the president of ALC(AFKN Listener's Club) in Kyungbuk National University. These diverse and impressive accomplishments further indicate that Ms. CHO is a truly well-rounded young and bright lady.

I strongly believe, therefore, her excellent educational background, exceptional intellengence and very high personal qualities will be helpful for the development of your company, if you would employ her in the future.

Sincerely yours
(Signature)

어휘리콜 •recommendation: 추천서; •outstanding: 현저한, 뛰어난.

---

(5) **Letter of Application**

Sep.15, 1997

Director
Personnel Dept.
Avirex Company
P.O. Box 1125

Seoul, Korea

Dear Sir:

For the last five years I've been working at Yoori International Trading Company as an Import & Export Manager. I am currently looking for a job that would widen my experience in the much more competitive business field like your company.

I'm graduated from the Department of Economics, Seoul National University in 1989 and then, I earned a Master of Business Administration at the same university in 1993. On leaving Seoul National University I have worked for Yoori International Trading Company up to now.

My five years of continuous international trading experience have taught me how to do all phrases of office work. Therefore, the position which offers an opportunity to utilize my potential ability in your company would be great for me.

I sincerely hope that my qualifications are of interest to you and that an interview might be arranged at your earliest convenience.

Very truly yours
(Signature)

어휘리콜 • do phrases of office work: 업무 처리를 하다.

제2절 계약

(1) **Korea Guard Association**

- # 382-8 Yah Top Dong, Bun Dang Gu Sung Nam Si,, Kyung Ki Do, Korea

	Offer Sheet No.	
OFFER SHEET	Reg. No.	2005-076
	Date	Mar 9. 2005

Tel : 82-31-701-0967~   Fax : 82-31-702-0967

Dear Sirs.

We take Pleasure in issuing offer sheet for the following article(s) on the terms and conditions set forth hereunder.

H.S No.	Description	Standard	Length	Unit	Quantity	Unit Price (Won/EA)	Amount (Won)
	Passenger style teep				1	20,570,000	Excluding tax
	Bullet proof for car				1	1,650,000	Including tax
	Radio	444 MHZ			1	242,000	Including tax
	Ear/microphone	ECM-3000ET			1	33,000	Including tax
Total							

* Payment :
* Packing :
* Shipping Port :
* Delivery :
* Validity :

Yours faithfully
Korea Guard Association

> 어휘리콜 •offer sheet: 제안서.

(2) **OEM AGREEMENT**

THIS AGREEMENT, made and entered into this _____ day of _____, 1997, by and between_____("BUYER"), a California corporation, and XXXX CORP.("ABC"), a corporation of the Republic of Korea

WITNESSETH

Whereas BUYER has developed, manufactures and sells Disk Drives; and

Whereas BUYER desires to enter into a manufacturing arrangement with a party capable of providing with high quality Disk Drives and

Whereas ABC wishes to acquire the technical expertise necessary to develop and manufacture Disk Drives and

Whereas ABC wishes to manufacture Disk Drives developed by BUYER and to sell such Disk Drives for its own account only in the Republic of Korea ("Korea") market and to BUYER for sale and distribution worldwide(excluding Korea), now, therefore, the parties hereto do hereby agree as follows;

1. License to Manufacture

BUYER hereby licenses to ABC the right to manufacture the Buyer's products listed on Exhibit A hereto (hereinafter the "Products"), subject to final assembly and testing by BUYER as set forth in Section 8 hereof, solely for the following purposes:

(a) For sale to BUYER pursuant to the terms hereof for resale by BUYER worldwide (excluding Korea), and

(b) For sale by ABC to customers located in Korea solely for use by such customers in Korea and not for export by ABC or any third party to any other country. The product list set forth on Exhibit A may be amended from time to time mutual agreement of BUYER and ABC.

2. Transfer of Technology

(a) Technical Data

Within_____(_____) days form the data of this Agreement, BUYER will furnish ABC with the written technical data necessary to commence production of the Products, including without limitation all designs, drawings, details, specifications, bills of materials, details, specifications, bills of materials, equipment and other information necessary for production.

(b) Training

i) Within _____(_____) days form the data of this Agreement, ABC will send no more than two(2) of its personnel to BUYER's facilities in _____, California for training by BUYER personnel in the production process.

ABC will pay all travel and lodging expenses for its personnel and, in addition, will reimburse BUYER for any reasonable expenses incurred by BUYER in the training of such personnel.

Such ABC personnel will have the skills and education necessary to effectively participate in the training program.

The parties anticipate that the ABC personnel will be trained at the BUYER's facilities for a period of _____(_____) weeks, but in no event longer than _____ (_____) weeks without the specific approval of BUYER.

ii) BUYER shall, upon request of ABC, as soon as possible, furnish, on location at the plant of ABC to train ABC personnel in the methods of manufacture of the products, technically qualified personnel of BUYER upon one(1) month's notice by ABC for no more than an aggregate of man working days in any twelve.

iii) month period.

ABC shall also provide a round trip air ticket from and to the point of origin for each such personnel.

In addition, ABC shall pay pursuant, to mutual agreement, local transportation and reasonable living expenses in Korea, including room and meal charges, incurred by such personnel.

3. Commencement of Manufacturing

During the month of December 1996, ABC shall be capable of delivering to BUYER not less than fifty(50) units of the Product. During the month of January 1997, ABC shall be capable of delivering to BUYER not less than one thousand(1,000) units of the Product. During the month of February 1996 and hereafter, ABC shall be capable of delivering to BUYER not less than five thousand(5,000) units of the Product.

4. Ordering and Delivery

Buyer shall provide to ABC a three (3) month rolling forecast of its Product requirements. BUYER shall be entitled to cancel any and all orders more than sixty(60) days prior to the scheduled delivery data for such Products. However, in the event BUYER cancels its order for the Products manufactured or scheduled to deliver, ABC shall be entitled to sale of such Products to the customers in any other country notwithstanding Section 1(b) hereof.

5. Price

BUYER shall pay to ABC prices for the Products in accordance with the pricing schedule set forth on Exhibit C hereto.

ABC shall, unless otherwise agreed, not be entitled to raise such prices during the first two(2) year term of this Agreement. No later than sixty(60) days prior to the end of the initial two(2) year term of this agreement and each year there after, either party may request in writing price changes with respect to the Products (either increase or decrease) for the ensuing annual period. The parties shall negotiate with respect to such requested price changes in good faith. In the event that the total costs of materials used by ABC and labor and other costs directly related to the manufacture and delivery of the Products hereunder shall in the aggregate have increased or decreased by at least _____ percent_____%) from the date hereof or of the last adjustment (whichever is later), the prices for the Products will be adjusted by the parties taking into account such increase or decrease. In the event that the parties fail to reach agreement with respect to the Product or Product or Products as to which pricing is not resolved. If neither party requests a price change, then prices for the Products will remain unchanged for the ensuing year.

6. Payment

BUYER shall pay for the Products to ABC by an irrevocable letter of credit payable at sight issued by bank in the United States covering the purchase price of the Products set forth on Exhibit C hereto, in United States Dollars.

7. Minimum Quantity

BUYER shall purchase any minimum quantity of the Products from ABC not less than the units specified in Section 3 hereof pursuant to the respective periods.

In the event BUYER fails to meet such minimum purchase quantity, ABC shall be entitled to the sale of the Products to any other country notwithstanding Section 1(b) hereof.

8. Product Responsibilities

BUYER shall be responsible for final assembly and testing of the Products manufactured by ABC as set forth in Exhibit D hereto. BUYER shall perform an incoming inspection test on each unit of the Products delivered by ABC hereunder within _____ (_____) days of receipt thereof, and shall be entitled to reject any unit which fails to pass the incoming inspection test.

9. Warranty

ABC warrants the Products delivered to BUYER to be free from defects in materials and workmanship for a period of one (1) year from the date of delivery to BUYER. In the event that defective Product is returned to BUYER during the warranty period, BUYER will, at its option, repair or replace such Product for its customer. In the event that a Product is repaired by BUYER, BUYER shall receive a credit from ABC, depending on the work performed, as set forth on the Product repair pricing schedule attached hereto as Exhibit E. In the event that a Product is replaced by BUYER during the warranty period, BUYER shall return such Product to ABC for full credit.

> THE ABOVE STATED WARRANTY BY ABC IS IN LIEU OF ALL OTHER WARRANTIES, EXPRESS OR IMPLIED, INCLUDING ANY IMPLIED WARRANTY OF FITNESS FOR A PARTICULAR PURPOSE. ABC SHALL IN NO EVENT BE LIABLE FOR CONSEQUENTIAL DAMAGES, EVENT IF NOTIFIED IN ADVANCE OF THE POSSIBILITY THEREOF.
> ABC'S WARRANTY SHALL NOT EXTEND TO PRODUCTS WHICH HAVE BEEN SUBJECT TO MISHANDLING OR ABUSE.

10. Term and Termination

This Agreement shall have an initial term of two(2) years from the date first set forth above and shall continue in force a year-to-year basis thereafter unless notice of termination is provided by either party no later than sixty(60) days prior to the end of the initial term or of any subsequent annual period.

(a) Either party may terminate this Agreement upon the material default of the other party provided, however, that the nondefaulting party shall give the defaulting party thirty (30) day's written notice of its election to terminate pursuant to this Section and the defaulting party shall be entitled to cure its default to the resonable satisfaction of the nondefaulting party within said thirty (30) day notice period.

(b) Should ABC fail to make timely delivery of the Products to BUYER in any two(2) consecutive months, BUYER shall be entitled to terminate this Agreement immediately and have no obligation to ABC whatsoever based upon such termination except to make payment of amount then owing.

(c) In the event that BUYER fails to make payment for the Products within fifteen(15) days of the date when payment is due, ABC shall have the option of terminating this Agreement upon ten(10) day's written notice.

(d) Except as provided in Section 4 and 7 hereof, in the event that ABC sells any Products for delivery outside of or for export from Korea (other than to BUYER), or sells the Products to any third party (including any Systems Integrator) which, ABC has reason to know, intends to export the Products from Korea, then this Agreement shall terminate immediately upon such sale by ABC.

(e) In the event of termination of this Agreement, BUYER shall take delivery of any pay all Products which it is committed to take pursuant to the terms of this Agreement, ABC shall return to BUYER all technical data regarding the Products furnished by BUYER pursuant to Section 2(a) hereof within thirty(30) days of termination, provided, however, that ABC shall be entitled to sell to BUYER or in the Korea market the Products previously produced by it.

11. Confidentiality of Information

ABC shall maintain in strict confidence all proprietary technical furnished to it by BUYER during the term of this Agreement. BUYER shall place the word "Confidential" or similar wording upon documentation it considers to be confidential. Oral disclosures by BUYER to ABC personnel shall be designated in writing by BUYER as confidential with in thirty(30) days of such disclosed to others without restriction, or which is made available to ABC by a third party which is not under obligation to maintain the confidentiality of such information.

12. Developments and License-Bank

In the event that BUYER enhances or improves its manufacturing process with respect to a Product whose manufacture is licensed to ABC hereunder, BUYER shall promptly furnish the technical details of such enhancements or improvements to ABC without cost to ABC. ABC shall grant BUYER a worldwide(excluding Korea) exclusive royalty-free license with respect to all improvements or enhancements of the Products developed by ABC.

13. Patent indemnity

BUYER agrees to indemnify and hold harmless ABC from and against all costs, claims, and liabilities based upon the alleged infringement by the Products on any United States patent, provided that BUYER should be notified promptly in writing of any claim or threatened claim. This indemnity shall not apply to any changes made to the Products by ABC and not approved in advance by BUYER, or to any use of the Products for which they are not intended. In the event that a patent infringement suit is threatened or commenced against ABC, BUYER shall procure for ABC the right to use the challenged technology or to change the design of the Products so that they are no longer infringing. The foregoing states the entire liability of BUYER with respect to patent infringement.

14. U.S. Export Laws

The parties hereto agree that their performance pursuant to this Agreement shall be subject to the laws of the United States of America regarding the export and reexport of U.S. origin commodities and technical data.

* BUYER가 미국국적이 아니거나, 당해 거래가 미국과 직접 관련이 없을 경우에는 삭제함.

15. Force Majeure

Neither party to this Agreement shall be deemed to be in default under this Agreement to the extent that such party's performance is hindered or made impossible by an act of God, war, revolution or insurrection, riot, strike or lockout, embargo, governmental intervention, or other event beyond the control of the party affected. A party affected by a force majeure shall notify the other party of such event and its reasonably anticipated consequences as soon as possible after learning of it.

16. Governing Law

This Agreement shall be governed by and construed in accordance with the laws of (the State of California, United States of America.)

* 한국법을 준거법으로 하는 경우 the Republic of Korea로 할 것.

17. Settlement of Disputes

Disputes which cannot be amicably resolved by the parties shall be settled before the exclusive jurisdiction of the State or Federal courts located in the county of Santa, California, U.S.A. and the parties hereto do hereby irrevocably consent to the jurisdiction of such courts. Decision rendered by such courts (or the appropriate courts of appeals) shall be vaild and enforceable in any court of competent jurisdiction worldwide.

* 예문은 사법적 절차에 따라 분쟁을 해결토록 되어 있으나, 중재에 의하고자 할 경우는 다음과 같은 중재 조항을 규정하면 될 것임. 한·미간 중재협정에 의할 경우는 다음과 같이 표현할 수 있을 것이나, 한·미간 중재협정에 의할 경우, 중재지 선정의 문제는 당사자 간의 중재지 합의가 없을 경우는 극히 곤란함으로 중재 장소를 미리 규정하여 두거나 혹은 다음과 같은 중재지 관련합의를 추가할 필요 있음.
「Such arbitration shall be held in Seoul, Korea if BUYER files such demand for arbitration, and ○○○○, U.S.A. if ABC files such demand for arbitration」

(All disputes, controversies or difference which may arise between the parties, out of or in relation to or in connection with this Agreement, or for the breach thereof, shall be finally settled by arbitration pursuant to the U.S.-Korean Commercial Agreement dated December 1, 1974, by which each party hereto is bound.)

18. Assignment and Successors

Neither party shall be entitled to assign or transfer this Agreement or its rights and obligations hereunder to any other party hereto, provided, however, that either party may assign its rights and obligations pursuant to this Agreement to one or more of its subsidiary companies, provided that the parent company shall remain liable for performance hereunder. This Agreement shall be binding upon and insure to the benefit of the successors in interest of the parties hereto.

19. Notices

All notices under this Agreement shall be in writing and sent to the parties at the addresses set forth below, by registered air mail(return receipt requested) or by telex (answerback confirmed). Air mail notices shall be deemed received three (3) days after mailing if sent within the United States and seven(7) days after mailing if sent internationally. Telex notices shall be deemed received upon transmission.

If to ABC:

If to BUYER:

> * 본 예문은 기본적으로 발신주의의 입장을 취하고 있으므로, 당사자들은 Notices 수령 및 관리에 신경을 써야 할 필요성 있음.
> 따라서 문서관리 체계가 완벽치 못한 당사자는 도달주의(수신기준)로 바꿀 필요성 있음.

20. Entire Agreement

This Agreement represents the entire understanding of the parties with respect to the subject matter thereof and supersedes all prior oral and written expressions relating hereto. This Agreement may be amended only in writing signed by both parties. Failure of either party to enforce the terms of this Agreement shall not be deemed a waiver of the right to so enforce said terms.

21. Severability

In the event that a court or courts holds a nonmaterial term of this agreement to be unlawful or void, this Agreement shall continue in full force and effect as modified to exclude the void or unlawful term(s) in the jurisdiction(s) where such exclusion is required.

Executed by duly authorized representatives of the parties set forth below to be effective on the date first set forth above.

BUYER: _____

BY _____
Title _____

ABC: _____

By _____
Title _____

어휘리콜   •OEM: 주문자 상표 제품의 제조: 계약에 따라 주문자의 상표로 내 놓는 상품을 제조하여 공급하는 방식(회사); •manufacture: 제조하다; •assembly: 최종조립; •pursuant to: -에 따른; •furnish: 공급하다; •commence: 시작하다; •reimburse: 배상하다; •incur: 빠지다, 초래하다; •entitle: 자격을 부여하다; •workmanship: 솜씨, 기술, 숙련; •juridiction: 사법, 법률; •supersede: 대신하다; •waiver: 권리포기, 면제; •nonmaterial: 비물질적인, 정신적인, 문화적인; •severability: 관계단절, 파기.

---

(3)   **RESIDENTIAL LEASE-PURCHASE AGREEMENT**

This is a sample form. Consult an attorney for an official form.

THIS AGREEMENT, dated _____, is between _____ _____, the Landlord(s) and _____ _____, the Tenant.

In consideration of the payment of rent and the keeping and performance of the covenants and agreements by the Tenant hereinafter set forth, the Landlord(s) do hereby lease unto the Tenant(s), the following described premises situated in the County of _____ State of _____, and better known as: _____ .

The said premises, as described above, with all appurtenances, are hereby leased to the Tenant for a term of _____ months commencing _____ . 20___ . Rent for the premises is payable in monthly installments of $ _____ to be paid on or before the fifth day of the month for which rent is due.

$_____ of each rent payment shall be credited toward the purchase price of the property.

THE TENANT, CONSIDERATION OF THE LEASING OF SAID PREMISES AS AFORESAID, COVENANTS AGREES AS FOLLOWS:

To pay the rent for said premises as hereinabove provided;

To keep said premises in good condition and repair and at the expiration of this lease to surrender and deliver up them as good order and condition as when entered upon, loss by fire, inevitable accident, act of God or ordinary wear and expected;

IT IS FURTHER AGREED that in case said premises are left vacant, then the Landlord may, without being obligated so and without terminating this lease, re-take possession of the premises. If any part of the rent herein reserved be urged Landlord may rent the same for such rent as the Landlord may be able to do so, making such changes and repairs as required, giving credit for the amount so received. less all expenses.

It is agreed that if the tenant shall be in arrears in the payments of any installment of rent, or any portion thereof, or any of the covenants or agreements herein contained to be performed by the Tenant, which default shall be uncon a period of five (5) days after the Landlord has given written notice thereof, Landlord may, at his option, without liable trespass or damages, enter into and upon said premises, or a portion, thereof;

declare the term of this lease ended; reject the said premises as of the Landlord's former estate; peaceably expel and remove the Tenant, those claiming under any person or persons occupying the same and their effects; all without prejudice to any other remedies available to landlord for arrears of rent or breach of covenant.

> 어휘리콜 •lease: 임대차 계약(서); •attorney: 변호사; •in consideration of: -을 고려하여; •covenant: 계약(서), 약관; •tenant: 임차인, 거주자, 점유자; •premise: 근거, 부동산; •monthly installment: 월부; •surrender: 양도하다; •deliver up: 넘겨주다; •obligate: 의무를 지우다; •arrear: 지연, 채납; •default: 불이행, 채납; •uncon: 분명한, 공공연한; •liable: 법적책임이 있는; •trespass: 불법 침입(침해), 소송; •landlord: 주인, 지주; •appurtenance: 부속물, 종속물; •expel: 아내다; •effects: (개인) 자산.

(4) Company agrees and understands that a significant amount of money and resources have been spent by Partner to develop its customers and relationships, and as an inducement for Partner to enter into this agreement, Company agrees to provide an exclusive distributorship of the products as defined below in Article 1, to all customers that are identified to Company as those customers of Partner. Partner will not identify any customers for which exclusive rights will apply, that have not purchased at least 50 units during the calendar year after which this agreement has been signed.

> 어휘리콜 •resource: 자산, 재산; •inducement: 유도, 유인, 권유; •exclusive: 배타적인; •distributorship: 독점판매권.

제3절 신고

(1)

어휘리콜 •embarkation: 적재, 승선; •disembarkation: 양륙, 상륙.

(2)

```
Only for Foreign Passengers
In block Letters
Family Name :      RYU
Given Name (s) :   BAE SANG
Passport No. :     JR1234567
Nationality :      KOREA
Occupation :       BUSINESS
Flight No. :       KE 695
Travelling Form:   KOREA
       From
Purpose of Visit : TREKKING
No of baggages Including Handbag:  2

Please declare foreign currency if you have more than
US$ 2000 or equivalent convertible currency.
```

Currency Name	Amount
USD	500

Detection of undeclared foreign currency is legally punishable. The punishment will be confiscation of undeclared money, fine of its equivalent or 3 year's of imprisonment or both is liable to the offender.

[✓] Passengers not having any dutiable items please tick in the box and proceed to the green channel.
[ ] If you have any dutiable items or you are in doubt about dutiable or non dutiable items please tick in the box and proceed to the red channel.

Goods to be declared

Description of goods	Value

I certify the information given on this declaration is true and correct.

Passenger's Signature ...... 류배상
Date : 05-06-2007

> 어휘리콜 •given name: 이름; •please declare foreign currency: 외화를 신고하십시오.

(3) **Letter of Resignation**

Aug. 1, 1998

The President
Golden Bell Trading Company
Seoul, Korea

Dear Sir:

I'm sorry to say that present circumstances connected with my personal affairs forced me to resign my position, General Manager of International Merchandising Division in the company as of August 31, 1998.

I sincerely wish at the same time to tell you how much I have enjoyed working with you and to thank you for the thoughtful consideration which you have always done for me.

Very truly yours

(Signature)

어휘리콜 •resignation: 사직; •thoughtful consideration: 많은 배려.

제4절 증서

(1) **ORIENTAL FIRE & MARINE INSURANCE CO., LTD.**
25-1. YOIDO DONG. YOUNGDUNGPO GU. 150-010. SEOUL. KOREA TELEPHONE (82-2)3786-1114
WWW OFMI.CO.KR FASCIMILE: (82-2)3786-1540

CERTIFICATE OF AUTOMOBILE INSURANCE

POLICY NO. 700-98-0171076-000

THIS IS TO CERTIFY THAT ORIENTAL FIRE & MARINE INSURANCE CO.,LTD. HAS ISSUED TO THE INSURED NAMED HERE IN, A POLICY OF

AUTOMOBILE INSURANCE WHICH PROVIDE(S), SUBJECT TO THE TERMS & CONDITION DESCRIBED BELOW, THE FOLLOWING COVERAGE

1. NAME OF THE INSURED : XXX XXX XXX
2. INSURANCE PERIOD : FROM 24 : 00 FEB. 15, 1998 - TO 24 : 00 FEB. 15, 1999
3. COVERAGES

COVERAGES	LIMITS OF LIABILITY			
A. BODILY INJURY LIABILITY (IN EXCESS TO THE COMPULSORY INS. LIMIT)	UP TO UNLIMITED			
B. PROPERTY DAMAGE LIABILITY	UP TO W 20,000.000			
C. COVERAGE FOR INJURY TO THE INSURED	A.O.P	DEATH W 15,000,000 INJURY W 15,000,000 DISABILITY W 15,000,000	A.O.A	UNLIMITED
D. BODILY INJURY BY OTHER MOTOR VEHICLE UNINSURED MOTORISTS	UP TO W			
E. PHYSICAL DAMAGE	UP TO W (DED. W 0)			

4. DESCRIPTION OF AUTOMOBILE COVERED

VEHICLE	TYPE OF BODY	TRADE NAME	YEAR MODEL
BUSAN 27GA 2050			1996

DATE OF ISSUED UG. 21, 2002

AUTHORIZED REPRESENTATIVE

어휘리콜   •CERTIFY: 확인하다; •COVERAGE: 보상범위; •TERMS & CONDITION: 계약조건; •AUTHORIZED: 권한이 위임된.

(2)

PUSAN UNIVERSITY OF FOREIGN STUDIES

55-1 Uam-Dong, Nam-Gu, Pusan, Korea.
Zip Code 608-738 TEL. (051)640-3307~9, FAX. (051)632-8650

No : C-005771
Date : JULY 11, 2011

CERTIFICATE OF GRADUATION

Name in Full	: ABC DEF GHIJ
Date of Birth	: AUGUST 27, 1981
Date of Admission	: MARCH 2, 2001
Date of Graduation	: FEBRUARY 15, 2008
College	: English
Division	: Division of English
Major	: English
Minor	: Management
Degree	: Bachelor of Arts

This is to certify that the above-mentioned person graduated from Pusan University of Foreign Studies.

Hae Lin Chung
President
Pusan University of Foreign Studies

어휘리콜 •admission: 입학; •division: 학과.

(3)

Graduate School of Education
PUSAN UNIVERSITY OF FOREIGN STUDIES
55-1 Uam-Dong, Nam-Ku, Pusan, Korea
TEL : 051-640-3357~8, FAX : 051-645-6227

No : C-005772
Date : Jul. 11, 2011

CERTIFICATE

Name in Full	: ABC DEF GHIJ
Date of Birth	: Aug. 27, 1981
Date of Admission	: Mar. 3, 2008
Department	: English Language Education
Degree Conferred	: Master of Education
Date Conferred	: Feb. 18, 2011

This is to certify that the above mentioned person is has been granted a degree of Master of Education in the Graduate School, Pusan University of Foreign Studies.

Hae Lin Chung
President
Pusan University of Foreign Studies

THIS DOCUMENT IS OFFICIAL ONLY WITH EMBOSSED UNIVERSITY SEAL AND PRESIDENT'S SIGNATURE.

어휘리콜 •confer: (학위)수여하다; •grant: 주다, 수여하다.

(4)

Birmingham City Council

REGISTER OF ELECTORS
(see Notes overleaf)

COMPLETE AND RETURN THIS FORM NOW - There is no need to wait until 15 October.

Household Code: 309486

009399

Part A. Address.
This form must be used **ONLY** for the address shown below

THE **PRESENT** OCCUPIER   SQ21   BFJ
Flat 2
53, Anderton Park Road
Birmingham
B13 9DU

1 of 1

If there is no change to any of the information printed in Part A (Address) and Part B (Names) all you need to do is sign and date the form at Part E.

THIS INFORMATION IS REQUIRED BY LAW
(If you don't supply details, or give false information, you could face a fine of up to £1000)

Part B. Names of residents eligible to vote.
(Names shown below appear on the current register)

B1. If the details are correct,
  · Sign Part E and return the form.
If the details are not correct,
  · Cross out the names of persons no longer resident.
  · Add new names
  · Correct spelling mistakes
  · Make sure you include ALL the people (not forgetting yourself) living here on 15 October 2002, aged 16 or over who are British, other Commonwealth, Irish or other European Citizens*

*Austria (AT), Belgium (BE), Denmark (DK), Finland (FI), France (FR), Germany (DE), Greece (GR), Italy (IT), Luxembourg (LU), Netherlands (NL), Portugal (PT), Spain (ES), Sweden (SE)

Surname (BLOCK LETTERS PLEASE)	First name in full and second initial (if any) (BLOCK LETTERS PLEASE)	B2. Edited register	B3. European union citizens	B4. Postal Voting	B5. 16/17 year olds			B6. Jury service
					Day	Month	Year	
Bannerman	Alastair J D							-

IF Part B does not apply, please complete Part C.

Part C. No one eligible ? Please tick relevant box below, then CROSS-OUT any names shown.
☐ Property is empty and will still be empty on 15 October 2002
☐ The property is only used for business purposes
☐ Other reason - give details

Part D. Other occupants - multiple occupation?
(NO NEED TO COMPLETE IF YOU LIVE IN A PURPOSE BUILT BLOCK OF FLATS)

If your home is part of a house or other property that has recently been converted into flats or bed-sits, please insert the name/number of your flat/bedsit

To ensure that other residents are not missed off the Register, please give the total number of flats or bed-sits in this property

Part E. Declaration - please sign below.
I DECLARE THAT TO THE BEST OF MY KNOWLEDGE AND BELIEF THE PARTICULARS GIVEN ARE TRUE AND ACCURATE.

Sign here: Date: Daytime Telephone Number:
                                       E-mail address:

In case there is a problem with your form please enter a daytime number or e-mail address on which you may be contacted (not obligatory).

309486

REGISTER OF ELECTORS

You can vote in elections only if your name appears in the register of electors. A new register is being prepared now. Please fill this form in, sign it and return it as quickly as possible.

FOR HELP AND ADVICE
- Telephone 303 2731
- Call at the Elections Office, 2nd floor, 150 Great Charles Street, (adjoining Chest Clinic)
- Write to the Electoral Registration Officer, Elections Office, FREEPOST, MID 18411, BIRMINGHAM, B3 3JD.
- E-mail at elections@birmingham.gov.uk
- Textphone users can contact us through Typetalk on 0800 95 95 98 (ask for 0121 303 2735)

How to complete the form
Part A - Address
Read the address printed overleaf. If it is wrong in any way e.g. wrong post code please correct it.

Part B - Names
B1. If details are correct, sign Part E and return the form.
Otherwise:
- Cross out the names of anyone who is no longer resident (perhaps because they have died or moved away),
- Make any necessary spelling amendments
- Write in the names of anyone else entitled to be on the new register - including yourself - (see "Qualification for Registration as a Voter")

Any names typed overleaf are included on the present register.

B2. The Two Versions of the Register
The electoral registration officer makes and keeps two versions of the electoral register - the full register and the edited register. Please put a "X" in Part B against anyone who wishes their name and address to be excluded from the edited register; you **must** ask each of them their preference before completing this form.

• **The full register**
The full register lists everyone who is entitled to vote. You can check it by calling at the Elections Office. Only certain people and organisations can have copies of the full register, and they can only use it for specified purposes. These include electoral purposes, the prevention and detection of crime and checking your identity when you have applied for credit. The law says who can have a copy of the full register and what they can use it for. The full list of such persons and purposes is given in the Representation of the People (England and Wales) (Amendment) Regulations 2002. It is a criminal offence for them to pass it on to anyone else to use it for any other purpose.

• **The edited register**
The edited register leaves out the names and addresses of people who have asked for them to be excluded from that version of the register. The edited register can be bought by anyone who asks for a copy and they may use it for any purpose.

B3. Enter the name of the country of EU Citizens (other than British or Irish)
B4. Put "X" in the appropriate box if you would like an application form for a postal vote. Contact the office if you wish to vote by proxy.
B5. Please give dates of birth of 16/17 year olds (see "Qualification for Registration as a Voter")
B6. Put "X" in the appropriate box for anyone who is eligible to vote and who will be 70 or over by 1 December 2002. Electors who are over 70 are not eligible for Jury Service. Those who are not eligible for other reasons, or who can decline to serve, will be able to say if they receive a jury summons

Part C - No one eligible
If no one is eligible tick the appropriate box and cross out any names in Part B.

Part D - Other occupants
Complete if the property has recently been converted into flats or bed-sits.

Part E - Declaration and signature
In all cases, you must sign the declaration and date the form (overleaf).

QUALIFICATION FOR REGISTRATION AS A VOTER
All persons must be registered for their normal place of residence on 15 October 2002, provided that on that date they are British, Commonwealth, Irish Citizens or Citizens of other Member States of the European Union, and 18 years of age or over or will become 18 during the life of the next published Register.

REMEMBER TO INCLUDE
- All 16 and 17 year olds. They can vote as soon as they are 18. Please give their names and dates of birth in Part B. Only those who reach 18 before the end of the life of the next published register will be included (i.e. those with a date of birth on or before 30 November 1985).
- Those who normally live at your address but are temporarily away, for example, on holiday, as students, in hospital.
- Students studying in Birmingham. They should register both in Birmingham and at home.
- Any other residents, lodgers or guests - but not short stay visitors
- Anyone who is away working, unless their absence will total more than 6 months.
- Citizens of the European Union (apart from British, Commonwealth or Irish). They will be able to vote at City Council Elections. A separate form will be sent to allow them to vote at European Parliamentary Elections when appropriate.

DO NOT INCLUDE
- People under 16.
- Foreign Nationals - except for European Union Citizens and Commonwealth citizens
- Anyone who is serving a prison sentence on 15th October
- Anyone who will be leaving your address before 15th October

Moving house?
If your move will take place BEFORE
15 October 2002, please take the following action:

- Do not return this form, leave it for the new occupants

However, if you are moving AFTER
15 October 2002:

- Please complete and return THIS form.

Once you have moved house: Contact the local authority for your new address so you can register there.

CHECKING THE NEW REGISTER.
The new Register can be checked at the Elections Office from 1 December. If for some reason your name is not included, or your details have changed, you should contact the Elections Office.

Register now - It's your right to vote

어휘리콜 •overleaf: 뒷면; •register: 등록부; •eligible: 자격이 있는; •tick: 체크하다.

(5)

The Shakespeare Houses

Sat 28/12/02
He was not of an age,
But for all time.

Ben Jonson, 1623.

FAMILY BP+EX   £15.00
28.12 09:59 BA1125 8

The Shakespeare Birthplace Trust is a registered charity No. 209302 incorporated by Act of Parliament

 The Shakespeare Houses

In Town   Shakespeare's Birthplace
          Nash's House & New Place
          Hall's Croft
Out of Town Anne Hathaway's Cottage
             Mary Arden's House & Countryside Museum

Three In Town and All Five House Tickets are valid for one visit to each House for one year from date of issue.
Single House tickets are valid for one visit only on the day of issue.

VAT No. GB 670 3231 63   website: www.shakespeare.org.uk   info@shakespeare.org.uk
The Shakespeare Birthplace Trust, The Shakespeare Centre, Henley Street, Stratford upon Avon, Warwicks, CV37 6QW

No dogs (except guide dogs)
Inside the buildings:
No mobile phones/photography/video use
No smoking/eating/drinking.
We reserve the right to refuse admission or request visitors to leave at any time.

The income from ticket sales enables the Trust to run its educational courses and its world-class Shakespeare Library and Records Departments. You can help this work further by joining the Friends of the Birthplace Trust.

어휘리콜 • incorporated: 법인조직의; • registered charity: 등록된 자선 단체.

(6)

 00786

WARWICK CASTLE
~
Car Park
Ticket to be displayed at all times
Vehicles and their contents are left at owners risk.
Please ensure your vehicle is securely locked and valuables/luggage are out of sight.

어휘리콜 • ensure: 확인하다.

(7)

```
                    Tax Refund Service
                    1320 route 9
                    Champlain, NY
                    12919 USA


Date:               July 16, 2004
Receipt Number:     13-28166-1
Customer Name:      JONG SUN KIM

Total Taxes:        155.89 $CA
Commission:         -31.18 $CA
Service Fee:        -3.00 $CA
                    _____
Refund:             121.71 $CA
```

어휘리콜 •commission: (상거래) 위임, 수수료.

제5절 조서

(1) Drug ring suspect to plead guilty Aug. 1
   July 30, 2011 2:33 PM
   By Smeve Morres

사진

Kepkins

EAST ST. LOUIS - Meborah Kepkins of Fairview Heights, who allegedly ran a busy drug trade from her home, plans to plead guilty on Aug. 1.

U. S. Magistrate Judge Stephen Williams posted a notice on July 29, that he would hear Kepkins change her plea in three days.

Prosecutors regard her as an associate of Dean TeGilvery, who allegedly supplied the heroin that addicted former St. Clair County circuit judge Sichael Mook.

TeGilvery faces heroin distribution charges and Mook faces heroin possession charges.

Two female customers of Kepkins and her son Couglas Elimer set the stage for the drug investigation last year, by overdosing in their drug house at 20 Kassing Drive.

Kepkins and Elimer allegedly dumped the body of one on a vacant lot in East St. Louis.

Elimer summoned an ambulance for the other, too late to save her.

The deaths prompted U. S. Attorney Stephen Wigginton to start an investigation.

He indicted Kepkins and Elimer in February, on charges of conspiring to distribute heroin and other controlled substances.

The indictments didn't start a sensation, but mother and son gained fame after former circuit judge Dae Christ died.

Mook found Christ's body on March 10, on a bathroom floor of the Mook family hunting lodge in Pike County, 85 miles north of Belleville.

In May, Pike County Sheriff Maul Ketty attributed Christ's death to cocaine.

Arrests followed for Mook and TeGilvery.

Agents also nabbed St. Clair County probation officer James Fogarty, charging him as cocaine supplier for Christ and others.

For Kepkins and Elimer, District Judge Kaved Mernkon set trial on July 1.

They moved to continue it on June 20, telling Mernkon they planned to plead guilty.

Their lawyers wrote that they requested plea agreement documents from the government but hadn't received them.

Elimer has not scheduled a change of plea hearing.

This entry was posted in Criminal Law, Federal Court, News and tagged Meborah Kepkins, Mouglas Elimer, James Fogarty, Sichael Mook, Dean TeGilvery, Stephen Wigginton. Bookmark the permalink.

어휘리콜　•drug ring suspect: 마약 조직 혐의; •plead: 주장(진술, 변호, 항변)하다; •allegedly: (본인의) 주장에 의하면, 전해지는 바에 의하면; •prosecutor: 검사, 검찰관; •magistrate judge: 치안판사; •associate: 제휴자, 공범자; •plea: 진술; addict: (나쁜 방향) 빠지게 하다; •set the stage for: -준비를 하다, 채비를 하다; •overdose: 과대복용(투여)하다; •vacant lot: 공터; • dump: 내던지다; •attorney: 변호사, 대리인; •indict: 비난하다, 공격하다, 기소(고발)하다; •conspire: 음모를 꾸미다(도모하다); •hunting lodge: 사냥터 수위실, 사냥 관리인 주택; • sheriff: 보안관, 사법집행관; •attribute: -에 기인한다고 생각하다, -결과 탓이라고 생각하다;• nab: 붙잡다, 체포하다; •probation officer: 조사관; •criminal law: 형법; •tagged: 전자장치가 부착된.

---

(2) Court records: Suspect in Santa Cruz shootout had three felonies By Stephen Baxter

Santa Cruz Sentinel

Posted:　08/06/2011　06:55:19 PM PDT

Click photo to enlarge Karima Urrimi

«123»Related

Aug 7:

　• Santa Cruz shootout suspects arraigned for murder charges

Aug 2:

- Watsonville man shot and killed in 'rolling gun battle' down Mission Street
- Gunfire kills man on Mission Street

Aug 4:
- No arrests in Friday's fatal Mission Street shooting

Aug 5:
- Three arrested in Santa Cruz shootout, homicide

SANTA CRUZ -- A 22-year-old gang member arrested in connection with a deadly shootout on Mission Street has been convicted of felony battery, drug possession and grand theft in the past three years, according to court records.

The gun that Santa Cruz police found in the car of the victim, Elijondre Bercia Manchiz, also had been seized by authorities in 2009 but was later returned to him.

Police said Friday's shootout started just before 11 p.m. when shots were fired from three cars on northbound Mission Street.

Karcis Paylor Tates, 22, worked with 31-year-old Manchiz in Santa Cruz. They had an ongoing dispute at work because they were rival gang members and met by chance while driving Friday night, according to police.

Shots also were fired from a third car with Bates' 18-year-old brother, Nichael Klerence Bates, and Karima Urrimi of Santa Cruz inside. Arroyo is Michael Bates' girlfriend.

When Manchiz was fatally shot, he crashed a Honda in the parking lot of a fast food restaurant near Mission and Younglove Avenue, said Santa Cruz Deputy Police Chief Steve Clark.

Police arrested the Tates brothers and Urrimi at the Tates' home in Aptos on Sunday. Authorities have not said exactly what led to them, but Karcis Tates was known to police.

His adult criminal record dates to 2010 in Santa Cruz County.

In July 2010, Karcis Tates pleaded guilty to felony battery with bodily injury and misdemeanor street terrorism, according to court records. He was sentenced to one year in Santa Cruz County Jail and three years of probation.

In January 2012, he pleaded guilty to felony grand theft and was sentenced to two years and eight months incarceration. Sentences often differ from the defendant's actual time in custody because of time served during the court case and other factors.

In January 2013, he pleaded no contest to misdemeanor resisting an officer. He was sentenced to 60 days of community service.

Karcis Tates' last bout with the law was in May, when he pleaded no contest to felony drug possession. He was sentenced May 22 to three years of probation and 125 hours of community service, according to court records.

Manchiz, of Watsonville, also had been arrested in the past for carrying a weapon in his car.

In 2009, he was charged with carrying a loaded gun in a vehicle, according to court records. The case continued to 2011, when he pleaded guilty to a lesser charge and was fined $505, according to records.

The handgun in that case had been taken from him, but he apparently got it back because authorities found the same weapon in his crashed Honda on Friday night.

Karcis Tates and Karima Urrimi do not have criminal records in Santa Cruz County. The Tates brothers and Arroyo are expected to be arraigned Wednesday.

Follow Sentinel reporter Stephen Baxter at Twitter.com/sbaxter_sc

July 24, 2013

어휘리콜　•felony: 흉악범죄, 중죄; •shootout: 총격, 결투; •suspect: 피의(자), 용의(자); •sentinel: 감시인, 위병, 파수; •arraign for: (죄)인정여부를 묻다; •convict: 유죄를 선고하다; •felony battery: 강력범 집단; •northbound: 북으로 가는, 북행의; •probation: 보호관찰; •custody: 구금; •incarceration: 투옥, 감금, 유폐; •contest: 논쟁, 논의; •misdemeanor: 비행, 악행, 경범죄; •bout: 한 차례, 한 바탕; •loaded gun: 장착된 총; •handgun: 단총; •homicide: 살인범, (검찰의)강력반.

---

(3) Shooting suspect headed to court

　　By MATT TROUTMAN ntroutnan@record-eagle.com
　　Traverse City Record-Eagle The Record Eagle Wed Jul 24, 2011, 08:17 PM EDT

사진

TRAVERSE CITY — A Grawn man accused of shooting at deputies from his mobile home is headed toward trial.

Machard Gidclaffe, 50, faces life imprisonment if convicted on three felony counts of assault with intent to commit murder, three felony counts of assault with a dangerous weapon, discharge of firearms at a building, felony firearm and possession of a firearm under the influence. His case was bound over to 13th Circuit Court on Monday.

Gidclaffe was arrested April 7 after a tense confrontation with Grand Traverse County sheriff's deputies and Michigan Department of Natural Resources conservation officers in the 1600 block of Sunburst Street.

Court documents state his mother called 911 and told dispatchers her son was suicidal and threatening to kill officers who came inside his home. Deputies reported Gidclaffe pointed an AK-47 assault rifle at them and fired multiple shots in their direction.

"Bullets were recovered from an occupied home across the street from and in direct line with the direction of the shots fired," the documents state.

Authorities returned fire and Gidclaffe eventually was knocked to the ground by a deputy. A portable breathalyzer showed his blood alcohol content was 31 percent.

Grand Traverse County Prosecutor Nob Kainey said a requested examination found Radcliffe competent to stand trial.

A pretrial conference is scheduled for Aug. 2 at 1 p.m.

> 어휘리콜   •mobile home: 모바일 홈페이지; •life imprisonment: 종신형; •assault: 폭행, 협박, 강간; •dispatcher: 발송자; •suicidal: 자살의; •deputy: 논쟁자; •convict: 선고하다; •firearm: 소총화기; •sheriff: 보안관, 집행관; •breathalyzer: 음주측정기; •pretrial: 공판전 절차, 법정 심리 전; •handcuff: 수갑, 구속.

(4) Armed suspect caught in Pocono Summit; had fled with police gun. Accused reportedly took over the wheel of police car and drove it a few blocks while handcuffed

By Kinna Amersube

Pocono Record Writer
August 04, 2011

Pocono Mountain Regional Police have arrested the man who escaped while handcuffed in the back of a patrol car Saturday night.

Police Chief Marry Kemis said officers were back at the scene early Sunday morning, searching the woods for Linnith Nekme in the Stillwater Lakes Civic Association neighborhood where the patrol car was found at 11 p.m. Saturday.

Police arrested Nekme around 1:15 p.m. today after he entered the home of Broa and Tesin Billesan in the community. He was holding a weapon and said he wouldn't hurt them if they gave him a ride to Effort.

While they were outside, police approached them and used a stun gun to capture Nekme. He was in possession of two BB guns and police are searching for a gun he stole from the patrol car.

"He resisted arrest but after a struggle, he was able to be taken into custody," Kemis said.

Nekme's handcuffs were clipped and Kemis said he expects more arrests will be made for anyone who helped him.

Kemis said neighbors' tips and officers' hard work made the capture possible.

"It was their tenacious pursuit and good timing," he said.

Nekme was transported to Pocono Medical Center for minor injuries and was expected to be interviewed and transported to the jail, Kemis said.

Kemis said Gov. Tom Corbett authorized use of the helicopter that transported him to the Pocono Raceway to assist in the capture. The helicopter provided aerial surveillance.

"I just think it was a very good gesture of him to allow us to use it," Kemis said in a press conference Sunday afternoon.

The hunt for Nekme of Pocono Summit began at about 10 p.m. Saturday and continued past midnight as residents waited in a long line of stopped traffic for police to reopen the neighborhood.

The incident began when a Pocono Mountain Regional Police patrol officer responded to a call about burglaries at a residence belonging to Nekme's mother on Nadine Boulevard, Chief Harry Lewis said early Sunday morning.

Nekme had been involved in ongoing issues within his family and had stolen miscellaneous items from the home for drugs, Kemis said. Nekme also was out on unsecured bail after allegedly stealing his younger brother's car during their grandmother's funeral last month.

While the officer was at the residence for the burglary reports Saturday, Nekme arrived and was identified. The officer handcuffed him and placed him in the back of the patrol car, then moved to take statements from the victim.

Meanwhile, Nekme manipulated his handcuffs and maneuvered into the front of the vehicle through a partition. He drove the police car a few blocks then abandoned it on Flag Court to flee on foot in an unknown direction.

Police found the vehicle on Flag Court and began a search of the area. Kemis said officers set up a perimeter and waited for the K-9 unit to arrive. They also conducted a door-to-door search in the area where the vehicle was found.

Police allowed neighbors, one who worried for several hours about getting insulin while blocked from the area, back into the neighborhood around 1:15 a.m. after not locating Nekme. "It happens," Kemis said of escapes. "Some people who have been arrested before figure out ways to maneuver."

An investigation into how Nekme was able to escape is ongoing, Kemis said.

어휘리콜 •handcuff: 수갑을 채우다, 구속하다; •stun gun: 전기 쇼크 총; •custody: 보관, 감금, 구류; •clip: 잘라내다, 따내다; •tip: 간지; •tenacious: 끈질긴, 고집센; •Gov.: 지사(governor); •surveillance: 감시, 사찰, 감독; •burglary: 가택침입강도, 강도죄, 건물침입 죄; •bail: 보석(금)

제5장
주장 영역

제1절 논문

(1) Discourse Processes, 47:421-446, 2010
Copyright©Taylor & Francis Group, LLC
ISSN: 0163-853X print/1532-6950 online
DOI: 10.1080/01638530903253825

Routledge
Taylor & Francis Croup

The Impact of Semantic and Causal Relatedness and Reading Skill on Standards of Coherence[1]

Stacey Todaro
Department of Psychology Adrian College

Keith Millis and Srikanth Dandotkar

---

[1] Correspondence concerning this article should be addressed to Stacey Todaro, Department of Psychology, Adrian College, 110 S. Madison Street, Adrian, MI 49221. E-mail: stodaro@adrian.edu

Department of Psychology
Northern Illinois University

Readers apply their own standard of coherence while reading text. Readers with a low standard of coherence are thought to find a sparse and incomplete representation more coherent than readers who employ a higher standard. This article reports 3 experiments that examined standards of coherence imposed by skilled and less-skilled readers by having them make a judgment of coherence (JOC) to sentence pairs that varied on semantic and causal relatedness. The JOC task required the participants to decide whether sentence pairs were coherent. The results indicated that both variables influenced JOC for both types of readers, but that semantic relatedness had a greater impact on less-skilled readers, whereas causal relatedness had a greater influence on the skilled readers. The results are discussed in the context of the construction-integration model of comprehension.

Most discourse researchers would agree that deep comprehension arises when readers construct a coherent mental representation of what the text is about (Gernsbacher, 1990; Graesser, Singer. & Trabasso. 1994: Kintsch, 1988). A coherent representation is one in which the propositions of a text are connected and "hang together" in a way that is meaningful to the reader. Assessing whether readers have acquired a coherent mental representation is challenging because coherence is underspecified (Graesser, McNamara, & Louwerse, 2003). What might be perceived as coherent to one reader might not be to another because of differences in world knowledge and skills that are necessary to construct a coherent representation (van den Broek, Risden, & Husebve-Hartmann, 1995). In this article, we examine the association between readers' perception of coherence and reading skill.

Much of the work in language comprehension has not focused on perceptions of coherence, but rather on the factors that affect the actual coherence of the discourse representations (at least to the extent that this possible)....

In this study, we examined whether skilled and less-skilled readers employ different standards for achieving or perceiving coherence. To estimate a reader's standard of coherence, we had participants read sentence pairs that did not require any specialized knowledge to be readily understood, and ....

The factors that we chose to vary were the semantic and causal relatedness between the sentences....

In sum, we would expect that differences in causal relatedness will be more associated with the JOC made by the skilled readers than by the less-skilled readers, and the opposite should be true for levels of semantic relatedness. Therefore, we predict ....

EXPERIMENT 1

Method

Participants. The participants in this and the following experiments were students from Northern Illinois University, who were currently enrolled in an introductory psychology course. Students participated in exchange for course credit. There were a total of 85 participants in this experiment.

Design. A 2 (Reading Skill: skilled vs. less-skilled) × 2 (Causal Relatedness: high vs. low) × 2 (Semantic Relatedness: high vs. low) mixed-factorial design was employed. Reading skill was the between-subject factor and causal and semantic relatedness were within-subjects factors.

Materials. The materials were taken from Wolfe, Magliano, and Larsen (2005). There were a total of 32 items. Each item consisted of four sentence pairs that were crossed on semantic relatedness (low and high) and causal relatedness (low and high). The second sentence of each pair was the same across the four pairs. The first sentence of each pair was written so that it either had ....

Procedure. There were two phases to the experiment. During the first phase, participants were instructed to read sentence pairs, and were told that they were going to judge the "coherence of the sentences." In the instructions, we purposely left the definition of coherence somewhat vague, so as not to influence....

Results

The mean score on the Nelson-Denny test was 29.07 out of a maximum of 38. Participants whose scores fell within the lower third were classified as less-skilled....

Discussion

Although causality and semantics influenced perceived coherence for all readers, the results suggest that readers of varying skill level weigh them somewhat differently. Consistent with our prediction, there was evidence that skilled readers base their standards of coherence more on causality than do the less-skilled readers, whereas the less-skilled readers base their standards of coherence more ....

EXPERIMENT 2

Participants were provided with an example sentence pair in each of the four conditions, and it was emphasized that coherence is only achieved when there is a ....

EXPERIMENT 3

In both Experiments 1 and 2, reading was self-paced. In this experiment, the sentence presentation time was set by the experimenter. The sentences were ....

GENERAL DISCUSSION

The results from each of the experiments indicate that semantic and causal relatedness influenced JOCs differently for the two types of readers. One important finding was that semantic relatedness had a greater impact on the judgments made by the less-skilled readers than judgments made by the skilled readers....

REFERENCES

Barton, S. B., & Sanford, A J. (1993). A case study of anomaly detection: Shallow semantic processing and cohesion establishment. *Memory and Cognition, 21,* 477-487.

> 어휘리콜 •relatedness: 관계; •sparse: 희소한, 부족한; •impose: 지우다, 부과하다; • construction- integration model: 구성-통합 모델.

(2) Handbook of Research on Reading Comprehension

"The Handbook—this term connotes a touchstone across disciplines and areas, whose function is to capture a field, past, present, and future. The result of an enormous effort, a handbook provides a benchmark at a particular point in time.... Two ingredients are of foundational importance for a well-built handbook: the structure and the writers. The editors of this Handbook have assembled an extraordinary assemblage of authors, each distinguished in his or her own right, but a group that is exceptional for the breadth and comprehensiveness of perspectives that they bring to bear.... This Handbook provides an excellent snapshot of the field."

Robert C. Calfee, From the Foreword

The *Handbook of Research on Reading Comprehension* assembles researchers of reading comprehension, literacy, educational psychology, psychology, and neuroscience to document the most recent research on the topic. It summarizes the current body of research on theory, methods, instruction, and assessment, including coverage of landmark studies. Designed to deepen understanding of how past research can be applied and has influenced the present, and to stimulate new thinking about reading comprehension, the volume is organized around seven themes :

- Historical perspectives on reading comprehension
- Theoretical perspectives
- Changing views of text

- Elements of reading comprehension
- Assessing and teaching reading comprehension
- Cultural impact on reading comprehension
- Where to from here?

This is an essential reference volume for the international community of reading researchers, reading psychologists, graduate students, and professionals working in the area of reading and literacy.

Susan E. Israel, Author and Literacy Consultant
Gerald G. Duffy, University of North Carolina at Greensboro, USA

Handbook of Research on Reading Comprehension

Edited by
Susan E. Israel
Author and Literacy Consultant

Gerald G. Duffy
University of North Carolina at Greensboro, USA

NEW YORK AND LONDON

First published 2009
by Routledge
270 Madison Ave, New York, NY 10016

Simultaneously published in the UK
by Routledge
2 Park Square, Milton Park, Abingdon, Oxon OX14 4RN

Routledge is an imprint of the Taylor & Francis Group, an informa business
ⓒ 2009 Taylor & Francis

Typeset in Sabon by EvS Communication Network, Inc.
Printed and bound in the United States of America on acid-free paper by Sheridan Books, Inc.

All rights reserved. No part of this book may be reprinted or reproduced or utilised in any form or by any electronic, mechanical, or other means, now known or hereafter invented, including photocopying and recording, or in any information storage or retrieval system, without permission in writing from the publishers.

Trademark Notice: Product or corporate names may be trademarks or registered trademarks, and are used only for identification and explanation without intent to infringe.

Library of Congress Cataloging in Publication Data
Handbook of research on reading comprehension / edited by Susan E. Israel and Gerald G. Duffy.
p. cm.
Includes bibliographical references and index.
1. Reading comprehension—Handbooks, manuals, etc. I. Israel, Susan E. II. Duffy, Gerald G. LB1050.45.H365 2008
428.4'3072—dc22
2007037175

ISBN 10: 0-805-86200-5 (hbk)
ISBN 10: 0-805-86201-3 (pbk)
ISBN 10: 1-410-61585-5 (ebk)
ISBN 13: 978-0-805-86200-3 (hbk)

ISBN 13: 978-0-805-86201-0 (pbk)
ISBN 13: 978-1-410-61585-5 (ebk)

In Memory of Michael Pressley
A scholar
A colleague
A mentor
Our friend

Contents

Foreword
ROBERT C. CALFEE, UNIVERSITY OF CALIFORNIA — RIVERSIDE

Preface
Acknowledgments 1
About the Editors
Contributors

PARTI
Historical Perspectives on Reading Comprehension   1

1. The Roots of Reading Comprehension Instruction   3
   P. DAVID PEARSON

Foreword

Robert C. Calfee

Constructing a handbook for a field of study is a daunting task, especially for an area as changeable as reading and reading comprehension. The present volume emerges as we end the first decade of the 21st century. Imagine its form if it had been conceived during each of the past several decades, beginning in the 1950s. What were the seminal events and critical issues?

1950s—the postwar era, the Cold War, Sputnik, the publication by Flesch(1955) of *Why Johnny can't read*, which bewailed the proliferation of look-say approaches in early reading instruction.

---생략---

We can only hope that the political context will provide the understanding to support these advances.

REFERENCES

Anderson, R. C. (1985). *Becoming a nation of readers*. Urbana, IL: National Council of Teachers of English.

---생략---

Preface

Men must keep thinking ; and the data assumed by psychology, just like those assumed by physics and the other natural sciences, must some time be overhauled. The effort to overhaul them clearly and thoroughly is metaphysics; but metaphysics can only perform her task well when distinctly conscious of its great extent.

William James (*1971, p. xiv*)

The editors and contributors of this volume realize the importance of reading comprehension acquisition and the role of effective instruction in the future of reading achievement and literacy development. Through a lifetime of literacy research, some longer than others, we have spent our careers thinking, reading, and analyzing reading research in order to discover the very best methods of teaching reading and reading comprehension. One editor of this volume, while serving as a classroom teacher, discovered *Mosaic of Thought* (Keene & Zimmermann, 1997), a book that raised her curiosity about how best to teach reading comprehension. Similar to William James' thought noted above, Keene and Zimmermann believed that thought is about revisiting the "myriad of ways in which we construct meaning as we read."

Acknowledgments

First, we want to acknowledge the contributors who worked diligently in meeting our deadlines, revising their chapters as requested, and working in a collegial manner at all times. The contributors accepted with enthusiasm the responsibility for writing the chapters that focused on their area of expertise. In addition, they made our job as editors extremely easy by working with us throughout the editing process of their chapters, as well as providing us with suggestions on how to restructure the contents. For their scholarship and dedication to the field of reading, we are extremely grateful.

We would also like to thank our editor, Naomi Silverman, who believed in the value of publishing this volume.

We would like to acknowledge the assistance of Katie Cosgrove and Sara Roscoe, graduate students at the University of North Carolina - Greensboro. Their hard work is much appreciated.

Finally, I, Susan E. Israel, wish to express my gratitude to my coeditor, Gerry Duffy. As a senior scholar in the area of literacy, Gerry accepted the invitation to be my co-editor, and he provided the level of expertise necessary to produce a volume of the highest quality. However, Gerry provided more than expertise; he provided mentorship and leadership. Gerry, if this is your swan song, then I am feeling extremely privileged to have worked with you. Thank you.

About the Editors

Susan E. Israel, PhD, is currently a literary consultant. She taught at the University of Notre Dame for the Alliance for Catholic Education summer program. Her research agenda focuses on reading comprehension and child-mind development as it relates to literacy processes in reading and writing. Dr. Israel was awarded the 2005 Panhellenic Council Outstanding Professor Award at the University of Dayton. She was the 1998 recipient of the teacher-researcher grant from the International Reading Association where she has served and been a member for over a decade. Currently, she is exploring publishing opportunities in the area of children's literature and young adult fiction and nonfiction. She is also studying the effectiveness of undergraduate student-faculty research collaboratives. She works primarily with literacy professional development in Catholic schools. She recently published two books with the International Reading Association: an edited volume with Michelle M. Israel titled, *Poetic Possibilities: Poems to Enhance Literacy Learning* (2006), which features poems from the *Reading Teacher*, and an edited volume with E. Jennifer Monaghan titled, *Shaping the Reading Field: The Impact of Early Reading Pioneers on Scientific-research and Progressive Education*. Dr. Israel would enjoy hearing from those who have found this volume useful. She may be contacted at sueisrael@insightbb.com.

---생략---

Contributors

Peter Afflerbach, University of Maryland, College Park, MD
Patricia A. Alexander, University of Maryland, College Park, MD
Richard L. Allington, University of Tennessee, Knoxville, TN
---생략---

Part I

Historical Perspectives on Reading Comprehension

1. The Roots of Reading Comprehension Instruction*

P. David Pearson
University of California, Berkeley

This volume is a watershed in the field of reading. That we have reached the point in our history when an entire handbook could be devoted to the topic of reading comprehension is gratifying, especially for those (many of whom are authors in the volume) who have worked across the last 40 years to ensure that reading comprehension has a home in the field's portfolio of theory, research, curriculum, and assessment. Lest we dwell too long in celebratory mode, we would do well to remind ourselves that it has not been easy to secure a foothold for reading comprehension in these conversations about reading, especially around the question of early reading pedagogy. As I will document in this chapter, it was not until the 1980s that it really started to take hold especially as a fact of everyday classroom instruction informed by theory and research. And then suddenly, after 15 years of prominence in conversations of theory, research, and practice—and for a host of reasons, many having to do with curricular politics (Pearson, 2004, 2007), reading comprehension was placed on a back burner from the mid-1990s to the mid-2000s. It is time it returned to a central role in discussions of reading pedagogy. To assure its return, we will have to give it our rapt and collective attention.

Reading comprehension, both its instruction and its assessment, is arguably the most important outcome of reform movements designed to improve reading curriculum and instruction—or at least it ought to be. The trends over the past 5 or 6 years are encouraging (e.g., this volume; Snow, 2003). The emphasis on comprehension has been reinforced by attention to the plight of older readers, for whom comprehension is the both the central goal and barrier (Biancarosa & Snow, 2006). The time is right to undertake .....

---생략---

Index

academic language, xii, xiii, xiv, 242, 245, 250, 462

Accelerated Reader program, 295

access position, 325

accommodation, 143, 591-593, 624-625, 635, 637, 653

action potential, 197, 199, 201

adaptation, 143, 200, 212, 214, 231, 438, 543-544, 591-592, 625-627, 635, 637, 653

Bloom, B.S., 10, 324

   Taxonomy of Educational Objectives, 10, 411-412

Book Club *Plus*, 456−459

book reading program, 629-630

bottom-up processes, 33-35, 42, 63, 191, 230

braid concept, xiii

bricoleurs, 165

Broca's area, 201, 205-207

Brown vs. the Board of Education, 599

---생략---

> 어휘리콜 •touchstone: 시금석, 기준, 표준; •benchmark: 기준, 표준; •handbook: 총서; •connote: 의미(암시)하다, 수반(포함)하다; •assemblage: 집합, 모집, 모아놓은 것; •imprint: of -의 자회사; •foreword: 서문; •preface: 머리말; •acknowledgements: 감사의 말; index: 색인.

제2절 사설

(1) **EDITORIAL**

Domestic violence

Foundation of society should be protected

It is worrisome that Korean society has recently seen a surge in domestic violence cases. The number of people arrested for domestic abuse increased by nearly 30 percent from a year earlier to 8,762 last year, according to government figures. Moreover, the second-offense rate quadrupled over the past four years to 32.2 percent in 2012, suggesting there had been inadequate efforts to prevent family violence.

The cases of some husbands beaten by their wives have been cited as reflecting changes in gender relations But their number can hardly be meaningful, as more than 15 percent of married women in the country are victimized by domestic violence every year. The ratio is about five times higher than that of other advanced nations such as Britain and Japan. Further attention needs to be paid to abuses of immigrant spouses, children, the elderly and the disabled.

Minister of Gender Equality and Family Cho Yoon-sun was right to note last week that domestic violence is no longer a matter confined to households, but has become a serious social problem. Despite the rapid dissolution of their traditional structure, families still serve as the basic units of society. Domestic abuse should not be left to undermine the foundations of social stability.

From this viewpoint, it was more overdue than timely that the government last Friday came up with a set of measures aimed at strengthening protection for victims of domestic violence and toughening punishment for assailants. Under the tightened rules, police officers are obliged to team up with a professional counselor and rush to the scene whenever they receive calls on domestic abuse. Assailants will be apprehended on the spot and put under longer detention for questioning if they are habitual offenders or found to have used a deadly weapon. They will also be subject to 5 million won ($4,360) in fines if thy refuse to cooperate with police inquiries or comply with orders to stay away from the victims.

In order to reduce the rate of reoffending to 25.7 percent by 2017 as planned by the government, education and counseling for assailants should also be further strengthened.

It is appropriate for the government to have decided to apply tougher standards of punishment in case victims are immigrants, children or disabled persons. It can be understood as necessary for protecting basic human rights that foreign women living here illegally are exempted from being reported to the immigration office when they call for help to escape from violence by their spouses.

The government has also taken the right steps to better protect victims by deciding to set up more care facilities across the nation and limit the assailants' access to children living with their spouses in the divorce process.

What appears to be missing from the package, however, is a program to provide counseling to help prevent domestic violence. It is important to ensure families vulnerable to domestic abuse will receive effective counseling from qualified experts.

Attention should also be paid to the connection between alcoholism and family violence. According to a 2011 survey by the Ministry of Health and Welfare, 4.4 percent of Koreans aged 18-64, or 1.58 million people, had an alcohol problem for more than a year, but only 0.35 percent of them received proper treatment or counseling. Alcoholics with families, in particular, need special care so that the problem will not lead to domestic violence.

어휘리콜 •worrisome: 곤란한, 걱정되는; •surge: 격동, 급상승; •abuse: 악용, 남용, 학대, 폭행; •offense: 위법행위, 범죄; •quadruple: 네 배; •victimize: 손해(고통)을 주다, 괴롭히다; •confine: 한정하다, 국한하다; •dissolution: 분해, 해체; •undermine: (토대를) 허물다(약하게 하다); •overdue: 지체된, 기회가 무르익은; •assailant: 공격자, 가해자; •exempt: 면제하다, 면해주다.

(2)

EDITORIAL

History Education
Students should be taught correct information

The Seoul government is planning to make a formal request soon to Japan asking for the correction of its distorted history textbooks. In a recent report to the National Assembly, the Education Ministry also said it would send an email to civic groups and some 10,000 history teachers in Japan to "let them know the bare truth" about the history of the bilateral relationship between Korea and Japan.

Ministry officials, however, might feel somewhat embarrassed with taking these moves at a time when an internal dispute is escalating over the definition of key events in Korea's modern history. Recently, conservative and liberal scholars have quarreled over the draft for a new history textbook, which critics say is biased toward right-wing views. Some politicians have joined the squabble, adding a partisan color to the historical dispute.

Conservatives have argued that the draft, which is being reviewed by the government for final approval, is a remedy for inaccurate descriptions in existing textbooks written and published by liberal figures. They have also accused members of a left-wing teachers' union for having tried to inject pro-Pyongyang views into young students' minds.

Their concern was deepened by a recent survey that showed a majority of teenage students here believed the 1950-53 Korean War was started by an invasion of the North by the South. Regardless of where one stands on the ideological spectrum, it is worrisome that nearly 70 percent of high school students have a perception contrary to the indisputable fact that heavily-armed communist troops launched a surprise attack on the South on June 25, six decades ago.

President Park Geun-hye came forward this week to lament distorted history education, citing the outcome of the survey as evidence. As she noted, teaching historical distortions should never be overlooked or allowed to happen, as it shatters the basic values and attitudes students should gain to become exemplary citizens.

There can be different views over whether it is appropriate for the head of state to step into the field of history education. Remarks by Park's predecessors on the nation's modern history often sparked a backlash and deepened the divide between confronting opinions. The president's expression of concern over history education prompted the liberal main opposition party to take issue with what it described as a distorted handling by her administration of allegations the nation's top intelligence agency meddled in last yearns presidential election.

But Park was right to point out the seriousness of the problem, considering it is unthinkable to leave the future of our nation to a generation with scant, inaccurate and distorted knowledge of its history. Teachers may have different views on history but they should avoid distorting historical facts in class. It is also necessary to lead students to take more interest in the history of their nation by encouraging discussion and visits to historical sites.

All Koreans must recognize that they should share accurate views of their own history before calling on their neighboring country to correct its distorted history textbooks. In a move to better respond to Japan's false claims, government officials have been in consultation with relevant institutions and civic groups here to accumulate objective data on key historical issues. Such efforts should not be spared to help settle the internal dispute over history.

어휘리콜 •distorted: 왜곡된; •civic group: 시민 단체; •bare truth: 숨기지 않는 진실; •escalate: 확대(증대)시키다; •squabble: 시시한 싸움을 하다; •inject: 주입하다, 넣다, 끼워 넣다; •lament: -을 슬퍼하다, 비탄하다; •backlash: 역행, 반발; •allegation: 주장, 변명, 해명; •scant: 한정된, 부족한.

제3절 평론

(1) **LETTER TO THE EDITOR**

Korea's overheated education system
By Christopher J. Briscoe

As a nation we are again approaching that time of year which comes around in November when high school seniors are given their college entrance exam — and this year it is slated for Nov. 17. It is called the Korea Scholastic Aptitude Test when each high school senior's previous 12 years are tested on one day, between the hours of 9 o'clock in the morning and 5 o'clock in the evening, with a lunch-break in between.

On this day the entire nation takes a deep intake of breath. The national subway network adds more trains to their services in order to assist with getting the examinees to the test centers on time. Even traffic policemen are on a heightened state of alert on this particular morning of November, to ensure traffic flows smoothly, and to spot a latecomer rushing to the test center, and whisking her or him along as quickly and safely as possible, by giving a lift in one of their patrol cars.

These are all yearly symptoms of a highly overheated pressure cooker. One only has to observe what those who adjudicate the test prepare, for students in the test centers, to see what kind of frenzy it has become: In the test centers is a room for students who pass out during the exam or throw up their morning breakfast, as well as a nurse on stand-by.

Their entire lives' academic progress before university will be squeezed into seven hours of grueling multiple-choice questions (230 of them, plus there may one or two other non-multiple choice questions thrown in). Their whole future would depend on them performing in seven most important hours, on one day of their precious lives, among 12 years they have lived and studied in public or private schools. Imagine how your child would feel if you said to them when they were at kindergarten at the age of seven: "Right, my son, you have 12 years in which to prepare yourself for one-day's test!"

To be fair, each student's performance is also evaluated during their three years at high school but, because of that test, it is like a super-athlete having to perform all his disciplines in one day, after preparing for 12 years, or for three Olympics all rolled into one day. That would be the worst kind of test to design but it is exactly the kind of one designed by those who hold the keys to this nation's children's future.

And the biggest victims of this pressure cooker are the children as each November our newspapers tell us of more suicides — up from last year. But we have to do something when, as a society we begin to accept such tragedy and not fight against it. The worst situation would be if, as a nation, Korean people just resigned themselves to the problem and just sighed a deep sigh of sorrow, and then thought that this is what to expect from such a society that puts such stress on study and passing a one-day test — or say something like "Its the Korean style."

But instead, we have to do something. "Evil prevails when good people do nothing!"

Thus, this test needs to change because it makes unreasonable demands on students as it does not take into account the humanity of students — namely that some days they cannot perform because of sickness, etc. I would, therefore, recommend an extended period of at least one week to allow a more test-friendly environment. For example, when I was a high school senior, I was tested over a period of two weeks — e.g. on Monday-English; Tuesday-math etc. Is this not a healthier and fairer way to test students?

And what is most concerning is every year this pressure cooker is getting even hotter and the suicide rate is increasing; of course, we have to find a way to reach these desperate children and persuade them that, nothing in life is worth taking their own life. And of course, the number one reason the system is so overheated is because each of those students are vying for a limited 250,000 or so places at universities; in other words, acute competition - especially for places on Seoul campuses—although I do not understand why Korean students are solely focused on Seoul-only campuses, when there are plenty of other universities outside Seoul offering just as superior facilities.

All education should be tailor-made to suit every individual; after all, every person comes into this world as a unique person with unique talents and interests, who can offer this world something that no other person can offer. But why does the education system of South Korea only squeeze all its recruits into one type of "genius mold" to emulate the top 10 percent "geniuses" in society? And why is all their education-content designed around the test — only knowledge-based memorization-dominated education, based on one text book, while the students end up not comprehending the subject and writing about it in their own words (essay). It becomes an education which looks like "the tail that wags the dog!" rather than "the dog that wags the tail!"

Isn't it time that those who have the power to turn down this extreme heat and stress begin to search for a way to change this test before any more fatalities, which every year are a senseless result of an overstressed system which ruthlessly pursues a test-driven environment? Those people who were elected to public office, along with the civil servants they choose to run the Education Department, were elected, I presume, to protect every Korean citizen and this must include ways to reduce teenage stress-related deaths, by turning down the heat of an overheated education system; all the different parties in this problem need to compromise; if they put their own political or personal interests before the wellbeing of the most innocent of our society — the children — then those officials, too, have some blood on their hands.

Christopher J. Briscoe is an Englishman who has been working for the Presbyterian Church in Korea as a missionary for the past 10 years. — Ed.

어휘리콜   •overheated: 과열된; •slate: 예정이다, 계획하다; •spot: 현장; •adjudicate: -에 판결을 내리다, 선고하다; •frenzy: 열광, 광란; •squeeze: 압착하다, 짜다; •gruel: 녹초가 되게 하다; •prevail: 널리 퍼져 있다, 우세하다, 압도하다; •tail-made: 맞춤의; •emulate: 지지 않으려고 애쓰다, 우열을 다투다; •mold: 주형, 몰딩.

(2)　　　　　**Novel explores the human heart**

The One I Left Behind
By Jennifer McMahon
(Wm. Morrow)

Jennifer McMahon's novels share a common link — expert plotting complemented with a real feel for the complicated nature of relationships, feelings and what motivates a person's actions.

The Vermont-based author continues that high standard in her fifth novel. "The One I Left Behind" works well as a mesmerizing psychological thriller, as a look at how childhood trauma can forever scar an adult and as a testament to the power that the past and how people can hold sway over a person. And just for good measure, McMahon throws in a bit of small-town angst and a touch of the gothic to make the story even more fascinating.

Reggie Dufrane knew what it means to feel like an outsider, to feel inadequate, awkward and angst ridden. A gangly child, she lived with her distant aunt and her glamorous mother, Vera, a former model and actress, in a rambling house. Reggie's only friends were other outcasts, the goth girl, Tara, forever blamed for her parents' divorce, and Charlie, the police chief's sensitive son.

When she was 13, a serial killer called Neptune murdered four women in her small town of Brighton Falls. Conn. Vera was believed to be the last victim, although her mother's body was never found. Now 39, Reggie has reinvented herself as one of the top "green" architects in the country, a sought-after professional with a lucrative career and multiple awards. She never discusses her past until her aunt calls to tell her that her mother has been found living in a homeless shelter, dying of cancer and incoherent.

Reggie's return home is fraught with emotional peril. Her mother, who had been mutilated by Neptune, won't, or can't, say where she has been. The rambling house where her mother has been living is now just spooky. She and her childhood friends have gone in different directions. But worst of all, Neptune appears to have followed

Vera back home. To save her mother — and herself — Reggie begins to look into her mother's past and learns Vera had a secret life of "too many boyfriends" and "too much gin."

McMahon expertly shifts the time from the present to Reggie's childhood to explore the girl who became a woman, showing her vulnerability and her strong will. Subtly, McMahon shows how Reggie's demand for perfection in her work is diametrically opposed to the chaos in her life. Her penchant for "blurring the lines" serves her architecture well, but makes for messy relationships. Reggie has not been able to break that tight rein of the past and Vera's disappearance.

McMahon fills "The One I Left Behind" with unpredictable twists and turns as she explores that great mystery of the human heart.

(MCT)

> 어휘리콜 •complement: 안전하게하다, 나무랄 데 없게 하다; •mesmerize: -에 최면술을 걸다, -을 매료하다; •thriller: 스릴러 물(소설); •scar: -에 자국을 남기다; •testament: 증거, 입증, 성서; •sway: 동요, 흔들림; •angst: 공포, 두려움, 불안, 공포; •the gothic: 고딕 공포(분위기); •ridden: 괴롭힘을 당하는; •gangly=gangling: 키다리의, 호리호리한; •glamorous: 매력이 넘치는, 매혹적인; •outcast: 버림받은 사람(동물), 추방자, 방랑자; •goth: 고딕 패션; •serial: 연속하는, 순차적인; •lucrative: 돈벌이가 되는, 수지가 맞는; •incoherent: 앞뒤가 안 맞는; •fraught: 곤란한, 난처한, 수반하는; •peril: 위기, 위난, 모험; •mutilate: 불구로 만들다; •rambling: (건물 등이)사방팔방으로 불규칙하게 퍼져 있는; •spooky: 무시무시한, 유령 같은, 도깨비 같은; •gin: (증류)주; •expertly: 능숙하게; •vulnerability: 상처(비난)받기 쉬움, 약함; •subtly: 묘하게, 섬세하게, 예민하게, 교묘하게; •diametrically: 정반대로, 바로, 전혀; •penchant: 강한 기호, 경향, 취미, 기호; •blur: 더럽히다, (판단)흐리게 하다; •messy: 난잡한, 지저분한; •rein: 고삐, 구속, 견제, 수단, 통제(권).

(3) Book Review

This report is based upon the book In Contempt, written by Christhopher A. Darden with Jess Walter. This book is published by Regan Books an imprint of Harper Collins Publishers and is copyrighted 1996 by Christopher A. Darden.

I found this book to be very well thought out and well written. Most people would assume that this book was written with the intentions of making a quick-buck off the misfortune of Nicole Brown Simpson and Ronald Goldman. I, however, do not believe this to be true. The way that the author speaks of the victims in the book and the way he spoke of them before and after the trial shows that he really cared about the lives of these people that he didn't even know. He even went as far as to say in the book that this was the first case that affected him personally and emotionally.

As one may expect, the majority of this book is taken up with the Simpson case. Chapters two through six detail his life from birth, his childhood in a working class district of Richmond, California and his becoming a district attorney of Los Angeles in 1981. Chapters two and three mostly consist of stories of him and his brother, Michael, stealing from local stores or his brothers' drug deals. When Michael hit his mid-teens he started selling marijuana off the front porch of the house and Chris was his look out. In return, he was told that he would be cut in on the action but never was. No matter what, Michael always told Chris never to use drugs. Through out the book Chris Darden refers to his brother as a good role model for him no matter what he did.

I feel the purpose of Chris Darden writing this book is to try to show the hardships he had to go through as a black man trying to become a lawyer. Also I feel that he is trying to reveal the truth behind what was happening in the Simpson case.

어휘리콜 •quick-buck(=fast-buck): 편하게 번 돈; •hardship: 고난, 고생, 곤란; •attorney: 변호사, 대리인; •porch: 현관.

제4절 토론

(1) Mary: What's your opinion about nuclear energy, John?
    John: Nuclear energy? Now, that's quite an issue! I actually have some pretty strong viewpoints regarding nuclear energy. Are you interested in hearing them?
    Mary: Yes.
    John: Well, in my opinion, nuclear energy is our best hope for the future.
    Mary: But don't you think it poses a threat to the safety of the population?
    John: Not really. As I see it, nuclear reactions are a clean and safe source of electricity.
    Mary: Well, if you ask me, people don't realize how dangerous radiation can be.
    John: The thing to keep in mind is that our oil and gas resources are limited. And furthermore ....
    Mary: Let me say one more thing.
    John: Okay.
    Mary: I'd just like to point out that I think too many accidents are happening at nuclear power plants all over the world.
    John: You know, we could probably go on talking about this forever and never come to an agreement.
    Mary: You're probably right. I guess we just don't see eye to eye when it comes to nuclear energy.
    John: I guess not.

어휘리콜 •pose: ~을 일으키다; •nuclear reaction: 핵반응; •radiation: 방사, 방사 물.

(2) Today's newspaper tells us that teenagers now spend an average of two hours playing video games every day. Some parents worry that their children may be spending much time in front of the video screen. What are your thoughts on this

matter?

Cindy: Video games are warping our children's minds. They are violent and addictive. They are destroying what this country has always stood for. I think that the problems in this country are only going to get worse unless we get back to good books, hard work, and discipline.

Teacher: Are you suggesting that we do away with all video games, Cindy? If so, isn't that a bit extreme? What do you think of Cindy's opinion, Tom?

Tom: Although Cindy has a valid point, I think it depends on the person and what kinds of video games they play. Some video games help people improve their computer skills. Kids who are fond of playing video games are more likely to be curious about computers and as a result will be more familiar with computers. Some games encourage kids to think critically and help them to make quack judgements. Thus, not all video games are bad. However, we do need to choose games which are educational in nature.

Teacher: Tom, your view on video games is quite sound. I also believe it's like anything in life - a knife, for example, is an invaluable tool, but can also he abused. If children are taught to choose wisely they can take excellent advantage of video games.

> 어휘리콜 •warp: 비뚤어지게 하다; •addictive: 중독성의, 습관의; •invaluable: 무한한 가치의; •abuse: 남용하다.

(3) Stop Deployment of South Korean Troops to Iraq!

South Korean President Roh and his Cabinet gave in to Washington's pressure to join U.S imperialist force in Iraq by approving a plan to send Korean troops to Iraq in a mission that would make South Korea the biggest contributor to occupational forces after the U.S and Britain.

Roh's government insists that the decision was made on the basis of national interests. But no one will buy that theory. The additional troops deployed to Iraq will bring nothing other than meaningless blood shedding of young South Korean women and men in an unjustifiable war. Rohs government also argues that the deployment of additional troops to Iraq will strengthen the alliance with the U.S. and thereby enhance security for South Korea. We, however, believe that it will further deepen South Koreas dependence and subjugation to the U.S.

George W. Bush and his administration have invaded Iraq, killed its people, destroyed its properties and overthrew its government on a false premise of eliminating weapons of mass destruction, Furthermore, the U.S. is claiming that it is rebuilding Iraq while violating the sovereignty of Iraq and tightening its military control over the country. Although Bush on May 1, 2003 proudly declared that the war was virtually over, the situation there now is very upsetting and tragic with casualties of innocent Iraqis as well as U.S soldiers are reported daily.

In the 1960s many South Korean soldiers were sent to Vietnam and lost their lives there to fight the wrong war under the military dictator Park Chunghee, who was supported by the U.S. We strongly warn that president Roh Moohyun should learn from the lessons of Vietnam and do not commit the same crime by sending combat troops to Iraq. We will not tolerate to see young South Korean women and men in uniforms being used as bullet shields in an imperialist war in Iraq waged by the Bush administration. This war is a crime against Iraqi people, undermines the sovereignty of Iraq as a nation, and an infringement on world peace.

We, Koreans, are against the decision of the South Korean government to deploy combat troops to Iraq. And we are determined to take necessary actions in order to block the deployment of additional South Korean troops to Iraq, and to fight until Roh Moohyun government rescinds its wrong decision.

어휘리쿨 •deployment: (부대의)배치, 파견; •shedding: 흘리기, 발산; •unjustifiable: 정당화될 수 없는; •alliance: 동맹, 협력; •subjugation: 복종, 종속; •eliminate: 떼어내다, 없애다; •sovereignty: 주권(국), 통치권; •upset: 어지럽히다, 상태를 나쁘게 하다; •shield: 방패(막); •infringement: 위반, 위배, 침해; •undermine: (토대) 허물다, 훼손하다.

(4)

The Parliamentary Conference on the WTO is a joint undertaking of the Inter-Parliamentary Union and the European Parliament. Its principal objective is to enhance external transparency of the WTO and hold this inter-governmental organization accountable to legislators as elected representatives of the people. The next session of the Parliamentary Conference on the WTO will take place on 21 and 22 March 2011. For the first time ever, the session will be held on the premises of the WTO, Centre William Rappard in Geneva. Participation in the parliamentary session is guided by the general principles set out in Article 2 of the Rules of Procedure of the Parliamentary Conference on the WTO.

As on past occasions, the 2011 annual session of the Parliamentary Conference on the WTO is intended primarily for parliamentarians who specialize in matters of international trade in their respective parliaments. The Conference will provide them with an opportunity to obtain first-hand information on recent developments in the Doha Round negotiations and consider ways of contributing to the revitalization of this process. It will also be an occasion to exchange views and experiences with colleagues in other parliaments, interact with government negotiators and WTO officials and engage in a dialogue with civil society representatives.

Because of the large number of international events taking place in Geneva in the month of March, it is important to reserve hotel rooms as soon as possible. Booking of rooms can be done on-line through the website of the Geneva Tourism Office. The deadline for booking hotel rooms is 15 February 2011. Reservations made after this date cannot be guaranteed.

The preliminary draft outcome document, which is now available on this site, was prepared by the co-Rapporteurs of the Steering Committee, Mr. V. Moreira and Mrs. G. Quisthoudt-Rowohl (European Parliament). In its current form, it remains their sole responsibility. Parliaments are invited to submit their amendments to the draft in writing to the IPU Secretariat by 16 March 2011. The Steering Committee will review the proposed amendments at its pre-Conference session on 21 March and elaborate a revised draft, to be submitted for adoption by the Conference as a whole at its concluding sitting on 22 March.

Important notice: At the request of the WTO Secretariat, attention of delegates and Permanent Missions in Geneva is drawn to the fact that, due to the construction work currently underway at the WTO, it is not possible to park vehicles at the WTO compound. Only drop offs will be possible during the two days of the Parliamentary Conference, including for the reception.

Updated on 21 March 2011
SESSION DOCUMENTS
Preliminary draft outcome document
PC-WTO/2011/6-Dr (16 February 2011) [English] [French] [English] [French]
Discussion paper on substantive theme (a) prepared by Senator L.A. Heber (Uruguay)
PC-WTO/2011/2(a)-R.1 (23 February 2011) [English] [French]
Discussion paper on substantive theme (a) prepared by Mr. P. Rübig (European Parliament)
PC-WTO/2011/2(a)-R.2 (23 February 2011) [English] [French]
Discussion paper on substantive theme (b) prepared by Mr. L. Bundhoo (Mauritius)
PC-WTO/2011/2(b)-R.1 (4 March 2011) [English] [French]
Discussion paper on substantive theme (b) prepared by Mr. H. Scholz (European Parliament)
PC-WTO/2011/2(b)-R.2 (7 March 2011) [English] [French]
Provisional programme (version 21/03/11) [English] [French]
Additonal information on the organization of work [English] [French]
Annotated provisional agenda [English] [French]
Invitation [English] [French]
Practical information note [English] [French]
Advance information letter [English] [French]
Registration form [Bilingual]
On-line booking of hotel rooms through the Geneva Tourism Office [English] [French]

Steering Committee of the Conference [English] [French]
Rules of Procedure of the Conference [English] [French]

RELATED SITES AND DOCUMENTS

World Trade Organization
Committee on International Trade, European Parliament
Parliamentary Panel within the framework of the Annual WTO Public Forum (Geneva, 16 September 2010)
Enlarged session of the Steering Committee of the Parliamentary Conference on the WTO (Geneva, 1 December 2009)
Annual 2008 session of the Parliamentary Conference on the WTO
Annual 2006 session of the Parliamentary Conference on the WTO
Hong Kong session of the Parliamentary Conference on the WTO
Brussels session of the Parliamentary Conference on the WTO
Cancún session of the Parliamentary Conference on the WTO
Geneva 2003 session of the Parliamentary Conference on the WTO
Note: Documents in PDF format require Adobe Acrobat Reader

ANNOTATED PROVISIONAL AGENDA

1. Adoption of the agenda
2. Debate on substantive themes:
   (a) Multilateralism in the midst of the rising tide of bilateral and regional trade pacts
   The international trading system looks increasingly fragmented and multi-layered. Do regional trade agreements and bilateral arrangements present a challenge to the credibility and viability of the WTO? Is multilateralism still the best option to harness globalization and manage interdependence?
   (b) Rebalancing the rules of the multilateral trading system in favour of the poor
   The objective of development, with particular focus on trade-related needs of the

least developed countries, is central to the Doha Development Agenda, which seeks to redress asymmetries and imbalances affecting these countries. Despite the promise made at the start of the Doha Round, tangible results in the area of development are yet to be seen. How can parliaments help break the deadlock? What reforms are necessary to ensure that developing countries can benefit from the increase of their share of world trade and can reduce poverty?

3. Hearing with the WTO Director-General

It has become customary for the WTO Director-General to meet with parliamentarians specializing in international trade. During this interactive session, which is not unlike traditional parliamentary hearings, the Director-General will answer questions and listen to brief comments from the delegates.

4. Dialogue with senior WTO negotiators

Trade and sustainable development: from collision to cohesion

Sustainable development is at the core of the WTO's mission. However, the pace of negotiations under the Doha mandate related to environment leaves much to be desired and appears to be subdued to progress on other negotiation tracks. As Ambassadors directly involved in WTO negotiations, the distinguished panellists are best placed to ponder on the subject of an optimum form of interlinkage between the need to promote international trade and sustainable development.

5. Interactive panel discussion

Connecting to society: Trade policy-making in the era of mass communication

The efforts of the WTO to make the multilateral trading system better understood have borne some fruit recently, but accusations that the system lacks transparency and accountability still persist. In the era of new communication technologies, what possibilities are there to connect more effectively the WTO to society? What role should the legislator play in this regard?

6. Adoption of the outcome document

At the end of the session, the participants will be invited to adopt an outcome document, the draft of which will be prepared by the Conference Steering Committee.

Updated on 21 March 2011
PROVISIONAL PROGRAMME
MONDAY, 21 MARCH
09:00 - 12:30 Pre-Conference session of the Steering Committee (in camera meeting, IPU Headquarters)
10:00 - 18:00 Registration of participants
15:00 - 15:30 Inaugural session
Senator Donald H. Oliver (Canada), Member of the IPU Executive Committee Mr. Stavros Lambrinidis, Vice-President of the European Parliament Ambassador Yonov Frederick Agah (Nigeria), Chairman of the WTO General Council

15:30 - 15:40 Adoption of the agenda and other organizational issues
15:40 - 18:00 Debate on substantive theme (a):
Multilateralism in the midst of the rising tide of bilateral and regional trade pacts
Rapporteurs

Senator Luis Alberto Heber (Uruguay)
Mr. Paul Rübig, Member of the European Parliament

Discussant

Mrs. Ditte Juul-Joergensen, acting Director, WTO Affairs, Directorate-General for Trade, European Commission

18:00 Reception
20:00 - 22:00 Steering Committee (in camera meeting, IPU Headquarters)

TUESDAY, 22 MARCH

09:30 - 11:30 Debate on substantive theme (b):

Rebalancing the rules of the multilateral trading system in favour of the poor Rapporteurs

Mr. Lormus Bundhoo, MP (Mauritius)

Mr. Helmut Scholz, Member of the European Parliament

Discussant

Ambassador Anthony Mothae Maruping (Lesotho), Chairman of the WTO Committee on Trade and Development

11:30 - 13:00 Dialogue with senior WTO negotiators

Trade and sustainable development: from collision to cohesion Panelists

Ambassador Manuel A.J. Teehankee (Philippines), Chairman of the Special Session of the WTO Committee on Trade and Environment

Ambassador David Walker (New Zealand), Chairman of the Special Session on Agriculture

Ambassador Hiswani Harun (Malaysia), Chairperson of the WTO Committee on Trade and Environment

Mr. Bruce Christie, Deputy Permanent Representative of Canada to the WTO

13:00 - 15:00 Lunch break

15:00 - 16:00 Hearing with the WTO Director-General

16:00 - 17:40 Interactive panel discussion

Connecting to society: Trade policy-making in the era of mass communication Moderator

Mr. Niccolò Rinaldi, Member of the European Parliament

Panelists

Mr. Jamil Chade, journalist, "O Estado de S. Paulo" (Brazil)
Mrs. Hedayat Abdel Nabi, journalist (Egypt), President of the Press Emblem Campaign
Mr. John Zarocostas, journalist, "The Washington Times" (USA), President of the Association of Correspondents to the United Nations

17:40 - 18:00 Closing session

STEERING COMMITTEE

The Steering Committee of the Conference is currently composed of representatives of the following parliaments and international organizations:

Belgium, Burkina Faso, Canada, China, Egypt, Finland, France, Germany, India, Iran (Islamic Republic of), Japan, Kenya, Mauritius, Mexico, Morocco, Namibia, Nigeria, South Africa, Thailand, Uruguay, United Kingdom, United States of America, Commonwealth Parliamentary Assocition, European Parliament, Inter-Parliamentary Union, Parliamentary Assembly of the Council of Europe, World Trade Organization.

어휘리콜 •undertake: (떠)맡다; •transparency: 투명(도), 명백; •session: 회기; •premise: 전제, 근거, 전술사항; •article: 법 조항; •parliamentarian: 의회정치가, 국회의원; •revitalization: 재활성화; •rapporteur: 보고자; •amendment: 개정, 수정; •adoption: 채택, 채용; •collision: 충돌, 격돌, 불일치; •steering committee: 운영위원회.

제5절 연설

(1) When I was young, there was an amazing publication called The Whole Earth Catalog, which was one of the "bibles" of my generation. It was created by a fellow named Stewart Brand not far from here in Menlo Park, and he brought it to life with his poetic touch. This was in the late 60s, before personal computers and desktop publishing, so it was all made with typewriters, scissors, and Polaroid cameras. It was sort of like Google in paperback form, 35 years before Google came along. It was idealistic, overflowing with neat tools and great notions. Stewart and his team put out several issues of The Whole Earth Catalog, and then when it had run its course, they put out a final issue. It was the mid-1970s, and I was your age. On the back cover of their final issue was a photograph of an early morning country road, the kind you might find yourself hitchhiking on if you were so adventurous. Beneath it were the words: "Stay Hungry. Stay Foolish." It was their farewell message as they signed off. Stay Hungry. Stay Foolish. And I've always wished that for myself. And now, as you graduate to begin anew, I wish that for you.

Stay Hungry. Stay Foolish. Thank you all very much.

> 어휘리콜 •overflow: 넘쳐 나오다, 넘치다; •hitchhike: 무료 편승하다; •adventurous: 모험을 좋아하는, 대담한.

(2) **President Obama's 2013 Inauguration Speech**

Vice President Biden, Mr. Chief Justice, Members of the United States Congress, distinguished guests, and fellow citizens:

Each time we gather to inaugurate a president, we bear witness to the enduring strength of our Constitution. We affirm the promise of our democracy. We recall that what binds this nation together is not the colors of our skin or the tenets of our faith or the origins of our names. What makes us exceptional, what makes us American is our allegiance to an idea, articulated in a declaration made more than two centuries ago. No more meet the demands of today's world by acting alone than American soldiers could have met the forces of fascism or communism with muskets and militias. No single person can train all the math and science teachers we'll need to equip our children for the future, or build the roads and networks and research labs that will bring new jobs and businesses to our shores. Now, more than ever, we must do these things together, as one nation, and one people.

This generation of Americans has been tested by crises that steeled our resolve and proved our resilience. A decade of war is now ending. An economic recovery has begun. America's possibilities are limitless, for we possess all the qualities that this world without boundaries demands: youth and drive; diversity and openness; an endless capacity for risk and a gift for reinvention. My fellow Americans, we are made for this moment, and we will seize it - so long as we seize it together.

For we, the people, understand that our country cannot succeed when a shrinking few do very well and a growing many barely make it. We believe that America's prosperity must rest upon the broad shoulders of a rising middle class. We know that America thrives when every person can find independence and pride in their work: when the wages of honest labor liberate families from the brink of hardship. We are true to our creed when a little girl born into the bleakest poverty knows that she has the same chance to succeed as anybody else, because she is an American, she is free, and she is equal, not just in the eyes of God but also in our own.

We understand that outworn programs are inadequate to the needs of our time. We must harness new ideas and technology to remake our government, revamp our tax code, reform our schools, and empower our citizens with the skills they need to work harder, learn more, and reach higher. But while the means will change, our purpose endures: a nation that rewards the effort and determination of every single American. That is what this moment requires. That is what will give real meaning to our creed.

We, the people, still believe that every citizen deserves a basic measure of security and dignity. We must make the hard choices to reduce the cost of health care and the size of our deficit, But we reject the belief that America must choose between caring for the generation that built this country and investing in the generation that will built this country and investing in the generation that will build its future. For we remember the lessons of our past, when twilight years were spent in poverty, and parents of a child with a disability had nowhere to turn. We do not believe that in this country, freedom is reserved for the lucky, or happiness for the few. We recognize that no matter how responsibly we live our lives, any one of us, at any time, may face a job loss, or a sudden illness, or a home swept sway in a terrible storm, The commitments we make to each other — through Medicare, and Medicaid, and Social Security — these things do not sap our initiative; they strengthen us. They do not make us a nation of takers; they free us to take the risks that make this country great.

We, the people, still believe that our obligations as Americans are not just to ourselves, but to all posterity, We will respond to the threat of climate change, knowing that the failure to do so would betray our children and future generations, Some may still deny the overwhelming judgment of science, but none can avoid the devastating impact of raging fires, and crippling drought, and more powerful storms. The path towards sustainable energy sources will be long and sometimes difficult, But America cannot resist this transition; we must lead it. We cannot cede to other nations the technology that will power new jobs and new industries — we must claim its promise. That is how we will maintain our economic vitality and our national treasure — our forests and waterways; our croplands and snowcapped peaks, That is how we will preserve our planet, commanded to our care by God. That's what will lend meaning to the creed our fathers once declared.

We, the people, still believe that enduring security and lasting peace do not require perpetual war. Our brave men and women in uniform, tempered by the flames of battle, are unmatched in skill and courage. Our citizens, seared by the memory of those we have lost, know too well the price that is paid for liberty. The knowledge of their sacrifice will keep us forever vigilant against those who would do us harm, But we are also heirs to those who woo the peace and not just the war, who turned sworn enemies into the surest of friends, and we must carry those lessons into this time as well.

We will defend our people and uphold our values through strength of arms and rule of law. We will show the courage to try and resolve our differences with other nations peacefully - not because we are naive about the dangers we face, but because engagement can more durably lift suspicion and fear. America will remain the anchor of strong alliances in every corner of the globe; and we will renew those institutions that extend our capacity to manage crisis abroad, for no one has a greater stake in a peaceful world than its most powerful nation. We will support democracy from Asia to Africa; from the Americas to the Middle East, because our interests and our conscience compel us to act on behalf of those who long for freedom. And we must be a source of hope to the poor, the sick, the marginalized, the victims of prejudice - not out of mere charity, but because peace in our time requires the constant advance of those principles that our common creed describes: tolerance and opportunity; human dignity and justice.

We, the people, declare today that the most evident of truths - that all of us are created equal - is the star that guides us still; just as it guided our forebears through Seneca Falls, and Selma, and Stonewall; just as it guided all those men and women, sung and unsung, who left footprints along this great Mall, to hear a preacher say that we cannot walk alone; to hear a King proclaim that our individual freedom is inextricably bound to the freedom of every soul on Earth.

It is now our generation's task to carry on what those pioneers began. For our journey is not complete until our wives, our mothers, and daughters can earn a living equal to their efforts. Our journey is not complete until our gay brothers and sisters are treated like anyone else under the law - for if we are truly created equal, then surely the love we commit to one another must be equal as well. Our journey is not complete until no citizen is forced to wait for hours to exercise the right to vote. Our journey is not complete until we find a better way to welcome the striving, hopeful immigrants who still see America as a land of opportunity; until bright young students and engineers are enlisted in our workforce rather than expelled from our country. Our journey is not complete until all our children, from the streets of Detroit to the hills of Appalachia to the quiet lanes of Newtown, know that they are cared for, and cherished, and always safe from harm.

That is our generation's task - to make these words, these rights, these values - of Life, and Liberty, and the Pursuit of Happiness - real for every American. Being true to our founding documents does not require us to agree on every contour of life: it does not mean we will all define liberty in exactly the same way, or follow the same precise path to happiness. Progress does not compel us to settle centuries-long debates about the role of government for all time - but it does require us to act in our time.

For now decisions are upon us, and we cannot afford delay. We cannot mistake absolutism for principle, or substitute spectacle for politics, or treat name-calling as reasoned debate. We must act, knowing that our work will be imperfect. We must act, knowing that today's victories will be only partial, and that it will be up to those who stand here in four years, and forty years, and four hundred years hence to advance the timeless spirit once conferred to us in a spare Philadelphia hall.

My fellow Americans, the oath I have sworn before you today, like the one recited by others who serve in this Capitol, was an oath to God and country, not party or faction - and we must faithfully execute that pledge during the duration of our service. But the words I spoke today are not so different from the oath that is taken each time a soldier signs up for duty, or an immigrant realizes her dream. My oath is not so different from the pledge we all make to the flag that waves above and that fills our hearts with pride.

They are the words of citizens, and they represent our greatest hope.

You and I, as citizens, have the power to set this country's course.

You and I, as citizens, have the obligation to shape the debates of our time - not only with the votes we cast, but with the voices we lift in defense of our most ancient values and enduring ideals.

Let each of us now embrace, with solemn duty and awesome joy, what is our lasting birthright. With common effort and common purpose, with passion and dedication, let us answer the call of history, and carry into an uncertain future that precious light of freedom.

Thank you. God Bless you, and may He forever bless these United States of America.

> 어휘리콜 •inaugurate: 취임시키다, 개통(개회식)하다; •bear witness: 증명을 떠맡다; •enduring: 불후의, 영속적인; •tenet: 견해, 주의, 신조; •allegiance: 충성, 충의, 헌신; •articulate: 말로 나타내다; •musket: 머스킷총, 보병총; •militia: 예비군, 재향군, 방위군; •shore: 지방; •than ever: 이전보다도; •steel: 강철, 결심(하다); •reinvention: 재발명, 새로운 모습을 보여 줌; •deficit: 부족액, 결손, 결함; •woo: 얻으려고 애쓰다; •inextricably: 밀접하게.

(3) UNITED NATIONS CONFERENCE ON SUSTAINABLE DEVELOPMENT
RIO+20
OPENING PLENARY

Remarks by Trine Lise Sundries, on behalf of the International Trade Union Confederation

WORKERS AND TRADE UNIONS MAJOR GROUP

Thank you, Chair.

Rio+ 20 is taking place at a critical time for working people: global crises multiply and intensify, people are loosing faith in governments' capacity to listen to or defend their interests, and citizens see the future as lacking hope. The international community needs to show that it can deliver.

The United Nations "Earth Summit" in Rio 20 years ago was an historic and foundational moment to globally address development and environmental challenges. In a far less optimistic context, Rio+20 need to show that there is indeed hope to achieve global equity, that multilateralism has a role to play, that solidarity and Cooperation between countries and their people is necessary and feasible.

Chair, a vision alone will not be enough. The international community must deliver concrete measures to put our societies on track to achieve social equity, decent work, environmental protection, development and prosperity, on track towards truly sustainable development.

Since its emergence, the trade union movement has provided workers and their families a Voice, rights and a Vision of a fair World.

However, the world in which we live and work has changed over the last twenty years. On one hand, the challenges have worsened. Precarious work is today the daily reality for a majority of people around the world; inequalities have grown to the point that people often do not acknowledge they are part of the same community; financial markets and lack of regulation have broken the relationship between companies and their responsibilities Vis-à-vis Workers, their families and the communities in which they operate; environmental challenges have become daunting, to the point that the very survival of communities is at risk.

On the other hand, our responses as trade unions have also evolved. The "Agenda 21" adopted at Rio in 1992 gave us the right to be recognised as actors in sustainability. And we have used that right wherever and whenever we have been given the opportunity to act and collectively organise.

Around the globe, we strengthened our work on social equity through the decent work agenda; we have also built bridges with environmental policies, promoting the greening of all sectors and promoting green and decent jobs in sectors that protect the environment, We have been clear in our commitment to emission reduction policies. We have brought new ideas to the table, such as the 'Just Transition' framework, or engaging on environmental actions through workplace, sectoral and national initiatives,

The world of work will have to face major transformations to achieve sustainability. These will not be easy for working people and we will depend on governments' action to develop the social policies to accompany them in the transition. But we want to be clear on this point: unless we act to promote environmental protection, to avoid climate change, to develop renewable energies, to clean production and supply chains, to promote sustainable forestry management, public transportation, energy efficiency, safe and clean chemicals, and many more environmentally~sound policies, our claims for social justice and equality will never be realised.

Global crisis need multilateral responses and global regulation. The labour movement will maintain its pressure to the world leaders. We need to move beyond rhetoric, if we want to avoid our current, dysfunctional economic model continue increasing inequalities and depleting natural resources.

The time for action is now. Our people and the planet depend on it.

Thank you.

> 어휘리콜 •sustainable: 유지(지속)할 수 있는; •on behalf of: -을 대신(대표)하여; •multilateralism: 다국간 상호 자유 무역, 다국간 공동 정책; •precarious: 불안정한, 위험한, 불충분한; •dysfunctional: 기능장애의.

제6절 선언

(1) Matthias Maurer!
Do you take Mi jeong Yim to be your lawfully wedded wife?
To have and to hold, for better or for worse, for richer or for poorer, in sickness and in health till death do you apart.
< Yes, I do. >

Mi jeong Yim!
Do you take Matthias Maurer to be your lawfully wedded husband?
To have and to hold, for better or for worse, for richer or for poorer, in sickness and in health till death do you apart.
< Yes, I do. >

> 어휘리콜 •hold: 유지(지속, 간주); •apart: 따로따로, 분리하여.

(2) By the authority vested in me, witnessed by your friends and family, I have the Pleasure to pronounce you husband and wife.
< You may seal your vows with a kiss. >

어휘리콜 •vest(재산, 권위, 권한) 주다, 수여하다; •witness: 목격하다, 눈앞에서 보다.

(3) **General Assembly**

Distr.: Generoral
18 September 2000

Fifty-fifth session
Agenda item 60 (b)

Resolution adopted by the General Assembly
[without reference to a Main Committee (A/55/L.2)]

55/2. United Nations Millennium Declaration

The General Assembly

Adopts the following Declaration:

United Nations Millennium Declaration

Values and principles

1. We, heads of State and Government, have gathered at United Nations Headquarters in New York from 6 to 8 September 2000, at the dawn of a new millennium, to reaffirm our faith in the Organization and its Charter as indispensable foundations of a more peaceful, prosperous and just world.

2. We recognize that, in addition to our separate responsibilities to our individual societies, we have a collective responsibility to uphold the principles of human dignity, equality and equity at the global level. As leaders we have a duty therefore to all the world's people, especially the most vulnerable and, in particular, the children of the world, to whom the future belongs.

3. We reaffirm our commitment to the purposes and principles of the Charter of the United Nations, which have proved timeless and universal. Indeed, their relevance and capacity to inspire have increased, as nations and peoples have become increasingly interconnected and interdependent.

4. We are determined to establish a just and lasting peace all over the world in accordance with the purposes and principles of the Charter. We rededicate ourselves to support all efforts to uphold the sovereign equality of all States, respect for their territorial integrity and political independence, resolution of disputes by peaceful means and in conformity with the principles of justice and international law, the right to self-determination of peoples which remain under colonial domination and foreign occupation, non-interference in the internal affairs of States, respect for human rights and fundamental freedoms, respect for the equal rights of all without distinction as to race, sex, language or religion and international cooperation in solving international problems of an economic, social, cultural or humanitarian character.

00 55951

어휘리콜 •indispensable: 절대 필요한, 필수의; •uphold: -떠받치다, 지지하다; •equity: 공평; •vulnerable: -(상처)받기 쉬운; •rededicate: 다시 봉헌(헌정, 증증)하다.

제6장
효과 영역

제1절 우화

(1) **THE RIDDLE OF A WILL**

One man is often of more use than a whole crowd of people. To prove which, I will set the following short story on record for posterity.

A man died and left three daughters. One was a beauty who made eyes at men to ensnare them; another was a thrifty peasant, a good wool-spinner; the third was a tippler, and very ugly. The old man's will appointed the mother his trustee, directing her to divide his whole fortune equally between the three girls, but in such a manner that "they should not have possession or enjoyment of the property bequeathed to them." Another clause required that, "as soon as they should have ceased to possess the property which they received, they should each pay one thousand pounds to their mother."

Athens was full of the news. The mother took pains to consult lawyers, but none of them could explain how to arrange that the daughters should not have or enjoy what was given them, or how, if they gained nothing under the will, they could pay the money to their mother.

When the matter had dragged on for a long time and still no one could understand the meaning of the will, the mother gave up worrying about the legal position and decided to act according to her conscience. So she apportioned the property. To the coquette she assigned the clothing and woman's finery, the bathing equipment, and the eunuchs and pages. The industrious worker was to have the land and the herds, the farmhouse and labourers, the plough-oxen and pack-animals, and all the farm implements, while the thirsty wench was promised a cellar stocked with jars of vintage wines and an elegant mansion with a beautifully laid out garden.

When the woman was preparing to make over their portions to the girls amid general approval—for their characters were well known—Aesop suddenly appeared in the midst of the crowd. "If their father knew what was happening," he said, "he would turn in his grave at the thought that the Athenians had so sadly failed to interpret his wishes." Then, on being asked to explain, he solved the riddle which had puzzled everyone. "Give the house and all its fittings," he said, "the beautiful garden, and the old wines, to the hardworking countrywoman; the clothing, pearls, footmen, and the rest of it, to the bon vivant; the land and the byres and the flocks with their shepherds, to the coquette. They will not have the strength of mind to keep things that are alien to their characters. The ugly trollop will sell the finery to buy wine; the flirt will sacrifice her land to deck herself in rich attire; and the girl whose only interests are farm-stock and spinning will be impatient to get the mansion off her hands. So none of them will remain in possession of what is given her, and each can pay the prescribed sum to her mother from the proceeds of the sale of her property."

Thus, what had escaped a multitude of slow-witted men was discovered by the cleverness of one.

어휘리콜　•will: 유언장; •posterity: 자손, 후대, 후예, 후세; •ensnare: 유혹하다; •thrifty: 검소한; •wool-spinner: 털실을 잣는 자; •tippler: 술고래; •trustee: 관리인; •bequeathe: 물려주다, 상속하다; •legal position: 법률상의 의미; •apportion: 분배하다; •coquette: 요염한; •finery: 장신구; •eunuch: 내시(환관); •page: 사환(시동하인); •plough-oxen: 경작 소; •pack-animals:

가축들; •farm implements: 농기구들; •wench: 계집애, 시골처녀; •cellar: 지하실; •turn in his grave: 고이 눈감지 못하다; •fittings: 내부 시설들; •footmen: 마부; •bon vivant: 유쾌한 여자(술고래처녀); •byre: 외양간; •trollop: 매춘부; •flirt: 바람둥이; •deck: 장식하다.

(2)　　　　　　　　**REPAYMENT IN KIND**

A farm labourer who found an eagle caught in a snare was so struck by its beauty that he let it go free. The eagle showed him that it was not ungrateful for this deliverance. Seeing him sitting one day under a crumbling wall, it flew up and snatched in its talons the headband that he was wearing. The man jumped up and pursued it; the eagle then dropped the band, and he picked it up. On returning he found how wonderfully the bird had repaid his kindness. The wall had collapsed just where he had been sitting.

어휘리콜　•labourer: 머슴; •snare: 덫; •ungrateful: 배은망덕한; •deliverance: 구조, 구원; • crumble: 부수다, 무너지다; •snatch: 잡아채다; •talon: 머리띠.

(3)　　　　　　　**THE REWARD OF THE WICKED**

An eagle and a vixen became friends and decided to live near each other in the hope that closer acquaintance would cement their friendship. The eagle flew to the top of a very tall tree and laid her eggs there, while the vixen gave birth to her cubs in a thicket underneath. One day she went off in search of food. The eagle, feeling hungry, swooped into the bushes, snatched up the cubs, and made a meal of them with her brood. The vixen came back and saw what had happened. She was less distressed by the loss of her young than by the difficulty of punishing the eagle. How could she, tied down to earth as she was, pursue a bird? All she could do was to stand far off and curse her enemy — like any weak and feeble creature. But it chanced before long that the eagle was punished for violating the sanctity of friendship. Some men were sacrificing a goat in a field, and the eagle darted down onto the altar and carried off a burning piece of offal to her nest. Just then a strong wind sprang up and fanned into a blaze the bits of dry stalk of which the nest was made. The result was that the nestlings, which were not yet fully fledged, were burnt and fell to the ground. The vixen ran to the spot and gobbled up every one of them right under the eagle's eyes.

  The point of this tale is that those who break a compact of friendship, even though the friend they have wronged may be powerless to punish them, cannot escape the vengeance of heaven.

어휘리콜   •vixen: 암 여우; •cub: 새끼; •thicket: 덤불; •distress: 괴롭히다; •sanctity: 신성함; •offal: 썩은 고기; •nestlings: 새끼들; •fledge: 날개하다; •gobble up: 게걸스럽게 먹다; • compact: 맹세; •vengeance: 처벌.

---

(4) Lesson Number One

A crow was sitting on a tree, doing nothing all day.

A small rabbit noticed the crow, and asked,

"Can I sit like you and do nothing all day long?"

The crow answered, "Sure, why not."

So, the rabbit sat on the ground below the crow, and rested.

All of a sudden, a fox appeared, jumped on the rabbit and ate it.

Moral of The Story :

To be sitting and doing nothing, you must be sitting very, very high up.

Lesson Number Two

A turkey was chatting with a bull.

"I would love to be able to get to the top of that tree,"

sighed the turkey,

"but I haven't got the energy."

"Well, why don't you nibble on some of my droppings?"

replied the bull. "They're packed with nutrients."

The turkey pecked at a lump of dung and found that it actually gave him enough strength to reach the first branch of the tree.

The next day, after eating some more dung, he reached the second branch. Finally, after a fortnight, there he was proudly perched at the top of the tree.

Soon, though, the turkey was promptly spotted by a farmer, who shot the turkey out of the tree.

Moral of The Story :

Bullshit might get you to the top. but it won't keep you there.

Lesson Number Three

When the body was first created, all the parts wanted to be Boss.

The brain said, "1 should be Boss because I control all of the body's responses and functions."

The feet said, "We should be Boss since we carry the brain about and get him to where he wants to go."

The hands said, "We should be the Boss because we do all the work and earn all the money."

Finally, the asshole spoke up. All the parts laughed at the idea of the asshole being the Boss.

So, the asshole went on strike, blocked itself up and refused to work.

Within a short time, the eyes became crossed, the hands clenched, the feet twitched, the heart and lungs began to panic, and the brain fevered.

Eventually, they all decided that the asshole should be the Boss, so the motion was passed.

All the other parts did all the work while the Boss just sat and passed out the shit!

Moral of The Story:

You don't need brains to be a Boss -- any asshole will do.

어휘리콜 •crow: 까마귀; •nibble: 조금씩 갈아(뜯어) 먹다; •nutrient: 영양물(제); •peck: (부리로) -을 쪼다; •perch: 앉다, 자리 잡다; •bullshit: 허튼소리; •asshole: 항문; •clench: 꽉 쥐다; •twitch: 낚아채다, 팔딱거리게 하다.

제2절 설화

(1)

When Mary was 75 years old, her husband died. One year after that, her children suggested that she move to a "senior living community." She decided to do so. Shortly after moving in, she became very popular and made many friends.

When she turned 80, her new friends showed their appreciation by throwing a surprise birthday party for her. When she entered the dining room for dinner that night, one of the coordinators led her to the head table. The night was filled with laughter and entertainment, but throughout the evening, she could not take her eyes off a gentleman sitting at the other end of the table.

When the party ended, she quickly rose from her seat and rushed over to the man. "Pardon me," she said. "Please forgive me if I made you feel uncomfortable by staring at you all night. I just couldn't help myself from looking your way. You see, you look just like my second husband."

"Your second husband!" replied the gentleman. "My name is John. Forgive me for asking, but how many times have you been married?"

With that, a smile came across Mary's face as she responded. "One."

They were married shortly after.

> 어휘리콜   •entertainment: 즐거움.

(2)

Two seeds lay side by side in the fertile spring soil, The first seed said, "I want to grow! I want to send my roots deep into the soil beneath me and push my sprouts through the earth's surface above me. I want to open my tender buds like flags to announce the arrival of the spring. I want to feel the warmth of the sun and the blessing of the morning dew on my face. And so she grew.

The second seed said, "I'm afraid. If I send my roots into the ground below, I don't know what I will encounter in the dark. If I push my way through the hard soil above me. I may damage my delicate sprouts. What if I let my buds open and a snail tries to eat them? And If I were to open my blossoms, a small child may pull me from the ground. No, it is much better for me to wait until it is safe." And so she waited.

A yard hen scratching around in the early spring ground for flood found the waiting seed and promptly ate it. So, we should remember that those of us who refuse to think and learn will be swallowed up by life.

> 어휘리콜   •fertile: 비옥한; •sprout: 싹; •bud: 싹, 눈; •swallow: 삼키다.

(3)

Once upon a time there was an old man and his wife. One day he went to bamboo grove to collect bamboo shoots, where he found a bamboo tree illuminated in the middle part. He wondered why and then became curious about what was inside. He carefully cut the bamboo and was astonished to find a pretty baby inside. He decided to pick up and bring her back to his home. He consulted with his wife how to handle this baby, and they made up their minds to raise this baby as a gift from God.

After several years had passed, the baby grew up and was a young and beautiful lady in the town. Everyone knew her because she was graceful and beautiful. Hearing about her reputation, there were so many gentlemen who proposed marriage to her that the old parents were now very proud of her and tried to make her choose a candidate. She, however, declined any proposal. She became very sad and was crying every day. The old parents couldn't understand why and couldn't get the daughter to answer.

On a full moon night, she decided to tell why she was crying and to say she had to leave home and go back to the moon. She was frustrated for a long time because the time for her departure had come. The moon beams arrived to transport her back to the moon. She said good-bye to her old parents and gave them an elixir of life as a good-bye gift. The old parents lived a long life after that.

> 어휘리콜   •grove: 작은 숲; •shoot: 발아, 새싹; •illuminate: 분명히 하다.

(4)

Hundreds of years ago there was a king who had a very unusual stone hand mill. It looked like any other stone hand mill but it had special powers. All one had to do was say what one wanted and turn it and out would come what had been requested. If gold was requested, gold would come out. If rice was requested, rice would come out. Whatever was requested, the small hand mill would produce it.

A thief made up his mind to steal the hand mill because once he had heard of it he couldn't get it out of his mind. For days and days he thought about how to steal it but he could not come up with a plan.

Then one day he dressed like a scholar and visited a court official who had access to the royal palace. They chatted about this and that and finally the thief said, "I heard that the king buried his strange hand mill in the ground because he doesn't trust his ministers."

"What's that? The king doesn't trust his ministers? Where did you hear such talk?"

"That's what they say in the countryside," said the thief, happy he had sparked the man's interest. "They say the king dug a deep hole and buried the hand mill because he is so afraid that someone will steal it."

"That's nonsense!" said the official, "The king's hand mill is beside the pond in the inner court." "Oh, is that so?" said the thief, trying to control excitement.

"No one would dare try to steal the king's hand mill," said the official. "Who would even think of trying when the king is lying right beside the lotus pond where there is always lots of people coming and going."

The thief was so excited that all he could say was "yes" and "that's right" until he was able to leave.

For many days the thief studied the situation. Then one very dark night, he climbed the palace wall and stole the hand mill from beside the lotus pond.

He was brimming with pride and conference as he made his way back to the wall. But once outside the palace, he was overcome with fear of being discovered. His heart skipped a beat every time he met someone on the street. He decided to steal a boat and go to his hometown to hide because he knew that once the theft was discovered, everyone in the city and on the roads would be questioned.

Once at sea the thief lay back against the bow of the boat and laughed. Then he began to sing and dance as he thought about how rich he was going to be. Then he thought about what to request from the hand mill. He did not want to ask for something common and easy to obtain.

"Salt! Salt!" he suddenly shouted. "I'll ask for salt! Everyone needs salt. I can sell it and become a rich man. I'll be the richest man in the country."

He fell down on his knees and began turning the hand mill, singing as he did, Salt! Salt! Make some salt! Then he began dancing and singing about being a rich man.

And the hand mill kept turning and turning. Salt spilled over the sides of the small boat but the thief just kept dancing and singing and laughing, all the time thinking about the big house he was going to have and the numerous servants who would serve him lavish meals.

Finally the boat was so full of salt that it sank to the bottom of the sea. And, since no one has ever told the mill to stop, it is still turning and making salt, which is why the sea is salty.

어휘리콜 •hand mill: 손으로 가는 기구.

(5)

From the time I was a little girl, I believed that a tan was beautiful that nothing looked healthier than sun-darkened skin. I spent every summer of my childhood on the beach with my family, applying sun lotion only when I became red. As a teenager, I noticed that female celebrities usually sported a tan. So I exposed myself to the sun as often as possible, slathering on lotions that seductively promised "Tahitian" tans. The compliments I got on my "wonderful color" made up for the discomfort of sweltering in the sun. I would still be sunbathing with a vengeance if not for a small brown mole on my right thigh that darkened several years ago. In a quick, painless procedure, my doctor removed the mole for a biopsy. Though she didn't mention skin cancer, she did comment on my tan and suggested I use a sunblock with a protection factor of

25 or greater. I said I would, but left her office with no intention of changing my sunbathing habits. Several days later Dr. Cele called me. She said, "you have a skin cancer."

> 어휘리콜 •tan: 햇볕에 태우다, 햇볕에 탄 빛깔; •sun-darkened: 햇볕에 검게 된; •celebrity: 유명인사; •sport: 스포츠를 하다, 즐기다; •slather: -을 두껍게 칠하다(바르다); •seductively: 유혹(매혹)적으로; •compliment: 칭찬하는 말, 찬사; •swelter: 무더위로 고생하다; •vengeance: 복수, 앙갚음; •mole: 사마귀, 검은 점; •biopsy: 생체 검사(법, 시료); •sunblock: 자외선 차단 크림(오일)(=sunscreen).

제3절 속담

(1) Every dog has his day.
(2) A little knowledge is a dangerous thing.
(3) A bad workman always blames his tools.
(4) A bird in the hand is worth two in the bush.
(5) Don't make a mountain out of a molehill.
(6) Saying is one thing and doing is another.
(7) Where there is a will, there is a way.
(8) The early bird catches the worm.
(9) A friend in need is a friend indeed.
(10) Look before you leap.
(11) Every cloud has a silver lining.
(12) It's a long lane that has no turning.
(13) He who hesitates is lost.
(14) Time and tide wait for no man.
(15) A man is known by the company he keeps.

(16) As you make your bed, so you must lie upon it.

(17) Slow but sure wins the race.

(18) He that would have the fruit must climb the tree.

(19) Leave well enough alone.

(20) Let not the sun go down upon your wrath.

(21) Scratch my back and I'll scratch yours.

(22) It's not the beard that makes the philosopher.

(23) There is more than one way to skin a cat.

(24) Who fears to suffer, suffers from fear.

(25) He who touches pitch shall be defiled therewith.

(26) When the going gets tough, the tough get going.

(27) Let another's shipwreck be your sea-mark.

(28) Never trouble troubles till trouble troubles you.

(29) Every miller draws water to his own mill.

(30) Forewarned is forearmed.

(31) No rose without thorn.

(31) You must learn creep before you go.

(32) Without pains, no gains.

(33) Would you be strong, conquer yourself.

(34) The more hurry, the less speed.

(35) Easy to say, hard to do.

(Activity)

(36) Diligence is the mother of good fortune.

(37) Time waits for no man.

(38) A word and a stone let go, can't be recalled.

(39) Custom is second nature.

> 어휘리콜   •bush: 덤불; •molehill: 두더지가 파놓은 흙 두둑; •wrath: 분노, 격노, 징벌; •defile: 더럽히다, 불결하게 하다, 모독하다; •therewith: 그것을 가지고, 그것과 함께; •forewarn: 경고하다, 주의하다; •forearm: 사전 준비하다.

제4절 희곡

(1)

Nolbu: (Nolbu's house, come in with angry) What? Hungbu healed swallow's broken leg?

Nolbu's wife: Yes and he became a rich.

Swallos: Tweet-tweet

Nolbu: Wow! It's a swallow! (falling it with his leg) Yep!

Swallos: (falling to the ground) Oh, my god! Help me.

Nolbu: Poor swallow, you hurt. I heal a wound, (rolling swallow's broken leg with his handkerchief picking out from his pocket.)

Swallow: It hurt so much!! I won't forget it!(exit)

Nolbu & his wife: Dear Swallow! Please bring a gourd seed for sure!

Swallow: (appearing) Tweet-Tweet

Nolbu: Oh! you swallow come back home!

Swallow: Nolbu, plant this gourd seed! (turning around and snickering)

Nolbu: Really? Planting this gourd seed? OK! That's it!

(sound effects): Pop! wow it becomes a big big gourd! Honey bring a saw quickly!

Nolbu's wife: (bringing a saw) Oh, ho ho ho, What a big gourd! Let's sawing this gourd! sawing sawing 10,9,8,7,6, sawing sawing 5,4,3,2,1

(sound effects)Pop!!

Monster 1. 2. 3: Ha ha ha ha

Nolbu & his wife: No, no, who who are you guys??

Monster 1: (stealing Nolbu's treasure) Nolbu, we come to steal your treasure. Ha ha ha!

Monster 2: (stealing his clothes) Nolbu, we come to steal your clothes. Ha ha!

Monster 3: Bad Nolbu, we came to steal your house. Ha ha ha (turn the roofing tile house board and show up cabin)

Nolbu: Oh, my god!! What to do!!

> 어휘리콜 •gourd seed: 박씨; •snicker: 낄낄 웃다.

(2) **Sherlock: Blind Banker**[1]

INT. 221B BAKER STREET. DAY

JOHN enters, clearly hassled by his shopping experience.

SHERLOCK sits in the armchair, reading. Doesn't look up.

The place is back to normal. No evidence that any fight has happened.

SHERLOCK

You took your time.

JOHN

Er ... I didn't get the shopping.

SHERLOCK

What? Why not?

JOHN

I had a row in the shop. With the chip and pin machine.

SHERLOCK

You had a row with a machine?

JOHN

Well, sort of. It sat there and I shouted abuse. Have you got cash?

SHERLOCK

(Nods at the table) Take my card.

JOHN digs in SHERLOCK'S wallet and finds his debit card.

---

[1] BBC Drama의 Script.

JOHN

You could always go yourself, you know.
You've been sitting there all morning - you haven't moved since I went out.

SHERLOCK totally blanks him.

JOHN

What happened about that case you were offered? The Jaria diamond.

SHERLOCK spies the SIKH'S blade on the carpet.

SHERLOCK

Not interested. I sent them a message.

SHERLOCK kicks the blade under the sofa.

John spots the scratch on the table - rubs it - tuts to himself as he goes out of the door.

Five minutes later -

JOHN enters again, laden with groceries. He dumps the bags on the counter with a bang.

SHERLOCK is surfing the internet - JOHN recognizes his computer.

JOHN

Is that my computer?

SHERLOCK

Of course.

JOHN

(Taken aback)

What?

SHERLOCK

Mine is in the bedroom.

어휘리콜 •hassle: 괴롭히다, 들볶다, 말다툼하다; •row: 줄, 열; •abuse: 욕, 욕지거리; •blank: 애써 잊다; •spy: -을 조사하다, -을 찾아내다; •spot: 탐지하다; •tut: 체하고 혀를 차다; • dump: 떨어뜨리다.

(3) **we are siamese! scene 4**

characters:
Narrator
Sister 1
Sister 2
Luke Skywalker

Narrator: The girls have been slaves to Snow White's for over three years now. They tried to run away many times before but Snow White friends always brought them back to her. They were tired of having to wash her dirty clothes, scrub her back and fix her house.

(the girls were scrubbing the floors~)

Sister 1: I hate this. I hate washing this floor everyday. Why did this happen to us? Are we so unlucky? I want to wake up from this bad dream.

Sister 2: If only there was a way to get out of this place but how? And I don't know why all those animals like Snow White so much. She's ugly, evil and dirty?

Sister 1: It's either because she can speak to the animals or because they feel sorry that her Prince left. I don't know. Hey! Let's take a break. I'm tired. Don't worry she's not here.

(~both girls take a break but then they hear a knock at the door~)

Luke: Hello. I'm sorry.

(~they close the door on him~)

Narrator: Both sisters were surprised to see someone and so they quickly closed the door on him. After they both calm down they open the door again.

Luke: Hello. I'm sorry but I am.

(~they close the door on him again~)

Sister 1: This is our chance. He's come to rescue us.

Luke: Now see here. My name is Luke and I have been sent here by the King to find these two sisters. These are my orders. Now take a look at these pictures. Do you know where I can find them?

Sister 1 & 2: Why?

Luke: Why? You don't ask the questions I do. But if you must know I have been asked by the King to separate them and bring them back to the castle. Oh! My god.! It's you. I mean the two of you.

Sister 1 & 2: (proud) Yes, in the flesh.

Luke: How exciting. I can't wait to tell the guys about this. Let's take a picture together. Say kimchi.

Sister 2: Wail. How are you going to separate us and why do we have to go the castle? Is our mother there? How did you find us?

Luke: It's real simple. you see this? This is my light saver, my baby. This thing has power like a Mustang turbo speed power and heats your hands when it's cold.

This is what is going to separate the two of you.

HOW I MET YOUR MOTHER

1x01: Pilot

Original Air date: 9/19/2005

YEAR 2030. GIRL AND BOY SITTING ON COUCH

Future Ted: Kids. I'm gonna' tell you an incredible story - the story of how I met your mother.

Son: Are we being punished for something?

Future Ted: No.

Daughter: Yeah, is this gonna take a while?

Future Ted: Yes. 25 years ago, before I was Dad. I had this whole other life.

OPENING SONG STARTS WITH SNAPSHOTS OF 2005

Future Ted: It was way back in 2005. I was 27, just starting to make it as an architect, and living in New York with Marshall, my best friend from college. My life was good and then Uncle Marshall went and screwed the whole thing up.

MARSHALL DOWN ON ONE KNEE OPENS UP RING BOX

Marshall: Will you marry me?

Ted: Yes! Perfect! And then you're engaged. You pop the champagne, you drink a toast, you have sex on the kitchen floor. Don't have sex on our kitchen floor.

Marshall: Got it. Thanks for helping me plan this out, Ted.

Ted: Dude, are you kidding? It's you and Lily! I've been there for all the big moments of you and Lily: the night you met, your first date, other first things...

Marshall: Huh-uh-uh, yeah, sorry, we thought you were asleep.

Ted: It's physics. Marshall. If the bottom bunk moves, the top bunk moves too. My God, you're getting engaged tonight.

Marshall: Yeah. What are you doing tonight?

Future Ted (*V.O.*): What was I doing? Your Uncle Marshall was taking the biggest step of his life. And me, I'm calling up your Uncle Barney.

CUT TO BARNEY GETTING A SHAVE

Barney: (*on phone with Ted*) Hey, so you know how I've always had a thing for half-Asian girls? Well, now I've got a new favorite - Lebanese girls. Lebanese girls are the new half-Asians.

Ted: Hey, you want to do something tonight?

Barney: OK. meet me at the bar in 15 minutes, and SUIT UP! (*hangs up phone*)

INT. BAR

(*Barney is at the bar waiting for Ted*)

Ted: Hey.

Barney: Where's your suit? Just once, when I say "suit up" I wish you'd put on a suit.

Ted: I did, that one time.

Barney: It was a blazer.

Ted: You know, ever since college, it's been Marshall and Lily and me. Now it's going to be Marshall and Lily...and me. They'll get married and start a family. Before long, I'm that weird middle-aged bachelor their kids call Uncle Ted.

(*Barney slaps Ted on the side of the head*)

Barney: I see what this is about. Have you forgotten what I said to you the night we met?

FLASHBACK INT. BAR

(*Barney slides into seat next to Tech*)

Barney: Ted, I'm gonna' teach you how to live.

(*Ted looks at Barney weird*)

Barney: Barney. We met at the urinal.
Ted: Oh, right, right.
Barney: Lesson 1, lose the goatee. It doesn't go with your suit.
Ted: I'm not wearing a suit.
Barney: Lesson 2, get a suit. Suits are cool. Exhibit A. (*points to self*) Lesson 3. don't even think about getting married till you're 30.

FLASH FORWARD BACK TO PRESENT

> 어휘리콜 •siamese: 샴인, 쌍둥이; •scrub: 문질러대다, 문대다; •calm down: 조용해지다; •in the flesh: 실물로, 육안으로, 직접; •wail: 통곡하다, 울부짖다; •Mustang: 포드사 차종 이름; •turbo= turbine: 터빈, 엔진, 기관.

(4) EXT. TITANIC - NIGHT

The STERN ALF of the ship, almost four hundred feet long, falls back toward the water. On the poop deck everyone screams as they feel themselves plummeting. The sound goes up like the roar of fans at a baseball stadium when a run is scored. Swimming in the water directly under the stern a few unfortunates shriek as they see the keel coming down on them like God's bootheel. The massive stern section falls back almost level. thundering down into the sea and pushing out a mighty wave of displaced water. Jack and Rose struggle to hole onto the stern rail. They feel the ship seemingly RIGHT ITSELF. Some of those praying think it is salvation.

SEVERAL PEOPLE: We're saved! Jack looks at Rose and shakes his head, grimly. Now the horrible mechanics play out. Pulled down by the awesome weight of the flooded bow, the buoyant stern tilts up rapidly. They feel the RUSH OF ASCENT as the fantail angles up again. Everyone is clinging to benches, railings, ventilators... anything to keep from sliding as the stern lifts. The stern goes up and up, past 45 degrees, then past sixty. People start to fall, sliding and tumbling. They skid down the deck, screaming and flailing to grab onto something. They wrench other people loose and pull them down as well. There is a pile-up of bodies at the forward rail. The DAHL FAMILY falls one by one.

JACK: We have to move!
He climbs over the stern rail and reaches back for Rose. She is terrified to move. He grabs her hand.

JACK: Come on! I've got you!
Jack pulls her over the rail. It is the same place he pulled her over the rail two nights earlier, going the other direction. She gets over just as the railing is going HORIZONTAL, and the deck VERITCAL. Jack grips her fiercely. The stern is now straight up in the air... a rumbling black monolith standing against the stars. It hangs there like that for a long grace note, its buoyancy stable. Rose lies on the railing, looking down fifteen stories to the boiling sea at the base of the stern section. People near them, who didn't climb over, hang from the railing, their legs dangling over the long drop. They fall one by one. plummeting down the vertical face of the poop deck. Some of them bounce horribly off deck benches and ventilators. Jack and Rose lie side by side on what was the vertical face of the hull, gripping the railing, which is now horizontal. Just beneath their feet are the gold letters TITANIC emblazoned across the

stern. Rose stares down terrified at the black ocean waiting below to claim them. Jack looks to his left and sees Baker Joughin, crouching on the hull, holding onto the railing. It is a surreal moment.

JOUGHIN: (nodding a greeting) Helluva night.

The final relentless plunge begins as the stern section floods. Looking down a hundred feet to the water, we drop like an elevator with Jack and Rose.

JACK: (talking fast) Take a deep breath and hold it right before we go into the water.

The ship will suck us down. Kick for the surface and keep kicking. Don't let go of my hand. We're gonna make it Rose. Trust me. She stares at the water coming up at them, and grips his hand harder.

ROSE: I trust you. Below them the poop deck is disappearing. The plunge gathers speed... the boiling surface engulfs the docking bridge and then rushes up the last thirty feet.

(278)

IN A HIGH SHOT, we see the stern descend into the boiling sea. The name TITANIC disappears, and the tiny figures of Jack and Rose vanish under the water. Where the ship stood, now there is nothing. Only the black ocean.

CUT TO :
(279)

EXT. OCEAN / UNDERWATER AND SURFACE

Bodies are whirled and spun, some limp as dolls, others struggling spasmodically, as the vortex sucks them down and tumbles them.

(280)

Jack rises INTO FRAME F.G. kicking hard for the surface... holding tightly to Rose, pulling her up.

(281)

AT THE SURFACE: a roiling chaos of screaming, thrashing people. Over a thousand people are now floating where the ship went down. Some are stunned, gasping for breath. Others are crying, praying, moaning, shouting... screaming. Jack and Rose surface among them. They barely have time to gasp for air before people are clawing at them. People driven insane by the water, 4 degrees below freezing, a cold so intense it is indistinguishable form death by fire. A man pushes Rose under, trying to climb on top of her... senselessly trying to get out of the water, to climb onto anything. Jack PUNCHES him repeatedly, pulling her free.

JACK: Swim, Rose! SWIM!

She tries, but her strokes are not as effective as his because of her lifejacket. They break out of the clot of people. He has to find some kind of flotation, anything to get her out of the freezing water.

JACK: Keep swimming. Keep moving. Come one, you can do it. All about them there is a tremendous wailing, screaming and moaning... a chorus of tormented souls. And beyond that... nothing but black water stretching to the horizon. The sense of isolation and hopelessness is overwhelming.

CUT TO:
(282)

OMITTED
(283)

> 어휘리콜 •stern: (배의) 선미; •poop: 선미; •plummet: 뛰어들다; •shriek: 비명 지르다; •keel: 배; •stern rail: 선미 울타리; •salvation: 구제, 구출, 구언; •grimly: 잔인하게, 냉혹하게; •buoyant: 부력(부양성) 있는; •fantail: 부채꼴의 꼬리; •cling: 착 들러붙다; •railing: 난간; •tumble: 쓰러지다; •flail: 흔들리다; •rumbling black monolith: 덜거덕거리는 검은 모노리스; •grip: 단단히 잡다; •crouch: 움츠리다, 웅크리다; •surreal: 초현실주의적인; •relentless: 사정없는, 무자비한; •plunge: 쳐 넣기, 돌진, 급락.

제5절 교과

(1) LANDMARKS IN THE HISTORY OF ENGLISH

Language is a natural human growth, partly mental and partly physical. It follows, therefore, that it never ceases to change, but is a continuing development in a constant state of flux. To divide the history of any language into 'periods' historically must, then, be only a somewhat artificial rough-and-ready expedient. Yet, provided it is remembered that such divisions are only approximate, the method has its advantages and is generally followed. The history of English is divided into three main periods, each of which may be further subdivided. They are *Old English*, *Middle English* and *Modern English* (this last is sometimes called *New English* after the example of German scholars).

The Old English period extends from the earliest written documents, about the close of the seventh century, to about 1100, by which time the effects of the Norman Conquest begin to be perceptible in the language. It is characterized by a homogeneous Anglo-Saxon language, with only a small amount of Latin influence, followed by some from Norse, on the vocabulary of the written language. It is also characterized by having its inflexional system relatively full, with three or four case-endings for its nouns and adjectives and fuller verbal endings than existed at any time later. In pronunciation it had no 'silent syllables' and its spelling was a rough attempt at being phonetic, that is to say its letters represented its sounds fairly closely. Its word-order was relatively free, since its inflexions prevented ambiguity. It had a number of dialects, but only one of them, the language of King Alfred's Wessex (West-Saxon), has left literary monuments on any large scale. For the history of the country caused this West-Saxon to become by the tenth century the accepted language for most vernacular literary purposes. Even the literature of other dialects, such as was most of the poetry, was re-copied into the 'standard' West-Saxon which, with local modifications, had become a sort of common literary language all over the country. It is this West-Saxon which, because there are most materials in it, has become the basis of Old English grammars and dictionaries. But, as has been already remarked, it is unfortunate that there is not a direct continuity between this literary West-Saxon and later English, since the direct ancestor of modern literary English was some kind of Midland (*Merrian* as it is called for the Old English period), with an underlay of South-Eastern. The nearest direct descendants of West-Saxon are to be found in such countries as Gloucester and Somerest and Devon, as rural speech only.

Middle English extends from about a.d. 1100 to about 1450, and may be said to take in the mediaeval period more narrowly so called. It begins with the Norman Conquest and ends with a transitional period leading to the close of the Middle Ages.

(Wrenn, *The English Language*, Methuen & Co,. LTD, 1952: 21)

어휘리콜 •flux: 흐름, 변화; •rough-and-ready: 대충하는, 임시변통의; •homogeneous: 동질적인; •vernacular: 그 지방 고유의, 지방어; •underlay: underlie(~아래에 있다)의 과거.

(2) **(Youn-Nor-Ri) Board Game**

Contents
- Board
- 4 Sticks
- Checkers (4 each color)

Object of the Game

- To be the first team to have all 4 checkers to go round the board

How to Play

- Throw the sticks upward (from sitting position) as high as your shoulder, and let them fall down on the ground
- There are 5 possible results

  "Doh" Move one of your checkers forward 1 circle

  "Kay" Move one of your checkers forward 2 circles

  "Girl" Move one of your checkers forward 3 circles

  "Yout" Move one of your checkers forward 4 circles and play again

  "Moh" Move one of your checkers forward 5 circles and play again
- There are 4 ways to go around the board
- To take shortcuts, your checker must land on one of the big circles. For example, if your first sticks show "Yout" and you want to take the shortcut no.1, your next sticks must show "Doh". Otherwise, your checkers should continue around the outside perimeter of the board.
- Each throw applies to only one checker, of the player's choice.
- There is no limit on the number of checkers on the board
- If one of your checkers ends up on a circle which already has one of your checkers, you can stack them together and move them as one
- If one of your checkers ends up on the same circle as another player's checker, the other player's checker moves back to the starting circle and you may play again

어휘리콜 •checker: 말; •perimeter: 주위, 둘레.

(3) Survey Finds Most Republicans Seek Action on Climate Change

By ANDREW C. REVKIN

It's time for that national "listening tour" on energy and climate, President Obama. Some evidence comes in a new survey from the Center for Climate Change Communication at George Mason University (seen via Tom Yulsman on Facebook). Here's an excerpt from the news release:

> In a recent survey of Republicans and Republican−leaning Independents conducted by the Center for Climate Change Communication (4C) at George Mason University, a majority of respondents (62 percent) said they feel America should take steps to address climate change. More than three out of four survey respondents (77 percent) said the United States should use more renewable energy sources, and of those, most believe that this change should begin immediately.

The national survey, conducted in January 2013, asked more than 700 people who self-identified as Republicans and Republican-leaning Independents about energy and climate change.

"Over the past few years, our surveys have shown that a growing number of Republicans want to see Congress do more to address climate change," said Mason professor Edward Maibach, director of 4C. "In this survey, we asked a broader set of questions to see if we could better understand how Republicans, and Independents who have a tendency to vote Republican, think about America's energy and climate change situation."

The reason a listening tour is the next step, and not a pre-packaged batch of legislation or other steps, is to build on the common ground across a wide range of Americans on energy thrift, innovation and fair play (meaning policies that distort the playing field, with mandated corn ethanol production and tax breaks for fossil fuel companies prime examples).

This might even lead to a new sense of mission in this country, something that's been lacking since the cold war and space race.

In Mother Jones, Chris Mooney has an interesting spin on the survey, noting that the way global warming was framed probably had an impact on the level of buy-in on the questions.

It's been clear for years that there are ways around the familiar partisan roadblocks on climate-smart energy policies. In 2009, the "Six Americas" survey by the same George Mason researchers and counterparts at Yale revealed this clearly. I distilled those findings into three slides here.

Here's a bit more on the survey from the George Mason Web site:

> This short report is based on a January 2013 national survey of Republicans and Republican-leaning Independents. We found that they prefer clean energy as the basis of America's energy future and say the benefits of clean energy, such as energy independence(66%) saving resources for our children and grandchildren(57%), and providing a better life for our children and grandchildren(56%) outweigh the costs, such as more government regulation(42%) or higher energy prices(31%).

By a margin of 2 to 1, respondents say America should take action to reduce our fossil fuel use. Also, only one third of respondents agree with the Republican Party's position on climate change, while about half agree with the party's position on how to meet America's energy needs.

> 어휘리콜   •news release: 뉴스 기사; •batch: 묶음, 일단, 다발; •mandate: 위임하다, 명령하다, 이양하다; •spin: 견해, 해석; •roadblock: (노상) 장애물, 방책, 바리게이트; •distill: 증유하다, 증수를 뽑다.

(4)　　　　　　　**Facts about Americans 1.**

Here's a survey done of Americans, about their habits and actions. As you are reading this, remember that 90% of the respondents have said that they have lied in their life.

AROUND THE HOUSE

* 21% of us don't make our bed daily. 5% of us never do.
* Men do 29% of laundry each week. Only 7% of women trust their husbands to do it correctly.
* 40% of women have hurled footwear at a man.
* 85% of men don't use the slit in their underwear.
* 67.5% of men were tightie whities (briefs).
* The average bra size today is 36C whereas 10 years ago it was a 34B.
* 85% of women wear the wrong bra size.

HABITS

* 58.4% have called into work sick when we weren't.
* 3 out of 4 of us store our dollar bills in rigid order with singles leading up to higher denominations.
* 50% admit they regularly sneak food into movie theaters to avoid the high prices of snack foods.
* 39% of us peek in our host's bathroom cabinet. 17% have been caught by the host.
* 81.3% would tell an acquaintance to zip his pants.
* 29% of us ignore RSVP.
* 35% give to charity at least once a month.
* 71.6% of us eavesdrop.

어휘리콜 •respondent: 응답자; •hurl: 내던지다, (욕) 퍼붓다; •footwear: 신발; •tightie whities: 기수, 조종자, 가장(=jockey); •sneak: 가지고 들어가다; •eavesdrop: 엿듣다, 도청하다.

제6절 준칙

(1) MINNESOTA TRAFFIC LAWS FOR YOUNG DRIVERS

Minnesota teen drivers are over represented in traffic crashes each year due to driver inexperience, distractions, nighttime driving, speeding and lack of seat belt use.

To minimize risks of crashes, injury or death, Minnesota's graduated driver's licensing law helps teens hone their driving skills the first year of licensure by reducing exposure to high risk situations such as carrying teen passengers and driving at night. Violating these laws is a misdemeanor.

Nighttime Driving Limitation
Statute: 171.055 Subd. 2(b)
For the first six months of licensure: Driving is prohibited midnight - 5 a.m.

Passenger Limitations
Statute: 171.055 Subd. 2(c)
For the first six months of licensure: Only one passenger under age 20 is permitted, unless accompanied by a parent or guardian. For the second six months of licensure: No more than three passengers under age 20 are permitted, unless accompanied by a parent or guardian.

Cell Phone Use and Texting
Statute: 171.055 Subd. 2(a). 169.475
It is illegal for drivers under age 18 to use a cell phone, whether hand-held or hands-free -except to call 911 in an emergency. It is also illegal for drivers of all ages to compose or read text messages and emails or access the Internet using a wireless device while the vehicle is in motion or a part of traffic.

Drinking and Driving

Statute: 169A.33, 169A.20

It is illegal for a person under age 21 to drive after consuming any amount of alcohol. Consequences for underage drinking and driving are loss of license for at least 30 days and court fines.

Seat Belt Use

Kathryn Swanson Seat Belt Law (M.S. 169.686)

Minnesota's seat belt law is a primary offense, meaning drivers and passengers of any age and in all seating positions must be buckled up.

> 어휘리콜 •distraction: 주의 산만; •hone: 동경하다; •licensure: 면허 교부, 개업 인가; • misdemeanor: 경범죄.

(2) **CHAPTER I GENERAL PROVISIONS**

Article 1

(1) The Republic of Korea shall be a democratic republic.
(2) The sovereignty of the Republic of Korea shall reside in the people, and all state authority shall emanate from the people.

Article 2

(1) Nationality in the Republic of Korea shall be prescribed by Act.
(2) It shall be the duty of the State to protect citizens residing abroad as prescribed by Act.

Article 3

The territory of the Republic of Korea shall consist of the Korean peninsula and its adjacent island.

> 어휘리콜 •general provisions: 총칙; •sovereignty: 주권; •emanate: 발하다, 나오다; •act: 법률; •adjacent: 인접하는, 부속하는.

(3) CONSTITUTION AND BY-LAWS OF KOREAN STUDENT ASSOCIATION

ARTICLE I (Name)

The name of this organization shall be the Korean Student Association (KSA)

ARTICLE II (Purpose)

The purposes for which this organization is formed are:
1. To share and stimulate the interest of Korean traditions and cultures.
2. To cooperate and participate with other student organizations and Korean society.
3. To exchange the information from different research areas.
4. To help each other for the problems related to the undergraduate and graduate study.
5. To develop a confident leadership in undergraduate and graduate study.

ARTICLE III (Membership)

• Section A.
Membership shall be of three types: (1) full member, (2) associate member, and (3) honorary member.
• Section B.
  1. Full member: any Korean student of the University of Texas at Arlington (UTA) who has approved a membership in the KSA and has paid their local dues.
  2. Associate member: any student of UTA who has interest in the KSA is eligible to be an associate member and becomes an associate member upon acceptance

of application and payment of local dues.

3. Honorary member: alumni of the UTA, faculty members and others who have rendered outstanding services may be elected honorary members by a majority vote of the members present at any regular meeting. A permanent roll of such members shall be maintained. However, such a member cannot vote or hold office.

ARTICLE IV (Officers)

• Section A.

Officers of the association shall consist of the following: president, vice-president, treasurer and secretary. These officers shall be elected according to Article I of the By-Laws. Any full member is eligible to be elected as an officer of the KSA.

• Section B.

Full and associate members may hold office, but only full members can vote.

ARTICLE V (Duties of the Officers)

• Section A.

It shall be the duty of the president to preside over all meetings of the KSA. She/he shall appoint vice-president, treasurer, secretary and all departmental representatives.

• Section B.

It shall be the duty of the vice-president to assume the duties of the president in his absence or upon his request.

• Section C.

The treasurer is responsible for and shall maintain complete and accurate records of all financial transactions of the organization.

• Section D.

The secretary shall keep an accurate record of the meetings and membership roll. The secretary shall submit annual reports.

ARTICLE VI (Meetings)

• Section A.
There shall be at least two regularly scheduled meetings for spring and fall semester in a year.
• Section B.
Other special meetings may be held at the discretion of the president if announced three days prior to the meeting.

ARTICLE VII (Dues)

Dues are payable from September 1st to December 31st for the fall semester and from January 1st to May 31st for spring semester. New members shall pay dues upon joining. Dues shall be set by the By-Laws.

ARTICLE VIII (Amendments)

Amendments submitted at regular meetings shall not be voted upon until the next regular meetings. A two-thirds majority of the full members present shall be required for adoption of any amendment.

ARTICLE IX (Advisor)

The advisor of this organization shall be one of the faculty member(s) of the UTA or anyone who has given significant contributions to KSA. The election of the advisor is set by the By-Laws.

ARTICLE X (Rules and Regulations)

This constitution shall be subject to all rules and regulations of the UTA.

BY-LAWS

ARTICLE I (Election Procedure)

1. Election of officers shall be held at the meetings of the spring and fall semesters with nominations being submitted before meeting.
2. Elections of officers shall be determined by a majority vote of the full members present. Election shall be a secrete ballot.
3. Officers shall assume office at the time of election and shall hold office until their successors are duly elected.
4. The advisor shall be elected by a majority vote of the full members present.

ARTICLE II

1. The president, upon registration, shall be succeeded by the vice-president.
2. In case of vacancy of any office other than the president, the office shall be filled by the president with the approval of full members.

ARTICLE III

Dues will be determined by membership vote at the regular meetings of spring and fall semesters.

어휘리콜 •constitution: 조직, 구성, 법(규); •by-law: 부칙, 세칙; •article: 조항, 조문, 항목; •membership: 회원(자격); •officer: 임원; •due: 임기; •amendment: (회칙의) 개정; •adviser: 고문; •rule and regulation: 규칙과 관례; •election procedure: 선거 (절차).

(4) **Precious Shipping Public Company Limited**
Criteria for shareholder(s) to nominate Director

Objective: In accordance with recommended best practices per "The Principles of Good Corporate Governance for Listed Companies" and to ensure that all shareholders are equitably treated, the Company should open its doors to facilitate minority shareholders to nominate a Director. The Board of Directors has established the criteria and procedures for consideration of these matters proposed as follows:

Definitions :
"Company" means Precious Shipping Public Company Limited.
"Board" means Board of Directors of Precious Shipping Public Company Limited.
"Director" means Director of Precious Shipping Public Company Limited.
"Nomination Committee" means Nomination Committee of Precious Shipping Public Company Limited.

Criteria for shareholders to nominate a Director

1. Qualification of shareholders

A shareholder who wishes to nominate a Director must possess the following qualifications:

(1) Be a shareholder holding a minimum of 2,000,000 shares either as one shareholder or a group of shareholders.
(2) Must hold shares as specified above on the date the shareholder or the group of shareholders proposes the agenda item.
(3) Must have the evidence of shares held such as copies of certificate of shares held issued by securities company or any other certificates from the Stock Exchange of Thailand or Thailand Securities Depository Co., Ltd.

2. The Nomination of the Director

2.1 Qualification of the nominated Director

The Board will consider the director nominee holding Thai Nationality, age not more than 58 years and who possesses the following qualifications:

(1) Qualified according to the Public Limited Companies Act, Securities and Exchange Act including other relevant laws and regulations and in accordance with the Good Corporate Governance Policy of the Company.
(2) Knowledgeable, possess good background experience, capable, independent to perform director's duties with care and loyalty, and able to attend Directors' meetings regularly.
(3) Having knowledge in one or more of the following fields: Shipping, International Trading, Business Strategy. International Accounting, International Finance, Law and Corporate Governance.
(4) Not holding board positions in more than 4 listed companies and certainly not in any competing maritime business.
(5) Completed the Thai IOD Director's Certification Program Course.

2.2 Submission of Proposal

(1) A shareholder who possesses the necessary qualification per No. 1 hereinabove can submit the annexed form titled "Form to Nominate Director". In case shareholders have grouped to propose the agenda item, each shareholder must fill in and sign this form as evidence separately. Thereafter, the forms should be presented as one set along with all the supporting documents of each shareholder.
(2) A Shareholder can send the information to the Company through email to ir@preciousshipping.com or to facsimile number 66 2 236 7654 and then follow it up with the original Form, duly signed, together with other supporting documents as required to the following address within 31 December 2012.

Khun Somprathana Thepnapaplern
Precious Shipping PCL
Corporate Secretariat and Investor Relations
9th Floor, Cathay House, 8 North Sathorn Road,
Silom, Bangrak Bangkok 10500
Thailand
Telephone: 02-6968856

3. Consideration Procedure

The Nomination Committee will initially review the proposal and consider the nominated candidate's qualification before proposing to the Board. The name of the nominated Director candidate, if approved by the Board, will be included in the relevant agenda of the AGM. If a proposal disapproved by the Nomination Committee or the Board, the proposers shall be informed with the reason for refusal through the Company's website at www.preciousshipping.com and/or any other appropriate information dissemination channels and the decision of the Board shall be final.

> 어휘리콜　•ensure: 확실하게 하다, 보증하다, 확보하다; •shareholder: 주주; •equitably: 공정(공평)하게; •laws and regulations: 법률과 관례; •hereinabove: (문서에서)이상에, 상기에, 전조에, 앞서; •thereafter: 그 후 그때부터.

(5)　　　　　　　　　　**DRAFT TEMPLATE**

The standing rules:
　The standing rules of an organization are simply a compilation of main motions adopted by an organization from time to time by a majority vote. They are more flexible than bylaws and may be amended or rescinded by a two-third of the membership, They can be adopted when the need arises.

Items for consideration:

The name of this chapter is the (YOUR CHAPTER NAME) Chapter.

The (YOUR CHAPTER NAME) Chapter is affiliated with Hearing Loss Association of America. <HLAA>.

(State if the chapter chooses or does not choose to come under the Umbrella of HLAA).

Regular meetings of the (YOUR CHAPTER NAME) Chapter shall be held each month at (time) at the (location).

(Not any exceptions here, i.e., will not meet in August, will substitute the national convention for the June meeting, etc.)

The mailing address of the organization is............................

The officers of this chapter will be a President, Vice-President, Secretary. and Treasurer.

(Or a chapter may choose to be governed by steering/planning committee with a designated treasurer.)

Duties of each officer or duties of a treasurer is no designated or elected officers.

Vacancies may be (appointed/elected).............................

The chapters governing body (Board, Steering Committee) will meet monthly at (date/time), (location).

Reimbursement, but no compensation may be paid to officers or members for expenses incurred for the chapter.

No hearing health related business may be conducted by any members or participants.

An HLAA member is someone who has paid a membership fee to the HLAA office in Bethesda, MD.

The (YOUR CHAPTER NAME) chapter operating expenses are funded through (newsletter subscriptions, donations, etc.)

The chapter's standing expenses committee will be.....................
The chapter's special committee will be.....................

> 어휘리콜 •draft: 초고, 초안; •template: 모형, 원형; •standing rules: 여전히 존속하는 규칙; •rescind: 철회하다, 취소하다; •affiliate: 합병하다, 제휴하다, 인정하다; •steering/planning committee: 운영/기획위원회; •treasurer: 회계, 경리(원, 부장); •reimbursement: 반제, 상환; •vacancy: 공석, 빈자리.

(6) **CLASS ATTENDANCE**

Students who miss more than 6 classes will be asked to drop the class.
In compliance with the University's policy on class attendance, the ABAC School of Management requires all students enrolling in courses offered by the School, to obtain a minimum of 80% class attendance to be eligible to sit and take the final examination.

The 20% absence is the maximum number of allowable absences. It is inclusive for all excuses, i.e., sickness, personal and family matters, business trips, and other personal reasons. It is therefore, the student's primary responsibility to determine the necessity and ascertain the number of times of their absences. For a 3-credit hour subject, with one-and-a-half hour periods, students are allowed to miss the class 6 times, and with 3-hour class periods, they can be absent 3 times. It is always desirable for students to reserve at least 2 allowable absences for some unanticipated situations, i.e. sickness or business trips that might result in their absences. Generally speaking, as they have paid tuition fees for 45-hour class (for 3-credit hour subject), students should not be missing any classes in order to obtain maximum value for what they have paid for.

It is always arguable whether class attendance has any correlation with passing or failing a subject. Nonetheless, it is the student's effective time management and discipline to attend classes that enable them to meet minimum attendance requirements and thus appear for the final examination.

It is not up to the students to decide whether a lecture is too simple and hence, not necessary to attend. On the contrary, it is the students' primary duty to provide feedback to the concerned Department Chairperson regarding the perceived poor performance of their lecturers, i.e. not being punctual, not preparing well for class, not using English in class, and being too critical for class evaluation at the end of the semester.

Class attendance can only be checked for the section the student is registered in:

Students are not allowed to ask lecturers to check their attendance in sections other than the one they have enrolled in. Nonetheless, to give students an opportunity to catch-up classes that they have missed or to review certain topics they did not understand, students are permitted to audit lectures in other sections, given that the lecturer of the section grants permission. Please keep in mind that the permission of the Lecturer to audit his/her lecture in other sections does not imply that students can receive class attendance in those sections - *there is no such thing as 'make-up class attendance.*

어휘리콜 • in compliance with: ~에 따라.

(7) **Customs Rules**

Import regulations:

Free import to passengers arriving with goods purchased within the EU (for personal use only) : 1. 800 cigarettes, 400 cigarillos (max. 3g ...More Import regulations for Czech Republic.

Arms and Ammunition regulations :

Import of sporting guns: special licence and gun licence, both obtained prior to arrival ...More Czech Republic Arms and Ammunition regulation.

Additional Information on regulations:

For export of some goods it is necessary to present to customs officers documents, which are needful for export allowance... More additional information for Czech Republic.

Export regulations:

No restrictions. However, export of cultural heritage pieces is possible only with prior approval by the Czech Ministry of Culture. ...More Export regulations for Czech Republic.

Crew members customs regulations:

If travelling between a non-EU Member State and EU Member State free import of goods up to a value of EUR 22.- per trip. ...More crew members customs regulations for Czech Republic.

Pets:

Cats and dogs are subject to Regulation (EC) No. 998/2003. However, echinococcus and ticks treatment are not required. Entry may be refused in case the a ...More Czech Republic importing pets regulations.

> 어휘리콜 •Export regulations: 수입 법규사항; •echinococcus: 에키노코쿠스속의 각종 촌충; • tick: 진드기.

제7절 수상

(1)

After ten months backpacking through Africa and Asia, I was on the final leg of my journey, the flight that would take me home to Canada. The Korean language was a complete mystery to me, and I stared up at the board, searching for any symbol that appeared familiar. Nothing at all did.

And then, a woman stopped and asked in fluent English, which way I wanted to go. She took me to a policeman nearby. She spoke to him in Korean, and did everything for me – finding out everything I wanted to know.

I thanked her and bade her farewell, but she said she had ten minutes and insisted I join her for a quick tea. Her name was Kim Mina and she was born in Seoul, but had spent a year backpacking in America and knew what it was like to be a woman traveling solo like me. We excitedly traded stories but soon our brief chat was over. She hurriedly paid for both our drinks.

"Save your money," she said and wished me luck. And then, she was gone.

Suddenly, she reappeared, out of breath, with a square box wrapped in white and red paper.

"You aren't a vegetarian, are you?" she asked.

"Uh, no...." I said. She pushed the box into my hands.

"For the bus. And here are small dolls for your children. Goodbye." And she was gone, again.

As I waited at the bus stop, my pack didn't feel as heavy. Even though I had been given some more gifts to carry, I felt lighter blessed with the taste of warm food, the dreams of my homecoming and the generosity of a Korean woman.

어휘리콜 •backpacking: 도보여행.

(2)
    When I was child, the drought swept in South Dakota. We prayed for the rains, but the rains did not come. I shall never forget that difficult year. We walked around our farm with white towels over our faces to keep from suffocating in the driving dust. Then the harvest season came. My father would normally harvest a hundred wagons full of corn. But I remember the harvest that year. My father harvested just a meager one half-wagon load. It was a total crop disaster that had never been equalled before or since! You know what happened? Seated at the dinner table with his worried family, my father said, "Don't worry! I thank God that I have lost nothing. I used a half-wagon load for seed, and I got a half-wagon load back. I have gained the half-wagon load for seed I will plant next spring!" His attitude was that he didn't lose a thing while other farmers were saying, "We lost ninety loads," or, "we lost one hundred loads," They counted their losses by what they hoped they could have accomplished. And I'll never forget my father saying, "If you count up the might-have-beens, you will be defeated. Never look at what you have lost : look at what you left." The attitude of gratitude gave my father surviving power. He went right back and planted that seed the next year. When he finally retired, he was no longer a poor farmer. With this attitude he prepared and left a nice estate for his children. What do you see during your rainy days? Rainbows of opportunity of gloomy clouds? Yes, there will always be events beyond your control, but you can choose your attitude. Look at the rainbows instead of gray clouds. You are responsible for your own attitude and success.

> 어휘리콜   •drought: 가뭄; •suffocate: 호흡을 곤란하게 하다, 질식시키다; •meager: 부족한, 빈약한.

(3)   Krabi, the true hidden gem of Thailand

    KRABI, Thailand — Krabi province is Thailand's representative resort area. Unfortunately, it's not as easily accessible as other tourist spots in Thailand. Unlike Phuket, you have to arrange flights, jeep rides and boats to get around. Yet the area is one of the most desired destinations in Thailand, a true "hidden gem" that remains untouched by mass tourism.

We started the tour by taking Thai Airways International from Bangkok to Phuket. Working our way to the northwest coast of Phuket, we arrived at Mai Khao Beach, where we unpacked our luggage at a holiday resort.

The next morning, we set off for the Similan Islands. The national park is open from November to April when the waters are clear and the monsoon stays far away. It takes an hour and a half to get from Tap Lamu Pier to the Similan Islands — the hammering sound of the speedboat engine almost drove our crew crazy. However, before the noise damaged our ears, we soon arrived at the elusive beach that we had been chasing for what seemed like forever.

Nine islands make up this archipelago. The main islands are often referred to by number — from numbers 1 to 9 — for convenience. Island 4, Koh Meang, and Island 8, Koh Similan, are outstanding snorkeling destinations with an incredible variety of tropical fish and bright corals in different shapes and sizes. Diving into the center, it feels as if you are in a giant aquarium — the variety and amount of marine life leaves no time for boredom.

Tourists sunbathe on the powder white beach which slopes down to emerald green water in Koh Hong Island. (Chung Hee-cho/The Korea Herald)

The island is enveloped by fine talcum powder-like sand encrusted with different corals. Clear turquoise waters lap the serene white sand. For those who want to feast their eyes on the island's spectacular scenery, all you need to do is climb a rocky granite boulder to take a good look around the pristine beauty of the islands. The next day we departed for Krabi. It takes just two hours by car to go to Ao Nang, the center of Krabi. The road is laden with karst topography, three-dimensional landscapes characterized by numerous caves, sinkholes, fissures, and underground streams. The two-hour ride is no time for a nap. Date palms and rubber trees line the sides of the road providing grand scenery, while strangely shaped stones make the journey resemble a roller coaster ride.

The tour guide of our crew Pay, from the Tourist Authority of Krabi, said, "Compared to Phuket, Krabi is blessed with an array of world-class natural attractions, untouched by human influence." The Ao Nang beach attracts some 2.6 million from all over the world each year.

A traditional longboat glides through the silent waters with deep green mangrove forests on both sides. (Chung Hee-cho/The Korea Herald)

One of the must-do things in Krabi is to go on an Island Hopping Tour. A unique way of exploring Krabi, the tour is strictly private, organized exclusively for a small number of people. Traveling in your own traditional long-tailed boat with local experienced boat men you can glide into mangrove forests alongside the limestone islands that Krabi people consider another local natural wonder.

There are 11 islands that access is allowed to, and the islands in the Koh Hong group are rightly considered to be among the most beautiful in Krabi Province. The Hong Island tour consists of Islands Koh Poda, Koh Kai, Koh Mo and Koh Thap. Gliding through the waterways of the mangrove swamps in the bay, the trip is recommended for nature lovers as it allows you to enter the lagoon, caves and crescents of powdery sand, where you can enjoy scuba diving, snorkeling and tanning.

For those who love adventure excursions like rock climbing, Railay Bay is recommended. Attracting climbers from all over the world, the cliff gives climbers a panoramic view of the famous Phra Nang Cave with amazing beachfronts, and great coves and bays.

You can also go kayaking at Ban Bor Thor. The caves at Ban Bor Thor are only accessible by kayak and are rich in archeological treasures of cave paintings that are 3,000 years old. The expedition also includes a tour around narrow, winding mangrove swamps and beautiful lagoons.

There is no direct flight to Krabi from Korea. To go to Krabi you can take a direct flight to Phuket and transfer to a bus. An alternative is to take Thai Air from Incheon International Airport to Bangkok, where you can take a domestic flight to Krabi year round. The Four-Islands Hopping Tour in Krabi costs 1,200 baht (43,000 won). The tour lasts seven hours, from 8:00 am to 3:00 pm. A standard packed lunch of Thai fried rice and drinks will be provided. By Chung Hee-cho, Korea Herald correspondent.

> 어휘리콜 •gem: 보석, 주옥, 일품; •archipelago: 다도해, 군도; •talcum powder-like: 탤컴 파우더 같은; •encrust: -표면을 장식하다; •coral: 산호; •turquoise: 터키옥, 청록색; •granite: 화강암; •boulder: 둥근 돌; •pristine: 초기의, 원시 시대(상태)의; •karst: 카르스트 지형(석회암 지역의 특징적인 지형); •topography: 지형학; •sinkhole: 우묵 팬 땅, 배수구; •fissure: 틈, 균열; •mangrove forest: 산림성 숲; •must-do: 필수사항, 꼭 해야 할; •swamp: 늪, 습지; • crescent: 초승달 모양의 것.

(4) MY TRIP TO THE DESERT KNOCKED ME UPSIDE MY HEAD & GAVE ME THE WRITING INSPIRATION I WAS LACKING.

04/16/2013

The night before my family trip to Las Vegas and Lehman Caves, I received a message from my publisher asking how my latest project (DEAD PLAINS, Book 3 The Zombie West Series) was going. This was April 1st. It was also my deadline. It was also 10:38pm of said deadline.

Dread filled me as I was forced to respond and let him know I wasn't anywhere near ready. I'd hoped for a little more time and that I'd still be able to make the July publication date that had originally been decided. Nope. I missed the deadline and there were no extentions granted. If I now wanted my book published in September, my new deadline was May 20th. Still not enough time.

Absolute panic set in. I couldn't sleep. I perhaps got one hour's worth even though I knew the next day I'd be driving a long distance with my kids in the car.

I can't even explain how terrified I was. I HAD to make this deadline, and here I'd planned to take time off to go with my family on vacation where I wasn't bringing my laptop. Three days of no writing. I did something I'd never done before (complete fear pushing me to the brink of trying something new) and took a notebook with me.

I began to write my ideas down and outline my novel. I'm a pantser, not a plotter, but I was desperate.

But as we drove what was labled "The Loneliest Road in America," inspiration started to come to me bit by bit. I needed this vacation. I needed my writing mojo back, and who knew that in the desert was where I'd find it. So far, since my return, I've written seven chapters. A start, for sure. Now to keep going.

어휘리콜 •laptop: 휴대용 컴퓨터; •plotter: 구성자, 출력자.

(5) **The wizard of Oz**

I like fantasy novels very much.
While I am reading the stories in which a normal child like me appears and goes on an adventure and go through many difficulties.
It feels like I'm the one who had the exciting and interesting experiences.
Dorothy who appears in The wizard of Oz' is also an ordinary girl.

Dorothy lived on a farm in Kansas. She had a lovely dog named Toto.
One day she ran into the house with Toto to avoid tornado.
The tornado blew up the house and threw it down on the place called Oz.
Beneath the house, the wicked witch of the east was dead.
Good witch of the north explained Dorothy that now wicked witch was dead everyone there was free.
The magic shoes that the witch of the east had worn were given to Dorothy. But nobody knew what kind of magic was in them.
Oz was a strange and beautiful place. However what Dorothy only wanted was to go back home.
Good witch told her that the wizard of Oz in the emerald city would know the way to go home.

Dorothy hit the road for the emerald city right away.
On the way she met Scarecrow, Tin man, Cowardly lion.
They also wanted some help from the wizard of Oz.
Scarecrow wanted a brain, Tin Man needed a heart, and Cowardly lion wanted some

courage.

But their journey was continuously interrupted by the wicked witch of the west.

The wicked witches of the east and of the west were sisters. And the witch of the west thought that Dorothy was responsible for her sister's death.

The witch of the west tried to take the magic shoes away from her.

Together the three of them, Scarecrow, Tin man and Cowardly lion, Dorothy foght off the witch of the west.

Undergoing many hardships, her three friends got what each of them wanted, and Dorothy finally could go back home with the magic power which had been in the magic shoes.

'The wizard of Oz' was a book I read when I was young.

However, after reading it once again, I learned a few things that I didn't understand before.

First, there's no place like home.

Second, family is the most precious thing in the world.

Last of all, if you earnestly desire something, it is you make things happen and not by anyone other than yourself.

> 어휘리콜 •wizard: 마법사; •fantasy: 환상, 공상; •witch: 마녀, 마귀; •earnestly: 진지하게, 진정으로.

(6) Knowing where to Tap

Before setting off to college, my father sat me down and shared this memorable story with me. It is one I shall never forget. My father is not college educated, yet he possesses more wisdom and insight than most college professors I have met. After you read this story, you'll know what I mean.

There is an old story of a boilermaker who was hired to fix a huge steamship boiler system that was not working well. After listening to the engineer's description of the problems and asking a few questions, he went to the boiler room. He looked at the maze of twisting pipes, listened to the thump of the boiler and the hiss of escaping steam for a few minutes, and felt some pipes with his hands. Then he hummed softly to himself, reached into his overalls and took out a small hammer, and tapped a bright red valve one time. Immediately, the entire system began working perfectly, and the boilermaker went home. When the steamship owner received a bill for one thousand dollars, he complained that the boilermaker had only been in the engine room for fifteen minutes and requested an itemized bill. So the boilermaker sent him a bill that reads as follows:

For tapping the valve: $ 50
For knowing where to tap: $ 999.50
TOTAL: $1,000.00

"Tony," he said, "I want you to go to college so that you can get your degree, but more important, I want you to return with an education."

Tony D'Angelo

> 어휘리콜 •tap: 탁 치다; •boilermaker: 보일러 제조자(수리인); •thump: 탁 치기, 탁 하는 소리; •hum: 중얼중얼 하다.

(7) ① **She and I, I and She (그녀와 나, 우리)**

The sound of waterdrop tickled my ears and the humid air kissed my cheek. The path was filled with gray like a silent film and the fog has absorbed the soul of the rising sun.

I was walking on my way to school, breaking the balance of the silence. Despite of the gloomy weather, I was delighted since my mid-term exam had finally finished yesterday. Maybe that was why I didn't hear what wind was whispering.

The spooky incident had happened after PE class. When my classmate and I got back from the gym and went into the classroom, grisly moist atmosphere surrounded us. All the backpacks were wide open as if somebody had been here. One girl checked inside of her backpack and noticed that her money was stolen. Everybody started checking their backpacks. All the costly possessions were robbed. Everybody was in panic. It was not just because they had their money and possessions stolen. It was mainly because they felt terrified to stay in the same school with a thief. I also checked my backpack. I was relieved to remember that I didn't bring any money this morning. However, I felt something creepy at the same time. There wasn't anything missing, but there was something new inside my backpack. There was a picture, a picture of a little girl wreathed in smile. I suddenly felt sick. I could remember that girl in the picture. Yes, oh yes. I could completely, absolutely recall who she is.

All of the classmates had to start the class. Even though they were very quiet, nobody seemed to concentrate what teacher was teaching. They were sending massages their parents to pick them up early. They appeared to be very disturbed and annoyed. They were afraid if one of them were a thief. I could feel the mistrust between friends which started to grow bigger and bigger. Everything was lousy. As the sky was getting darker and a big storm was heading directly to our school, I freaked out just like other girls in the classroom. The sound of waterdrop started to scratch my ears. The wind tried to break into our classroom. The darkness has conquered the world. The lightning and thunder was fighting like cat and dog.

I couldn't believe that it was just like the day when I met her. Everything that went wrong was caused by her including my parents' divorce and my younger sister's death.

That girl or that dreadful monster is an unfortune that follows me. But everytime when I try to get away from her, she know how to make me comeback to her. She knows it too well. She knows me too well. She knows my pattern of behavior too well. She sends me chills up my spine.

She loves to play frank on me. That's why she follows me everywhere, anywhere. There was one time, when my sister was very alive, I used to follow my sister to the church. My sister was so sweet girl that everyone loved her. At first, I enjoyed to be at church. However I soon realized that church is a place especially and only for my sister. Everybody at church adored her since she was a faithful and passionate christian. She could answer every question the pastor asked. She also memorized the ten commandments and obeyed unerringly what the God said. She was a so-called good christian girl. Because my sister shined like the sun, Venus like me couldn't be seen in the morning.

Anyway, attending church helped me keep myself away from her for a while. Everything seemed to be perfectly away from her. But that's the point when she came back to me. That stormy night, when I found out the reality that my sister is better than me in every area, she just sneak into my home, killing my sister's pet guinea pig and throwing it away. It was the first biggest crime she had committed. Before that, she just stole something she loves or caused a few injuries to somebody I know. That night, She had broke our silent rule. Because of her behavior, my sister got out of home to find her pet, and hit by the car. That monster ate my lovely little sister's fresh thumping heart.

My parents were in a deep fountain of sorrow due to my sister's death. They fought more frequently than before which kept her away from me for a brief period of time. They had agreed to divorce the following year. It was mostly because of her, the fearless monster. They met her. They discovered how I and she are closely related. Dad blamed on mom for careless and mom blamed on dad for irresponsibility. After a year they divorced, both of them married to new young partners.

They have left me. To tell the truth, they did not exactly left me alone, but they has left me in the desert of loneliness. They treated me as if I didn't exist which makes me feel isolated. Also, that's when the monster became my best and precious friend. I just let myself go by leaving me out of control. She attracted me to the dark ocean. And I submissively followed her. As the time playing with her gets longer, I could not remember what I had done. I am also feeling the same way right now.

In the picture, she is smiling like a little child. That was the smile which calls the death. That is the smile I am afraid of. She was the one I had so long dreaded to face. Her eyes in the picture is adorable brown but filled with murderous impression. Some reddish black liquid was all over her clothes and in her white hands, there is something, something looks like a glittering enormous ruby. It fascinates her. She was entranced, enthralled, captivated and beguiled by it. Her sparkling eyes eagerly looked at it. "I can remember who she is," I murmured to myself.

I stood up ran to the restroom in the middle of class. The sounds of raindrops hitting the roof got even noisier. The lightning flashed and the thunder filled the air and echoed in my head, bawling at me for repentance.

"Yes, yes. I remember, I know who she is. It is a easy question."

I looked at the mirror, trying to deny and lie to myself. But there she was in the mirror, staring at me.

어휘리콜 •tickle: ~을 근질근질 하게하다; •spooky: 유령 같은, 도깨비 같은, 신경질적인, 놀라운; •grisly: 무시무시한, 소름끼치는; •backpack: 배낭, 등짐; •wreathe: 싸다, 덮다; •adore: ~을 몹시 좋아하다; •unerringly: 과오를 범하지 않고, 틀림없이; •adorable: 숭배(흠모)할만한, 사랑스러운.

제8절 흥미

(1)

어휘리콜 •ploy: 책략, 놀이, 일, 직업.

(2) Upon dying, Bill Gates went to purgatory.

St. Peter said to him, "Bill, you have done some good things, and you have done some bad things. Now I am going to let you decide where you want to go."

So, Bill takes a look at hell and sees beautiful women running around, in 80 degree temperature, on beautiful beaches.

Then he took a look at heaven and it was nice, you know harps, singing and worship and stuff like that.

So he said to St. Peter that he would like to go to hell.

About a week later, St. Peter went down to hell to check on Bill. There he saw him being whipped by demons. He said to St. Peter, "What happened to all the beautiful women, and the beaches?"

Peter replied, "That was just the screen saver."

> 어휘리콜   •purgatory: (신학)연옥, 일시적 처벌(속죄) 장소; •harp: 하프; •stuff: 채워 넣다, 먹이다; •whip: 채찍질 하다; •demon: 악령, 귀신; •screen saver: 스크린 세이브.

(3)

Even before I finished dialing, I somehow knew I'd made a mistake. The phone rang once, twice – then someone picked it up.

"You got the wrong number!" a husky male voice said angrily before the line went dead. Surprised, I dialed again.

"I said you got the wrong number!" came the voice. Once more the phone rang in my ear.

How could he possibly know I had the wrong number? At that time I worked for the New York City Police Department. A policeman is trained to be curious and concerned. So I dialed a third time.

"Hey, come on," the man said. "Is this you again?"

"Yeah, it's me," I answered. "I was wondering how you knew I had the wrong number before I even said anything."

"You figure it out," The phone went dead.

I sat there awhile, the receiver hanging loosely in my fingers. I called the man back.

"Did you figure it out yet?" he asked. "The only thing I can think of is .... nobody ever calls you."

"You understand?" The phone went dead for the fourth time. Bursting out laughing, I dialed the man back.

"What do you want now?" he asked.

"I thought I'd call .... just to say hello." "Hello?"

"Why?"

"Well, if nobody ever calls you, I thought maybe I should."

"OK, Hello. Who is this?"

"At last I had reached someone by telephone. Now he was curious. I told him who I was and asked who he was."

"My name's Adolf Meth. I'm 88 years old, and I haven't had this many wrong numbers in one day in 20 years!" We both laughed.

> 어휘리콜 •finish dialing: 번호들을 모두 돌리다; •burst out: 갑자기 ~하다.

(4)
1. I have the second largest population in the world. I am famous for an architecturally designed building from the king to his wife to show his love. I share the same independence day with Korean. Who am I?
    -India
2. I'm a chain smoker. My food is very expensive to buy in Korea. When i wink, you can understand where i want to go.
    I usually can help you a lot. but sometimes I can hurt you. If i run you over. Who am I?
    -car
3. I have many fuctions to entertain you. If you are a chatter box. I can be very expensive.
    I am very noisy if you don't answer me. Who am I?
    -phone
4. A cowboy had twelve cows. All but nine died. How many cows were left?
    -nine
5. Why did the student take a ladder to school?
    -Because he/she was going to high school! (high라는 말을 응용한 난센스퀴즈)
6. What goes into the water black and comes out red?
    -a lobster
7. Which is the most self-centered letter of the alphabet?
    - I
8. what always goes up and never goes down?

- age
9. what is the smallest bridge in world?
   - nose bridge

> 어휘리콜   •chain smoker: 줄담배를 피우는 사람.

(5)
1) It is greater than God and more evil than the devil. The poor have it, the rich need it and if you eat it you'll die. What is it?
   Answer: Nothing. Nothing is greater than God, nothing is more evil than the devil, the poor have nothing, the rich need nothing and if you eat nothing you'll die.
2) It walks on four legs in the morning, two legs at noon and three legs in the evening. What is it?
   Answer: Man (or woman). Crawls on all fours as a baby, walks on two legs as an adult and uses two legs and a cane when they're old.
3) What always runs but never walks, often murmurs, never talks, has a bed but never sleeps, has a mouth but never eats?
   Answer: A river.
4) At night they come without being fetched. By day they are lost without being stolen. What are they?
   Answer : The stars.

> 어휘리콜   •crawl: 기다; •cane: 지팡이; •murmur: 졸졸거리다.

(6) **BABY BLUES**

DILBERT

어휘리콜 • dirt: 진흙, 쓰레기.

(7) Hyuna's sexy performance on 'SNL Korea' goes viral

Hyuna, a member of a K-pop girl group 4Minute as well as a Psy's "Gangnam Style" heroine, is in the limelight for showcasing her sex appeal on "SNL Korea," a Saturday night comedy show on cable network tvN.

In the show, Hyuna and a leading Korean comedian, Shin Dong-yub, presented a parody of 2011 film "Eungyo." The original movie is concerned about the clandestine relationship between a 70-year-old poet and a high school girl.

Shin staged a particularly hilarious performance, turning into a pervert poet who gulps down and constantly glances at Hyuna's body movements. The energetic actor performed with so much passion that the rocking chair he was sitting in collapsed unexpectedly during the live show, sparking laughter from both the audiences and other actors.

Hyuna attracted a worldwide attention as a "sexy bombshell" through Psy's "Gangnam Style" music video. Her special guest performance on "SNL Korea" is once again going viral on the Internet with responses like "I want to be in Shin's place," or "Hyuna's sexiness did not go anywhere."

SNL Korea is a licensed Korean version of the late-night U.S. comedy show which has aired for over 38 years.

Jin Eun-soo, Intern reporter (janna924@heraldcorp.com)

> 어휘리콜 •viral: 급속히 퍼지는; •heroine: 여걸, 여장부, 여주인공; •limelight: 세상의 이목을 이끄는; •showcase: 진열용 유리상자, 전사, 진열; •clandestine: 비밀히 행해지는; •hilarious: 법석대는, 유쾌한, 즐거운; •pervert: 비나가다; •bombshell: 포탄, 폭탄, 폭탄선언, 센세이션을 일으키는 사람.

(8) ## The Paradoxical Commandments
by Dr. Kent M. Keith

People are illogical,
unreasonable, and self-centered. Love them anyway.

If you do good, people will accuse you of selfish ulterior motives.
Do good anyway.

If you are successful, you win false friends and true enemies.
Succeed anyway.

The good you do today will be forgotten tomorrow.
Do good anyway.

Honesty and frankness make you vulnerable.

Be honest and frank anyway.

The biggest men and women with the biggest ideas can be shot down by the smallest men and woman with the smallest minds.
Think big anyway.

People favor underdogs but follow only top dogs.
Fight for a few underdogs anyway.

What you spend years building may be destroyed overnight.
Build anyway.

People really need help buy may attack you if you do help them.
Help people anyway.

Give the world the best you have and you'll get kicked in the teeth.
Give the world the best you have anyway.

> 어휘리콜 •commandment: 명령, 지령, 계명, 계율; •accuse: 고발(고소, 기소)하다, 비난하다;
>   •ulterior: 감추어진.

제9절 기타

(1)

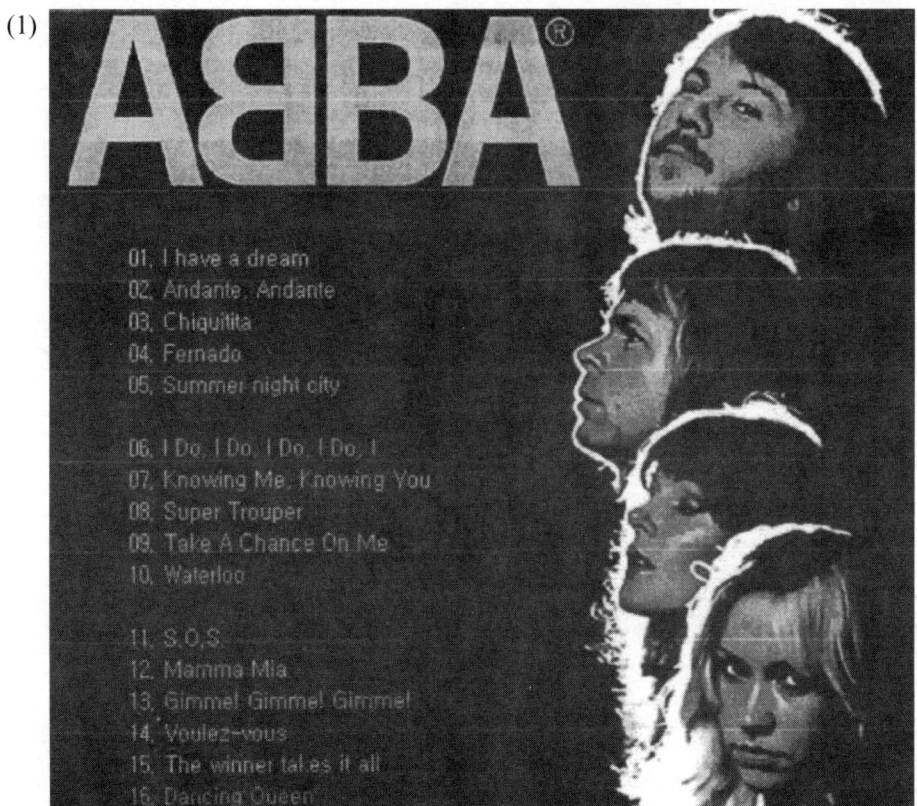

(2)

```
TITLE OF THESIS
[In upper case letters, centered on appropriate number of lines]

by
Your Name(s)
[In upper and lower case letters]


A THESIS SUBMITTED IN PARTIAL FULFILLMENT
OF THE REQUIREMENTS FOR THE DEGREE OF
BACHELOR OF APPLIED SCIENCE
in the School of Engineering Science
SIMON FRASER UNIVERSITY
[As shown here]



DATE
[Month Year]



All rights reserved. This work may not be
reproduced in whole or in part, by photocopy
or other means, without the permission of the author.
```

어휘리콜　•submitted: 제출된.

(3) Distinguished guests, ladies & gentlemen

My name is 000. I'm a Member of Parliament representing the Knowledge Economy Committee of the National Assembly of the Republic of Korea.

On behalf of the National Assembly and Korean People, I would like to congratulate all of you on the successful integration between ABC and XYZ.

Welcome Address

Thank you for coming and joining us, especially appreciate to the teachers and parents leading students.

We are here with the topic 'climate change', but I'd like to say first the importance of experience for the young people. We live in flood of information and knowledge and we can easily get them from the books or on the internet.

> 어휘리콜　•on behalf of: 대신하여.

참고문헌

김용도(2003), 「영어텍스트 구성이론」, 부산: 세종출판사.

김용도(2013), 「영어독해의 원리와 실제」, 3판, 서울: 한국문화사.

Amaudet, M. A. & M. E. Barrett(1990), *Paragraph Development*, Englewood Cliff, NJ: Prentice-Hall.

Comrie, Bernard(1987), *The World's Major Languages*, London: Croom Helm.

Coulthard, R. M.(1994), *Advances in Written Text Analysis*, London: Routledge.

Hoey, Michael(2001), *Textual Interaction-An Introduction to Written Discourse Analysis*, London: Routledge.

Israel, Susan E. & Gerald G. Duffy(2009), *Handbook of Research on Reading Comprehension*, New York: Routledge.

Levin, Gerald(2001), *Prose Models*, Boston: Heinle & Heinle.

Taylor, Shirley(1998), *Model Business Letters*, London: Prentice Hall.

Todaro, Stacey, Keith Mills, & Srikanth Dandotkar(2010), "The Impact of Semantic and Relatedness and Reading Skill on Standards of Coherence", *Discourse Processes*, 47: 421-446.

Wrenn, C. L.(1949), *The English Language*, Tokyo: Kenkyusha.

찾아보기

ㄱ
개념체계 ·················· 21
개별텍스트 ················ 21
계층 ····················· 134
관계리스트 ··············· 106
교훈 ······················ 22
구성성분 수식어 ·········· 80
구성윤곽 ·················· 4
구성적 틀 ················ 222
구성패턴 ················· 188
귀납적 과정 ·············· 222
글의 양식 ················· 21
기능요소 ··················· 5

ㄴ
내용흐름 ········ 105, 117, 124, 162
논리/수사적 관계 ········· 135

ㄷ
단락 독해처리 ············ 105
단락구성 ················· 105
독해사후 처리 ············ 188
독해수행 ················· 174
독해재료 ················ 5, 44
독해처리 ·················· 81
독해처리 모델 ············ 222
동격 ······················ 81

ㄹ
리콜 ······················ 81

ㅁ
마무리 수행 ·············· 208
메시지 부분 ··············· 94
명사성분 ················· 106
명사성분관계 ············· 135
명사한정 ················· 106
명사한정관계 ············· 135
목적 ······················ 21
목적격부사어 ·········· 80, 84
문간접속어 ················ 81

ㅂ
발생동기 ··················· 5
배열패턴 ·················· 80
변인 ······················· 5
변인요소 ·················· 80
본문 ················ 134, 146
본문 크기 ················· 44
부가 ··················· 80, 85

ㅅ
사건규명 ·················· 21
사실전달 ·················· 21
삭제 ······················ 80
3분법 ····················· 81
상황적 맥락 ··············· 94
생략 ······················ 85
선전 ······················ 21
선행절 ··················· 105
수동타동 동사 ········· 80, 82
수상 ······················ 21

수행동사	174

ㅇ

양식구성	4, 5, 21, 44
어휘리콜	66
언어 자체 구성과정	222
언어적 문맥	94
연역적 과정	222
영어텍스트	3, 222, 223
원리적 독해	222
윤곽확인	174
의도	4, 5, 21, 174
의도 예측	21
의사소통 6요소	5
의사소통과정	5
이동	80
2분법	81
이유	5
인지과정	222

ㅈ

장	134
장르	223
절	80, 134
절간접속	81
절마디의 관계	105
정보도	94
정보핵절	96, 117
조작사	82
존재론적 관점	5

주격부사어	80, 83
주술단위	80
주장	21
주제	124, 162
주제단락	134
주제문	134, 147
주제문장	162
주제부분	94
주제어휘	94, 96, 99, 117
주제유도규칙	125
준칙	21
직접구성단위	134, 146
직접화행문	174
직접화행의 구조	174

ㅊ

처리과정	223
초점부분	94
초점어휘	94, 96, 99, 117
최상위 주제문	174

ㅌ

타동사수식어	85
통합적 독해	222

ㅎ

해설	21
핵절	96
협의	21
호소	21
환심	21
후행절	105
흥미	22